CW00322455

"[The Berkeley Guides are] brimming with ... low-budget traveler—material delivered in ... irreverent way."

". . . hip, blunt and lively . . . . these Cal students boogie down and tell you where to sleep in a cowboy bunkhouse, get a tattoo and eat cheap meals cooked by aspiring chefs." **—Atlanta Journal Constitution**

". . . Harvard hasn't yet met 'On the Loose's' pledge to plant two trees in Costa Rica for every one felled to print its books—a promise that, given the true grit of these guides, might well mean a big new forest in Central America." **—Newsweek**

"[The Berkeley Guides] offer straight dirt on everything from hostels to look for and beaches to avoid to museums least likely to attract your parents . . . they're fresher than Harvard's Let's Go series." **—Seventeen**

"The books are full of often-amusing tips written in a youth-tinged conversational style." **—The Orlando Sentinel**

"So well-organized and well-written that I'm almost willing to forgive the recycled paper and soy-based ink." **—P.J. O'Rourke**

"These guys go to great lengths to point out safe attractions and routes for women traveling alone, minorities and gays. If only this kind of caution weren't necessary. But I'm glad someone finally thought of it."

—Sassy

"The very-hip Berkeley Guides look like a sure-fire hit for students and adventurous travelers of all ages. This is real budget travel stuff, with the emphasis on meeting new places head on, up close and personal . . . . this series is going to go places." **—The Hartford Courant**

"The guides make for fun and/or enlightening reading."

—The Los Angeles Times

"The new On the Loose guides are more comprehensive, informative and witty than Let's Go." **—Glamour**

OTHER BERKELEY GUIDE TITLES

California 1995
Central America
Eastern Europe
Europe 1995
France 1995
Germany & Austria 1995
Great Britain & Ireland 1995
Italy 1995
London 1995
Mexico 1995
Pacific Northwest & Alaska
Paris 1995
San Francisco 1995

the BERKELEY guides

THE BUDGET TRAVELER'S HANDBOOK

LONDON

ON THE LOOSE

1995

WRITTEN BY BERKELEY STUDENTS IN COOPERATION WITH THE
ASSOCIATED STUDENTS OF THE UNIVERSITY OF CALIFORNIA

ISBN 0–679–02782–3

First Edition

LONDON ON THE LOOSE

Editors: Chris Hoffpauir, Rachael Myrow
Editorial Coordinators: Laura Comay Bloch, Sharron S. Wood
Executive Editor: Scott McNeely
Production Editor: Laura M. Kidder
Map Editor: Robert Blake
Creative Director: Fabrizio La Rocca
Cartographers: David Lindroth, Inc.; Eureka Cartography
Text Design: Tigist Getachew
Cover Design and Illustration: Rico Lins Studio

SPECIAL SALES

The *Berkeley Guides* and all Fodor's Travel Publications are available at special discounts for bulk purchases for sales promotions or premiums. Special editions, including personalized covers, excerpts of existing guides, and corporate imprints, can be created in large quantities for special needs. For more information, contact your local bookseller or write to Special Markets, Fodor's Travel Publications, 201 E. 50th Street, New York, NY 10022. Inquiries from Canada should be directed to your local Canadian bookseller or sent to Random House of Canada, Ltd., Marketing Department, 1265 Aerowood Drive, Mississauga, Ontario L4W 1B9. Inquiries from the United Kingdom should be sent to Fodor's Travel Publications, 20 Vauxhall Bridge Road, London SW1V 2SA, England.

MANUFACTURED IN THE UNITED STATES OF AMERICA

10 9 8 7 6 5 4 3 2 1

Contents

We Go Where You Go.

Photo Credit: Rick Steves

Lowest student/budget airfares anywhere

International Student ID Cards
International Youth ID Cards
Eurail and Britrail passes
issued on the spot

Hostel Cards
Work Abroad Programs
Travel Gear and Guidebooks
Expert travel advice

Council Travel is a travel company of the Council on International Educational Exchange

What the Berkeley Guides Are All About

Three years ago, a motley bunch of U.C. Berkeley students spent the summer traveling on shoestring budgets to launch a new series of guidebooks—the *Berkeley Guides.* We wrote the books because, like thousand of travelers, we had grown tired of the outdated attitudes and information served up, year after year, in other guides. Most important, we thought a travel guide should be written by people who know what cheap travel is all about.

You see, it's one of life's weird truisms that the more cheaply you travel, the more you inevitably experience. You're bound to experience a lot with the *Berkeley Guides,* because we believe in living like bums and spending as little money as possible. You won't find much in our guides about how a restaurant prepares its duck á l'orange or how a hotel blends mauve curtains with green carpet. Instead, we tell you if a place is cheap, clean (no bugs), and worth the cash.

Coming from a community as diverse as Berkeley, we also want our books to be useful to *everyone,* so we tell you if a place is wheelchair accessible, if it provides resources for gay and lesbian travelers, and if it's safe for women traveling solo. Many of us are Californians, which means most of us like trees and mountain trails. It also means we emphasize the outdoors in every *Berkeley Guide,* from info on hiking to tips on protecting the environment. To further minimize our impact on the environment, we print our books on recycled paper using soy-based inks.

Most important, these guides are for travelers who want to see more than just the main sights. We find out what local people do for fun, where they go to eat, drink, or just hang out. Most guidebooks lead you down the tourist trail, ignoring important local issues, events, and culture. In the *Berkeley Guides* we give you the information you need to understand what's going on around you—whether it's the latest on John Major and the IRA or yet another royal scandal.

The *Berkeley Guides* began by covering Eastern Europe, Mexico, California, and the Pacific Northwest and Alaska. During the first year of research, our student writers slept in whorehouses in Mexican border towns and landed bush planes above the Arctic Circle. The second year was no different: Our writers weathered guerrilla attacks in the Guatemalan Highlands, motorcycle wrecks in Ireland, and a strange culinary concoction in Belize known as "greasy-greasy." The result was five new guidebooks, covering Central America, France, Germany, San Francisco, and Great Britain and Ireland. This year, things were even crazier. One writer got an ulcer, one lost her skirt on a moped, two crashed their motorbikes, and another spent hours digging through a dumpster to find a lost manuscript batch. Bloodied but unbowed, the *Berkeley Guides* brings you four new guidebooks, covering Europe, Italy, Paris, and London, not to mention completely revised and updated editions of our first- and second-year guides.

We've done our best to make sure the information in the *Berkeley Guides* is accurate, but time doesn't stand still: prices change, places go out of business. Call ahead when it's really important, assuming, of course, that the place has a phone.

Thanks to You

Putting together a guidebook that covers all of London is no easy task. From fig-uring out the British Museum to getting the lowdown on Camden's café scene, our writers and editors relied on helpful souls along the way. We'd like to thank the following people—as well as the hundreds of others whom our writers met briefly on the streets, on the Underground, and in strange unprintable places—for their advice and encouragement. We would like you to help us update this book and give us feedback. Drop us a line—a postcard, a note scrawled on a piece of toilet paper, whatever—and we'll be happy to acknowledge your contribution below. Our address is 515 Eshleman Hall, University of California, Berkeley, CA 94720.

Mary Bahr (Berkeley); Gunnar Bendiksen (Norway); Andy Brandt (Oakland); the staff and residents at Brighton Backpackers (Brighton); Sandy Crockett (London); Dave (London); Everton Davies (London); Sarah Edelstenin (Avalon); April Gertler (San Francisco); Ann, Joan, and Adam Grant (West Derby Village); Margaret Hall (Canterbury); David Hepler and Ann (San Diego); Paul Kavanaugh (Penzance); Martin Keady and family (Greenwich); Olivier Kobel (Switzerland); Baty Landis (New Orleans and Paris); Leila Hudson (London); Nicole Löcse (Germany); Sue McLeish (London); everyone at Megatripolis (London); Matt, Miles, and Richard (London); Julie Morfee (Berkeley); Bola Ogunlaru (London); Liz Procter (Hull); Phil Psilos (Universal); the Rasta family (London); Richard Selby (London); Sonya Shechter (London); Tim Snyder (Oxford); David Thomas (St. Albans); Penny Whittingham (Rye); Marin Van Young and the Homies (BADA, London); Helga Varden (Norway); Rich Vary (Winchester); and Viken Ververian (Los Angeles).

We'd also like to thank the Random House folks who helped us with cartography, page design, and production: Bob Blake, Ellen Browne, Mike Costa, Denise DeGennaro, Tigist Getachew, Laura M. Kidder, Fabrizio La Rocca, Linda Schmidt, and Bob Shields.

Berkeley Bios

Behind every restaurant blurb, write-up, lodging review, and introduction in this book lurks a student writer. You might recognize the type—perpetually short on time, money, and clean clothes. Three writers spent the summer in London researching and writing this book. Every two weeks they sent their manuscript back to Berkeley, where a two-person editorial team whipped, squashed, and pummeled it into shape.

The Writers

Lara Harris first became acquainted with English food 24 years ago when she was born in London. Her desire to write about it took shape at age eight when she was terrorized by classmates over her mother's packed lunches of rabbit and quail's eggs. Sixteen years later, Lara finally got the chance to cover London's dining scene from her flat in Belsize Square. Overworked but still smiling (sort of), she's currently enjoying a stint in Thailand practicing her tai chi.

After being propelled down the street Mary Poppins—style by gale-force winds and *twice* breaking into tears (literally) after being served frightening British meals, **Emily W. Miller** realized that she'd had enough. As a cowriter of the Trips From London chapter, she took a fast train to the West Country, sat writing in the sun, ate whole trout and Cornish pasties, and slept in a tiny cottage atop a cliff. Emily became so envious of long-distance walkers with mud on their boots that she made her way to the Peak District with fellow writer Mark Rosen. They stopped only long enough to eat lunch and snap kitschy "Hills Are Alive" pictures among the sunflowers. Soon after, she was back behind her computer editing *The Berkeley Guide to the Pacific Northwest and Alaska* and wondering whether she'd ever left in the first place.

After coediting *The Berkeley Guide to Central America* and *The Berkeley Guide to Italy*, **Caitlin Ramey** set off across the Atlantic to get a master's degree in international political economy at the London School of Economics. Little did she know that it would take much more than moving abroad to escape the greedy clutches of *The Berkeley Guides*. Against her better judgment, she signed on to write about her new home, and she very nearly had a nervous breakdown trying to meet all the deadlines slamming her from every direction. But, thanks to strong tea and weekly techno/trance dancing at Megatripolis, she survived (sanity more or less intact), and ended up falling 100% head-over-heels in love with London and Londoners. She was last seen headed for the Colombia School of Journalism.

The wretched state of the Bay Area job market drove **Mark S. Rosen** to enlist with *The Berkeley Guides* for a third go-round. The true glory of traveling off-season, however, was almost nullified by Britain's so-called springtime. Faced with Easter snow flurries in Wales, Mark hid his rattling bones under a massive, coffee-color jacket known colloquially as El Café. With a trusty copy of *Melody Maker* perennially draped over his arm, he learned to love and hate the Next Big Thing bands with nearly as dry a wit as the Brits. Mark is currently back in the Bay Area, awaiting a vision of what comes next.

Rashmi Sadana, who wrote three chapters for *The Berkeley Guide to France 1995,* had the near impossible task of finding London's cheapest beds and breakfasts. The sog and soot of the city didn't quite match up to the deep blue Corsican skies, but Rashmi managed to find many kindly proprietors and a few rooms with views. Informed by local sources that the rite of passage for any true Londoner is finding a good place to sleep, Rashmi now feels she has the necessary experience to fit right in with her fellow city dwellers. Rashmi recently finished her master's degree at London School of Oriental and African Studies and plans to stay in London for at least another year.

Special thanks to **Elke Wangen** for running around London helping to "research" the Pubs and After Dark chapters. Surprisingly, no arm twisting was necessary.

The Editors

Chris Hoffpauir hasn't been able to live down his old driver's license photo ever since it was stolen from his wallet, photocopied, and passed around the office. At least his hair and taste in music have grown a lot since then (and the photo's now safely under lock and key). When he's not busy sneaking in allusions to Keats or Shelley, Chris spends his time writing songs, scouring the used record bins at Amoeba in Berkeley, and savoring the unexpected perks of his *Berkeley Guide* position—a beautiful new Mission District flat and flatmate.

When **Rachael Myrow** was born, she bore a striking resemblance to Winston Churchill ("We shall fight them on the beaches . . . "), so it came as no surprise to relatives and close friends when she began editing *The Berkeley Guide to London* and *The Berkeley Guide to Great Britain and Ireland*. Fortunately, her looks have matured, as has her sense of humor. After mentally traveling about the United Kingdom for the Berkeley Guides, Rachael's return to the real world has been impeded by jet-lag and graduate school. Should anyone wish to offer her a job writing on a remote Scottish island, please send details to 515 Eshleman Hall.

What to do when your *money* is done traveling before you are.

Don't worry. With MoneyGram,℠ your parents can send you money in usually 10 minutes or less to more than 15,500 locations in 75 countries. So if the money you need to see history becomes history, call us and we'll direct you to a MoneyGram agent closest to you.

USA: 1-800-MONEYGRAM • Canada: 1-800-933-3278
France: (331) 47-77-70-00 • Germany: (0049) Ø*-69-21050
England: (44) Ø*-71-839-7541 • Spain: (91) 322 54 55
When in Europe, contact the nearest American Express Travel Service Office.

MoneyGram℠
INTERNATIONAL MONEY TRANSFERS.

Introduction

Visitors to London often arrive with more preconceptions than luggage. Like it or not, countless images and symbols of England's capital have become ingrained in the global subconscious, some from contact with Shakespeare, Dickens, and Shaw, others from the Beatles, the Stones, and the Smiths. Even people who've never set foot in London have vivid images of Big Ben, Tower Bridge, red double-decker buses, and pasty white people brandishing raincoats and umbrellas. Newcomers, however, should be prepared to throw most preconceptions out the window. Now that the British empire has come home to roost, large factions of former subjects have relocated to London, and the presence of so many international influences is changing the very essence of what it is to be English. The buses are still here—as are Big Ben and Tower Bridge—but modern London is far more diverse and complex than Dickens could ever have imagined.

With a population of almost seven million, London is both quintessentially English and an eccentric aberration. For every traditional pub serving bangers and crisps, there's a Bengali, Vietnamese, or Caribbean restaurant vying for tourist dollars. For every patriotic Londoner ranting and raving from a Speakers' Corner soapbox about the relative worth of monarchy, there are impassioned activists pressing for equitable treatment of gays, people with disabilities, and others living in the margins of mainstream British society. Unlike the traditional picture of England presented by a film like *The Remains of the Day* (adapted, ironically, from the novel by Kazuo Ishiguro, an Englishman of Japanese descent), modern London is perhaps best summed up by nontraditional—even apocalyptic—films like Mike Leigh's *Naked* and Stephen Frears's *Sammie and Rosie Get Laid*.

> *Asked for his impression of English civilization, Mahatma Ghandi reputedly said, "I think it would be a good idea."*

This is not to say that all Londoners are embracing the changes wrought by multiculturalism. White supremacist groups, which are exerting their influence in working-class neighborhoods that have been hard hit by unemployment, are criticizing unchecked immigration and crying, "England for the English." Since the reign of Margaret Thatcher in the 1980s, government economic policy has been unsubtly skewed to the benefit of London's white upper classes, as much from ignorance as from prejudice. Within a week of arriving in London, you'll no doubt hear at least one wisecrack about "those stupid Irish," Yorkshiremen who do it with sheep, or Bengali shopkeepers who "just don't belong."

Yet if you make the mistake of coming to London with generalizations about how bland, uptight, and close-minded the English are, you deserve to have a bland, uptight, close-minded experience. Part of London's appeal is discovering the reality behind the preconceptions and prejudices. The ritual of cream tea surprises you for being tangible and, after the scrumptious clotted cream, strawberry jam, and scones have been safely tucked away in the tummy, the ritual takes on a new meaning. The same goes for the English pub, for cricket and rugby, and for scrappy kids eating fish-and-chips wrapped in greasy newspaper. These images ring hollow as stereotypes, but if you look beyond London's heavily trod tourist trails, you'll discover that they are common, real, and meaningful aspects of modern British society.

As great a city as London is, few people fall madly in love with it at first sight. Even after a few weeks, people can remain noncommittal. Maybe it's the dreary weather, or maybe it's that the fabled British reserve just doesn't see the need to celebrate itself. But don't be deterred: London *can* inspire a fierce, if classically understated, love and loyalty. This is especially true of "foreigners" who call London home—people who, having scratched below the gray stone and overcast weather, find a wealth of things to do. Shopping in the rain on Camden Lock can be a romantic novelty, whether you're here for a week, a month, or a year. The same goes for something as mundane as hailing a black cab on a soggy winter evening. Locals rarely take to the bridges over the Thames to gaze at the skyline, but it's exactly this sort of wide-eyed approach that shows London

If you dare to suggest that you can eat well in London, or that some Londoners can be as fashionable and outgoing as anyone else, people twitch, unable to admit it may actually be true

in its best light. "All bright and glittering in the smokeless aire," wrote William Wordsworth after standing upon Westminster Bridge one morning, and he was right. London is sort of beautiful.

Don't skip the classic sights: A peek at the spoils of the empire that are housed within the British Museum reveals more about English imperialism than a stack of history books ever could. By the same token, a stroll around the grounds of Buckingham Palace gives a better sense of royal wealth, power, and influence than a thousand stories in the *Sun* and other tabloids. On the other hand, don't get sucked into the tour-package version of the city that narrowly focuses on traditional and royal London—a Disneyesque montage of busbied sentries, Beefeaters, and pomp and circumstance. Instead, grab the latest copy of *New Musical Express* and a Thermos full of strong Earl Grey, and plant yourself on Trafalgar Square in the wee hours of a Sunday morning, when the all-night clubbers are waiting for the last buses home. This, after all, is the real London, the London that sucks you in and keeps you coming back for more.

PRESENTING AN INDEPENDENT APPROACH TO TRAVEL.

If you have independent ideas about travel, we specialize in putting you *exactly* where you want to be. And with over 100 offices worldwide, we'll take care of you when you're there. So when it's time to plan your trip, call us at 1.800.777.0112.

New York: 212-477-7166
Washington DC: 202-887-0912
Philadelphia: 215-382-2928
Boston: 617-266-6014
Los Angeles: 213-934-8722
San Francisco: 415-391-8407

STA TRAVEL

We've been there

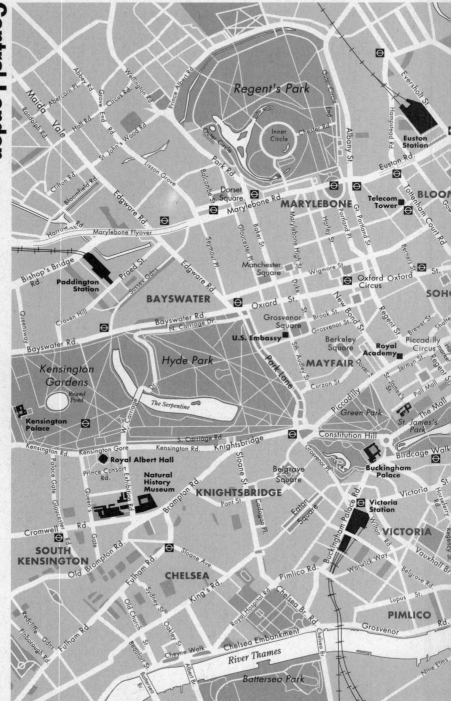

Regent's Park

Inner Circle

Outer Circle

Chester Rd.

Albany St.

Eversholt St.

Euston Station

Hampstead Rd.

Euston Rd.

Maida Vale

Randolph Rd.

Clifton Rd.

Bloomfield Rd.

Abercorn Pl.

Hall Rd.

Abbey Rd.

Grove End Rd.

Circus Rd.

St. John's Wood Rd.

Wellington Rd.

Prince Albert Rd.

Outer Circle

Park Rd.

Dorset Square

Balcombe St.

Marylebone Rd.

MARYLEBONE

Gt. Portland St.

Portland Pl.

Harley St.

Telecom Tower

Tottenham Court Rd.

BLOOM

Gow

Harrow Rd.

Edgware Rd.

Marylebone Flyover

Bishop's Bridge Rd.

Paddington Station

Praed St.

Sussex Gdns.

Edgware Rd.

Seymour Pl.

Gloucester Pl.

Baker St.

Marylebone High St.

Wigmore St.

Manchester Square

Oxford Circus

Oxford

St.

SOHO

BAYSWATER

Craven Hill

Queensway

Bayswater Rd.

N. Carriage Dr.

Bayswater Rd.

Oxford

St.

Grosvenor Square

U.S. Embassy

Brook St.

Grosvenor St.

Sth. Audley St.

New Bond St.

Berkeley Square

MAYFAIR

Curzon St.

Royal Academy

Jermyn St.

Regent St.

Dover St.

Piccadilly Circus

Brewer St.

Shafte

market

Regent

Pall Mall

St. James's

The Mall

Kensington Gardens

Royal Pond

The Serpentine

W. Carriage Dr.

Kensington Palace

Kensington Rd.

Kensington Gore

Prince Consort Rd.

Royal Albert Hall

Natural History Museum

Exhibition Rd.

Kensington Rd.

S. Carriage Rd.

Knightsbridge

Sloane St.

Belgrave Square

Constitution Hill

Grosvenor Pl.

Green Park

St. James's Park

Buckingham Palace

Birdcage Walk

Cromwell Rd.

Palace Gate

Gloucester Rd.

Queen's Gate

Brompton Rd.

Pont St.

Cadogan Pl.

KNIGHTSBRIDGE

Eaton Square

Buckingham Palace Rd.

Victoria Station

Victoria

Wilton Rd.

VICTORIA

Horseferry Rd.

Vauxhall Br.

Regency St

SOUTH KENSINGTON

Old Brompton Rd.

Fulham Rd.

Sloane Ave.

CHELSEA

King's Rd.

Pimlico Rd.

Warwick Way

Belgrave Rd.

Lupus St.

PIMLICO

Grosvenor

Redcliffe Gdns.

Finborough Rd.

Fulham Rd.

Old Church St.

Sydney St.

Oakley St.

Royal Hospital Rd.

Chelsea Br. Rd.

Chelsea Br.

Beaufort St.

Battersea Br.

Cheyne Walk

Albert Br.

Chelsea Embankment

River Thames

Battersea Park

Nine Elms

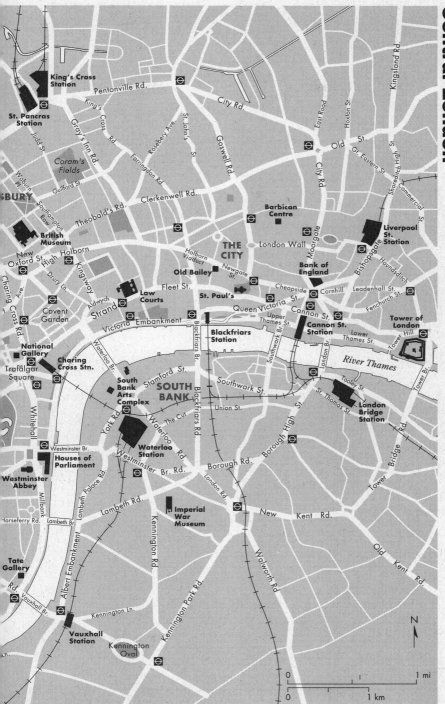

Central London

King's Cross Station

St. Pancras Station

Pentonville Rd.

City Rd.

King's Cross Rd.

Gray's Inn Rd.

Rosebery Ave.

Goswell Rd.

City Rd.

Old St.

East Road

Hoxton St.

Kingsland Rd.

Gt. Eastern St.

Shoreditch High St.

Commercial St.

Coram's Fields

Judd St.

Woburn Pl.

Guilford St.

Southampton Row

Farringdon Rd.

St. John's

Clerkenwell Rd.

Theobald's Rd.

Barbican Centre

Liverpool St. Station

SBURY

British Museum

New Oxford St.

High Holborn

Kingsway

Holborn Viaduct

Newgate St.

London Wall

Moorgate

Bishopsgate

Houndsditch

THE CITY

Bank of England

Old Bailey

St. Paul's

Cheapside

Cornhill

Leadenhall St.

Fenchurch St.

Charing Cross Rd.

Drury Ln.

Aldwych

Law Courts

Fleet St.

Queen Victoria St.

Upper Thames St.

Cannon St.

Lower Thames St.

Tower of London

Covent Garden

Strand

Victoria Embankment

Blackfriars Br.

Blackfriars Station

Cannon St. Station

London Br.

Tower Hill

Tower Br.

National Gallery

Charing Cross Stn.

Waterloo Br.

Southwark Br.

River Thames

Trafalgar Square

Stamford St.

SOUTH BANK

Southwark St.

Tooley St.

St. Thomas St.

London Bridge Station

South Bank Arts Complex

York Rd.

Waterloo

The Cut

Blackfriars Rd.

Union St.

Borough High St.

Tower Bridge Rd.

Whitehall

Waterloo Station

Westminster Br.

Houses of Parliament

Westminster Br. Rd.

Borough Rd.

London Rd.

Westminster Abbey

Lambeth Palace Rd.

Lambeth Rd.

Imperial War Museum

New Kent Rd.

Old Kent Rd.

Millbank

Horseferry Rd.

Lambeth Br.

Albert Embankment

Kennington Rd.

Kennington Park Rd.

Walworth Rd.

Tate Gallery

Vauxhall Br.

Kennington Ln.

N

Vauxhall Station

Kennington Oval

0   1 mi

0   1 km

xvii

TOP 5 Ways to Save Money While Traveling

5. Ship yourself in a crate marked "Livestock." Remember to poke holes in the crate.

4. Board a train dressed as Elvis and sneer and say "The King rides for free."

3. Ask if you can walk through the Channel Tunnel.

2. Board the plane dressed as an airline pilot, nod to the flight attendants, and hide in the rest room until the plane lands.

1. Bring a balloon to the airline ticket counter, kneel, breathe in the helium, and ask for the kiddie fare.

But if you're serious about saving money while you're traveling abroad, just get an ISIC--the International Student Identity Card. Discounts for students on international airfares, hotels and motels, car rentals, international phone calls, financial services, and more.

BASICS

1

If you've ever traveled with anyone before, you know the two types of people in the world: the planners and the nonplanners. You also know that travel brings out the very worst in both groups. Left to their own devices, the planners will have you goose-stepping from attraction to attraction on a cultural blitzkrieg, while the nonplanners will invariably miss the flight, the bus, and the point. The following pages offer you a middle ground, because like any big city, London respects the traveler who knows what's up. Bear in mind that telephone numbers change, companies go out of business, and sometimes the particular person answering the phone just doesn't know. And hey, we're only too human; as one Nixon official so eloquently said, "mistakes have been made."

Planning Your Trip

WHEN TO GO

The main tourist season runs from mid-April to mid-October, but the real hordes arrive in June, July, and August—prepare for the crunch. In summer, prices predictably go up, and many hostels and cheap hotels stop offering weekly rates. Even so, the daffodils and crocuses are in full bloom, and British high society hits its stride with events like Wimbledon and the Royal Ascot. In winter, London doesn't hibernate simply because all the tourists have gone home. In fact, you're more likely to get an honest—albeit a cold and wet—view of the city during the off-season, without the troops of Americans, Australians, French, Japanese, and everyone else who "does London" in two days as part of "Le Grand Tour."

CLIMATE Every 10 years, London is blessed with a summer so wonderful that it helps everyone through the next nine years of gray skies. (Unfortunately, the summer of 1994 was one such glorious period, with temperatures in the 80s and 90s.) Though the temperature rarely falls below freezing in winter, the air is damp, and the cold seems to go right to your bones. The fact that London's B&Bs and hostels have yet to come to grips with central heating does little to help matters. In spring, the weather is incredibly schizophrenic: Sun, rain, and hail can follow one another in rapid succession. London's average highs and lows stack up as follows: **January** 39°F/43°F, **July** 56°F/71°F.

Even in summer, rain is a threat and layering is de rigueur. Summer also means long, long days—sunrise by 6:30 AM, sunset by 10:30 PM.

PUBLIC HOLIDAYS Banks, shops, and almost everything you depend on close on the following national holidays: **January 1** (New Year's Day); **Good Friday** (two days before Easter); **Easter Sunday; Easter Monday** (Mon. after Easter); the first and last Mondays in May (bank holidays); the last Monday in August (bank holiday); **December 25–26** (Christmas and Boxing Day).

FESTIVALS London has more festivals, street parties, and royal parades than you can shake a scepter at; check *Time Out* magazine and other local publications for info on seasonal events. Many events listed below are free, though some—like Wimbledon—are most definitely not.

➣ **JANUARY** • Trafalgar Square hosts a huge **New Year's Eve** celebration. On the last Sunday in January, Londoners dress up in 17th-century garb to celebrate the **Charles I Commemoration** at the Banqueting House in Whitehall, held on the anniversary of the monarch's execution.

➣ **FEBRUARY** • London's large Chinese community (primarily from Hong Kong) throws a big bash on Gerrard Street to usher in the **Chinese New Year.** The main festivities—lion and dragon dancers, street performers, and lots of firecrackers—usually take place on the Sunday following Chinese New Year; ring 0171/437–5256 for a schedule of events. Although the English don't give a hoot about groundhogs, they're crazy about dogs, especially during the first weekend in February at the **Cruft's Dog Show** (Earl's Court Exhibition Centre, Warwick Rd., tel. 0171/493–6651).

➣ **MARCH** • The **Camden Jazz Festival** hits this north London neighborhood early each March; look for posters around town or check *Time Out* for ticket info. An **Easter Day Parade** with floats and marching bands marks the holiday in Battersea Park.

➣ **APRIL** • Trusty steeds pound the pavement at the **London Harness Horse Parade** (tel. 01733/234451), held on the Inner Circle in Regent's Park. Londoners don medieval garb and parade from Southwark Cathedral to the Tower of London for the one-day **Chaucer Festival** in early April (tel. 01227/470379). The fete continues at the Tower, with food, jugglers, and strolling minstrels galore. Late April's **London Marathon** (tel. 0171/620–4117) is one of the great spectacles of the running world, with enthusiastic crowds and more than 25,000 giddy participants. The best place to watch is at Tower Bridge, where the starting and finishing lines are. The **Boat Race,** the annual contest between the rowing "eights" of Cambridge and Oxford, is held on a Saturday in late March or early April. The race down the Thames starts at Putney (take the tube to Putney Bridge) and finishes at Mortlake.

➣ **MAY** • Held late in the month, Britain's ultra-hyped **Chelsea Flower Show** (tel. 0171/834–4333) is the be-all and end-all of flowers and gardening in a country that takes both very seriously. **Beating the Bounds** (tel. 0171/488–4772) is a remnant from the days when school parish boundaries were marked by schoolboys who ran around the Tower of London; one boy is even dangled by his ankles to smack the boundary line on the Thames.

➣ **JUNE** • Tickets are sold out months in advance for **Wimbledon** (tel. 0181/944–1066 or 0181/946–2244 for recorded info), the world's most prestigious tennis competition. But you can still get in if you're prepared to wait in line (some people bring sleeping bags); take the tube to Southfields or Wimbledon Park and follow the crowds. **The Trooping of the Colour** (tel. 0171/930–4466) celebrates the official birthday of the queen and features a small contingent of troops in charmingly archaic outfits performing—with much pomp and circumstance—for their fearless leader. Another June staple is the **Beating Retreat Ceremony** (tel. 0171/930–4466), a floodlighted spectacle of marching bands and soldiers on horseback. Europe's largest music fete, the **Capital Radio Music Festival,** happens from mid-June to mid-July. Look for posters around town or in *Time Out* for details on who's playing where.

In late June, London's huge Gay Pride Festival rallies, parties, and parades around Regent's Park, Hampstead Heath, or Hyde Park; check the local gay press for this year's venue.

➢ **JULY** • Held during the first three weeks in July, the **City of London Festival** is all about music, theater, poetry, and art. The venues change from year to year, so check for posters or in newspapers for the latest details. At the **Royal Tournament** (tel. 0171/373–8141) in late July, it's Las Vegas meets the armed forces with military pageantry and jingoism. Held in the Royal Albert Hall, the **Henry Wood Promenade Concerts** (tel. 0171/765–4296), nicknamed the "Proms," is one of the world's premier classical-music events. The concerts begin in mid-July and continue through September. The South Bank Arts Centre (tel. 0171/928–3232) hosts the **Summerscope Festival of Performing Arts** in July and August, with film, theater, dance, classical music, and most anything else you can think of.

➢ **AUGUST** • Bottoms up—hundreds of beers are available to sample for a mere £3 during the **Great British Beer Festival** (tel. 01727/867201), held the first week of August. At the end of the month, the **Notting Hill Carnival** (tel. 0181/964–0544) is the biggest street festival in Europe. The flavor is strongly Afro-Caribbean, with live music, floats, food, and spliffs galore. London's buskers congregate once a year along with overseas colleagues for mid-August's **International Street Performers Festival** in the Covent Garden Piazza.

➢ **SEPTEMBER** • The **Chinatown Mid-Autumn Festival** (tel. 0171/437–5256), held on Gerrard Street in Soho, is a smaller but no less colorful version of the Chinese New Year festival (*see above*). The Pearly Kings and Queens, representatives of costermongers (fruit and vegetable vendors), gather at the Church of St. Martin-in-the-Fields for **Costermonger's Pearly Harvest Festival** (tel. 0171/930–0089). The prestigious **Horse of the Year Show** (tel. 01298/72272) features show jumping and other equestrian hijinks in Wembley Arena. On **Horseman's Sunday** (tel. 0171/262–1732), the good vicar of the Church of St. John and St. Michael sits on horseback and blesses more than 100 horses, which then proceed to trot through Hyde Park. You can spend the rest of the afternoon at a show-jumping competition at Kensington Paddock.

➢ **OCTOBER** • The influential but long-dormant **Soho Jazz Festival** (tel. 0171/437–6437) is trying to make a comeback and slowly succeeding. It's usually held the first week of October. Later in the month, or in early November, the queen rides in a coach from Buckingham Palace to the Houses of Parliament to read a speech. The procession and the pep talk that follows marks the **Opening of Parliament.**

➢ **NOVEMBER** • November 5 marks **Guy Fawkes Night,** a fireworks and bonfire celebration commemorating a foiled attempt to blow up Parliament in 1605. (It all started when James I of Scotland inherited the English throne and began making nasty comments about Catholics. Several plots were hatched against the new king, and just before the 1605 session of Parliament, Guy Fawkes and his accomplices were found in a cellar beneath the House of Lords with enough gunpowder to blow it to bits. The MPs were not amused, and Guy was hanged.) The best place to see fireworks and attend a bonfire is Primrose Hill near Camden Town. On the second Saturday in November, the **Lord Mayor's Show** (tel. 0171/606–3030) makes a big deal of the person who still has some sort of vestigial sovereignty over the one-square-mile chunk known as the City. A bunch of floats make a ceremonial trek from Westminster to the Law Courts, where the Lord Mayor makes a speech, accepts his duties, and so forth. The evening brings fireworks along the Thames. For something a little more modern, make your way to the National Film Theatre at the South Bank Arts Centre for the smashing **London Film Festival** (tel. 0171/815–1320).

GOVERNMENT TOURIST OFFICES

➢ **IN THE UNITED STATES** • The **British Tourist Authority (BTA)** answers queries and provides maps and printed travel info about England, Wales, Scotland, and Northern Ireland. *Main office: 551 5th Ave., New York, NY 10176, tel. 800/462–2748.*

➢ **IN CANADA** • *111 Avenue Rd., Suite 450, Toronto, Ont. M5R 3J8, tel. 416/925–6326.*

➢ **DOWN UNDER** • Australia: *8th Floor, University Centre, 210 Clarence St., Sydney, NSW 2000, tel. 02/267–4413.* **New Zealand:** *Suite 305, Dilworth Bldg., Queen and Customs Sts., Auckland 1, tel. 09/303–1446.*

BUDGET TRAVEL ORGANIZATIONS

Student Travel Australia (STA) has 120 offices worldwide and offers low-price airfares to destinations around the globe. It also sells rail passes, books car rentals, and issues the International Student Identity Card (ISIC) and the STA Travel Card to anyone 35 or under. STA also issues offer IYC (International Youth Card), AYH (American Youth Hostel), and ITC (International Teacher Card) cards (*see* Student I.D. Cards, *below*). Call for free pamphlets on services and rates.

Council on International Educational Exchange (CIEE) is a nonprofit organization dedicated to the pursuit of work, study, and travel abroad. Through its two subsidiaries, **Council Travel** and **Council Charter,** CIEE offers discounted airfares, rail passes, accommodations, and guidebooks. It issues the ISIC, IYC, ITC, and youth hostel cards (*see* Student I.D. Cards, *below*). **Council Charter** (tel. 212/661–0311 or 800/223–7402) buys blocks of seats on commercial flights and sells them at a discount. *205 E. 42nd St., New York, NY 10017, tel. 212/661–1414.*

Travel CUTS is a full-service travel agency that sells discounted airline tickets to Canadian students and issues ISIC, IYC, and HI cards. Their 25 offices are on or near college campuses. *187 College St., Toronto, Ont. M5T 1P7, tel. 416/979–2406.*

Hostelling International (HI) is the grandmammy of hostel associations, offering cheap (£5–£12 per night), single-sex, dorm-style beds ("couples" rooms and family accommodations are available at certain HI hostels) plus kitchen facilities at more than 250 locations in Britain (London alone has seven HI hostels). Membership in the Youth Hostel Association of England and Wales (YHA) allows you to stay in any HI-affiliated hostel at member rates. Members also have priority if the hostel is full. Annual membership, available to travelers of all ages, costs $25 for adults, $10 for those under 18, and $35 for families; renewals are $20. Lifetime membership will set you back $250, and if you're not sure you want to commit, a one-night guest membership is only $3. *733 15th St. NW, Suite 840, Washington, DC 20005, tel. 202/783–6161.*

Other associations aiding and abetting hostel-goers include **American Youth Hostels (AYH)** (733 15th St., Suite 840, Washington, DC 20005, tel. 202/783–6161); **Canadian Hostelling Association (CHA)** (1600 James Naismith Dr., Suite 608, Gloucester, Ont. K1B 5N4, tel. 613/748–5638); **Youth Hostel Association of England and Wales (YHA)** (Trevelyan House, 8

STA Offices

- **UNITED STATES. ARIZONA:** *Scottsdale (tel. 602/596–5151 or 800/777–0112).* **CALIFORNIA:** *Berkeley (tel. 510/642–3000); Los Angeles (tel. 213/934–8722); San Francisco (tel. 415/391–8407); Santa Monica (tel. 310/394–5126); Westwood (tel. 310/824–1574).* **MASSACHUSETTS:** *Boston (tel. 617/266–6014); Cambridge (tel. 617/576–4623).* **NEW YORK:** *East Village (tel. 212/477–7166); Columbia University (tel. 212/854–2224).* **PENNSYLVANIA:** *Philadelphia (tel. 215/382–2928).* **WASHINGTON DC** *(tel. 202/887–0912).*

- **INTERNATIONAL. AUSTRALIA:** *Adelaide (tel. 08/223–2426); Brisbane (tel. 07/221–9388); Cairns (tel. 070/314199); Darwin (tel. 089/412955); Melbourne (tel. 03/349–2411); Perth (tel. 09/227–7569); Sydney (tel. 02/212–1255).* **FRANCE:** *Paris (tel. 01/4325–0076).* **HOLLAND:** *Amsterdam (tel. 020/626–2557).* **NEW ZEALAND:** *Auckland (tel. 09/309–9995); Christchurch (tel. 03/379–9098); Wellington (tel. 04/385–0561).* **UNITED KINGDOM:** *London (tel. 0171/938–4711).*

St. Stephen's Hill, St. Albans, Herts. AL1 2DY, England, tel. 01727/855215); **Australian Youth Hostels Association (YHA)** (Box 61, Strawberry Hills, Sydney 2012, New South Wales, tel. 02/212–1266); and **Youth Hostels Association of New Zealand (YHA)** (Box 436, Christchurch 1, tel. 03/799970).

STUDENT I.D. CARDS

The **International Student Identity Card (ISIC)** entitles students to special fares on local transportation as well as discounts at museums, theaters, sporting events, and many other attractions. If purchased in the United States, the $17 card also buys you $3,000 in emergency medical coverage, limited hospital coverage, and access to a 24-hour international, toll-free hot line for assistance in medical, legal, and financial emergencies. In the United States, apply to CIEE or STA. In Canada, the ISIC is available for C$15 from Travel CUTS (*see* Budget Travel Organizations, *above*). In the United Kingdom, students with valid university I.D.s can purchase the ISIC at any student union or student-travel company. Applicants must submit a passport-type photo as well as proof of current full-time student status, age, and nationality.

The **STA Travel Card** is available to travelers ages 35 and under for $6. With it, you're eligible for a book of dollars-off coupons that are good at a limited number of subscribing businesses, discount student fares, and access to the "Discount Counter." Purchase the card from STA *before* departing on your trip.

The **Youth International Educational Exchange Card (YIEE)** is issued to travelers (students and nonstudents) under age 26 by the Federation of International Youth Travel Organizations (FIYTO). It provides services similar to those given by the ISIC card. The card is available for $16 from CIEE or FIYTO. *81 Islands Brugge, DK-2300 Copenhagen S, Denmark.*

Council Travel Offices

ARIZONA: Tempe (tel. 602/966–3544). CALIFORNIA: Berkeley (tel. 510/848–8604); Davis (tel. 916/752–2285); La Jolla (tel. 619/452–0630); Long Beach (tel. 310/598–3338 or 714/527–7950); Los Angeles (tel. 310/208–3551); Palo Alto (tel. 415/325–3888); San Diego (tel. 619/270–6401); San Francisco (tel. 415/421–3473 or 415/566–6222); Santa Barbara (tel. 805/562–8080). COLORADO: Boulder (tel. 303/447–8101). CONNECTICUT: New Haven (tel. 203/562–5335). FLORIDA: Miami (tel. 305/670–9261). GEORGIA: Atlanta (tel. 404/377–9997). ILLINOIS: Chicago (tel. 312/ 951–0585); Evanston (tel. 708/475–5070). INDIANA: Bloomington (tel. 812/330– 1600). LOUISIANA: New Orleans (tel. 504/866–1767). MASSACHUSETTS: Amherst (tel. 413/256–1261); Boston (tel. 617/266–1926 or 617/424–6665); Cambridge (tel. 617/497–1497 or 617/225–2555). MICHIGAN: Ann Arbor (tel. 313/998–0200). MIN- NESOTA: Minneapolis (tel. 612/379–2323). NEW YORK: New York (tel. 212/661–1450, 212/666–4177, or 212/254–2525). NORTH CAROLINA: Chapel Hill (tel. 919/942– 2334). OHIO: Columbus (tel. 614/294–8696). OREGON: Portland (tel. 503/228–1900). PENNSYLVANIA: Philadelphia (tel. 215/382–0343); Pittsburgh (tel. 412/683–1881). RHODE ISLAND: Providence (tel. 401/331–5810). TEXAS: Austin (tel. 512/472– 4931); Dallas (tel. 214/363–9941). UTAH: Salt Lake City (tel. 801/582–5840). WASH- INGTON: Seattle (tel. 206/632–2448 or 206/329–4567). WASHINGTON DC (tel. 202/ 337–6464).

INTERNATIONAL STUDENT EXCHANGE ID CARD!!!

ise CARDS®

- Special Student Airfares to Europe/Asia

- Special Discounts Abroad, Accommodations/Museums Exhibitions

- International Medical Insurance

- 24 Hour Hotline

- Scheduled Major Airlines/ No Charters

- 75 U.S. Departure Cities/ 183 Foreign Destinations

- Groups and Individuals

- Eurail and Britrail Passes

- International Youth Hostel Cards

- International Student Exchange ID Cards

- International Faculty ID Cards

☐ **YES!** Rush me my ISE Card! I want to save money when I fly in the U.S. or overseas. I understand that if I'm not 100% satisfied, I can return my Card within 60 days, and receive a full refund of the price I paid.

SEND CARD TO:

Name _____

Address _____

City/State/Zip _____

Name of Your School _____

Your Birthdate Nationality _____

Phone Number (____) _____ - _____

I am a... ☐ Student ☐ Faculty Memeber

METHOD OF PAYMENT:

☐ Check enclosed for $15.00 (Card only)
☐ Check enclosed for $17.95 (Card plus Handbook)

Charge to my ☐ VISA ☐ MasterCard
☐ American Express ☐ Discover

Card Number _____

Exp. Date _____ / _____ / _____

I certify that I am currently, or have been during the last 12 months, a student or facutly member at the School stated above.

Signature X _____

ISE Cards, Inc. P.O. Box 22111, Phoenix, Arizona 85028. (602) 951-2157

PASSPORTS AND VISAS

Visas are not required for U.S., Canadian, Australian, or New Zealand citizens for stays of up to three months in the United Kingdom. If you plan to stay for more than three months, you'll almost certainly need a visa; talk to the British consulate before you leave home. If you discover that you just can't bear to leave your new English lover, contact immigration officials or the local police well before your three months is up.

OBTAINING A PASSPORT

➤ **U.S. CITIZENS** • You must apply for a passport in person if: you're a first-time applicant; your most recent passport was issued more than 12 years ago or before you were 16; your passport has been lost or stolen; or you are between 13 and 17 years old (in which case a parent must accompany you). Other renewals can be taken care of by mail. Apply at one of the 13 U.S. Passport Agency offices a *minimum of five weeks* before your departure; local county courthouses, many state and probate courts, and some post offices also accept passport applications. For fastest processing, apply between August and December. If you blow it, you can have a passport issued within five days of departure if you have your plane ticket in hand. This method usually works, but if there's one little glitch in the system, you're out of luck. Have the following items ready when you go to get your passport:

• A completed passport application (form DSP-11), available at courthouses, some post offices, and passport agencies.

• Proof of citizenship (certified copy of birth certificate, naturalization papers, or previous passport issued in the past 12 years).

• Proof of identity with your photograph and signature (for example, a valid driver's license, employee I.D. card, military I.D., student I.D.).

• Two recent, identical, 2-inch-square photographs (black-and-white or color head shots).

• A $55 application fee for a 10-year passport ($30 for those under 18 for a five-year passport). First-time applicants are also hit with a $10 surcharge. If you're paying cash, exact change is necessary; checks or money orders should be made out to Passport Services.

If you're lucky enough to be able to renew your passport by mail, send a completed form DSP-82 (available from a passport agency); two recent, identical passport photos; your current passport (less than 12 years old); and a check or money order for $55 ($30 if under 18) to the nearest passport agency. Renewals take three to four weeks.

For more information or an application, contact the **Department of State Office of Passport Services** (tel. 202/647–0518) and dial your way through their message maze. Passport applications can be picked up at U.S. post offices, at federal or state courts, and at U.S. Passport Agencies in Boston, Chicago, Honolulu, Houston, Los Angeles, Miami, New Orleans, New York, Philadelphia, San Francisco, Seattle, Stamford, and Washington, DC.

➤ **CANADIAN CITIZENS** • Canadians should send a completed passport application (available at any post office or passport office) to the **Bureau of Passports** (Suite 215, West Tower, Guy Favreau Complex, 200 Rene Levesque Blvd. W, Montréal, Qué. H2Z 1X4, tel. 514/283–2152). Include C$35; two recent, identical passport photographs (as specified on the application); and proof of Canadian citizenship (original birth certificate or other official document as specified). You can also apply in person at regional passport offices in many locations, including Edmonton, Halifax, Montreal, Toronto, Vancouver, and Winnipeg. Passports have a shelf life of five years. Processing takes about two weeks by mail and five working days for in-person applications.

➤ **AUSTRALIAN CITIZENS** • Australians must visit a post office or passport office to complete the passport application process. A 10-year passport for those over 18 costs AUS$76. The under-18 crowd can get a five-year passport for AUS$37. For more information, call toll-free in Australia 008/026022.

➤ **NEW ZEALAND CITIZENS** • Passport applications can be found at any post office or consulate. Completed applications must be accompanied by proof of citizenship, two passport-size photos, and a letter from a friend confirming the applicant's identity. The fee is NZ$50 for a 10-year passport. Processing takes about three weeks.

LOST PASSPORTS If your passport is lost or stolen while traveling, immediately notify the local police and nearest embassy or consulate. A consular officer should be able to issue you a new one, or at least get you back into your country of origin without one. The process will be slowed considerably if you don't have some other forms of identification on you, so you're well advised to carry a driver's license, a copy of your birth certificate, and a student I.D. separately from your passport. For good measure, tuck a few photocopies of the front page of your passport in your luggage and/or a traveling companion's pockets.

To deal with lost and stolen passports, the Canadian embassy or consulate requires a police report, any form of I.D., and three passport-size photos; you must also have a guarantor with you (someone who has known you for at least two years, lives within the jurisdiction of the consulate or embassy, and is a mayor, practicing lawyer, notary public, judge, magistrate, police officer, signing officer at a bank, medical doctor, or dentist). Since most travelers don't know anyone fitting this description, there's also the option of paying an officer of the consulate/embassy to be your guarantor (proving once again that throwing enough money at a problem usually makes it go away). A replacement passport usually takes five working days. New Zealand officials ask for two passport-size photos, and Australians require three, but both usually replace passports within 24 hours.

MONEY

CURRENCY The unit of currency in Great Britain is the pound, broken into 100 pence. Exchange rates change daily, but at press time £1 was equal to $1.56 and $1 was equal to 64p. In Great Britain, pound notes (nobody calls them "bills") come in denominations of £5, £10, £20, and £50. Coins are available in denominations of 1p, 2p, 5p, 10p, 20p, 50p, and £1. Older coins you may come across include the one-shilling coin (worth 5p) and the two-shilling coin (worth 10p). A heavy new £2 coin, currently just a collector's item, may become widely available toward the end of next year. Remember that coins, no matter how valuable, are *not* exchangeable outside the borders of the United Kingdom.

HOW MUCH IT WILL COST For travelers with American dollars, prices in Britain are almost double what they are in the United States. It's more than just a bad exchange rate—the Brits themselves can hardly afford to live in the country. Even if you stay in hostels and eat only pub grub and cheap Indian food, be prepared to drop $50 a day. If you plan to stay in hotels and eat in restaurants, your daily bill could top $100 per person. To add insult to injury, the British government slaps a whopping 17.5% Value Added Tax (VAT) on almost everything. VAT is usually included in prices, but not always—be sure to ask. Lodging will be your greatest expense. Expect to pay around £8–£12 for a bed in a hostel, £15–£20 per person for a room in a B&B. Hotels are extremely expensive (£20 and up), and often lack the charm and friendliness of B&Bs.

In England, you only tip if the service is excellent. Standard practice is to tip 10% in taxis and restaurants (unless service is included). Bartenders are rarely tipped.

TRAVELING WITH MONEY Cash never goes out of style, but traveler's checks and a major credit card are the safest way to pay on the road. Strike a balance with these three forms of currency, and protect yourself by carrying your cash in a money belt or "necklace" pouch, by keeping accurate records of traveler's checks' serial numbers, and by recording credit card numbers and emergency numbers for reporting the cards' loss or theft. Since most budget establishments only accept cash, bring some U.S. currency in small denominations; changing dollars is easier and often cheaper than cashing traveler's checks.

CHANGING MONEY Bureaux de change are everywhere in London—at banks, airport booths, and tiny kiosks on street corners and near city center tube stations. If you find a "fabulous" exchange rate, ask if they charge a commission; most bureaux de change in London take

2%–3% for themselves (some bloodsuckers actually skim 5%). If you have American Express or Thomas Cook traveler's checks (*see below*), you don't pay commissions *if* you exchange the checks at one of their respective offices. It's always cheaper to buy pounds in Britain rather than at home—though you might want to change $30 or so before arriving, just in case the exchange booth at the train station or airport is closed or has an unbearably long line.

TRAVELER'S CHECKS Traveler's checks can be used in the same way as personal checks (always ask first), or they can be exchanged for cash at banks, some hotels, tourist offices, American Express offices, and currency-exchange offices. American Express checks are the most widely accepted; other brands—even Visa checks—are sometimes refused. Some banks and credit unions will issue checks free to established customers, but most charge a 1%–2% commission fee. Members of the American Automobile Association (AAA) can purchase American Express traveler's checks from the AAA commission-free. Buy the bulk of your traveler's checks in small denominations (a pack of five $20 checks is the smallest); many establishments won't accept large bills, and, even if they do, breaking a large check for small purchases leaves you carrying too much cash. Unlike cash, lost or stolen traveler's checks *can* be replaced or refunded *if* you can produce the purchase agreement and a record of the checks' serial numbers (especially of those you've already cashed). Common sense dictates that you keep the purchase agreement separate from your checks. Caution-happy travelers will even give a copy of the purchase agreement and checks' serial numbers to someone back home.

American Express (tel. 800/221–7282 in the United States and Canada) cardholders can order traveler's checks in U.S. dollars and six foreign currencies by phone, free of charge (with a gold card) or for a 1% commission (with the basic green card). Even if you don't have an AmEx gold card, you can still get American Express Traveler's Checks free with an AAA membership (talk to the cashier at your local AAA office). AmEx also issues **Traveler's Cheques for Two**, checks that can be signed and used by either you or your traveling companion. If you lose your checks or are ripped off, true to Karl Malden's repeated pledges, American Express has the resources to provide you with a speedy refund—often within 24 hours. Stop by a London AmEx office (*see* Staying in London, *below*) to write a personal check in exchange for traveler's checks, report lost or stolen checks, exchange foreign currency, or pick up mail.

Citicorp traveler's checks are available from Citibank and other banks worldwide in U.S. dollars and some foreign currencies. For 45 days from the date of check purchase, you have access to the 24-hour **International SOS Assistance Hot Line** (tel. 800/645–6556 in the United States or 813/623–1709 collect from abroad), which can provide referrals for interpreters and English-speaking doctors or lawyers; assistance with loss or theft of travel documents; traveler's check refund assistance; and an emergency message center.

CREDIT CARDS Major credit card companies have tightened requirements and aren't passing out $1,000 credit lines to students and low-income applicants the way they did in the material-world '80s. If you want plastic, check at university bookstores or student unions for special student offers from American Express and other companies. If a more economically sta-

Making the Most of Your Parents' Credit Card

Even if you have no job, no credit, no cards, and no respect, you can still tap into fabulous services offered by the Visa Assistance Center if one of your parents has a Visa Gold or Business card. You just have to be younger than 23 and at least 100 miles from home. Write down the card number in a safe place and call the center for emergency cash service, emergency ticket replacement, lost luggage assistance, medical and legal assistance, and an emergency message service. Helpful, multilingual personnel await your call 24 hours a day, seven days a week. In the United States call 800/759–6262; from overseas call 919/370–3203 collect.

BASICS

ble family member is willing, they may apply for a second card for you that's linked to their account. For a survey that details annual fees and interest rates, send a SASE to the nonprofit outfit **Consumer Action** (116 New Montgomery St., Suite 233, San Francisco, CA 94105, tel. 415/777–9635).

GETTING MONEY FROM HOME

Provided that there is money at home to be had, there are at least six ingenious ways to get it:

• Have it sent through a large **commercial bank** that has a branch in London. If there isn't one, you'll have to initiate the transfer at your own bank—slow and expensive.

• **American Express** cardholders can cash a personal check at an American Express office for up to $1,000 ($2,500 for gold cardholders) every 21 days; you'll be paid in U.S. traveler's checks or, in some instances, in foreign currency. **Express Cash** allows American Express cardholders to use automated teller machines (ATMs) and withdraw as much as $1,000 every 21 days from their personal checking accounts. (*see* Cash Machines, *below*).

• An **American Express MoneyGram**^{SM} can be a dream come true if you can convince someone back home to go to an American Express MoneyGram^{SM} agent and fill out the necessary forms. You don't have to be an AmEx cardholder: Simply pay up to $1,000 with a credit card or cash (and anything over that in cash) and, as soon as 10 minutes later, it's ready to be picked up. Fees vary according to the amount of money sent, but they range from 3% to 10%. You have to get the transaction reference number from your sender back home and show I.D. when picking up the money. For MoneyGram^{SM} agent locations call 800/926–9400; from overseas call 303/980–3340 collect or contact the nearest AmEx agent (*see* Staying in London, *below*).

• **MasterCard** and **Visa** cardholders can get cash advances from many banks, even in small towns. The commission for this handy-dandy service is about 6½%. If you get a personal identification number (PIN) number for your card before you leave home, you might even be able to make the transaction from an ATM machine.

• Have funds sent through **Western Union** (tel. 800/325–6000). Fees range from 4% to 10%, depending on the amount sent. If you have a MasterCard or Visa, you can have money sent up to your card's credit limit. If not, have someone take cash or a cashier's check to a Western Union office. The money will reach the requested destination in minutes but may not be available for hours or days, depending on the whim of the local authorities.

• In extreme emergencies (arrest, hospitalization, or worse) there *is* one more way U.S. citizens can receive money overseas: by setting up a **Department of State Trust Fund.** A friend or family member sends money to the Department of State, which then transfers the money to the U.S. embassy or consulate in London (tel. 0171/499–9000). Once this account has been established, you can send and receive money through Western Union, bank wire, or mail, all payable to the Department of State. Talk to the Department of State's Citizens' Emergency Center (tel. 202/647–5225).

CASH MACHINES Virtually all U.S. banks belong to a network of **ATMs,** which gobble up bank cards and spit out cash 24 hours a day around the world. Some are affiliated with the Cirrus system, some with PLUS and Exchange, and a very few with STAR. ATMs, however, are better in theory than practice. For one thing, if the transaction can't be completed (a common occurrence), chances are the computer lines are busy (especially on Friday afternoons), and you just have to try again later. Another problem is that some British ATMs only accept PINs of *four or fewer* digits; if your PIN is longer, ask your bank about changing it, and make sure you memorize the *numerical* code if you know your PIN as a word—some ATM keypads only show numbers. On the plus side, you can get British currency instantly at a generally excellent rate of exchange. Because some banks charge a 1%–3% fee per ATM transaction, consider withdrawing larger chunks of cash. To find out if there are cash machines in a given city, contact your bank's international banking department, or call **Cirrus** (tel. 800/424–7787) for a list of worldwide locations.

Gain 500 pounds within minutes.

Sometimes there's no such thing as unwanted pounds. At those times, it's nice to know that with Western Union you can receive money from the States within minutes, in case the situation arises. Plus it's already converted into pounds.

So just call either the toll-free number in London, 0-800-833-833*, or the United States, 1-800-325-6000*, and then pick up your money at any Western Union location.

Traveling can be a lot easier if you're packing a few extra pounds.

WESTERN UNION | MONEY TRANSFER
The fastest way to send money worldwide.^{SM}

A **Visa** or **MasterCard** can also be used to access cash through certain ATMs (provided you have a PIN for it), but the fees are usually higher than bank-card fees. Also, a daily interest charge usually begins to accrue immediately on these credit-card "loans," even if your monthly bills are paid up. Check with your bank for information on fees and on the daily limit for cash withdrawals.

Express Cash allows AmEx cardholders to withdraw up to $1,000 in a seven-day period (21 days overseas) from their personal checking accounts via a worldwide network of ATMs. Gold cardholders can receive up to $2,500 in a seven-day period (21 days overseas). Each transaction carries a 2% fee, with a minimum charge of $2 and a maximum of $6. Apply for a PIN and set up the linking of your accounts at least two or three weeks before departure. Call 800/CASH–NOW for an application.

STAYING HEALTHY

HEALTH AND ACCIDENT INSURANCE Some general health-insurance plans cover health expenses incurred while traveling, so review your existing health policies (or a parent's policy, if you're a dependent) before leaving home. Most university health-insurance plans stop and start with the school year, so don't count on school spirit to pull you through. Canadian travelers should check with their provincial ministry of health to see whether their resident health-insurance plan covers them on the road.

Organizations such as STA and CIEE (*see* Budget Travel Organizations, *above*), as well as some credit-card conglomerates, include health-and-accident coverage with the purchase of an I.D. or credit card. If you purchase an ISIC card (*see* Student I.D. Cards, *above*), you're automatically insured for $100 a day for in-hospital sickness expenses, up to $3,000 for accident-related medical expenses, and $10,000 for emergency medical evacuation. Otherwise, several private companies offer coverage designed to supplement existing health insurance for travelers.

Carefree Travel Insurance is, in fact, pretty serious about providing coverage for emergency medical evacuation and accidental death or dismemberment. It also offers 24-hour medical phone advice. *100 Garden City Plaza, 5th Floor, Garden City, NY 11530, tel. 516/294–0220 or 800/323–3149.*

International Association for Medical Assistance to Travellers (IAMAT) offers free membership (donations are much appreciated) and entitles you to a worldwide directory of qualified English-speaking physicians—on 24-hour call—who've agreed to a fixed-fee schedule. *417 Center St., Lewiston, NY 14092, tel. 716/754–4883; 40 Regal Rd., Guelph, Ont. N1K 1B5 Canada, tel. 519/836–0102; Box 5049, Christchurch 5, New Zealand.*

International SOS Assistance provides emergency evacuation services, worldwide medical referrals, and optional medical insurance. It also covers the return of "mortal remains." Plan A (medical insurance extra) costs $50 for up to 31 days, $95 for up to four months, $120 for up to six months. *Box 11568, Philadelphia, PA 19116, tel. 215/244–1500 or 800/523–8930.*

Medic Alert offers an internationally recognized identification bracelet and necklace that indicate the bearer's medical condition, drug allergies, or current medication information. It also provides the number of Medic Alert's 24-hour hot line, through which members' medical histories are available. Lifetime membership costs $35–$75. *Medic Alert Foundation International, Box 1009, Turlock, CA 95381, tel. 800/432–5378; in Canada, tel. 416/696–0142 or 800/668–1507; in Australia, tel. 09/277–9999 or 08/274–0422; in New Zealand, tel. 05/288219; in the U.K., tel. 0171/833–3034.*

Travel Guard offers a variety of insurance plans, many of which are endorsed by the American Society of Travel Agents. Most policies include coverage for sickness, injury (or untimely death), lost baggage, and trip cancellation. *1145 Clark St., Stevens Point, WI 54481, tel. 715/345–0505 or 800/782–5151.*

PRESCRIPTIONS Bring as much as you need of any prescription drugs as well as your written prescription (packed separately). Ask your doctor to type it and include the following information: dosage, the generic name, and the manufacturer's name. To avoid problems clearing customs, diabetic travelers carrying syringes should have handy a letter from their physician confirming their need for insulin injections. No matter where you're traveling in Britain most cities have at least one all-night pharmacy.

FIRST-AID KITS For about 97% of your trip, a first-aid kit may mean nothing to you but extra bulk—but in an emergency you'll be glad to have it. Packaged kits are available, but you can pack your own: bandages, waterproof surgical tape and gauze pads, antiseptic, cortisone cream, tweezers, a thermometer in a sturdy case, an antacid (e.g., Alka-Seltzer), something for diarrhea (Pepto Bismol or Immod-

After arriving in London, remember to adjust timed medications like insulin or birth-control pills.

ium), and, of course, aspirin. If you're prone to motion sickness, take along some Dramamine. Women: If you're prone to yeast infections, you can now buy over-the-counter medication (Monistat or Gynelotrimin) that will save you prolonged grief on the road. However, self-medicating should only be relied on for short-term illnesses; seek professional help if symptoms persist or worsen.

CONTRACEPTIVES AND SAFE SEX AIDS and other STDs (sexually transmitted diseases) don't respect national boundaries, and protection when you travel takes the same forms as it does at home. If you're contemplating an exchange of bodily fluids, condoms ("rubbers," "johnnys," "macs," and "sheaths" in Britain) or dental dams and condoms are the best forms of protection against STDs. Pack condoms or diaphragms in a pouch or case where they won't be squashed or damaged. The most reputable British condoms are Mates and Durex.

As Billy Bragg says, "Safe sex doesn't mean no sex; it just means use your imagination."

DIABETIC TRAVELERS If you have diabetes, consider contacting one of the following organizations for resources and medical referrals: **American Diabetes Association** (1660 Duke St., Alexandria, VA 22314, tel. 703/549–1500 or 800/232–3472), **Canadian Diabetes Association** (15 Toronto St., Suite 1001, Toronto, Ont. M5C 2E3, tel. 416/363–3373), and **International Diabetes Federation** (International Association Centre, rue Washington 40, B-1050 Brussels, Belgium, tel. 032/2647–4414, fax 032/2649–3269).

RESOURCES FOR WOMEN

This being a notoriously polite culture, women can breathe a bit easier in London than, say, in Rome or Paris. Of course, urban precautions are still necessary, and men do still get "friendly" in pubs and clubs—practice saying "Piss off!" They should catch your drift at that point.

PUBLICATIONS *Spare Rib,* a monthly available at newsagents throughout London, covers women's groups and centers; its classifieds have details on women-friendly lodging and events. Excluding the lesbian-oriented *Women's Traveller* and *Are You Two...Together?* (*see* Resources for Gay and Lesbian Travelers, *below*), the only major travel publication for women is *Women Travel: Adventures, Advice, and Experience* ($12.95), published by Prentice Hall. More than 70 countries receive some sort of coverage, with journal entries and short articles. It offers few details on prices, phone numbers, and addresses, however. Thalia Zepatos' *A Journey of One's Own* ($13), subtitled "Uncommon Advice for the Independent Woman Traveler" is fun to read, and a good resource for general travel information, but has little specific info on London or the United Kingdom.

ORGANIZATIONS **Women's Aid** (tel. 0171/251–6537) and **London Rape Crisis Centre** (tel. 0171/837–1600) both offer round-the-clock emergency counseling and support. **Women Welcome Women (WWW)** (Contact F. Alexander, 8A Chestnut Ave., High Wycombe, Buckinghamshire HP11 1DJ, England), a nonprofit organization aimed at bringing together women of all nationalities, can put you in touch with others around the globe interested in every variety of women's issues.

RESOURCES FOR GAYS AND LESBIANS

London has a strong gay community and a large variety of social venues where alternative sexual orientations can be fully expressed. Of course, Brits can be bigots with the worst of them, but the general atmosphere is one of tolerance. **Old Compton Street** in Soho, near the Leicester Square tube station, and the surrounding area are the equivalents of San Francisco's Castro district: lots of gay cafés, nightspots, businesses, and services.

PUBLICATIONS London has a multitude of publications with info on things like meetings, cultural events, gay businesses, and entertainment. Many are free—among them *The Pink Paper, Capital Gay,* and *MX,* available at cafés and some newsstands around town. Other names to watch for are *Shebang* (lesbian focus), *Boyz* (gay focus) and, as always, *Time Out* magazine, which devotes an entire section each week to gay goings-on around town—and they're close to unbeatable when it comes to London's gay club scene.

Are You Two...Together?, published by Random House, is the best known, and perhaps most detailed, guide for lesbians who are traveling in Europe. Although it's anecdotal and funny, it's slightly out-of-date, and it skimps on practical details like prices. It makes an excellent read for $18, though. Another resource for lesbians is *Ferrari's Places for Women* ($13 plus shipping), a worldwide women's travel guide with listings of gay resorts, bars, and bookstores. It also features an events calendar. Contact Renaissance House (Box 533, New York, NY 10014, tel. 212/674–0120) for more info.

ORGANIZATIONS **Gay's the Word** (66 Marchmont St., tel. 0171/278–7654; Tube: Russell Sq.) is a social and intellectual center for London's gay and lesbian community, with books, magazines, music, a bulletin board—even coffee and tea. Stuff for lesbians to do by and amongst themselves is a bit harder to find, but the **Drill Hall** (16 Chenies St., tel. 0171/631–1353; Tube: Goodge St.) is a good start. Aside from hosting women-only Monday nights, the rest of the week it serves as a cultural center and presents theater and live music.

The National AIDS Helpline (tel. 0800/567123) is a toll-free, 24-hour service offering advice and referrals.

And hot lines? The **Lesbian and Gay Switchboard** (tel. 0171/837–7324) is the main 24-hour info and advice line in the London area. If their lines are busy you can call **London Friend** (tel. 0171/837–3337), which provides confidential phone counseling for lesbians and gay men daily 7:30 PM–10 PM. They also run a special **London Friend Women's Line** (tel. 0171/837–2782) open Tuesday–Thursday during the same hours. The **Lesbian Line** (tel. 0171/251–6911) is there for women Monday to Thursday 7 PM–10 PM, Friday 2 PM–10 PM. There are even more specific hot lines for lesbians and gays who are Jewish, Catholic, in legal trouble, or worried about protecting themselves on the streets; ask any of the folks listed above.

RESOURCES FOR TRAVELERS WITH DISABILITIES

London is ahead of the rest of the country in considering the needs of people with disabilities, as long as you've given up on the *budget* part of travel for lodging and transportation. Whenever possible, our reviews will indicate whether lodgings and tourist sites are wheelchair accessible. The best advice is to call ahead. Plan your trip and make reservations far in advance, as companies that provide services for people with disabilities go in and out of business regularly. Also, always ask if discounts are available, either for you or for a companion; you may be pleasantly surprised.

The good news: Many of the big tourist sights and entertainment venues have wheelchair access. Some museums and parks have special attractions, such as touch-tours for the vision-impaired and interpreted events for the hearing-impaired. And at the front of most London phone books is an **"Arts Access"** section with lots of cool hints on what to do and how to do it. You can pay a small fee to a tourist information center for a key that will give you access to wheelchair-accessible bathrooms throughout the country.

So, you're getting away from it all.

Just make sure you can get back.

AT&T Access Numbers
Dial the number of the country you're in to reach AT&T.

*AUSTRIA†††	022-903-011	*GREECE	00-800-1311	NORWAY	800-190-11
*BELGIUM	0-800-100-10	*HUNGARY	00◇-800-01111	POLAND†♦²	0◇010-480-0111
BULGARIA	00-1800-0010	*ICELAND	999-001	PORTUGAL†	05017-1-288
CANADA	1-800-575-2222	IRELAND	1-800-550-000	ROMANIA	01-800-4288
CROATIA†♦	99-38-0011	ISRAEL	177-100-2727	*RUSSIA† (MOSCOW)	155-5042
*CYPRUS	080-90010	*ITALY	172-1011	SLOVAKIA	00-420-00101
CZECH REPUBLIC	00-420-00101	KENYA†	0800-10	S. AFRICA	0-800-99-0123
*DENMARK	8001-0010	*LIECHTENSTEIN	155-00-11	SPAIN•	900-99-00-11
*EGYPT¹ (CAIRO)	510-0200	LITHUANIA♦	8◇196	*SWEDEN	020-795-611
*FINLAND	9800-100-10	LUXEMBOURG	0-800-0111	*SWITZERLAND	155-00-11
FRANCE	19◇-0011	F.Y.R. MACEDONIA	99-800-4288	*TURKEY	00-800-12277
*GAMBIA	00111	*MALTA	0800-890-110	UKRAINE†	8◇100-11
GERMANY	0130-0010	*NETHERLANDS	06-022-9111	UK	0500-89-0011

Countries in bold face permit country-to-country calling in addition to calls to the U.S. **World Connect**℠ prices consist of **USADirect**® rates plus an additional charge based on the country you are calling. Collect calling available to the U.S. only. *Public phones require deposit of coin or phone card. ◇Await second dial tone. †May not be available from every phone. †††Public phones require local coin payment through the call duration. ♦Not available from public phones. • Calling available to most European countries. ¹Dial "02" first, outside Cairo. ²Dial 010-480-0111 from major Warsaw hotels. ©1994 AT&T

Here's a travel tip that will make it easy to call back to the States. Dial the access number for the country you're visiting and connect right to AT&T. It's the quick way to get English-speaking AT&T operators and can minimize hotel telephone surcharges.

If all the countries you're visiting aren't listed above, call **1 800 241-5555** for a free wallet card with all AT&T access numbers. Easy international calling from AT&T. **TrueWorld Connections.**

AT&T

All the Best Trips Start with Fodor's

COMPASS AMERICAN GUIDES
Titles in the series: Arizona, Canada, Chicago, Colorado, Hawai'i, Hollywood, Las Vegas, Maine, Manhattan, New Mexico, New Orleans, Oregon, San Francisco, South Carolina, South Dakota, Utah, Virginia, Wisconsin, Wyoming.

"A literary, historical, and near-sensory excursion."—*Denver Post*

"Tackles the 'why' of travel...as well as the nitty-gritty details."—*Travel Weekly*

FODOR'S BED & BREAKFASTS AND COUNTRY INN GUIDES
Titles in the series: California, Canada, England & Wales, Mid-Atlantic, New England, The Pacific Northwest, The South, The Upper Great Lakes Region.

"In addition to information on each establishment, the books add notes on things to see and do in the vicinity."
— *San Diego Union-Tribune*

THE BERKELEY GUIDES
Titles in the series: California, Central America, Eastern Europe, Europe, France, Germany, Great Britain & Ireland, Italy, London, Mexico, The Pacific Northwest & Alaska, Paris, San Francisco.

The best choice for budget travelers, from the Associated Students at the University of California at Berkeley.

"Berkeley's scribes put the funk back in travel." — *Time*

"Fresh, funny and funky as well as useful." — *The Boston Globe*

EXPLORING GUIDES
Titles in the series: Australia, Britain, California, Caribbean, Florida, France, Germany, Ireland, Italy, London, New York City, Paris, Rome, Singapore & Malaysia, Spain, Thailand.

"Authoritatively written and superbly presented, they make worthy reading before, during or after a trip. "
— *The Philadelphia Inquirer*

"A handsome new series of guides, complete with lots of color photos, geared to the independent traveler."
— *The Boston Globe*

Visit your local bookstore, or call 24 hours a day 1-800-533-6478
Fodor's The name that means smart travel.

GETTING AROUND

➤ **TO AND FROM LONDON** • Most major airlines are happy to help travelers with disabilities make flight arrangements, provided you notify the airlines up to 48 hours in advance. **Air Canada** (tel. 800/776–3000 outside Canada or 800/361–8071 in Canada), **Delta** (tel. 800/221–1212, TDD 800/831–4488), and **USAir** (tel. 800/428–4322, TDD 800/245–2966) offer discount "companion fares." Ask about them and check-in protocol when making reservations.

➤ **WITHIN LONDON** • **London Regional Transport** publishes a number of helpful pamphlets, one of the best being "Access to the Underground." Wheelchair-accessible **Mobility Bus** services (tel. 0171/918–3312), numbered in the 800 and 900 series, run (albeit infrequently) in many parts of London. Fares are generally the same as for the regular bus. **Stationlink** (tel. 0171/918–3312) is a wheelchair-accessible minibus with hourly circular service that links Waterloo, Victoria, Paddington, Marylebone, Euston, St. Pancras, King's Cross, Liverpool Street, Fenchurch Street, and London Bridge stations. It also connects with the wheelchair-accessible **Airbus A1** at Victoria and **A2** at Euston for Heathrow airport.

PUBLICATIONS *Access in London* (£2.25), published by Nicholson, is the premier travel guide in the genre; it's available in most larger bookstores and at many travel bookshops. The London Tourist Board also puts out a guide, *London Made Easy* (£2.25). The **Greater London Association for Disabled People** (336 Brixton Rd., SW9, tel. 0171/274–0107) publishes a free, comprehensive book-sized pamphlet, the "London Disability Guide."

ORGANIZATIONS **Royal Association for Disability and Rehabilitation (RADAR)** (25 Mortimer St., W1N 8AB, tel. 0171/637–5400) is command central for everything people with disabilities could need to know about living and traveling in London. Open 9–5 weekdays, it publishes both travel information and periodicals on political issues. If you're planning an extended stay, check out the **Greater London Association for Disabled People (GLAD)** (336 Brixton Rd., tel. 0171/274–0107), which can put you in touch with folks in your particular neighborhood.

There's no lack of hot lines, either. The **Disability Information and Advice Service** (tel. 0171/275–8485) and the **Handicapped Helpline** (tel. 0171/473–2270) are tops for general info. The **Artsline** (tel. 0171/388–2227), open weekdays 9:30–5:30, can clue you in on accessible goings on around town. For info about accessible sports activities, call the **British Sports Association for the Disabled** (tel. 0171/383–7229), which operates a 24-hour hot line.

WORKING ABROAD

Getting a job in London and the United Kingdom is no easy matter—prepare for massive piles of red tape, lengthy booklets of rules and tax regulations, and little respect from British employers who just don't like American and Aussie accents. The most common scenario is perhaps the most bleak: You're in London for a few weeks, decide you love it, and want to stay. Now you need a job. Unless you have a passport from an EU country, however, your only real hope is under-the-table work at pubs and restaurants. These types of thankless positions pay £3–£5 per hour if you're lucky, and don't count on making much in tips. Some people simply walk in the door, introduce themselves to the manager, and see if he or she needs assistance (just hope that they don't ask for your papers). If you want to go the legal route, contact one of the following organizations *before* you arrive in London.

PUBLICATIONS The U.K.-based Vacation Work Press publishes two first-rate guides to working abroad: ***Directory of Overseas Summer Jobs*** (£9) and Susan Griffith's ***Work Your Way Around the World*** (£12). The first lists more than 45,000 jobs worldwide; the second has fewer listings but makes a more interesting read. Look for them at bookstores, or contact the publisher directly. *9 Park East End, Oxford OX1 1HJ, tel. 01865/241978.*

CIEE (*see* Budget Travel Organizations, *above*) publishes two excellent resource books with complete details on work/travel opportunities. The most valuable is ***Work, Study, Travel Abroad: The Whole World Handbook*** ($13.95), which gives the lowdown on scholarships, grants, fellowships, study abroad programs, and work exchanges. Also worthwhile is CIEE's **Going Places: The High School Student's Guide to Study, Travel, and Adventure Abroad** ($13.95). Both books can be shipped to you at book rate ($1.50) or first class ($3).

International Jobs: Where They Are, How to Get Them ($12.95) is a somewhat dated guide to working abroad; what makes it useful is its list of international companies and agencies that coordinate work exchanges for foreigners. Look for it at your local bookstore. And believe it or not, the U.S. government publishes a useful pamphlet about looking for jobs in foreign countries: **"Employment Abroad: The Facts and Fallacies"** ($8.50), available from the U.S. Department of Commerce. Send a check or a money order and a SASE. *1615 H St. NW, Washington, DC 20062.*

ORGANIZATIONS AIESEC is a nonprofit organization that arranges for full-time graduate and undergraduate students to work abroad for from four weeks to 18 months. Companies in more than 70 countries participate in the program, offering leadership and training and work-experience opportunities. To participate you must join your local AIESEC chapter; contact the main U.S. office for details. *135 W. 50th St., 20th Floor, New York, NY 10020, tel. 212/757-3774.*

Au Pair Abroad arranges boarding and lodging for people ages 18–26 who want to work as nannies for up to four months in Britain and Europe. All applicants must go through a somewhat lengthy interview process. *1015 15th St. NW, Suite 750, Washington, DC 20005, tel. 202/408-5380.*

The **CIEE Work Abroad Program** arranges work permits valid for three to six months, and it can help you find short-term employment in Britain. Pick up CIEE's "Work Abroad" pamphlet from any Council Travel office (*see* Budget Travel Organizations, *above*). Trouble is, the program is only for U.S. students. Canadians should contact **Travel CUTS,** which has similar programs for Canadian students who want to work abroad for up to six months.

The **YMCA** oversees a variety of international work exchanges in more than 25 countries, including the **Volunteers for Europe** and **International Camp Counselor Program Abroad.** The programs rarely last longer than a summer, and participants stay at local YMCAs or with families. Don't expect to make much money. Write for the brochure. *356 W. 34th St., New York, NY 10001, tel. 212/727-8800.*

STUDYING ABROAD

You may choose to study through a U.S.-sponsored program, usually via an American university, or to enroll in a program sponsored by a European organization. Do your homework, because programs vary greatly in terms of expense, academic quality, level of contact with local students, and living conditions. The easiest way, of course, is to make arrangements through your local university.

CIEE's **University Programs Department** (205 E. 42nd St., New York, NY 10017, tel. 212/661-1414) manages study abroad programs at various European universities. It also distributes the excellent *Work, Study, Travel Abroad: The Whole World Handbook* ($13.95). **World Learning** (Kipling Rd., Box 676, Brattleboro, VT 05302, tel. 800/451-4465) offers more than 100 semester abroad programs, many structured around home stays.

The **American Institute for Foreign Study** and the **American Council of International Studies** arrange semester and year-long study programs in universities throughout the world. Applicants must be enrolled as full- or part-time students at an American college to qualify. Fees vary according to the country and length of stay. *313 E. 43rd St., New York, NY 10017, tel. 800/727-2437.*

The Information Center at the **Institute of International Education** (IIE) publishes the helpful *Academic Year Abroad* ($42.95), which lists more than 1,900 study-abroad programs for undergraduates and graduates. If you're more interested in summer-abroad and living-abroad programs, check out IIE's *Vacation Study Abroad* ($36.95). Order either from IIE Books (tel. 212/984-5412). *809 U.N. Plaza, New York, NY 10017, tel. 212/984-5413.*

Coming and Going

CUSTOMS AND DUTIES

ARRIVING IN LONDON When going through customs, looking composed and presentable expedites the process. The United Kingdom is under daily threat from terrorism, and doesn't take it lightly; you may be asked to play your Walkman or show a customs official the inside of your camera. If you're bringing in any foreign-made equipment such as cameras or video gear, carry the original receipt or register it with customs before you leave the United States (ask for U.S. Customs Form 4457). Otherwise, you may end up paying duty when you return.

Don't even think about smuggling drugs into the United Kingdom. Being arrested for drug possession is no joke, and embassies and consulates can't or won't do much to persuade officials to release accused traffickers.

Travelers age 17 or over may bring into the United Kingdom the following duty-free goods: 200 cigarettes or 100 cigarillos or 50 cigars or 250 grams of tobacco; 1 liter of alcohol over 22% volume or 2 liters of alcohol under 22% volume; 2 liters of still table wine; 50 grams of perfume and 250 milliliters of toilet water; and other goods worth up to £32. If you're arriving from another EU country, you can import the following, provided they were *not* bought in a duty-free shop: 300 cigarettes or 150 cigarillos or 75 cigars or 400 grams of tobacco; 1.5 liters of alcohol over 22% volume or 3 liters of alcohol under 22% volume; 5 liters of still table wine; 75 grams of perfume and 375 milliliters of toilet water; and other goods worth up to £250.

RETURNING HOME

➤ **U.S. CUSTOMS** • You're unlikely to have run-ins with customs as long as you *never* carry any illegal drugs in your luggage. When you return to the United States, you have to declare all items you bought abroad, but won't have to pay duty unless you come home with more than $400 worth of foreign goods, including items bought in duty-free stores. For purchases between $400 and $1,000, there's a 10% duty tax. You also have to pay tax if you exceed your duty-free allowances: 1 liter of alcohol or wine (for those 21 and over), 100 non-Cuban cigars (sorry, Fidel) or 200 cigarettes, and one bottle of perfume. A free leaflet about customs regulations and illegal souvenirs, "Know Before You Go," is available from the **U.S. Customs Service** (Box 7407, Washington, DC 20044, tel. 202/927–6724).

➤ **CANADIAN CUSTOMS** • Exemptions for returning Canadians range from C$20 to C$300, depending on how long you've been out of the country. For two days out, you're allowed to return with C$100 worth of goods; for one week out, you're allowed C$300 worth. Above these limits, you'll be taxed 20% (more for items shipped home). In any given year, you are only allowed one C$300 exemption. Duty-free limits are: up to 50 cigars, 200 cigarettes, 2.2 pounds of tobacco, and 40 ounces of liquor—all must be declared in writing upon arrival at customs and must be with you or in your checked baggage. To mail back gifts—which is a great deal, since you're not taxed on things you mail back and you can mail one package per addressee per day—label the package: "Unsolicited Gift—Value under C$60." For more details, request a copy of the Canadian Customs brochure "I Declare/Je Declare" from **Revenue Canada Customs, Excise and Taxation Department** (2265 St. Laurent Blvd. S, Ottawa, Ont., K1G 4K3, tel. 613/957–0275).

➤ **AUSTRALIAN CUSTOMS** • Australian travelers 18 and over may bring back, duty free: 1 liter of alcohol; 250 grams of tobacco products (equivalent to 250 cigarettes or cigars); and other articles worth up to AUS$400. If you're under 18, your duty-free allowance is AUS$200. To avoid paying duty on goods you mail back to Australia, mark the package: "Australian goods returned." For more rules and regulations, request the pamphlet "Customs Information for Travelers" from a local **Collector of Customs** (GPO Box 8, Sydney NSW 2001, tel. 02/226–5997).

➤ **NEW ZEALAND CUSTOMS** • Although greeted with a *"Haere Mai"* ("Welcome to New Zealand"), homeward-bound travelers face several restrictions. Travelers over age 17 are allowed, duty-free: 200 cigarettes or 250 grams of tobacco or 50 cigars or a combo of all three up to 250 grams; 4.5 liters of wine or beer and one 1.1-liter bottle of spirits; and goods with a combined value up to NZ$700. For more details, ask a New Zealand consulate for the pamphlet "Customs Guide for Travelers."

GETTING THE BEST DEALS

When your travel plans are still in the fantasy stage, start studying the travel sections of major Sunday newspapers: Courier companies, charter flights, and fare brokers often list incredibly cheap fares. Travel agents are another obvious resource, as they have access to computer networks that show the lowest fares before they're even advertised. However, budget travelers are the bane of travel agents, whose commission is based on ticket prices. That said, agencies on or near college campuses—try STA or Council Travel (*see* Budget Travel Organizations, *above*)—actually cater to these pariahs and will help you find cheap deals.

Here are some hot tips you can use when you make your reservations: If the reservation clerk tells you that the least expensive seats are no longer available on a certain flight, ask to be put on the waiting list. If the airline doesn't keep waiting lists for the lowest fares, call them on subsequent mornings and ask about cancellations and last-minute openings—airlines trying to fill all their seats sometimes add additional cut-rate tickets at the last moment. Remember that off-season fares can be as much as 50% lower.

APEX TICKETS If you're not a student or the kind of person to spend days scouring newspapers, APEX tickets, bought directly from the airlines or from your travel agent, are the simplest way to go. If you know exactly when you want to leave (and it's not tomorrow or the next day), ask for the APEX fare when making your reservation: It'll save you a bundle and guarantee you a seat. Regular APEX fares normally apply to tickets bought at least 21 days in advance; you can get Super-APEX fares if you know your travel plans at least one month in advance. The catch: If you cancel or change flights, you pay a $50–$100 penalty.

CONSOLIDATORS Consolidator companies, also known as bucket shops, buy blocks of tickets at wholesale prices from airlines trying to fill flights. Check out a consolidator's reputation with the Better Business Bureau before you do business; most are perfectly reliable, but better safe than sorry. Then, register with the consolidator and work up a list of possible departure dates. The week before you leave, the consolidator should contact you and give you a list of the flights available to you. You're obligated to accept one of these flights, even if it wasn't your first choice. If you don't, the consolidator probably won't make much of an effort to get you on another flight. If everything works as planned, you'll save 10%–40% on the published APEX fare.

If possible, pay with a credit card, so that if the ticket never arrives, you don't have to pay. Bucket shops generally advertise in newspapers—be sure to check restrictions, refund possibilities, and payment conditions. One last suggestion: Confirm your reservation with the airline both before and after you buy a consolidated ticket. This not only decreases the chance of fraud, but it also ensures you won't be the first to get bumped if the airline overbooks. For more details, contact one of the following:

Airfare Busters. *5100 Westheimer Ave., Suite 550, Houston, TX 77056, tel. 713/961–5109 or 800/232–8783.*

Airhitch. *2790 Broadway, Suite 100, New York, NY 10025, tel. 212/864–2000; 1341 Ocean Ave., Suite 62, Santa Monica, CA 90401, tel. 310/458–1006; 870 Market St., Suite 1056, San Francisco, CA 94102, tel. 415/834–9192.*

Globe Travel. *507 5th Ave., Suite 604, New York, NY 10017, tel. 800/969–4562.*

Overseas Express. *2705 W. Howard St., Chicago, IL 60645, tel. 800/343–4873.*

UniTravel. *1177 N. Warson Rd., Box 12485, St. Louis, MO 63132, tel. 314/569–2501 or 800/325–2222.*

Up & Away Travel. *347 5th Ave., Suite 202, New York, NY 10016, tel. 212/889–2345.*

STANDBY AND THREE-DAY-ADVANCE-PURCHASE FARES Flying standby is almost a thing of the past. The idea is to purchase an open ticket and wait for the next available seat on the next available flight to your chosen destination. But most airlines have dumped these in favor of three-day-advance-purchase youth fares, which are open only to people under age 25 and can only be purchased within three days of departure. Return flights must also be booked no more than three days prior to departure. If you meet those criteria, expect a 10%–50% savings on published APEX fares.

CHARTER FLIGHTS Charter flights have vastly different characteristics, depending on the company you're dealing with. Generally speaking, a charter company either buys a block of tickets on a regularly scheduled commercial flight and sells them at a discount (the prevalent form in the United States) or leases the whole plane and then offers relatively cheap fares to the public (most common in the United Kingdom). Despite a few potential drawbacks—infrequent flights, restrictive return-date requirements, lickety-split payment demands, frequent bankruptcies—charter companies inevitably offer the cheapest tickets around, especially during high season when APEX fares are most expensive. Make sure you know the company's refund policy should either your trip or the flight be canceled. Summer charter flights fill up quickly and should be booked a couple of months in advance. You can minimize risks by checking the company's reputation with the Better Business Bureau and taking out enough trip-cancellation insurance to cover a potential failure.

Council Charter (tel. 212/661–0311 or 800/800–8222) has the scoop on hundreds of different charter and reduced-fare flights. **DER Tours** (Box 1606, Des Plains, IL 60017, tel. 800/782–2424) is a full-service travel store, with rail passes, discounted airfares, and listings of charter flights. **MartinAir** (tel. 800/627–8462) is an airline that operates like a charter. Restrictions apply, and availability is limited during summer. Definitely call a few weeks in advance. **Tower Air** (tel. 800/34–TOWER) specializes in domestic and international charters. On the upside, you get to deal with the airline directly. On the downside, Tower is notorious for overbooking. **Travel Charter** (tel. 810/641–9677 or 800/521–5267) caters to students bound for Europe, though some of their charters are loaded with restrictions. **Travel CUTS** (tel. 416/979–2406) is part of the CIEE umbrella, which means it's a reputable place for Canadian students to book their charter.

STUDENT DISCOUNTS Student discounts on airline tickets are offered through CIEE, the Educational Travel Center, STA Travel, and Travel CUTS (*see* Budget Travel Organizations, *above*). Keep in mind that you *won't* receive frequent-flyer mileage for discounted student, youth, or teacher tickets. To receive such discounts, carry an I.D. when you check in that proves your status: an ISIC, a Youth Identity Card, or an International Teacher Identity Card.

Campus Connection, exclusively for students under age 25, searches airline computer networks for the cheapest student fares. They don't always have the best price, but they deal with the airlines directly, so you won't get stuck with a heavily restricted or fraudulent ticket. *1100 E. Marlton Pike, Cherry Hill, NJ 08032, tel. 800/428–3235.*

COURIER FLIGHTS Restrictions and inconvenience are what you pay in return for colossal savings on airfare offered to air couriers—the shady, raincoat-and-sunglass-clad travelers who accompany letters and packages between designated points. It's simple: Courier companies list whatever flights are available for the next week or so. After you book the flight, you sign a contract with the company to act as a courier (some places make you pay a deposit, to be refunded after the successful completion of your assignment). On the day of departure, you arrive at the airport a few hours early, meet someone who hands you a ticket and customs forms, and off you go. After landing, you simply clear customs with the courier luggage, and deliver it to a waiting agent. Don't worry about what's in the luggage—we're talking business documents and the like, not drugs or SAM missiles.

The main restrictions are (1) flights can be booked only a week or two in advance, often only a few days in advance; (2) you're allowed one piece of carry-on luggage only, because the courier uses your checked-luggage allowance to transport the time-sensitive shipment; (3) you must return within one or two weeks, sometimes within 30 days; and (4) most courier companies only issue tickets to travelers over the age of 18.

Check newspaper travel sections for courier companies, or the yellow pages of your phone directory, or mail away for a directory that lists companies by the cities they fly to. One of the better publications is *Air Courier Bulletin* (IAATC, 8 S. J St., Box 1349, Lake Worth, FL 33460, tel. 407/582–8320), sent to IAATC members ($35 annually) every two months. *A Simple Guide to Courier Travel* gives tips on courier flying; send $15.95 (includes postage and handling) to Box 2394, Lake Oswego, OR 97035, tel. 800/222–3599. Another good resource is the newsletter put out by **Travel Unlimited** (Box 1058, Allston, MA 02134); the cost is $25 for 12 issues.

Discount Travel International offers courier flights to London and other major European hubs from Miami and New York. *169 W. 81st St., New York, NY 10024, tel. 212/362–3636; 801 Alton Rd., Suite 1, Miami Beach, FL 33139, tel. 305/538–1616.*

Now Voyager. Flights to London and the Continent depart from New York, Newark, or Houston. A nonrefundable $50 registration fee, good for one year, is required. *74 Varick St., Suite 307, New York, NY 10013, tel. 212/431–1616.*

BY AIR

On your fateful departure day, remember that check-in time for international flights is two hours before the scheduled departure. One more bulletin: International flights of more than six hours are smoking flights; if fumes make you queasy, book short air-hops or ask for seats as far away from the smoking section as possible.

FROM NORTH AMERICA Airlines that serve London with nonstop flights from major U.S. cities include **Aer Lingus** (tel. 800/223–6537) from Boston or New York; **American** (tel. 800/433–7300) from Boston, Chicago, Dallas, Los Angeles, Miami, New York, and Raleigh/Durham; **British Airways** (tel. 800/247–9297) from Atlanta, Boston, Chicago, Dallas/Ft. Worth, Detroit, Houston, Los Angeles, Miami, New York, Orlando, Philadelphia, Pittsburgh, Seattle, and San Francisco; **Continental** (tel. 800/231–0856) from Denver, Houston, and New York; **Delta** (tel. 800/241–4141) from Atlanta, Cincinnati, Detroit, and Miami; **TWA** (tel. 800/892-4141) from St. Louis; **United** (tel. 800/241–6522) from Los Angeles, New York, San Francisco, and Washington, DC; **USAir** (tel. 800/428–4322) from Philadelphia, Baltimore, and Charlotte; and **Virgin Atlantic Airways** (tel. 800/862–8621) from Boston, Los Angeles, Miami, New York, and Orlando.

FROM DOWN UNDER **Qantas** (tel. 800/227–4500 in the U.S. or 02/957–0111 toll-free from Sydney) flies from all major Australian cities to London via Bangkok or Kuala Lumpur. From New Zealand (tel. 0800/808767 outside Auckland or 09/379–0306 in Auckland), some flights fly via Australia, but some are nonstop.

TAKING LUGGAGE ABROAD You've heard it a million times. Now you'll hear it once again: Pack light. U.S. airlines allow passengers to check two pieces of luggage, neither of which can exceed 62 inches (length + width + height) or weigh more than 70 pounds. If your airline accepts excess baggage, it'll probably charge you. Foreign-airline policies vary, so call or check with a travel agent before you show up at the airport with too much stuff.

Foreign airlines have different policies but generally allow only one carryon in tourist class, in addition to a handbag and a bag filled with duty-free goodies. Call for the airline's current policy. Passengers on U.S. airlines are limited to one carryon bag, plus coat, camera, and handbag (women get a break here). Carry-on bags must fit under the seat in front of you or in the overhead compartment; maximum dimensions are 9 x 45 x 22 inches. Hanging bags can have maximum dimensions of 4 x 23 x 45 inches; to fit in an overhead bin, bags can be a maximum of 10 x 14 x 36 inches. If your bag is too porky for compartments, be prepared for the humiliation of rejection and last-minute baggage check.

BY TRAIN

London has eight major train stations (as well as a bunch of smaller ones). Each serves a specific part of the country (or the Continent), so be sure to figure out beforehand where your train leaves from. All eight stations have tourist and travel information booths (most close at 6 PM or 6:30 PM), rip-off bureaux de change, and luggage storage (£1–£5 per day). They are also all served by the London Underground, so it's easy to get around after you arrive in London. The **British Travel Centre** (*see* Visitor Information, in Staying in London, *below*) can provide you with full train schedules, ticket prices, and other information. The *British Rail Passenger Timetable* (£6), issued every May and October, contains details of all BritRail services; pick one up at any major train station.

Charing Cross (The Strand, tel. 0171/928–5100) serves southeast England, including Canterbury, Margate, and Dover/Folkestone. Charing Cross is on the Northern, Bakerloo, and Jubilee tube lines. **Euston** (Euston Rd., tel. 0171/387–7070) serves the West Midlands, north Wales, northwest England, and northwest and western Scotland. Trains to Birmingham and Glasgow leave from here. Euston is on the Northern and Victoria tube lines. **King's Cross** (York Way, tel. 0171/278–2477) marks the end of the Great Northern line, serving Yorkshire, northeast England, and Scotland. King's Cross is on the Circle, Metropolitan, Piccadilly, Hammersmith & City, Northern, and Victoria tube lines. **Liverpool Street** (Liverpool St., tel. 0171/928–5100) serves Cambridge and Norwich and is on the Central, Hammersmith & City, Metropolitan, and Circle tube lines. **Paddington** (Praed St., tel. 0171/262–6767) serves South Wales, Avon, and Cornwall, including Reading, Oxford, Worcester, and Bristol. Paddington is on the Circle, Bakerloo, District, and Hammersmith & City tube lines. **St. Pancras** (Pancras Rd., tel. 0171/387–7070) serves Leicester, Nottingham, and Sheffield. It's on the Victoria, Northern, Hammersmith & City, Circle, Piccadilly, and Metropolitan tube lines. **Victoria** (Terminus Pl., tel. 0171/387–7070) serves southern England, including Gatwick Airport, Brighton, Dover/Folkestone, and the south coast. Victoria is on the Circle, District, and Victoria tube lines. **Waterloo** (York Rd., tel. 0171/928–5100) serves southeastern destinations like Guildford, Portsmouth, and Southampton. Waterloo is on the Bakerloo and Northern tube lines.

RAIL PASSES If you plan to do even a moderate amount of traveling, it's probably worth investing in a **BritRail Pass,** since full-price tickets (especially one-way) are absurdly expensive. Also note that EurailPass is *not* accepted in Britain (though InterRail is), and that most BritRail passes cannot be purchased in the United Kingdom—you must get them *before* you leave home. An adult **second-class pass** costs $219 for eight days, $339 for 15 days, $425 for 22 days, and $495 for one month. If you're 16–25 years old consider a **BritRail Youth Pass.** It allows unlimited second-class travel in the following increments: $179 for eight days, $269 for 15 days, $339 for 22 days, and $395 for one month. Passes are available from most travel agents or from the **BritRail Travel Information Office** (1500 Broadway, New York, NY 10036, tel. 800/677–8585). About the only worthwhile pass available in Britain is the **Young Person's Railcard;** it costs £10–£20 from any BritRail office, and is good for ⅓ off most train tickets—an investment that will pay you back immediately. However, you must be under age 26 to purchase one.

BY BUS

London's main terminal for all long-distance bus companies is **Victoria Coach Station** (Buckingham Palace Rd. and Elizabeth St., tel. 0171/730–0202 or 0171/730–3466), just southwest of Victoria Station. Getting from Victoria Coach Station to Victoria Station is simple—just walk north up Buckingham Palace Road and turn right on Terminus Place. Victoria Coach Station has a bureau de change and luggage storage. Travelers with disabilities who need or will need mobility assistance should contact the **Help Point** (tel. 0171/730–3466, ext. 235).

You can save lots of money by taking a bus instead of a train. Prices offered by the various coach companies are almost identical, and **Economy Return** bus tickets can be 30% to 50% cheaper than train tickets. The catch: Economy tickets are only good Sunday through Thursday. Expect to pay about 20% more on Friday and Saturday for **Standard Return** fares. You can also buy APEX bus tickets, but you must book seven days in advance and adhere to exact times

TAKE THE TRIP THAT RANKS RIGHT UP THERE WITH KITTY HAWK, APOLLO 11 AND THE INAUGURAL CONCORDE FLIGHT.

Rail Europe invites you to be among the first to ride the Eurostar train through the Channel Tunnel.

Be one of the first to take the trip that will change the history of travel. Rail Europe and the high-speed, high-tech passenger train, Eurostar, can take you through the Channel

RIDE THE EUROSTAR
CALL 1-800-94-CHUNNEL

Tunnel from the center of London to the center of Paris in three short hours. All you do is relax, enjoy a drink or a meal and become part of history in the making.

For information on a variety of affordable Eurostar tickets call your travel agent or Rail Europe.

Rail Europe

EUROPE. TO THE TRAINED EYE.

and dates for departure and return. Book tickets on **National Express** (tel. 0171/730–0202) buses at Victoria Coach Station, or at one of their branch offices at 52 Grosvenor Gardens or 13 Regent Street. If you're age 16–25, get a **Young Person's Coach Card** (£7), valid for 30% off virtually all National Express fares anywhere in mainland Britain for a year. It may be cheaper to buy a bus pass—five-day passes cost £65, eight-day passes £90, 30-day passes £190—ahead of time in the United States; contact **British Travel Associates** (tel. 703/298–2232), which sells tickets over the phone and can quote you the latest price in dollars. In Britain, you can buy a pass at any National Express office or at the Heathrow or Gatwick bus stations.

BY FERRY

Ferries aren't the most pleasant way to get around, but they are the cheapest way to come from France, Belgium, or the Netherlands. They arrive at **Dover** and **Portsmouth** from the French ports of Calais, Boulogne, and Le Havre. The standard round-trip fare is £44, around £25 if you return in fewer than five days. Holland, northern Germany, and Scandinavia are best accessed from the East Anglia town of **Harwich,** via ferries bound for Hoek van Holland (Hook of Holland). The Welsh port town of **Holyhead** is the best place to catch ferries to Dublin (about £19 each way), though there's also service from the Welsh port of **Fishguard** to the Irish port of Rosslare, and from **Stranraer** (Scotland) to Belfast (Northern Ireland). For more info contact the ferry companies directly: **Hoverspeed and SeaCat** (tel. 01304/240241), **P&O Ferries** (tel. 01304/203388), and **Sealink** (tel. 01233/647047).

BY EUROTUNNEL

Since the early 1800s, visionaries have thought of building a tunnel between England and the European continent, but endless obstacles have stood in the way. The channel itself wasn't a problem; the chalk on the seafloor is actually quite firm and amenable to tunneling. The English psyche proved to be a far more formidable obstacle. Real and imagined fears of disease and unfettered Frenchness invading England have haunted Europhobes for centuries. To this day, the French are far more enthusiastic about the tunnel. The Brits have yet to build a high-speed rail link from London to Folkestone even, a necessity to encourage people to use the tunnel.

At press time, the Eurotunnel was not opened to the public (only VIPs like the queen and Mitterand are allowed to ride). For the latest info on the Eurotunnel and the passenger-only Eurostar line, contact **Eurostar Enquiries** (19 Worple Rd., Wimbledon, tel. 0181/784–1333). No one knows when the Eurotunnel will open to the public or how much it will cost when—if ever—it does.

The Slow Coach

To beat the high cost of bus travel in Britain, consider spending £69 on The Slow Coach, a new around-Britain bus service for travelers of all ages. Four coaches a week run a clockwise circuit from London to Windsor to Bath to Stratford to the Lake District to Edinburgh to York to Cambridge and back again to London. Coaches stop at YHA and SYHA hostels in the above destinations, and you can board and get off any time you like. Best of all, tickets are valid for two months and are completely transferable—in other words, any unused portion of your ticket can be given or sold to other travelers. Buy tickets from YHA and SYHA hostels en route, or write to The Slow Coach (71 Bradenstoke, Wiltshire, SN15 4EL, tel. 01249/891959).

HITCHING

Hitching from London is not difficult, though solo women hitchhikers should choose their rides carefully. Spring for a thick black pen and make a sign indicating your destination (it might con drivers into thinking you're a relatively responsible person). Get a good map of England, and determine which motorway out of London will lead to the area you want, then take a bus or the tube as close to that motorway as possible. You can also work thumb magic around major intersections on the edge of London's metropolis.

Loot, a want-ads paper available around London, Manchester, and Bristol, has a section to help those with the means of transport meet those in need of a lift. Also check out the **ride boards** at the University of London's Union (Malet St.) and at University College of London Union (Gordon St.), both of which are near the Euston Square tube station. Riders are usually expected to help pay for gas and any other expenses. If you wanna get organized about it, call **Freewheelers** (tel. 0191/222–0090), a ride-share agency that connects lift-seekers with lift-offerers. There is a £5 annual registration fee, plus £1 for each journey you take. Seekers should also expect to contribute around 2.5p per mile to the driver's costs—still but a fraction of bus, train, or plane fares.

Getting Around London

TO AND FROM THE AIRPORTS

HEATHROW INTERNATIONAL AIRPORT Heathrow (tel. 0181/759–4321) handles the vast majority of international flights to the United Kingdom. Heathrow has four terminals: **Terminals 1 and 2** are reserved for European and domestic flights; **Terminal 3** is for most intercontinental and Scandinavian flights; and **Terminal 4** handles all long-distance British Airways flights as well as shuttle flights between major British cities. **Tourist information** counters are located in every terminal, as are bureaux de change and accommodations services. Luggage storage, known here as **left luggage,** is also available at every terminal—but don't count on it being open during terrorist bombing campaigns. Passengers in transit or who have gone through passport control can take showers at Terminals 1, 3, and 4 in designated restroom areas for £1 (including towel and soap).

Don't let Heathrow intimidate you: Thanks to efficient train, tube, and bus service, you can be in central London within 90 minutes of deplaning.

Getting in and out of London from Heathrow is a piece of cake. The easiest and cheapest option is via the tube—the **Piccadilly Line** makes a loop through the airport before heading back to central London. The airport has two tube stations: One serves Terminals 1, 2, and 3, the other Terminal 4. Trains run every four to eight minutes from early morning until midnight; the 45-minute trip into town costs £2.80. However, if you plan to use the Underground again that day, consider an all-day **Travelcard** (£2.70–£3.70), which gives you unlimited use of the tube system. Also note: One of the biggest advantages of taking the tube is that the Piccadilly Line serves many of London's budget accommodation areas directly—among them Earl's Court, South Kensington, and Russell Square. To reach other cheap areas around Notting Hill Gate or Victoria Station, change to the **District Line** at Earl's Court.

Unfortunately, the Underground gets very crowded at rush hour (when many U.S. flights seem to land). In this case, consider London Transport's bright-red **Airbuses** (tel. 0171/222–1234), which make stops all over central London. For this 60- to 90-minute voyage to the city center, you pay a reasonable £5. From Heathrow, catch an Airbus outside any terminal—simply follow the AIRBUS or BUSES TO LONDON signs. If you're headed to the airport, **Bus A1** leaves Victoria Station every 15 minutes from 5:50 AM until 1 PM, then every half-hour until 8:35 PM; **Bus A2** runs from Russell Square, near Euston Station, every 15 minutes from 5:40 AM until 1:15 PM, then every half-hour until 9:50 PM.

GATWICK Gatwick (tel. 01293/535353), south of London, used to handle mainly charter flights, but it's been upgraded and now accommodates a steady stream of commercial flights from the United States and the Continent. It doesn't take any longer to reach London from Gatwick than it does from Heathrow, but it does cost £8 instead of £2–£5. Like Heathrow, Gatwick has a **tourist information** counter (tel. 01293/560108), left luggage and accommodation services, and a bureau de change—all in the International Arrivals Concourse.

BritRail's **Gatwick Express** (tel. 0171/928–5100 or 0171/928–2113) is your best bet for getting from Gatwick to London's Victoria Station. Trains leave every 15 minutes from 5 AM until 10 PM, and hourly at other times. The 35-minute trip costs £8.50. After you clear customs, just follow the signs to the trains, or ask at the information booth. **Flightline Bus 777** (tel. 0181/668–7261) offers hourly bus service between Gatwick and Victoria Coach Station, from about 5 AM to around 11 PM. The 75-minute trip costs £7.50.

STANSTED Stansted (tel. 01279/680500) opened in 1991 to alleviate the overcrowding at Heathrow. It serves mainly European destinations, plus American Airlines flights to Chicago, AirTransit flights to Toronto and Vancouver, and random charter flights. The airport has a **tourist desk** (tel. 01279/662520) and a bureau de change that's open daily 24 hours. To reach central London from Stansted, catch the **Stansted Express** train to Liverpool Street Station. Trains run every half-hour, and the 40-minute trek costs £9.80 one-way.

LONDON CITY AIRPORT The little-known **London City Airport** (tel. 0171/474–5555), in Silvertown, in southeast London, handles mostly European commuter flights. In the main terminal look for a left luggage service, a bureau de change, and a **tourist desk** for aid with accommodations, tours, and tickets. The best way to get from London City Airport to central London is by hopping the **BritRail** train at Silvertown station (a five-minute walk from the airport entrance) and changing at Stratford onto the Underground's Central Line. From here, the ride into central London takes about 45 minutes and costs £4.

BY UNDERGROUND AND BUS

London's Underground and bus networks are overseen by **London Regional Transport (LRT)** (tel. 0171/222–1234 for info or 0171/371–0247 for free maps and timetables). LRT info centers are located at all Heathrow terminals and in the following tube and BritRail stations: Euston, Victoria, King's Cross, Liverpool Street, Oxford Circus, Piccadilly Circus, and St. James's Park.

Don't ask Londoners where to catch the "subway." In Britain, a subway is an underground passage to allow pedestrians to cross under busy streets—ask for the "tube" or "underground."

Fares for both buses and the Underground are based on zones. LRT has divided London into six concentric rings, labeled Zones 1–6. With few exceptions, everything you want to see will be within **Zone 1** (which includes Westminster, Piccadilly Circus, Soho, Trafalgar Square, Covent Garden, the City, Victoria, Earl's Court, Kensington, and more) and **Zone 2** (which includes Camden, Hampstead, the East End, Brixton, and Greenwich Park).

The best deal for getting around London is the **Travelcard,** available at "Tickets and Assistance" windows at most tube and train stations, from some machines in Underground ticket halls, and from LRT Information Centres. The Travelcard gets you unlimited use of buses and the Underground for anywhere from one day to one year. The most popular is the Travelcard for Zones 1 and 2, which costs £2.70 daily, £13 weekly, and £50 monthly. You need a passport-type photo if you're buying a Travelcard good for a week or more, and a local address—a hostel or hotel address should work fine.

BY UNDERGROUND The Underground provides comprehensive service throughout central London and more sporadic service to the suburbs. Underground stations are marked by a large red circle with a blue banner that reads UNDERGROUND. London is served by 11 Underground lines, each color-coded, as well as by Docklands Light Railway and Network Southeast; it can seem extremely confusing until you get used to it, and you'll find yourself constantly referring to the Underground map.

London Underground

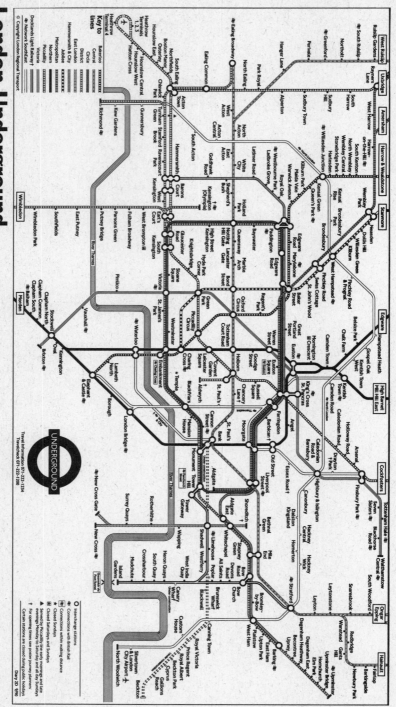

A wide variety of maps is available free at Tickets and Assistance windows in most stations, including the "Travelcard Zone Map," "Travelcard Seasons," "How to Travel in London," and the "Travelcard Journey Planner." The latter is a miniature version of the "Journey Planner" poster that stands near the entrance of every station and is usually issued when you buy your Travelcard. Larger stations—among them Victoria, Piccadilly Circus, Oxford Circus, St. James's Park, Liverpool Street, King's Cross, and Euston—have separate Travel Information counters where you can ask silly questions without the pressure of an anxious line behind you. Travelers with disabilities should get the "Access to the Underground" (70p) brochure from one of the above info counters. It provides details on lifts and ramps at the different Underground stations as well as Braille maps for the visually impaired.

Beware: Inspectors walk up and down tube trains slapping £10 "penalty fares" on riders without valid tickets.

If you don't plan to use public transport a lot, buy individual tickets for each journey—choose between single and return, the British equivalent of one-way and round-trip. Once again, fares are based on zones and range from 90p to £3.90 one-way. You can buy tickets at either the Tickets and Assistance windows or electronic vending machines built into the lobby walls of most stations. There are two types of machine: The newer, high-tech versions have huge banks of buttons with all the possible destinations labeled. Choose your category (adult or child, single or return) and then press one of the destination buttons. The older machines have four sets of prices for adults (90p, £1.30, £1.70, £2.80), one price for children (50p). If your ticket is worth at least £2.70, buy a Travelcard instead. And remember to hold on to your ticket, since you'll have to show it to a conductor to exit the Underground system.

The Underground gets going around 5 AM and closes between 11:30 PM and 12:30 AM, depending on which station you're in; check by the turnstiles for a notice board listing the time of the evening's last train. In terms of reliability, the tube is generally right on, and waiting more than 10 minutes is unusual. The Underground is fairly safe, too, possibly because it closes before the real crazies come out. Conversely, if you plan to party late, it pays to figure out London's Night Owl buses (*see below*).

BY BUS As with the tube, bus fares are based on zones: One-way fares start at 70p in Zone 1. Figuring out your bus route is also more difficult than figuring out your tube route. On transit maps—pick up the *Central London Bus Guide* free at travel info counters in larger tube stations—major intersections (often called "circuses") are represented by circles. Listed in these circles are the route numbers of up to two dozen buses. Compare the intersection nearest where you want to go with the intersection nearest where you are. If any route numbers match, you've found a direct bus; otherwise you'll need to transfer.

Out on the street, main bus stops are marked by plain white signs with a red LT symbol; buses *should* stop here automatically. Stops where you have to flag the bus down are known as request stops, marked by red signs with a white LT symbol and the word "request." At some of the main bus hubs (Trafalgar Square, Victoria, etc.) you'll have to look at one of the posted maps to find out *exactly* where you should be standing for the bus to your destination.

There are two ways to buy tickets. In the newer buses (the ones with flat, vertical fronts) tell the driver your destination and pay as you enter (exact change desired but not required). In older buses where the driver sits in a cab separate from the passengers, just hop on the back of the bus, take a seat, and a conductor will swing by to check your Travelcard or sell you a ticket from a coffee-grinder apparatus he wears around his neck. You can usually find a seat on the bus, even during rush hour (7–9:30 and 4–6:30), except on lines that pass through crowded areas like Whitehall, Trafalgar Square, Piccadilly Circus, and Oxford Street. To get off, pull the cord above the windows or press the button by the exit. For more info about London's buses, call 0171/222–1234 (routing help) or 0171/222–1200 (recorded info).

➤ **NIGHT OWL BUSES** • From 11 PM to 5 AM, some buses add the prefix "N" to their route numbers and are called **Night Owls.** They don't come as often and don't operate on quite as many routes as day buses, but at least they get you somewhere close to your destination. You'll probably have to transfer at one of the main night-bus terminals like Victoria, Westminster, Piccadilly Circus, or Trafalgar Square; the latter two are *the* main transfer stations for late-night buses. Note that weekly and monthly Travelcards are good for Night Owl buses, but daily ones *are not*. Night Owl single fares are also a bit more expensive than daytime ones. You should avoid sitting alone on the top deck of a Night Owl bus—it's prime mugging territory.

BY DOCKLANDS LIGHT RAILWAY

The massive Docklands area along the Thames east of central London is served by **Docklands Light Railway (DLR)**, which connects with the Underground at the following stations: Bank, Tower Hill, Shadwell, Stratford, and Bow Road. DLR trains use the same system of passes, zones, and fares as London's buses and Underground, and the DLR's two lines also show up on tube maps. Currently, DLR only runs on weekdays 5:40 AM–9:30 PM; on weekends they substitute bus services that follow basically the same routes and hours. The **Docklands Travel Hot Line** (tel. 0171/918–4000) offers info 24 hours a day.

BY TAXI

Cabs are the most expensive form of transportation in London, but they can be worthwhile if you share a ride with others. Traditional black cabs (they come in other colors as well) are the most reliable and least likely to rip you off. Drivers of these classy carriages have to pass a rigorous test known as "The Knowledge," and are required to take passengers on the shortest route possible (though some cabbies do take tourists for a ride). Every black cab also has a meter with a fare table so that you know exactly how much you should be charged. Weekday fares start at £1 and go up 20p per unit of distance/time (every 313.5 yards or 64 seconds). From 8 PM to midnight and on Saturday, the distance/time fare is 40p per unit, 60p per unit after midnight. It's 60p all day on Sunday and until 6 AM on Monday.

To hail a cab—fairly easy except on weekend nights and when it rains—look for the yellow "For Hire" light. You can also phone ahead, but many companies charge extra for "collections." **Radio Taxis** (tel. 0171/286–0286 or 0171/272–0272) is open 24 hours and uses black cabs only, but charges a "collection fee" depending on where you're getting picked up and where you're going. If you lose something in a black cab or have a complaint, call the **Public Carriage Office** (tel. 0171/230–1631).

If you're tired of being chatted up by creepy cab drivers, Lady Cabs (tel. 0171/272–1992) has taxis for women who'd rather be driven by women.

An alternative to the black cabs are minicabs—their fares are routinely cheaper, especially if you're traveling fairly long distances, at night, or on weekends. Run by private companies or individual drivers, they look just like regular cars. Although they can't legally pick up passengers on the street—you're supposed to call or walk into their office—it's quite the norm outside of clubs and in the West End. And bargaining is not out of the question. Obviously, this alternative is not as standardized; always remember to confirm both the company and the price with the driver *before* you get in. Some reputable and insured minicab companies include: **Abbey Car Hire** (west London, tel. 0171/727–22637); **Greater London Hire** (north London, tel. 0181/340–2450); **Newhame Minicabs** (south London, tel. 0181/472–0400); and **London Cabs Limited** (east London, tel. 0181/778–3000).

BY BOAT

Despite being a terribly touristy thing to do, sailing on the Thames is a neat way to see London's skyline. Expensive tour boats leave year-round from **Westminster Pier** (tel. 0171/930–4097) and **Tower Pier** (tel. 0171/488–0344); downstream boats chug past the Tower of London, Greenwich, and the Thames Barrier; upstream destinations include Kew Gardens, Richmond, and Hampton Court. Tickets for the 90-minute trips cost £2–£6 per person. For more info, call the Westminster Passenger Service Association (tel. 0171/930–4092); Catamaran Cruises (tel. 0171/987–1185 or 0171/839–3575); or Tidal Cruises (tel. 0171/928–9009).

Daily in the summer and on weekends in the winter, you can cruise in traditional narrow boats along Regent's Canal between Camden Lock (about 200 yards north of Camden Town tube station) and Little Venice (near Paddington Station). The **London Waterbus Company** (tel. 0171/482–2660) stops at the zoo in Regent's Park; the trips offered by **Jason's Trip** (tel. 0171/286–3428) also sail through Regent's Park. During April, May, and September there are two trips per day; June–August there are four. The 90-minute voyages cost £2–£3.50.

Staying In London

AMERICAN EXPRESS American Express has several offices in London, offering the usual array of services. Cardholders should have their mail sent to the main office in the Haymarket. *6 Haymarket, London SW1, tel. 0171/930–4411. Tube: Piccadilly Circus or Charing Cross. Open weekdays 9–5:30, Sat. 9–4 (until 6 for currency exchange), Sun. 10–4 (currency exchange only).*

Other American Express locations in London include **4–12 Lower Regent Street** (tel. 0171/839–2682; Tube: Piccadilly Circus); **78 Brompton Road** (tel. 0171/584–6182 or 0171/225–0055; Tube: Knightsbridge); **54 Cannon Street** (tel. 0171/248–2671; Tube: Cannon St.); **156A Southampton Row** (tel. 0171/837–4416; Tube: Russell Sq.); **89 Mount Street** (tel. 0171/499–4436; Tube: Bond St. or Marble Arch); **147 Victoria Street** (tel. 0171/828–7411; Tube: Victoria); and in the **Whiteleys Centre** on Queensway (next to Halifax Building Society, tel. 0171/221–7190; Tube: Queensway or Bayswater).

BUCKET SHOPS If you're looking for discount flights or cheap train, ferry, and bus tickets, buy a copy of the semi-tabloid *Evening Standard* or *Time Out* magazine, both available at newsstands; *TNT,* a budget-travel magazine with an Aussie bent, is available at newsstands in Earl's Court and the West End. They all have tons of listings, though it will take some leg- or phone work to track down the best deals. Most bucket shops here offer student discounts, InterRail passes (for those living in the United Kingdom longer than six months), as well as flights, ferries, and trains to the Continent, and more.

Campus Travel. Although this budget-travel agency occupies a little kiosk within YHA's Southampton Street headquarters, it's not affiliated with them. Call for quotes on airfares, rail passes, you name it. *14 Southampton St., tel. 0171/836–3343. Tube: Covent Garden or Charing Cross. Open Mon.–Wed. 10–5:30, Thurs. and Fri. 10–6:30, Sat. 9:30–5:30.*

Council Travel. This modest storefront off busy Oxford Street caters to young travelers with worldwide discount flights, train and coach tickets, car rentals, hotels, budget guides, and ISIC cards (£5). *28A Poland St., tel. 0171/437–7767. Tube: Oxford Circus. Walk 200 meters east down Oxford St., right on Poland St. Open weekdays 9–6 (Thurs. until 7), Sat. 10–5.*

The following bucket shops consistently offer some of the best prices in town: **London Student Travel** (52 Grosvenor Gardens, tel. 0171/730–3402; Tube: Victoria); **Top Deck Travel** (131–135 Earl's Court Rd., tel. 0117/370–4555; Tube: Earl's Court); **Touropa** (52 Grosvenor Gardens, tel. 0171/730–2102; Tube: Victoria); **STA Travel** (74 and 86 Old Brompton Rd., tel. 0171/581–4132; Tube: South Kensington); and **Trailfinders** (42–50 Earl's Court Rd., tel. 0171/937–5400; Tube: Earl's Court), which only handles flights.

BUREAUX DE CHANGE While bureaux de change are everywhere in London, actually using them is simply flushing money down the toilet—their exchange rates are 10%–15% worse than what the banks offer. The only exceptions are **Thomas Cook,** which has travel offices all over town, and **American Express** (*see above*), which charge bank rates for their respective checks. If you're desperate for cash after-hours, **Chequepoint** has two 24-hour branches, one at 222 Earl's Court Road (tel. 0171/373–9515; Tube: Earl's Court) and one at 2 Queensway (tel. 0171/229–4268; Tube: Queensway).

BUSINESS HOURS Business hours are strictly regulated in England, thanks to the Church. Standard business hours are Monday–Saturday 9–5:30. Outside tourist areas, most shops observe an early closing day once a week, often Wednesday or Thursday. Most **banks** open weekdays 9:30–3:30; some have extended hours Thursday evening, and a few are open Saturday morning. **Newsagents** are allowed to be open Sunday, and they sell papers until about noon. Every other type of business is *supposed* to be closed on Sunday, but some large supermarket chains have decided to blow the £10,000-per-store fine and make cool millions by staying open.

EMBASSIES Australian High Commission. *Australia House, The Strand, tel. 0171/379–4334 for general inquiries or 01891/600333 for visa info. Tube: Temple. Open weekdays 10–4.*

Canadian High Commission. *Macdonald House, 1 Grosvenor Sq., tel. 0171/258–6600. Tube: Bond St. Open weekdays 9–3, for visas 8:45–2, for passports 10–3.*

New Zealand High Commission. *New Zealand House, 80 Haymarket, tel. 0171/973–0366 for visas or 0171/930–8422 for passports and general info. Tube: Charing Cross or Piccadilly Circus. Open weekdays 10–noon and 2–4, for visas 12:30–4.*

United States. For passport and consular services (repatriation, expatriation, indigency), use the Upper Brook Street entrance around the corner from Grosvenor Square. *24 Grosvenor Sq., tel. 0171/499–9000. Tube: Marble Arch or Bond St. Open for visas Mon. and Wed.–Fri. 8:30–noon and 2–4, Tues. 8:30–noon; for consular services, weekdays 8:30–5:30.*

EMERGENCIES AND MEDICAL AID The general emergency number for **ambulance, police,** and **fire** is 999, and you don't need to deposit money to call. **Nightline** (tel. 0171/436–5561) confidentially gives all types of info and advice to students during termtime, 6 PM–8 AM. **Rape Crisis Line** (tel. 0171/837–1600) offers 24-hour emergency and nonemergency counseling. **The Samaritans** (tel. 0171/734–2800) can lend a helpful ear 24-hours a day to people who are in emotional crisis or feeling suicidal. **Women's Aid** (tel. 0171/251–6537) provides 24-hour advice, counseling, and referrals for women in crisis. The **National AIDS Helpline** (tel. 0800/567123) offers 24-hour counseling and info on AIDS and HIV; the call is free. The **Body Positive Helpline** (tel. 0171/373–9124), open daily 7 PM–10 PM, is another good source for info on the treatment of STDs, including AIDS. The **Pregnancy Advisory Service** (11–13 Charlotte St., tel. 0171/637–8962) offers pregnancy tests and advice on everything from adoption to abortion.

➤ **DOCTORS** • England has socialized medicine, and, happily, travelers can take advantage of this. Remember, your ISIC card also comes with hospitalization insurance—bring it with you, along with the summary-of-coverage card. You will not be charged by an English physician for a quick diagnosis and prescription, but you may be charged if you require other treatment (X-rays, shaman, witch doctor, etc.). For serious injuries, the following hospitals have 24-hour emergency wards:

Guy's. *St. Thomas St., tel. 0171/407–7600. Tube: London Bridge.*

Royal Free. *Pond St., Hampstead, tel. 0171/794–0500. Tube: Belsize Park.*

University College Clinic. *Gower St., tel. 0171/387–9300. Tube: Euston Sq. or Warren St.*

Westminster. *Dean Ryle St., tel. 0171/828–9811. Tube: Pimlico.*

➤ **DENTISTS** • Guy's Dental School accepts emergency dental visits, though for nonemergencies you must make an appointment. *St. Thomas St., tel. 0171/955–5000. Tube: London Bridge. Open weekdays 9–4, weekends 10–6 for emergencies only.*

➤ **PHARMACIES** • Chemists (equivalent to an American drugstore) are peppered throughout London; those with late hours include:

Bliss Chemists. *5 Marble Arch, tel. 0171/723–6116. Tube: Marble Arch. Also: 33 Sloane Sq., tel. 0171/730–4336. Tube: Sloane Sq. Both open daily 9 AM–midnight.*

Boots. *439 Oxford St., tel. 0171/409–2857. Tube: Bond St. or Marble Arch. Open weekdays 9 AM–10 PM, Sat. 9–9. Also: Victoria Station, tel. 0171/834–0676. Tube: Victoria. Open weekdays 8 AM–9 PM.*

LUGGAGE STORAGE If you're coming from Heathrow or Gatwick airports, the best place to store luggage is in **Victoria Station** (tel. 0171/928–5151, ext. 27514); it's open daily 7 AM–10 PM. You'll pay per piece £2.50–£5 per day (*see* Coming and Going, By Train, *above*). If you're arriving by bus, store your luggage in **Victoria Coach Station** (*see* Coming and Going, By Bus, *above*), which is slightly less expensive than the train station at £2–£3 per piece per day. Both are convenient to Victoria tube station. **Students-Tourists Storage,** with warehouses near Victoria, Earl's Court, and King's Cross, will store your stuff for £3 per item per week; call toll-free 0800/622–244 for the location nearest you.

MAIL Putting your precious cards and letters in the hands of the Royal Mail may not prove as wise as you'd hoped. Mail service is fairly reliable, but very slow. Expect your letter to North America to take up to four days longer to arrive than it takes to receive one. In London, look for post offices in butcher shops, liquor stores ("off-licenses"), or chemists. For locations near you, call **Customer Care** (tel. 0171/239–3040), or keep your eyes peeled for signs bearing a red oval with yellow lettering: POST OFFICE.

➤ **SENDING MAIL HOME** • Rates from the United Kingdom are 41p for an international airmail letter, 36p for an international aerogramme, and 35p for an international postcard. Prices for mail within the European Union are the same as domestic, first-class postal rates. Be sure to get the free PAR AVION/BY AIR MAIL stickers when you buy your stamps. If you're sending a letter, do it by air mail (a week to 10 days), because surface mail can take up to *nine weeks!* Surface mail is really for sending home gifts or heavy items you don't want to carry around. Boxes can be bought at office-supply stores like W. H. Smith and at some post offices. You'll need to fill out a small, green customs sticker that states the weight and contents (so much for surprise gifts).

➤ **RECEIVING MAIL** • You can receive those dear letters from home via poste restante at any post office—or, if you have an AmEx card, at one of their offices. Have people write "Poste Restante" and "Hold for 30 days" in the upper left corner of the box/envelope, and have them address it to the **Trafalgar Square Post Office.** They hold mail for up to one month; bring your I.D. to pick it up. *Trafalgar Square Post Office, 24 William IV St., WC2N 4DL, tel. 0171/930–4802. Tube: Charing Cross. Open Mon.–Sat. 8–8.*

PHONES Country Code: 44. British Telecom (BT) and Mercury are the only two phone companies operating in England. Mercury is the best deal for international calls; to use their phones, you'll need a plastic "phone card" that's worth a fixed number of 10p "units" (10p is the cost of a local call). Both companies' cards come in denominations of £2, £4, £10, and £20; to use them, lift the receiver, insert your card into the slot, and dial your number. An LED panel indicates how many units you've used. BT pay phones are easiest to find throughout London. The ones with a red stripe around them accept standard English coins, while phones with a green stripe require the phone cards, available at newsagents, train and bus stations, tourist-information centers, and numerous other locations. Look for signs saying PHONE CARDS SOLD HERE. To call the operator, dial 100; for directory inquiries (information) dial 142 (London) or 192 (the rest of Britain).

➤ **LOCAL CALLS** • London has two new area codes: 0171 for inner London, and 0181 for outer London. If you're phoning from one London area code to another, you must dial the area code. Local calls start at 10p. Modern pay phones display how fast your money is being gobbled up; older phones without displays beep when your money is about to run out. Pay phones will give back any unused coins fed into the slot, but they don't make change, so think twice about using a £1 coin for a local call.

➤ **INTERNATIONAL CALLS** • To dial direct from England, first dial 010 (or 00 after April 15, 1995), then dial the country code (1 for the United States and Canada, 353 for the Republic of Ireland, 61 for Australia, and 64 for New Zealand), then the area code and phone number. Calls to Northern Ireland from England, Scotland, or Wales can be dialed without the international codes. To dial direct or collect using American carriers, contact **AT&T USADirect**

London Postal Districts

SW6
EARLS COURT
W6
W12
W14
Kensington High St.
Holland Park Ave.
W11
W10
NW 10
NW6
W9
Maida Vale
W8
SW5
SW10
Cromwell Rd.
Old Brompton Rd.
Fulham Rd.
KNIGHTS-BRIDGE
SW7
Brompton Rd.
SW3
CHELSEA
Chelsea Embankment
River Thames
Battersea Park
KENSINGTON
Kensington Rd.
Notting Hill Gate
Westway A40(M)
PADDINGTON
W2
Bayswater Rd.
Edgware Rd.
Hyde Park
Knightsbridge
MAYFAIR
Piccadilly
Marylebone Rd.
MARYLEBONE
Baker St.
W1
Oxford St.
SOHO
Regent's Park
NW8
Wellington Rd.
NW1
VICTORIA
SW1
PIMLICO
WEST-MINSTER
Victoria St.
SW8
Vauxhall Br.
The Mall
ST. JAMES'S
Charing Cross Rd.
Tottenham Court Rd.
Gower St.
BLOOMS-BURY
WC1
High Holborn
HOLBORN
Euston Rd.
Gray's Inn Rd.
Everholt St.
FINSBURY
Pentonville Rd.
N1
City Rd.
Old St.
EC1
Westminster Br.
Lambeth Br.
LAMBETH
Lambeth Rd.
Waterloo Rd.
WC2
Strand
Fleet St.
EC4
Aldersgate
THE CITY
London Wall
EC2
E2
SE11
Kennington Pk. Rd.
BOROUGH
SE1
Cannon St.
London Br.
EC3
Kingsland Rd.
Whitechapel Rd.
Commercial Rd.
E1
SE5
WALWORTH
SE17
SE16
River Thames
SE15
N

32

(tel. 0800/890011), **MCI** (tel. 0800/890222), or **Sprint** (tel. 0800/877800)—the call to the carrier is free. Direct dialing is considerably more expensive from pay phones than from private ones, but many residential phone bills don't itemize calls, so it's difficult to reimburse your hosts. Have a phone card with lots of credit (at least 50 units) or a ton of change ready, especially £1 coins. To place an incredibly expensive collect call using BT, dial 155 to be connected with an operator.

VISITOR INFORMATION The main **London Tourist Information Centre** provides details on tube and bus tickets, theater, concert and tour bookings, and lodging. It doesn't have a public info line, though, so go in person and pick up a fistful of brochures. Otherwise, call 0171/824–8844 for an overpriced reservation in an overpriced lodging—they accept credit cards only and charge a hefty £5 reservation fee. Other information centers are located in **Harrods** (Brompton Rd.; Tube: Knightsbridge), **Selfridges** (Oxford St.; Tube: Marble Arch, Bond St.), **Heathrow Airport** (Terminals 1, 2, and 3), and **Gatwick Airport** (International Arrivals Concourse). *Main office: Victoria Station, no phone. Tube: Victoria. Open Mon.–Sat. 8–7, Sun. 8–5.*

The **British Travel Centre** provides details about travel and entertainment for the whole of Britain, and makes lodging reservations for a £5 fee. They have no phone line for public inquiries, so you must visit in person. *12 Regent St., no phone. Tube: Piccadilly Circus. Open May–Sept., weekdays 9–6:30, Sat. 9–5, Sun. 10–4; Oct.–Apr., weekdays 9–6:30, weekends 10–4.*

EXPLORING LONDON 2

By Caitlin Ramey

No matter how long you stay, it's tough to get bored wandering through the twisting streets of London's dense, distinctly flavored neighborhoods. Many residents are very neighborhood-oriented and fiercely proud of their minimilieus. Although Londoners venture out of their residential pockets, out of geographical necessity the districts function almost as self-contained, self-defined communities. Indeed, until the Industrial Revolution of the 19th century, what's now called London was a hodgepodge of villages—suburban satellites of the *original* City of London. This ancient core has evolved into what locals call "the City," the financial heart of London that sprawls along the banks of the River Thames.

Many of London's sights are in a relatively small area in the West End, and the most famous attractions—including Parliament, Westminster Abbey, and many of the palaces—are within walking distance of one another. Apart from a few sights on the outskirts, you're better off checking out London on foot. In the central area, tube stations are abundant and fairly close together, but if you *always* hop on the tube to travel between sights, you won't get a decent idea of the city's layout. Of course, it's a safe bet that on foot you'll end up hopelessly lost within minutes, so pick up a copy of the *London A to Z* street atlas (Brits pronounce it "A to Zed") that's sold at newsstands and schlock shops throughout the city. Buy the mini-London (£2.95) edition—just the right size to fit in your pocket. Locals, including cab drivers, swear by it.

GUIDED TOURS

If you don't mind feeling like a tourist, several companies offer interesting walking tours for around £4 per person. One of the best is **London Walks** (tel. 0171/624–3978), which has humorous, knowledgeable guides and a wide selection of routes from which to choose, including Shakespeare's London and all sorts of pub crawls. **City Walks** (tel. 0171/700–0738) operates the macabre (and sometimes downright silly) "Jack the Ripper Walk," following the serial killer's trail of death and destruction. It starts at the Tower Hill tube station every evening at 7 PM. **Cockney Walks** (tel. 0181/504–9159) will guide you around the East End, with a dual emphasis on the area's Jewish heritage and the working-class Cockney spirit. **Docklands Tours** (tel. 0171/512–1111) offers a somewhat pricey (£5–£8) guided coach tour of the developing (and struggling) business area along the Thames in the east.

Remember to look up every once in a while when you're walking around London. Many structures have magnificent old facades with busts of famous dead people tucked into the strangest of corners.

A more flexible (and cost-effective) way to structure your wanderings is to purchase one of the many self-guided walking tours available at most tourist offices for a few pounds. The **Silver Jubilee Walkway** covers 10 miles, passing most of the big-name attractions. The path is marked by a series of silver crowns set into the sidewalks; Parliament Square is a good starting point. The **London Wall Walk** follows the outer perimeter of the original city of London, passing recently excavated slabs of the old city's wall. You can follow the tour route from the Tower Hill tube station, right outside the Tower of London.

BY BUS If you feel more comfortable remaining seated while someone else points out the sights, a huge mass of companies are just begging for your tourist dollar. **London Transport (LT)** (tel. 0171/828–7395) offers 90-minute sightseeing tours on its double-decker buses; there are departures every half-hour 10–5 from Marble Arch, Victoria Station, Madame Tussaud's, and Piccadilly Circus. Buy your ticket from the driver for £9 or from the London Tourist Information Centre at Victoria Station for £8. Consider London Transport's VIP ticket (£12) if you'd prefer to hop on and off the tour bus at your whimsy for a full day. Between April and October **London General** (tel. 0171/646–1747) conducts 90-minute "London by Night" tours (£6) that leave from Victoria Station at 7 and 9 PM. If you can't make it to Victoria in time, flag down the London General bus at Paddington, Piccadilly Circus, or Oxford Circus.

BY BOAT If the weather doesn't suck, consider floating down the Thames in a glass-encased tour boat. Although ferries offer a more affordable way to get seasick on the Thames (*see* Getting Around in Chapter 1), an advantage of tour boats is the piped commentary that tries (sometimes in vain) to put London into historical perspective. Tour boats leave year-round from **Westminster Pier** (tel. 0171/930– 4097) and **Tower Pier** (tel. 0171/488–0344); get off the tube at Westminster or Tower Hill, respectively. Downstream boats chug past the Tower of London, Greenwich, and the Thames Barrier; upstream destinations include Kew Gardens, Richmond, and Hampton Court.

BY BIKE An exhilarating (although somewhat exhaust-filled) way to check out London is by bike. Weather permitting, the **London Bicycle Tour Company** (tel. 0171/928–6838) conducts mountain-bike tours of various London neighborhoods. Tours cost £9.95 per person but are scheduled only sporadically; call for the latest schedules. Another option is to rent your own

Sightseeing on the Cheap

If you prefer a motorized overview of central London, save some cash by joining London's commuters on a standard double-decker bus. You won't get the tape-recorded rundown on the sights, but you can use your plain ol' LT Travelcard (see Getting Around, By Bus in Chapter 1) for the following routes.

- *Bus 11: King's Road, Sloane Square, Victoria Station, Westminster Abbey, Houses of Parliament, Whitehall, Horse Guards, Trafalgar Square, the Strand, the Law Courts, Fleet Street, and St. Paul's Cathedral.*

- *Bus 12: Bayswater, Hyde Park, Marble Arch, Oxford Street, Regent Street, Piccadilly Circus, Trafalgar Square, Horse Guards, Whitehall, Houses of Parliament, Westminster Bridge.*

- *Bus 19: Sloane Square, Knightsbridge, Hyde Park Corner, Piccadilly Circus, Bloomsbury, Islington.*

- *Bus 88: Oxford Circus, Piccadilly Circus, Trafalgar Square, Whitehall, Houses of Parliament, Westminster Abbey, Tate Gallery.*

bike: For £6.95, London Bicycle Tour Company gives you a mountain bike for 24 hours, free maps, and advice on routes (*see* London by Bike in Chapter 8).

Major Attractions

The best and most famous museums in London are free, and the major sites that aren't generally offer student concessions. Carry your ISIC card at all times. As for the maddening crowds, arrive early in the day (or, even better, off-season) to avoid brushing up against some of the 5 million other tourists who charge through London every year. The best advice of all: Know when you've hit your limit, and head for the pub at the first sign of brain fade. It shows a measure of respect for the great metropolis, which has more to offer than you could possibly take advantage of in a day, a week, or even a year.

BRITISH MUSEUM

Anybody writing about the British Museum in Bloomsbury better have a large pail of superlatives close at hand: most, biggest, earliest, finest. This is the golden hoard of 2½ centuries of Empire, the booty bought—and flat-out stolen—from Britain's far-flung colonies. The first major pieces, among them the Rosetta Stone and Parthenon sculptures, were "borrowed" from the French, who "found" them in Egypt and Greece. The museum has since collected countless goodies of worldwide historical significance: the Elgin Marbles, the Black Obelisk, the Dead Sea Scrolls, the Magna Carta, the Lindow Bog Man. Hell, that only *begins* the list.

The collection spans the centuries as well as the globe, featuring artifacts from the prehistoric era, ancient Egypt and Assyria, right on through the Renaissance. The sheer magnitude of it all overwhelms; you need to make at least two visits for the most cursory overview of the museum and four or five visits to get any sort of handle on it. One good strategy is to spend £6 on a 90-minute guided tour and come back later to view whatever intrigued you most; ask at the info desk about tour times. Visually impaired visitors should ask about the special "touch tour" of Roman sculpture. If you absolutely must rush, make a beeline for the following: **Room 8** (the Elgin Marbles); **Room 12** (the tomb of Mausolus and what little remains of the Seven Wonders of the Ancient World); **Room 17** (carvings pilfered from the 7th-century BC ruins at Nineveh); **Room 25** (the Rosetta Stone); **Room 30** (handwritten poems and prose from Wordsworth, Donne, and Austen); **Room 35** (the perfectly preserved Lindow Bog Man, discovered in a peat bog); and **Room 41** (the Sutton Hoo Celtic art collection).

The **British Library Reading Room** (tel. 0171/323–7677), on the ground floor of the British Library, is a magnificent domed structure built in the 1850s. By royal decree, the British Library is entitled to receive one copy of everything published in the United Kingdom—from the Magna Carta and the Lindisfarne Gospels to trashy periodicals and daily newspapers. It's estimated that 2.1 miles of new shelving are needed each year to accommodate the ever-growing collection. Not surprisingly, England's number-one library is hurting for space, and sometime before 1997 it will move to a larger facility near St. Pancras. To see the **reading room**—where George Bernard Shaw and Karl Marx have warmed seats writing their magnum opuses—you must either obtain a research pass through your university or take the guided tour, which is currently given weekdays at 2:15 and 4:15 PM. The times are subject to change, so call to confirm. *Great Russell St., tel. 0171/636–1555 or 0171/580–1788 for recorded info. Tube: Tottenham Court Rd. Walk 1 block north on Tottenham Court Rd. (pass Burger King on your right), turn right on Great Russell St. Admission free (nominal charge for special exhibits). Open Mon.–Sat. 10–5, Sun. 2:30–6.*

The cafés and pubs south of the British Museum's main entrance are highly recommended. Just two blocks away, The Old Crown (33 New Oxford St., tel. 0171/836–9121) is an excellent pub that dishes out a fine plate of taquitos.

37

BUCKINGHAM PALACE

Since the reign of Queen Victoria, British monarchs have called this big gray fortress their London home. George III bought Buckingham House, as it was called then, in 1762 for a mere £28,000; following his reign, the palace proved to be a sinkhole for expensive remodeling efforts. When George IV took it over, he decided the palace looked far too bourgeois, and in 1824, he set architect John Nash to work on the structure. Nash is responsible for much of what you see now, although the heavy Portland stone facing is the fault of a 1913 remodeling effort—Edwardian architecture at its dullest.

The queen has her choice of 660 rooms, but occupies only a dozen on the first floor. It's easy to picture her there curled up in front of the telly with her corgis and a bag of crisps.

A flag bearing the Royal Standard flies whenever Queen Elizabeth II is in residence, usually on weekdays. The queen opened parts of Buckingham Palace to the public—for a fee, mind you—to pay for the restorations to Windsor Palace after the disastrous fire there in 1992. (The government initially offered the queen £90 million for restorations, but massive public outcry prompted Her Majesty to foot the bill.) With the high cost of castle restorations these days, it's likely the palace will remain open through the summer of 1998, but call for the latest word. They don't let you wander through the whole pad poking into medicine cabinets, but the **State Apartments** are open for viewing, including the throne room, picture galleries, and state dining room. *Tel. 0171/493–3175. Tube: Green Park or St. James's Park. From Green Park: walk ½ mile south on Queen's Walk. From St. James's Park: walk north on Queen Anne's Gate, turn left on Birdcage Walk, right on Spur Rd. Admission £8. Open Aug.–Sept., daily 9:30–4:30.*

QUEEN'S GALLERY Only a short distance down Buckingham Gate (which becomes Buckingham Palace Road), the Queen's Gallery houses rotating exhibits of pieces from her majesty's

Those Nutty Royals

Although the popularity of the monarchy has been declining for some time (especially among younger people), the sales of tabloids devoted to the royals shows that Brits are still passionately interested in their exploits—in much the same way people love to stop and stare at a car wreck. The last few years have certainly given Brits a fair amount to stare at: the fire at Windsor Castle, the breakup of the Duke and Duchess of York (complete with internationally published photos of a topless Fergie having her toes sucked poolside by a wealthy Texan), the public uproar over the family's tax-free status, and the increasingly ugly crash-and-burn of the marriage of Prince Charles and Princess Diana, leaving the eventual succession to the throne very much in doubt.

This last saga has dominated recent coverage of the monarchs, especially after the publication of transcripts of (supposedly) private conversations, first between Diana and confidant James Gilby (an affair known as "Dianagate"), and later between Charles and old flame Camilla Parker-Bowles (popularized as "Camillagate"). Diana's conversation, mainly expressing her unhappiness with her marriage and the family in general, was tame compared with Charles' steamy remarks detailing his desire to become a tampon so as to be as close to Camilla as possible. This caused the Prince more than a little embarrassment: The Italian press quickly dubbed him "Principe Tamponcino" (Little Prince Tampon).

private art collection. Gainsborough, Rembrandt, Reynolds, and Rubens are among the regulars featured. *Buckingham Palace Rd., tel. 0171/930–4832, ext. 3351. Admission: £3. Open Mar.–Dec., Tues.–Sat. 10–5, Sun. 2–5.*

ROYAL MEWS The Royal Mews houses the royal horsies, the liveried servants, and the gilded carriages. If you visit when both the Queen's Gallery and the Royal Mews are open, you can cop a slightly cheaper combined ticket for £5. *Buckingham Palace Rd., tel. 0171/930–4832, ext. 3351. Admission: £3. Open Apr.–Sept., Tues., Wed., Thurs. noon–4; Oct.–Mar., Wed. noon–4.*

GUARDS MUSEUM The Guards Museum occupies a set of underground rooms in Wellington Barracks, the regimental headquarters of the palace's Guards Division. The museum traces the history of the five Foot Guards regiments—Coldstream, Grenadier, Scots, Irish, and Welsh—from the 1660s through the Falklands War. The massive toy soldier shop is definitely worth a look, if you're into that kind of thing. *Wellington Barracks, Birdcage Walk, tel. 0171/930–4466, ext. 3430. Admission: £2, £1 students. Open Sat.–Thurs. and "sometimes" Fri. 10–4.*

CHANGING OF THE GUARD One of the biggest tourist shows in town is the Changing of the Guard ceremony, when the soldiers guarding the queen hand over their duties to the next watch. Marching to music, the old guard proceeds up the Mall from St. James's Palace to Buckingham Palace as the new guard approaches from Wellington Barracks via Birdcage Walk. When the two columns meet, they continue to march around to the music for a half-hour before the old guard symbolically hands over the keys to the palace. The ceremony takes place daily at 11 AM April–July, on alternating days August–March.

Be warned: Unless you arrive by 10:30 AM, you can forget about a decent frontal view of the pomp and circumstance. Latecomers should stand along Constitution Hill, the thoroughfare leading to Hyde Park Corner. Just press your nose between the iron fence around the Forecourt of the Palace. It's a side view, yes, but it beats the hell out of standing behind a crowd that's 15 people deep. If you don't mind the 48p charge, call the **Changing of the Guard Hot Line** (tel. 0171/930–4466) to find out when and if the guards will march, as they often cancel due to bad weather.

HOUSES OF PARLIAMENT

The Empire may be dead, but it's still fascinating to check out the site from which Britain once ruled with imperial impunity. The Houses of Parliament are officially known as the **Palace of Westminster,** symbolic of the heavy influence the monarchy held over Parliament for centuries. The media calls them Whitehall to distinguish Parliament from **Westminster Palace,** which was the principal royal residence from the time of William the Conqueror (1066–1087) until 1512, when Henry VIII moved into Whitehall Palace. Parliamentarians rebelled against Charles I during the English Civil War (1642–1648), but before then, they were very much at the beck and call of the monarch. In fact, many kings summoned Parliament only when they needed money (it was Parliament's responsibility to levy taxes) and then promptly dismissed it.

A major fire in 1834 destroyed almost everything but the massive **Westminster Hall,** built in 1097–1099 by William II and rebuilt by Richard II in 1394–1399. The only other remnants of the old parliamentary buildings are the **Crypt of St. Stephen's Chapel,** where the House of Commons met for 300 years, and the medieval **Jewel Tower** (*see below*), used to store Edward III's collections of furs, jewels, gold, and other royal knickknacks. After the blaze, a competition was held to design new Parliament buildings. The winners were Charles Barry, a classical architect, and his assistant, Augustus Pugin, a Gothicist. Not surprisingly, sparks flew between the two men over the new design, and the result is . . . well . . . a classical structure decorated with Gothic Revivalist details.

The best view of Parliament is probably the most traditional—from halfway across Westminster Bridge or from the Albert Embankment on the far side of the Thames. Then again, the vista entering Parliament Square via Whitehall has postcard written all over it, with views of Westminster Abbey, Big Ben, the Houses of Parliament, and Westminster Hall. The square itself features numerous statues of BMOC (Big Men of the Commonwealth), including Sir Robert Peel, Benjamin Disraeli, Oliver Cromwell, Jan Smuts, and Sir Winston Churchill.

HOUSE OF LORDS The House of Lords, the more prestigious but ultimately less powerful of Parliament's two houses, is composed of British ladies and lords who either inherited their titles or were elevated to their ranks by the queen. Periodically, left-wingers call for an overhaul of the Lords, asserting that no one should be allowed to serve purely on the basis of birth or title, and they've got a good point. Fortunately, the Lords wield little parliamentary power: Barring an inordinate amount of whining from the upper house, what the House of Commons decides becomes law.

The Lords chamber is a sumptuous affair, with lots of carved wooden paneling, gilding, and leather. Also, some of the public areas outside the chamber feature frescoes with scenes from British history. The line is always shorter to get into the House of Lords, but if you're looking for drama, forget it—unless, of course, you get off watching inbred aristocrats snoring and dribbling in a post-prandial coma.

HOUSE OF COMMONS The House of Commons, with roughly 700 elected members from around the country, is where the real power lies. Although the simple green benches of the Commons chamber are comparatively sober, catching a parliamentary session can be one of the best cheap thrills in London. Getting into the **Strangers' Gallery** for either house is tough however, and unless you plan ahead and manage to snag some tickets through your embassy, you might have to wait in line for several hours. The ultimate spectacle is the prime minister's **Question Time,** held in the House of Commons on Tuesday and Thursday between 3:15 and 3:30 PM. This is when the opposition leader has free rein to savage the PM—foreigners are *required* to secure tickets from their respective embassies, and Brits from their MPs. The extra effort can be worth it, though, as the repartee is always quick and cutting.

Arrange a special tour of the Houses of Parliament and Big Ben by contacting the Public Information Office (tel. 0171/219–4272) at least a month before your visit. If you take your chances and arrive at either Strangers' Gallery without a ticket, you're unlikely to get in until after 4:15.

Next best is either chamber's regular Question Time, held Monday–Thursday between 2:30 and 3:15 PM. There are other sessions and debates in both houses, but schedules are sketchy since they depend on what crisis the government is currently coping with. You're more likely to get into the Commons during an evening session—look for the light shining at the top of Big Ben to see if Parliament is sitting. *Tel. 0171/219–4272. Tube: Westminster. For Strangers' Galleries, line up at St. Stephen's Entrance (to the left for the Commons, to the right for the Lords). Admission free. House of Commons open Mon.–Thurs. 2:30–late, Fri. 9:30–3. House of Lords open Mon.–Wed. 2:30–late, Thurs. 3:30–late, Fri. 11 AM–late.*

BIG BEN AND VICTORIA TOWER The clock tower known as **Big Ben,** perhaps the most enduring symbol of both London and Britain, is actually named **St. Stephen's Tower.** To pick nits, it's only the 13-ton bell on top that's named Big Ben. Details aside, for the millions of colonials worldwide who've heard Big Ben strike the hour nightly on the BBC World Service, it evokes a wide range of emotions: home, security, a sense of belonging. Especially when lit up at night, Big Ben's stature dwarfs the other buildings in the Parliament complex, even though it's not the tallest. That distinction belongs to the 336-foot-high **Victoria Tower,** reputedly the largest square tower in the world. Very likely, it's also the most expensive to maintain, having just undergone a £7.5-million restoration. A Union Jack flies from the top of Victoria Tower whenever Parliament is in session.

JEWEL TOWER Sitting across from the Victoria Tower, the medieval Jewel Tower features various displays on the history of Parliament, with artifacts, photographs, and even videos of MPs duking it out. *Abingdon St., tel. 0171/222–2219. Admission: £2.10, £1.55 students. Open Easter–Oct., daily 10–1 and 2–6; Nov.–Easter, Tues.–Sat. 10–1 and 2–4.*

ST. PAUL'S CATHEDRAL

Just south of the Barbican in the heart of the City, St. Paul's is instantly recognizable by its huge dome, towering 218 feet above street level. The present structure, the third in a series of cathedrals erected on the site, was built by Christopher Wren between 1675 and 1710, shortly after the Great Fire ravaged London. Miraculously, the cathedral escaped major damage during World War II, when the rest of the city was reduced to little more than blazing rubble. The interior of the dome's base is encircled by the **Whispering Gallery;** whisper into the wall, and you'll be heard clearly 100 feet away on the other side of the gallery. For some great views of London, climb the staircase to the **Stone Gallery** outside the dome or the **Golden Gallery** at the top of the dome. Inside, the **crypt** is full of famous dead people, including military demigods Nelson, Wellington, and Kitchener. The tomb of the great builder himself, Christopher Wren, is adorned by his son's famous epi-

Prince Charles and Lady Di tied the fateful knot in St. Paul's. Ever since, Fleet Street tabloids have marked with relish their domestic decline. As one English columnist describes the Royals, "great weddings, shame about the marriages."

London Architecture

Great architectural achievements in London have often been motivated by extreme disaster or misfortune. After the Great Fire of 1666 destroyed four-fifths of a city still reeling from the onslaught of the Great Plague the preceding year, London required almost complete restoration. Nearly 300 years later, much of central and suburban London was again destroyed—this time by the German air raids of the early 1940s. The result of these intense civic reconstructions was that a few individuals had the opportunity to leave significant marks upon the city. Following are architects whose work will literally surround you as you wander through London.

- Inigo Jones (1573–1652), one of England's first great architects, was almost single-handedly responsible for the resurgence of classical styles of architecture in the early 17th century. Often directly modeling his work after that of Italian architect Andrea Palladio, Jones was highly influential during his time, as the Palladian style quickly spread throughout England. His most famous works include St. Paul's Church at Covent Garden and the magnificent Banqueting House in Whitehall.

- Sir Christopher Wren (1632–1723) was given the daunting task of overseeing the rebuilding of London following the Great Fire. His ambitious plans for a complete redesigning of the formerly medieval city were shot down by landowners, business people, and private citizens intent upon a quicker reconstruction, but he is still responsible for 51 new churches (all in the City), including the world's first Protestant cathedral, the amazing St. Paul's. Other examples worth checking out are St. Bride's (Fleet St.), St. Stephen Walbrook (Walbrook St.), and St. Martin Ludgate (Ludgate Hill).

- John Nash (1752–1835) completely redesigned a large section of the city stretching from the Mall northward to Regent's Park. He is largely responsible for the look of much of central London; it was his idea to clear Trafalgar Square of its royal stables to make room for the public space as it exists today. He also remodeled Buckingham Palace.

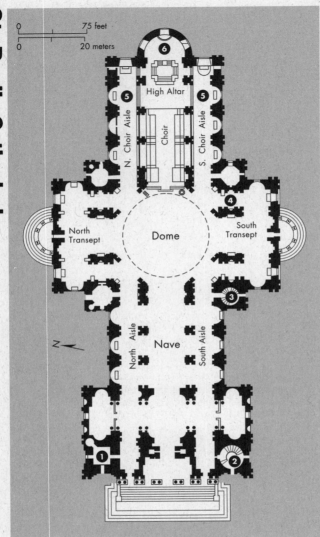

0 75 feet

0 20 meters

All Souls' Chapel, **1**
American Chapel, **6**
Crypt entrance, **4**
Geometric Staircase, **2**
Staircase to Dome, Whispering Gallery, and Golden Gallery, **3**
Tijou Gates, **5**

High Altar

N. Choir Aisle

Choir

S. Choir Aisle

North Transept

Dome

South Transept

North Aisle

Nave

South Aisle

taph: LECTOR, SI MONUMENTUM REQUIRIS, CIRCUMSPICE (Reader, if it is a monument you seek, look about you). In the ambulatory behind the high altar is the **American Chapel,** a memorial to the 28,000 Americans stationed in Britain who died during World War II.

St. Paul's most notable fine points are the choir stalls, hand-carved by Dutch artist Grinling Gibbons, and the iron screens by the French master Jean Tijou. If you want all the gory details, take a 90-minute **Supertour** (£3, £2 students) Monday–Saturday at 11, 11:30, 1:30, and 2. Organ recitals are given every Friday at 1:15 PM; check the posted listings. Admission to the cathedral is free, but admission is £2.50 (£2 students) to each of the galleries and £3 (£2.50 students) to the crypt, ambulatory, and American Chapel. A combo ticket for the crypt and galleries costs £5 (£4 students), but sauntering through the free gardens, especially when the roses are in bloom, can be just as satisfying. *St. Paul's Churchyard, tel. 0171/248–2705.*

Tube: St. Paul's or Mansion House. From St. Paul's: follow marked signs. From Mansion House: walk west on Cannon St., turn right on New Change. Open Mon.–Sat. 8:30–4:15; crypt and ambulatory open Mon.–Sat. 8:45–4:15; galleries open Mon.–Sat. 10–4:15.

TATE GALLERY

The Tate is one of the country's principal museums—less impressive than the National Gallery, perhaps, but much more contemporary and controversial. The artwork is divided into two collections: the British collection, which features British paintings from the 16th century to the present, and the modern collection, which features modern European and American works. The highlight of the British collection is the **Clore Gallery,** dedicated to J. M. W. Turner with more than 300 of his paintings, 300 personal sketchbooks, and 20,000 rough drawings. It goes without saying that the museum can't display all of Turner's works at once, so they're rotated, as is the art in the rest of the museum. Expect a complete rehanging about every nine months.

The Tate is far more famous—and infamous—for its modern collection, including works by van Gogh, Matisse, Picasso, Dali, Rothko, Moore, Johns, and Ernst, to name a few. Every now and then, the Tate gets itself into hot water by displaying an exhibit that, to the lay art-lover, is mind-numbingly dumb. Probably the most famous brouhaha occurred when the gallery paid an ungodly sum for a pile of bricks—nothing more, nothing less. Similar controversies have surrounded displays of such everyday items as milk bottles.

In the eyes of many Brits, a janitor couldn't leave a mop leaning against the wall at the Tate without museum patrons evaluating it with a critical eye.

Free guided tours are given daily. On weekdays, the gallery offers focused tours on British art before 1900 (11 AM), the Turner Collection (noon), early modern art (2 PM), and later modern art (3 PM). Saturday at 3 PM and Sunday at 3:45 PM the staff will guide you through the highlights of the collection. "Touch tours" of sculptures are also available for visually impaired visitors; call 0171/887–8724 for schedules. Free lectures, films, and video screenings take place almost daily in the auditorium; pick up a schedule at the info desk. The **café** in the basement of the main gallery offers cheap gourmet sandwiches, vegetarian dishes (£2–£4), pastries, and potent coffee. However, forget the posh restaurant: with £12 entrées, it speaks to a different crowd. *Millbank, tel. 0171/887–8726 or 0171/887–8008 for recorded info. Tube: Pimlico. Turn left on Bessborough St., left on Drummond, right at Vauxhall Bridge Rd. (a.k.a. Bessborough Gardens), left at Millbank (a.k.a. Grosvenor Rd.), and continue along river about 4 blocks. Admission free; special exhibits: £1–£5. Open Mon.–Sat. 10–5:50, Sun. 2–5:50. Wheelchair entrance on John Islip St.*

TOWER OF LONDON

The Tower of London actually refers to the 20 towers that comprise London's most famous medieval fortress, covering 18 acres on the banks of the Thames. Besides serving as the residence of every British sovereign from William the Conqueror (he built the original fortress in 1078) to Henry VIII in the 16th century, the Tower also houses a jewel safe, an armory, a zoo, and a garrison. It is most famous, however, for its role as a prison and place of execution. Some of England's most notable figures met their deaths here, including Sir Walter Raleigh, Sir Thomas More, Lady Jane Grey (crowned Queen of England in 1553 but deposed and executed after a week), and Anne Boleyn and Catherine Howard (Henry VIII's second and fifth wives, respectively).

The Tower of London draws more than 2 million visitors a year to wander up its winding staircases, into its tunnels, over its bridges, and through its narrow passages. Arrive early or perish in the teeming hordes.

The most impressive and oldest of the towers is **White Tower.** Finished in 1097, it was one of a number of fortified structures erected in London by the justifiably nervous William the Conqueror (angry Saxon kings craved Will's hide after he tanned theirs in 1066). Nowadays the White Tower houses the **Royal Armouries,** with floor upon floor of immaculately polished, beau-

43

Tower Hill

Moat

Outer Ward

N

Ticket
Office
and
Entrance
←

Casemates

The Parade

Casemates

Moat

8

7   6

5

4

3

1
2

9

10

Moat   Outer   Ward

Tower Wharf

Moat

Tower
Pier

0   200 feet

0   100 meters

River Thames

Beauchamp
Tower, **8**
Bloody Tower, **10**
Chapel of
St. John, **2**
Hospital Block, **3**
Jewel House, **7**
Martin Tower, **5**
Queen's House, **9**
Royal Fuseliers'
Museum, **4**
Waterloo
Barracks, **6**
White Tower, **1**

tifully crafted suits of armor, medieval small arms, pikes, and cannonballs. On the first floor of the White Tower is the tranquil **Chapel of St. John,** the oldest church in London, stunning in its simplicity and grace.

For a look at yet more weaponry, check out the **Oriental Armoury** in Waterloo Barracks. On display here are weapons taken from the various armies that clashed with His and Her Majesty's troops, including arms from North Africa, the Middle East, India (dig the elephant armor), Southeast Asia, and samurai armor and swords from Japan. To the east of Waterloo Barracks is **Martin Tower,** which contains a disappointingly teeny exhibit on torture instruments. The long queues are hardly worth the effort—better to go very early or very late in the day.

The Crown Jewels, housed in the **Jewel House** north of the White Tower, are the star attraction. The Royal Sceptre boasts the largest cut diamond in the world, a 530-carat monster from the Cullinan diamond. The Imperial State Crown, made for the coronation of Queen Victoria in 1838, is studded with 3,000 precious stones, including the second-largest diamond in the world, also cut from the Cullinan stone. Shiny objects tend to attract huge crowds, so it's best to visit immediately after the Tower opens or just before it closes. Make the mistake of going at a midday, especially on weekends, and the wait could last for hours.

West of the White Tower, to the left of the main entrance, **Beauchamp Tower** has more than 400 eerie notes and doodles left by prisoners of centuries past. South of the White Tower is **Bloody Tower,** where the so-called Little Princes, Edward V and his brother, were murdered in the 15th century, probably by henchmen of either Richard III or Henry VII. This is also where Sir Walter Raleigh spent 13 long years of imprisonment, during which he wrote the modestly titled *History of the World*. A reconstruction shows what his living quarters might have looked like.

Catch a free tour of the Tower of London, led by photogenic Yeoman Warders—better known as "Beefeaters"—dressed to the gills in Tudor costume. Tours leave from just inside the main entrance, near Byword Tower, at regular intervals throughout the day; the last tours leave at 3 PM in summer, 2:30 PM in winter. The trek lasts about 30 minutes, and they don't go in bad weather. *Tel. 0171/709–0765 or 0171/488–5718 for recorded info. Tube: Tower Hill. Walk south following signs. Admission: £7.95, £5.95 students under 18. Open Oct.–Feb., Mon.–Sat. 9–5, Sun. 10–5; Mar.–Sept., Mon.–Sat. 9–6, Sun. 10–6. Last admission 1 hr before closing (2 hrs before closing to the Jewel House).*

TOWER BRIDGE A three-minute walk along the Thames from the Tower of London brings you to Tower Bridge, a Gothic fancy built between 1885 and 1894. The hard-to-miss twin pillars now house exhibitions on the bridge's history and engineering, as well as on the history of London's bridges from Roman times onward. The two gangways across the top of the towers afford excellent views of Canary Wharf and the docklands to the east, and central London and Southwark to the west. (That said, the views of London are much better from the dome of St. Paul's Cathedral.) The bridge's gangways also feature boring phone histories (20p) of the HMS *Belfast* (*see* The South Bank in London Neighborhoods, *below*), London Bridge, and the Great Fire of 1666. At the bottom of the southern tower, the original steam and hydraulic machinery of the bridge is on polished display. *Tel. 0171/407–0922. Tube: Tower Hill. Admission: £5. Open Apr.–Oct., daily 10–6:30 (last admission 5:15); Nov.–Mar., daily 10–5:15 (last admission 4).*

TRAFALGAR SQUARE

Trafalgar Square, a broad, open plaza in the middle of a huge traffic circle, is the sentimental heart of London. Practically speaking, Trafalgar Square is the main terminus for late-night buses, which makes it one of the trippiest, coolest places in London at 4 AM on a Sunday, when clubbers, tourists, and night owls of every imaginable persuasion come stumbling by. The square also has a venerable history as the setting for riots, and it continues to be a favored venue for demonstrations. It's also a fine place for people-watching, especially after an exhaustive session at the nearby National Gallery and/or National Portrait Gallery.

Once home to the royal stables, Trafalgar Square was transformed into a public square in honor of naval honcho Lord Horatio Nelson in 1829. Nelson died in battle after decimating the French fleet at Cape Trafalgar (on the southwest coast of Spain) in 1805, after a long career of sanctioned and unsanctioned warring and wooing. Thirty-five years later, architect E. H. Baily began work on the 185-foot tall **Nelson's Column,** Trafalgar Square's most obvious landmark (and a sizable overstatement, considering wee "Baron Nelson of the Nile" measured only 5 foot

Men in Big Hats

Since 1485, the Tower of London has been guarded by a troop of Yeoman Warders, the so-called Beefeaters. They're the ones in skirt-length red suits, red stockings, and fancy black hats. Depending upon which source you want to believe, the term "Beefeater" either comes from the hefty ration of meat allotted to the Yeoman Warders by Henry VII, the founder of the regiment, or from the French word buffetier, a reference to the red-suited attendants who would serve the king at dinner. The modern Beefeaters are at their best in the Ceremony of the Keys, held nightly at 10 PM. Those lucky enough to get tickets are treated to low-key pomp and circumstance and a bugler who sounds the all-clear as the chief Yeoman bolts the front gate. For tickets send a SASE at least one month before arrival to: Resident Governor, Queen's House, Tower of London, London EC3.

4 inches in life). Four gigantic bronze lions were added by sculptor Sir Edward Landseer in 1868. It's of questionable legality, but agile tourists love climbing up on the lions to have their picture taken. The surrounding fountains are a favorite wallowing hole for the tanked on New Year's Eve. Since the large clocks around the square are perpetually out of sync, loopy New Year's crowds get confused, and the bacchanals end up celebrating the coming of midnight two or three times.

The pigeon-stained statue atop Nelson's Column portrays the admiral in his later years, minus his right arm, severed at the Battle of Santa Cruz (1797), and one of his eyes, lost in the Battle of Calvi (1794).

NATIONAL GALLERY Following the acquisition of one wealthy banker's private art collection early in the 19th century, Parliament felt compelled to start amassing a little (well, a lot of, actually) accredited culture. To accommodate the growing collection, Parliament bought a plot of land on the edge of Trafalgar Square in 1828 and began to build the National Gallery, a bland classical structure best known for its tall, sandy-brown columns. If you can get past the legions of pigeons guarding the front doors, you'll find one of the world's most impressive collections of Western European art inside, including works by Tintoretto, da Vinci, Caravaggio, della Francesca, Michelangelo, Monet, Titian, Rubens, van Dyck, van Eyck, Goya, Rembrandt, Constable, Turner, Gainsborough, Seurat, et cetera, et cetera. Ready yourself for a staggering number of Virgins and Sons. Pastorals are also well represented.

At the top of the main staircase, note the *Awakening of the Muses* floor mural by Boris Anerp: It depicts Virginia Woolf as the muse of history and Greta Garbo as the muse of song. The National Gallery itself is laid out in four wings. The **Sainsbury Wing** (paid for by the Sainsbury supermarket chain) displays medieval and early Renaissance works. The **West.Wing** is devoted to the High Renaissance, the **North Wing** to the Dutch masters, the **East Wing** to English portraiture and some of the better known Impressionists. Those brave souls who do decide to go it alone should pick up a floor plan at the entrance for basic orientation. This is where you'll also find listings of the day's free lectures (weekdays at 1 PM) and free guided tours (Mon.–Sat. only). The **café** in the main building is mellow and fairly cheap; sandwiches go for £1.50–£3.50. *Trafalgar Sq., tel. 0171/839–3321 or 0171/839–3526 for recorded info. Tube: Charing Cross. It's the huge building at top (northern) edge of the square. Admission free. Open Mon.–Sat. 10–6 (Wed. until 8 in July and Aug.), Sun. 2–6. Wheelchair access through Orange St. entrance.*

NATIONAL PORTRAIT GALLERY Painted faces, sculpted faces, drawn faces, photographed faces—the National Portrait Gallery is as much about portraiture as it is about the men and women who made Britannia great. The pieces are arranged chronologically from the top floor to the bottom; take the elevator up and wind your way down through the ages. The final leg of the exhibit brings you right up to the present, and walking out onto the streets of London afterward provides a nice sense of closure. Be warned: There are nominal charges for special exhibits. *St. Martin's Pl., tel. 0171/306–0055. Tube: Charing Cross. Cross Trafalgar Sq. to northeast cnr, walk 100 yds up St. Martin's Pl. Admission free. Open Mon.–Sat. 10–6, Sun. noon–6.*

Famous faces in the National Portrait Gallery include Chaucer, Shakespeare, Milton, Lord Byron, the Brontë sisters, and Virginia Woolf—but the largest crowds gather to gawk at the royal portraits: Diana in a morose moment, and Charlie looking rather silly in his polo suit.

ST. MARTIN-IN-THE-FIELDS In the northeast corner of Trafalgar Square stands the plain white-marble church of St. Martin-in-the-Fields, associated with the Academy of St. Martin-in-the-Fields orchestra. Free music recitals take place most weekdays at 1:05 PM—it's *not* the Academy of St. Martin-in-the-Fields orchestra playing, but it's usually good, and probably the best way to take in the church's grim memorials to British war dead. Evening concerts feature big-name ensembles. Tickets (£6 and up) are available at the door or at the bookshop in The Crypt (*see below*). Performance schedules are posted in the foyer as you enter the church.

Just underneath St. Martin's, rest your weary feet in **The Crypt,** an oasis of quiet amid the frenzy of Trafalgar Square. It's one of the most atmospheric places for coffee in all of London— dark and musty, with rough-hewn stone pillars and a floor tiled with worn tombstones. The **Crypt Café** (tel. 0171/839–4342) serves delicious but expensive meals; the hearty sandwiches (£2–£4) are more affordable. The crypt's **art gallery** and **bookstore** (tel. 0171/839–8362) are both heavy on religious themes. *East side of Trafalgar Sq., tel. 0171/930–0089. Admission free. Open Mon.–Sat. 10–7:30, Sun. 11–6.*

WESTMINSTER ABBEY

More than any other London monument, Westminster Abbey reflects the close relationship of church and state in Britain. The country's monarchs have been crowned and buried here since William the Conqueror assumed the English throne on Christmas Day, AD 1066. Burial in West-minster is one of the highest honors the country can bestow, and accordingly, a walk through this vast, ornate abbey is like perusing a *Who's Who* of British history. Among the deceased sovereigns buried here are Edward the Confessor, Elizabeth I, Mary Queen of Scots, Richard II, and Henry VII. Guided 90-minute **Supertours** (£6) are given twice in the morning and twice in the afternoon on weekdays, and twice on Saturday mornings if demand warrants. Book ahead by calling 0171/222–7110, or ask at the enquiry desk.

Behind the altar you'll find two of the most interesting areas of the abbey: the **Chapel of Edward the Confessor** and **Henry VII's Chapel.** Edward's chapel is home to the Coronation Chair, which is used during the crowning of Britain's kings and queens. The chair, built in 1300 and reputedly very uncomfortable, encloses the Stone of Scone (pronounced "Skoon"), which Edward swiped from Scotland in 1297. The Stone of Destiny, as it is also known, is a symbol of Scottish independence and has been a source of some friction between the two countries. Scottish nationalists stole back the stone in 1950, but Scotland Yard (a misnomer) recovered it six months later. In recent years, hooligans have managed to etch graffiti all over the wooden chair; when or if Prince Charlie is crowned, his royal derrière will rest on incisive comments like "C loves S forever" and "smoke dope."

Henry VII's Chapel is one of Britain's most beautiful examples of the rich Late Gothic style. The tomb of Henry VII and his wife, Elizabeth, was created by Italian artist Torrigiano, best known for popping Michelangelo on the nose during an argument (a blow that got Torrigiano banished from Florence). Nearly all the deceased greats of English literature are featured in Westminster's **Poets' Corner,** in the south transept. Geoffrey Chaucer was the first to be buried here in 1400. Memorial plaques pay homage to other luminaries like Shakespeare, T. S. Eliot, Byron, and Tennyson, whose actual remains lie elsewhere. Admission to West-minster Abbey is free, but surprise, surprise, it costs £4 (£2 students) to enter any of the royal chapels or the Poets' Corner—the coolest parts of Westminster Abbey. On the upside, admission is free to all parts of the abbey every Wednesday from 6 to 7:45 PM.

Real monks once wandered through **The Cloisters** on the south side of the nave. Open to the air, they retain a tranquility that the main portion of the abbey lacks after early morning hours. At the end of a passage leading from the Cloisters is the octagonal, spacious **Chapter House,** the original meeting place of England's Parliament. The **Pyx Chamber** and the **Abbey Treasure Museum** next door (open daily 10–4) feature a small collection of goodies like golden goblets and royal costumes from different historical periods, but frankly, with all the grand museums around town, £2.10 (£1.65 students) is too high a price for this rather puny display. *West-minster Abbey, tel. 0171/222–5152. Tube: Westminster. Cross Parliament Sq. and follow Broad Sanctuary. Admission free. Open Mon.–Sat. 7:30–6 (Wed. until 7:45), Sun. briefly btw services (10 AM, 3 PM, and 5:45 PM).*

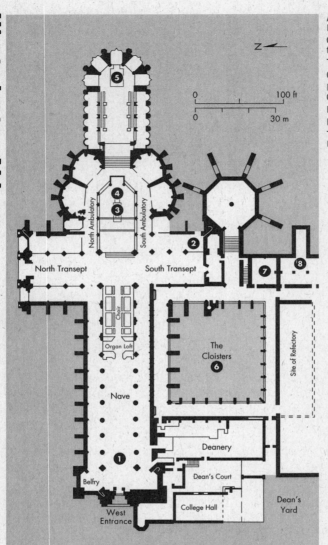

Abbey Treasure
Museum, **8**
Chapel of Edward
the Confessor, **4**
The Cloisters, **6**
Coronation Chair, **3**
Henry VII's
Chapel, **5**
Poets' Corner, **2**
Pyx Chamber, **7**
Tomb of the
Unknown Warrior, **1**

| 0 | | 100 ft |
| 0 | | 30 m |

North Ambulatory

South Ambulatory

North Transept

South Transept

Chapel

Organ Loft

The
Cloisters
6

Site of Refectory

Nave

Deanery

Dean's Court

Belfry

West
Entrance

College Hall

Dean's
Yard

London Neighborhoods

Like many of the world's great cities, London is best approached through its highly distinct, diverse neighborhoods, many of which were once towns or villages in their own right. Regardless of who you are or what you're after, London has a neighborhood to fulfill your every whim. If government buildings and famous monuments are what you want, **Whitehall** has more than enough for even the hardiest tourist. If you prefer a little boho culture, you might want to spend your time in **Camden, Nottinghill,** or **Hampstead.** For a vicarious taste of the good (or at least expensive) life, head to ritzy **Mayfair** or **Chelsea.** If you're interested in London's legal and financial institutions, make your way to **Holborn** and **the City,** respectively. There's great people-watching at **Covent Garden,** as well as in the various central squares. And for a taste of authentic, workaday London (and an earful of Cockneyspeak), check out the **East End.**

West London

KENSINGTON AND KNIGHTSBRIDGE

As a budget traveler, you're very likely to end up staying in the Kensington area, particularly in South Kensington or Earl's Court. If so, you'll rub shoulders with hordes of other American, European, and Australian shoestring travelers—Londoners themselves can be a bit thin on the ground around here. As you move toward central Kensington and Knightsbridge, however, the scene changes and prices go through the roof—only St. James's and Mayfair carry more snob value. If some fool has given you their credit cards, you might do some shopping here. For those without such pecuniary luck, there's always window-shopping; the best place to do it is on the long east–west thoroughfare of **Knightsbridge** and **Kensington High Street** (different names, same street). If shopping isn't your bag, the Knightsbridge/South Kensington area also doubles as museum central: In one large block, you'll find at least five major museums, many with a scientific bent. Just north of Knightsbridge lie two of London's best parks, Kensington Gardens and Hyde Park.

HOLLAND PARK Home to a major youth hostel (*see* Hostels in Chapter 3), Holland Park sits smack-dab in the middle of Kensington, just north of the intersection of Kensington High

Historical Houses

As you wander around London, you'll see lots of small blue plaques on the sides of buildings. These are historical markers that describe which famous person lived here in days gone by. For a complete list of the plaques throughout the city, pick up "The Blue Plaque Guide" at larger bookstores. Following are a few highlights:

- *Sir Winston Churchill (28 Hyde Park Gate, South Kensington).*

- *Charles Darwin (University College, Science Building, Bloomsbury).*

- *Charles Dickens (48 Doughty St., Bloomsbury).*

- *T. S. Eliot (3 Kensington Ct., Kensington).*

- *T. E. Lawrence (14 Barton St., Westminster).*

- *Karl Marx (28 Dean St., Soho).*

- *Sir Isaac Newton (87 Jermyn St., St. James).*

- *George Bernard Shaw (29 Fitzroy Sq., Marylebone).*

- *Percy Bysshe Shelley (15 Poland St., Mayfair).*

- *Oscar Wilde (34 Tite St., Chelsea).*

- *Virginia Woolf (51 Gordon Sq., Bloomsbury).*

Kensington and Knightsbridge

Natural History
Museum, **4**
Palace, **1**
Kensington
Harrods, **7**
Albert Memorial, **2**
Royal Albert Hall, **3**

Museum, **6**
Victoria and Albert
Science Museum, **5**

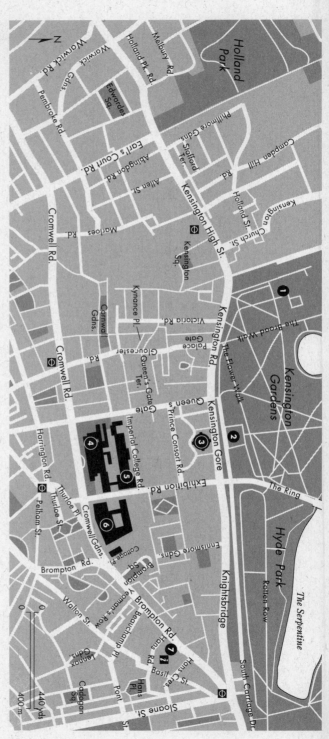

Street and Earls Court Road. Peacocks, ducks, rabbits, and chickens all run wild here, and the flower beds could make a nature-lover out of even the most unromantic oaf. If you're here in June and July, make a special trip just to smell the roses. Afterward you can find a number of good pubs near the northeast corner of the park, catering to the King's College student crowd. *Tube: Holland Park.*

KENSINGTON PALACE Although it's the official abode of Prince Charlie and Princess Di (with a heavy emphasis on the "official," nowadays), Kensington Palace is open to the public—at least, little bits of it are. Check out the **Court Dress Collection,** with clothes worn to regal soirées from 1750 until today, including Princess Diana's wedding dress. Visitors can also do the once-over of the **State Apartments** of Queen Mary II and William III. Beginning at 10 AM, free guided tours of the palace leave from the front desk every hour on the hour, the quarter hour, and the half hour. *Kensington Gardens, tel. 0171/937–9561. Tube: Queensway. Walk south to Kensington Gardens and head to far western end of park. Admission: £3.90, £2.95 students. Open Mon.–Sat. 9–5, Sun. 11–5; last admission 4:15.*

Royal aides, obviously terrified of potential headlines like "He Went Out With a Royal Flush," announced that King George II died in Kensington Palace on the throne. They didn't add that it was of the porcelain variety.

ROYAL ALBERT HALL A major-league concert venue, the Royal Albert Hall comes into its own in summer, when it hosts the Promenade Concerts (*see* Festivals in Chapter 1). The hall is named after Albert, Queen Victoria's hubby. The interior, a huge amphitheater done up in wine-red and gold, marks the height of Victorian imperial architecture. The hall is closed to the nonpaying public, but it's worth a quick look at the exterior, if only because it's mentioned in the Beatles song "A Day in the Life." Across from the hall is the grandiose **Albert Memorial,** commissioned by Queen Victoria in yet another expression of her obsessive reverence for her dead husband. Here Albert sits, 14 feet high, under an ornate canopy, holding a catalogue of the Great International Exhibition of 1851, which had been his brainchild. The base is decorated with 169 life-size figures of poets, composers, architects, and sculptors. *Kensington Gore, tel. 0171/589–8212. Tube: Knightsbridge. Walk west down Kensington Rd.*

SCIENCE MUSEUM Six floors detail the history of science and technology, with an emphasis on the industrial applications of past discoveries. Unless you're a major techno-buff, the thoroughness of the exhibitions may seem a bit dry. But some groovy highlights make it worthwhile, including The Launch Pad, a kiddie playpen with vaguely scientific games that big kids can also play with; the holograms in the optics section on the third floor; and the weird exhibits on the medical-history floor, including reconstructions of an open-heart surgery and a 1930s dentist's office (ouch). *Exhibition Rd., tel. 0171/938–8111. Tube: South Kensington. Walk north on Exhibition Rd. Admission: £4.50, £2.40 students; free daily after 4:30. Open Mon.–Sat. 10–6, Sun. 11–6.*

NATURAL HISTORY MUSEUM A really thorough collection of plants and animals, past and present, are housed in the visually impressive Earth and Life galleries of the Natural History Museum. Here we have fossils and reconstructed fossils; stuffed animals (in the literal sense) from every corner of the earth; explanations about the evolution of particular species; interactive exhibits such as a simulated earthquake—the whole shebang. Save some money and come during the free hours. *Cromwell Rd., tel. 0171/938–9123. Tube: South Kensington or Gloucester Rd. From South Kensington: walk north 2 blocks up Exhibition Rd., turn left on Cromwell Rd. From Gloucester Rd.: turn left as you exit station, walk ½-block north on Gloucester Rd., turn right on Cromwell Rd. Admission: £4.50, £2.20 students; free weekdays after 4:30, weekends after 5. Open Mon.–Sat. 10–5:50, Sun. 11–5:50.*

VICTORIA AND ALBERT MUSEUM Known as the V&A, this museum has a vast and eclectic collection of fine and applied art. The **Art and Design galleries** exhibit everything from Indian art to Renaissance Italian sculpture and Muslim carpets. The **Materials and Techniques galleries** illustrate different media of applied art such as jewelry, ornaments, and ceramics. Check out the two large rooms filled with cast-iron and plaster-of-Paris copies of Italian art; the

V&A was originally an art school, and Victorian youths learned to draw using these interesting reproductions as models. Also worth a stop is the **Fakes and Forgeries gallery** (Room 46), which has a great collection of honest-to-goodness bogus art. Some of the fakes are really good, and a few of the artists probably made some decent cash off their endeavors. Two varieties of free guided tours are offered daily: introductory tours leave from the info desk Tuesday–Saturday at 11, noon, 2, and 3; on Monday they leave at 12:15, 2, and 3. "Special tours"—covering a particular theme, country, or exhibit—leave Tuesday–Sunday at 11:30 and 1:30, Monday at 1:30 and 2:30. *Cromwell Rd., tel. 0171/938–8500 or 0171/938–8441 for recorded info. Tube: South Kensington. Walk 2 blocks north on Exhibition Rd., turn right on Cromwell Gardens. Donations requested. Open Tues.–Sun. 10–5:50, Mon. noon–5:50. Wheelchair entrance on Exhibition Rd.*

HARRODS This granddaddy of all London department stores is a magnet for every tourist on the planet. Don't come here to shop—it's incredibly expensive—but rather to browse. If you're here around Christmas, definitely check out the decorations and displays—they really do it up. Many of the upper floors are just like American department stores, so you're much better off moseying down to the lavish **food halls.** Mouthwatering meats and cheeses hang from the ceiling, smoked salmon is sliced oh-so-thin, and skilled butchers and fishmongers in white aprons make it all look even better. Vegetarians beware: There's plenty of carnage hanging from hooks and flukes. *87 Brompton Rd., tel. 0171/730–1234. Tube: Knightsbridge. Walk ½ block south down Brompton Rd. Open Mon., Tues., Sat. 10–6, Wed., Thurs., and Fri. 10–7.*

HYDE PARK AND KENSINGTON GARDENS

Hyde Park and Kensington Gardens are contiguous and really form one large 634-acre park—the biggest in London. Cool your heels leaning against a tree in the shade or lounging on the grass in the sun. Small boats cruise on the **Serpentine,** a long, thin lake that arcs through the middle of the two parks. You can rent a rowboat at the boathouse for a few quid. You're also duty-bound not to miss **Speakers' Corner** on the northeast edge of Hyde Park (Tube: Marble Arch). This is where anyone can get on their soapbox and rant and rave to their heart's delight. Spielers spiel, hecklers heckle, and free speech dovetails into street theater. It really hits full swing by about 2 or 3 PM on weekends. You could have as many as a dozen speakers declaiming to individual crowds of more than 100 people (mostly smiling tourists). Bible-thumpers form the largest contingent, with Afro-Caribbeans heaping shit on "dis racist society!" coming in a close second.

SERPENTINE GALLERY Across the Serpentine at the other end of the park, search out this tea pavilion turned art gallery that balances bright natural light with rotating exhibits of modern multimedia works. It's always worth consulting *Time Out* to see what's new here. Almost every Sunday at 3 PM the Serpentine has free "gallery talks," which give a taste of the current exhibit. *Kensington Gardens, tel. 0171/402–6075. Tube: Lancaster Gate or South Kensington. Admission free. Open daily 10–6.*

MAYFAIR

Mayfair is an ultra-ritzy residential neighborhood lined with beautiful 18th-century apartment blocks faced with deep-red brick. Many of London's wealthiest residents live in the area, but unless you have a ton of money, you're likely to get a bit bored here: Mayfair is one of those places where you become acutely aware of how poor you are (the sheer number of Rolls-Royces, Bentleys, and Jaguars is staggering). Even the delivery vans in Mayfair all seem to bear some royal coat of arms, proclaiming them to be purveyors of fine goodies for as long as anyone can remember.

BERKELEY SQUARE Shaded by tall plane trees and populated by cheeky squirrels, Berkeley Square (pronounced "Barkley") is a tranquil refuge in a sea of wealth. Robert Walpole (1676–1745), a former prime minister, and Clive of India (1725–1774) both lived here. On one side of the fenced-in park is a Rolls-Royce dealership that stays open late during the annual Berkeley Square Ball, in hopes that wealthy drunks might splurge for something to carry

Hyde Park and Kensington Gardens

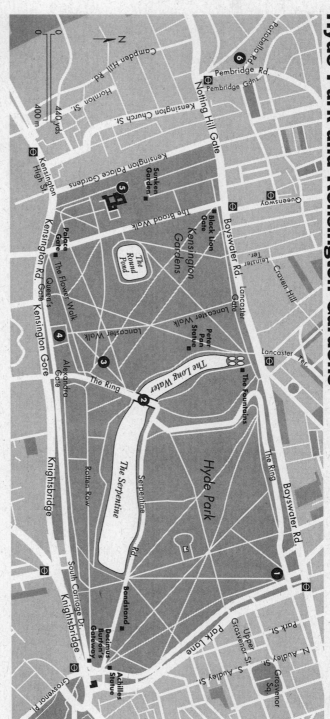

53

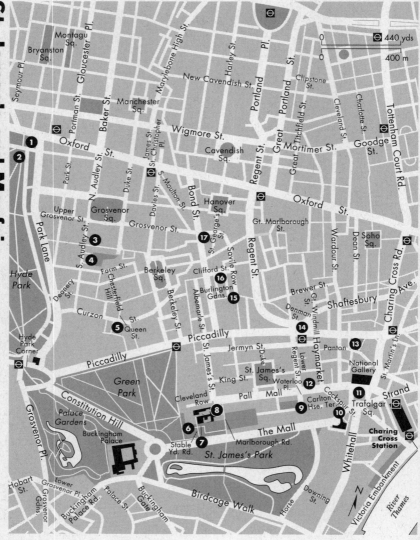

their Grey Poupon in. Just west of Berkeley Square, the **Mount Street Gardens** (also called St. George's Gardens) are a fine place for a picnic. Take a left out of the gardens, walk west along Mount Street, and you're headed straight for **Purdy's** (Mount St., at South Audley St., tel. 0171/499–1801), probably the most famous gun maker in Britain. The waiting list for Purdy guns is years long, and you could probably get a small tank for what you pay for one of their handcrafted shotguns. You're welcome to browse for free weekdays 9–5.

SHEPHERD'S MARKET The May Fair, the market that gave its name to the neighborhood, moved here in 1686 from the Haymarket and was famed for its ribald entertainment; later, the area became a popular haunt of prostitutes. Today, Shepherd's Market is a charming nest of pedestrian-only alleys loaded to the gills with cafés, wine bars, pubs, and expensive restaurants. It's tony, quiet, and an exceedingly pleasant place to while away an hour over a cappuccino. At one end, the market opens onto **Curzon Street,** where the British secret service (of 007 fame) has its unmarked headquarters. Look for a building with security cameras. Hint: The office is close to the swanky Mirabelle restaurant. *Tube: Green Park. Walk down Piccadilly toward Hyde Park Corner, turn right on Half Moon St., left on Curzon St.*

GROSVENOR SQUARE The largest square in London, Grosvenor Square has been ruined by the huge **American embassy,** the butt-ugliest government building in town. Not helping matters is the rather plain statue of Franklin D. Roosevelt, erected in 1948, that stands in the center of the square. Nearby, look for the plaque commemorating John Adams, first American ambassador to Britain and second President of the United States; he lived at the corner of Brook and Duke streets.

MARBLE ARCH This monument, modeled by Nash after the Arch of Constantine in Rome, originally stood in front of Buckingham Palace. It was intended to allow the monarch to make regal exits out of the palace up Constitution Hill. The only problem was that the arch was too narrow for the royal coach. In 1851, the arch was moved to its present location at the top of Park Lane, at the intersection with Oxford Street. The statue of George IV that was supposed to grace the top of the arch is now in Trafalgar Square. Go figure. *Tube: Marble Arch.*

OXFORD STREET Oxford Street, which runs from Marble Arch to Tottenham Court Road, is busy, noisy, and often quite tacky—lots of steak houses, souvenir shops, and cheapo clothing stores. The exceptions are the department stores near Marble Arch, including Marks & Spencer and Selfridges; you can get a decent, albeit expensive, snack at the food bar adjoining Selfridges' food halls. Another worthwhile detour is **South Molton Street,** a pedestrian arcade at the corner of Oxford and Davies streets. If you ferret around in the little alleys and passageways, you'll find some nice sandwich shops and a pub or two.

BOND STREET Perpendicular to Oxford Street, Bond Street may be the most expensive shopping street in London. It's divided into New Bond and Old Bond, but prices are very, very modern wherever you go. Jewelers, antiques stores, and art galleries predominate, and many of them won't give you a second look unless you're dressed to buy. If you want to play well-to-do for a day, attend an auction at **Sotheby's** (34–35 New Bond St., tel. 0171/493–8080) and see who you can fool. The schedule of auctions isn't set, but they usually have morning lots at least three days a week at 10, and sometimes an afternoon run at 2:30. Running parallel to Bond Street is **Cork Street,** the center of London's art trade (*see* Museums and Galleries, *below*), with a number of galleries open to the public. Two blocks farther east is **Savile Row,** famous for its many accomplished tailors. *Tube: Bond St., Green Park, or Piccadilly Circus.*

PICCADILLY CIRCUS Although Piccadilly Circus is a fine venue for people-watching, the crowd is all on its way somewhere, unlike in Trafalgar or Leicester squares, where people tend to mill around more. True, you can usually find some folks sitting on the steps of the famous **Eros** statue (actually a statue of Christian Charity), or on the wall of the fountain beneath the bronze **Horse of Helios** sculpture. Oddly enough, the seats on the second floor of the Burger King offer the best bird's-eye view of Piccadilly.

SOHO

Long one of the leading bohemian neighborhoods of London, Soho in the 1950s was a beatnik stomping ground and the heart of the London jazz scene. In the 1960s rock took over, and the area became home to a new counterculture, its clubs featuring headliners like the Rolling Stones, The Who, and The Kinks in their respective heydays. With the coming of punk and seminal bands like the Sex Pistols, Generation X, The Clash, and X-Ray Specs, King's Road replaced Soho as the home of London's pop culture, leading to a resurgence in the Soho jazz scene that continues to this day. Sadly, Soho has suffered from the yuppification and commercialization that is, ironically, so common in former bastions of urban hipness. The neighborhood is mostly an amalgam of clothing and shoe stores, hair salons, trendy cafés, theaters, nightclubs, and sex shops. Fridays after work, Soho pubs are packed with tourists, theatergoers, and young professionals from nearby offices—all hell-bent on having fun in one of London's main leisure zones.

Legend has it that Soho got its name from the hunting cry, "So-Ho!," when the area was part of the Palace of Westminster's hunting estate.

Soho has an international flavor that many of central London's neighborhoods lack; generally, you have to go to the city outskirts to find such a polyglot community. Greeks fleeing Turkish rule were probably the first foreigners to settle the area en masse, though Soho today displays more Chinese and Italian influences. The Chinese community is crowded around **Gerrard Street;** if you're looking for traditional Italian restaurants and cafés, head for **Old Compton Street,** which is also a major center for gay life in the city. If you catch the tube to Leicester Square, Piccadilly Circus, Tottenham Court Road, or Oxford Circus, you'll find yourself right on the edge of Soho.

LEICESTER SQUARE Leicester Square is often compared to New York's Times Square, but it isn't as big, as bright, or as sleazy. A small drug scene and some shady characters are par for the course in any major entertainment district, and Leicester (pronounced "Lester") has its fair share. Huge movie houses, many converted from grand old theaters, surround the square, showing the latest releases. Tacky tourist attractions line some of the side streets, and weird street theater is often staged on the pedestrian mall at the western edge of the square (although you may get tired of that punker playing the same six notes over and over on his sax). On the west side is the **Society of West End Theatres** ticket kiosk, where you can buy half-price, same-day tickets for many London shows (*see* Theater in Chapter 6).

Many of London's 50,000 Chinese residents live in Soho. Most came to Britain from Hong Kong in the '50s and '60s, and a new influx is likely as Britain prepares to hand Hong Kong over to China in 1997.

CHINATOWN Before you get excited, understand that London's Chinatown is very small. In fact, it's really only two streets, Gerrard and Lisle, in the area between Leicester Square and Shaftesbury Avenue. Known as **Tong Yan Kai** (Chinese Street) by residents, Chinatown has some purely tourist trappings—the telephone booths topped by pagodas, for example. Even so, it's fascinating to poke around in the tiny stores that sell Chinese herbs and unidentifiable produce, and to sit down for a meal of dim sum in one of the many restaurants. The closest tube to Tong Yan Kai is Leicester Square; head north on Charing Cross Road.

SHAFTESBURY AVENUE Cutting through the center of Soho, Shaftesbury Avenue is one of London's three principal theater streets (along with the Haymarket and Coventry Street). Built side by side in the early 1900s, many of the theaters survived the war and retain the grand look espoused by Edwardian theater. Noël Coward, John Gielgud, and Sir Laurence Olivier all made it big in Shaftesbury Avenue theaters like the Apollo, the Lyric, the Globe, and the Queen's. Today, you're likely to find these same theaters hosting the works of such playwrights as Tom Stoppard and Peter Shaffer. The closest tubes to the theaters of Shaftesbury Avenue are Piccadilly Circus and Leicester Square.

CARNABY STREET During the '60s, this pedestrian mall was a groovy place to hang out, buy flowery fashions, and pick up the latest tunes. All that's gone now, and the place survives solely on the basis of its past fame. Come in the late afternoon to miss the worst of the crowds, but don't spend much time on Carnaby Street itself—it's nothing more than trendy stores and tourist schlock. You're better off exploring the small alleys and streets to the east, which have

Soho and Covent Garden

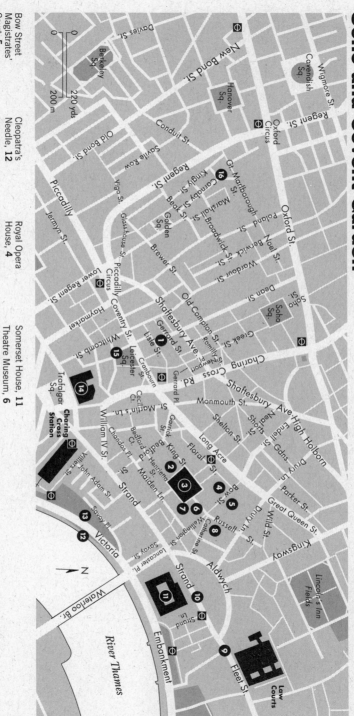

some hip clothing stores (particularly if you're in the market for leather) and tiny crafts shops; try Marshall and Broadwick streets. Carnaby Street runs parallel to Regent Street, south of the Oxford Circus tube; from the tube station, head south on Regent Street, take a left on Great Marlborough Street, and look for it on the right.

SOHO SQUARE Built in the 1670s to honor Charles II, Soho Square is one of the oldest public squares in London. Nowadays this pleasant village green is a welcome open space in the middle of hectic Soho. It's shared in perfect harmony by businessmen on their lunch breaks, babes in strollers, tourists, elderly folks, and homeless people—all under the watchful gaze of a dilapidated 19th-century statue of King Charles himself. To get here, take the tube to Tottenham Court Road and walk west along Oxford Street; it'll be on the left.

Central London

ST. JAMES'S

When Whitehall Palace burned down in 1698, all of London turned its attention to St. James's Palace, the new royal residence. In the 18th and 19th centuries, the area around the palace became *the* place to live, and many of the estates surrounding the palace disappeared in a building frenzy, as mansions were built, streets laid out, and expensive shops established. Today, St. James's—along with Mayfair and Sloane Square—remains London's most elegant and fashionable address. For a detail of the area, *see* the map for St. James's and Mayfair, *above*.

PALL MALL Pall Mall, pronounced "Pal Mal," is a corner of quiet and refined elegance that has managed to survive from more regal days. Both the street and the mall get their names from *paille maille*, a French version of croquet that was popular with Charles I and II. A number of gentlemen's clubs, those quintessentially snobby English institutions, line Pall Mall, including the Athenaeum, Whitehall, United Oxford and Cambridge University Club, Travellers' Club, and the Reform Club. Many clubs went under after World War II, though several made comebacks in the conservative, free-market '80s. Some, especially the Reform Club, are quite beautiful, but unless you've got a friend who's a member, you won't get past the front door. Women are allowed as guests into some clubs' dining rooms, but this kind of behavior is not encouraged, and the misogynistic climate is unmistakable. *Pall Mall runs almost parallel to the Mall from Trafalgar Sq., dead-ending at St. James's Palace. Tube: Charing Cross, Piccadilly Circus, or Green Park.*

ST. JAMES'S PALACE This elegant brick palace lies at the end of Pall Mall. It would be fitting if Princess Diana and Fergie, having fallen out of royal favor, decided to set up house in the palace, since it stands on the former site of a women's leper hospital (although Di would have to worry about bumping into her ex; the Prince of Wales currently uses a few rooms for his staff headquarters). The ever-sensitive Henry VIII bought the hospital in 1532 and erected a hunting lodge in its stead. Only the **Chapel Royal** and four-story **Gatehouse** remain of Henry's original manor—most of the palace was rebuilt after a fire in 1809. For much of its existence, the palace has played second fiddle to Whitehall Palace and Buckingham, though all foreign ambassadors to Britain are still officially accredited to "The Court of St. James's." Unfortunately, the palace is not open to the public. *Pall Mall at St. James's St. Tube: Green Park. Walk east on Piccadilly and go right at St. James's St.*

THE MALL The red-Tarmac Mall cuts a wide swath all the way from Trafalgar Square to Buckingham Palace. It was laid out in 1904, largely because it was felt that the British monarchy should have a processional route in keeping with its imperial status. After all, the French had the fine Champs-Elysées, and they didn't even have a sovereign any more. This 115-foot-wide Mall is no Champs-Elysées, though. Without a royal procession clomping down it, the Mall seems soulless. **Admiralty Arch,** a triumphal arch bordering Trafalgar Square, marks the start of the Mall. Built in 1911, the arch is opened only for royal processions. From here, the Mall sweeps past St. James's Park and **Carlton House Terrace,** a stately 1,000-foot-long facade of white stucco arches that is home of the ICA (*see* Museums and Galleries, *below*), a first-rate contemporary gallery. Farther down on the right is **Clarence House,** home of the Queen Mother. She alone seems to bob along high above the sex scandals, divorces, and assorted rubbish that have plagued the royal family recently. The Mall ends in front of Buckingham Palace at the **Queen Victoria Memorial,** an irritatingly didactic monument to the glory of Victorian ideals. The broad avenue of the Mall replaced a much smaller, gravel boulevard that now lies a little to the north. Together with St. James's Park, the Mall was *the* place to see and be seen in 17th- and 18th-century London. Nowadays the best time to explore the Mall is Sunday, when it's closed to traffic.

ST. JAMES'S PARK Sitting amid London's grandest monuments, the 93-acre park is remarkably peaceful—it enjoys an almost library-like quiet. This is a stroller's park, a place to wander among the flowers, feed the ducks, and sit and read. The focal point is an ornamental canal, added by Charles II and redesigned by George IV, filled with geese and lined with weeping willows. For the better part of the 17th and 18th centuries, the park was the playground for England's elite, who would gather here to stare down their noses at one another before heading off to be idle elsewhere. It's now a terrific place to bring a picnic lunch, be idle, and look down your nose at all the passing tourists. Try to visit at night, too, when illuminated fountains play, and Westminster Abbey and the Houses of Parliament are lit up—honestly breathtaking. *Tube: St. James's Park, Charing Cross, or Westminster.*

GREEN PARK Across the Mall from St. James's Park, Green Park is a grassy expanse crisscrossed by walking paths. You can never totally escape the traffic noise from Piccadilly here, but it's still a popular spot to doze in the sun or read the paper. Green Park tube station lets you off at the eastern edge of the park, at the top of Queen's Walk. This asphalt path leads south toward St. James's Park and the Mall, passing several large mansions behind protective fences. One of these mansions, **Lancaster House,** is used for government functions and negotiations. The talks that led to black-majority rule in Zimbabwe, formerly Rhodesia, were held here. *Tube: Green Park.*

WHITEHALL

Whitehall is both a street and a vast, faceless bureaucracy. Whitehall the street runs from Trafalgar Square to Parliament Square through the heart of official London—which means it's a major tourist stomping ground. Whitehall the bureaucracy can't be so easily defined. Essentially, the term applies to the central British government, whose ministries fill many of the buildings off Whitehall and around Carlton Terrace.

HORSE GUARDS AND PARADE GROUND As you walk down Whitehall toward Parliament Square, you pass the Horse Guards on the right. This low building, constructed between 1745 and 1755, is the backdrop for a smaller version of the **Changing of the Guard** performed at Buckingham Palace. Each day at 10:30 AM (9:30 on Sunday), a mounted contingent of the Household Cavalry clops its way down the Mall from Hyde Park Barracks to Whitehall. It takes about a half-hour before they arrive in front of Horse Guards and relieve the soldiers standing in sentry boxes facing the Banqueting House. If you don't feel like battling the crowds at Buckingham Palace, this is the next-best ceremonial relic. If it's raining significantly, the whole thing's canceled. For no apparent reason, two more sentries guard **Horse Guards Arch,** which leads to the **Parade Ground.** Once the site of Henry's VIII's jousting arena, this massive square looks a little bleak when nothing's going on. In late May or early June, however, the parade ground comes alive with some of London's biggest ceremonies—**Trooping the Colour** and **Beating Retreat** (*see* Festivals in Chapter 1). To the west of the parade ground lies St. James's Park, and the **Admiralty** building (look for all the incongruous high-tech antenna equipment on top) looms to the north.

BANQUETING HOUSE The Banqueting House is the only surviving building from the original Westminster Palace. Designed by Inigo Jones and built between 1619 and 1622, it's one of the earliest examples of Renaissance architecture in England. It started life as the venue for the court entertainments of Charles I, and in 1649 was the backdrop for his beheading. Now it's popular for state banquets. Today the chief attractions are Rubens' ceiling frescoes, which portray James I and Charles I in a favorable, even divine, light. Unless you get a wicked cramp

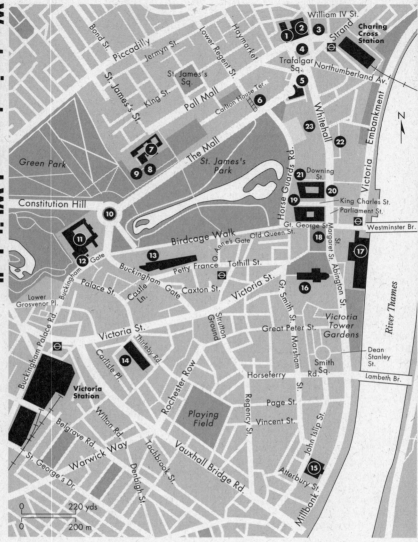

William IV St.

Charing
Cross
Station

Strand

Bond St.

Piccadilly

Jermyn St.

Lower Regent St.

Haymarket

St. James's
Sq.

Trafalgar
Sq.

Northumberland Av.

King St.

Pall Mall

Carlton House Ter.

Whitehall

Embankment

St. James's St.

St. James's St.

Green Park

St. James's
Park

The Mall

Constitution Hill

Victoria

King Charles St.

Parliament St.

Westminster Br.

Birdcage Walk

Q. Anne's Gate

Old Queen St.

Gt. George St.

Downing
St.

Horse Guards Rd.

Margaret St.

Abingdon St.

Buckingham Palace Rd.

Gate

Buckingham Gate

Petty France

Tothill St.

Caxton St.

Victoria St.

Gt. Smith St.

River Thames

Lower
Grosvenor Pl.

Palace St.

Castle
Ln.

Dean
Stanley
St.

Lambeth Br.

Victoria St.

Thirleby Rd.

Carlisle Pl.

Rochester Row

Strutton
Ground

Victoria
Tower
Gardens

Great Peter St.

Smith
Sq.

Horseferry
Rd.

Marsham
St.

Victoria Station

Wilton Rd.

Belgrave Rd.

Warwick Way

Tachbrook St.

Denbigh St.

Vauxhall Bridge Rd.

Playing
Field

Regency St.

Page St.

Vincent St.

John Islip St.

Atterbury St.

Millbank

St. George's Dr.

0   220 yds

0   200 m

N

Admiralty Arch, **5**

Banqueting
House, **22**

Buckingham
Palace, **11**

Cabinet War
Rooms, **19**

Cenotaph, **20**

Clarence House, **8**

Downing Street, **21**

Horse Guards and
Parade Ground, **23**

Houses of
Parliament, **17**

Institute of
Contemporary Arts
(ICA), **6**

Lancaster
House, **9**

National Gallery, **1**

National Portrait
Gallery, **2**

Nelson's Column, **4**

Parliament
Square, **18**

Queen Victoria
Memorial, **10**

Queen's Gallery and
Royal Mews, **12**

St. James's
Palace, **7**

St. Martin-in-the-
Fields, **3**

Tate Gallery, **15**

Wellington Barracks
(Guard's
Museum), **13**

Westminster
Abbey, **16**

Westminster
Cathedral, **14**

in your neck from looking at the ceiling, you can see the Banqueting House in just a few minutes. *Whitehall, across from Horse Guards Arch, tel. 0171/930–4179. Admission: £2.75, £2.10 students. Open Mon.–Sat. 10–5, last admission 4:30.*

DOWNING STREET If it weren't for the massive security measures and the ogling tourists, you would never suspect the importance of the rather ordinary homes on this street. The mammoth iron gate is the first hint, but the guys checking under every car for bombs are a dead giveaway. The prime minister lives at **10 Downing Street,** guarded by a black door and more than one policeman. The most recent occupant has been John Major, whose bland suburban demeanor looks right at home in this mundane setting—it's easy to picture him running next door to borrow a cup of sugar from the Chancellor of the Exchequer (Britain's finance honcho), who currently lives at **No. 11.** In 1992, the Irish Republican Army nearly decimated Mr. Major and friends with a well-aimed mortar that was fired from a nearby parked van. Instead of hitting Mr. Major, though, the bomb fell into the back garden of 10 Downing Street. The British have yet to catch those responsible for the blast; rumor has it that they're spending a few years laying low in Spain.

CENOTAPH Built in 1919, the Cenotaph is a simple white-stone memorial to those slain in World War I. This Whitehall monument is the focus of the annual Remembrance Day (equivalent to the American Veterans' Day) ceremonies. At 11 AM on the 11th day of the 11th month— the time of the World War I armistice—the nation observes two minutes of silence, and the queen lays a wreath of poppies on the Cenotaph. The blood red poppy, which proliferated on the battlefields of Flanders, has become a symbol for the nation's war dead. In another ceremony, the Royal British Legion drops a million poppies from the dome of the Albert Hall during a special Festival of Remembrance.

CABINET WAR ROOMS Winston Churchill, the Cabinet, and the Chiefs of Staff coordinated Britain's war effort from this fortified basement in a civil-service building—most definitely worth a few hour's exploration. A free audiotape tour guides you through rooms, which have been reconstructed to look as they did at the close of World War II, including a map covered with pushpins representing advancing Allied armies in the final weeks of the war. Old American vets and young German tourists roaming the war rooms together make for a curious spectacle beyond the exhibits. *Clive Steps, at end of King Charles St., tel. 0171/930–6961. Heading south down Whitehall, it's off to the right just past Cenotaph. Admission: £3.90, £2.80 students. Open daily 10–6, last admission 5:30.*

COVENT GARDEN

Just east of Soho lies Covent Garden, a nest of narrow streets, arcades, and pedestrian malls. For penniless budget travelers, this is one of the best places in London to come for free entertainment: Musicians, buskers, jugglers, and comics all perform in the streets and squares. The one bummer is that Covent Garden's pubs and restaurants are too expensive for vagabond travelers. Historically speaking, the original Covent Garden was just that—a plot of land used to grow fruit and veggies for the 13th-century Abbey of St. Peter at Westminster. In the 18th century, Covent Garden evolved into London's principal produce market, a bustling maze of stalls and shops selling everything from tulips to taters. This is where Eliza "My Fair Lady" Doolittle, the upwardly mobile flower girl of George Bernard Shaw's *Pygmalion,* was discovered by Professor 'iggins. Unfortunately, increasing traffic congestion forced the market to relocate south of the Thames in 1974. The original **Central Market Building** has been completely renovated, and is now filled with boutiques, health-food shops, and trendy restaurants. For a detail of the area, *see* the map of Soho and Covent Garden, *above.*

Facing away from the market, **St. Paul's** (entrance on Bedford St., tel. 0171/836–5221) is often called the "actor's church" because of the memorials to well-known thespians that line the walls. The rest of the church, built by Inigo Jones in 1631 and rebuilt in 1795 after a fire, is rather stark. The rear portico, though, serves as a great stage for the daily program of free entertainment—everything from theater to fire-eaters. On the southeast corner of the square are the **London Transport Museum** and **Theatre Museum** (*see* Museums and Galleries, *below*). The **Neal Street** pedestrian mall, just north of the market across Long Acre, has a young, laid-back, bohemian crowd and plenty of happy shoppers—good vibes overall. Have a pint in front of one of the many pubs and take a gander at the folks who walk by.

East of the market is Bow Street, famous for the **Royal Opera House,** home to the Royal Ballet and the Royal Opera Company (*see* Opera and Ballet in Chapter 6). Opposite the Opera House stands the **Bow Street Magistrates' Court** (tel. 0171/379–4713), established in 1749 by Henry Fielding, who was a magistrate, journalist, and author (he wrote *Tom Jones*). Fielding employed a group of detectives known as the "Bow Street Runners," and paid them with fines levied by the court. Eighty years later, Home Secretary Sir Robert Peel used the Bow Street Runners as the basis for his newly formed battalion of London police, called "bobbies" after his name.

North London

MARYLEBONE AND REGENT'S PARK

It may not come as a shock that Marylebone (pronounced MARRA-le-bun), one of the main tourist zones outside the West End, is boring and crowded. Its few redeeming features include the pleasant cafés along **Marylebone High Street** and the cheap take-out stands north of Marylebone Road. Get off at the Baker Street tube station to reach some of the area's schlockiest tourist traps. For reasons unknown, people have been flocking to **Madame Tussaud's Wax Museum** (Marylebone Rd., tel. 0171/935–6861) for eons. Save the staggering £7.95 admission and go to the movies instead. If our warning means nothing, Madame Tussaud's is open weekdays 10–5:30, weekends 9:30–5:30. The **London Planetarium** in the same building as Tussaud's is less hokey, but did you really come to London to look at a simulation of the night sky? In case you did, shows start every 40 minutes, and tickets are £4.20 (£9.95 for combined ticket with wax museum).

REGENT'S PARK Developed in the early 19th century by the Prince Regent as an elite residential development for his aristocratic buddies, Regent's Park is today one of central London's biggest parks. It has a small lake and an even tinier pond, both of which can be traversed by rented rowboats, paddleboats, and canoes. The **Inner Circle,** a perfectly round lane, encloses the beautiful **Queen Mary Gardens.** The presence of the **London Central Mosque,** on the western edge of Regent's Park, ensures that on weekends large numbers of Muslims from the ex-dominions are out promenading in their finest getups. *Tube: Baker St., Regent's Park, or Great Portland St.*

LONDON ZOO The northern end of Regent's Park is the site of the **London Zoo,** reputedly the oldest zoo in the world. The most direct way to get here is Bus 274, heading west from the Camden Town tube station (get off the bus at Ormonde Terrace). Inside is a vast array of captive animals, bugs, and fish. The reptile house is impressive, as is the aquarium—definitely worth the price of admission. *Regent's Park, tel. 0171/722–3333. Tube: Baker St. or Camden Town. Admission: £6.50, £5.50 students. Open daily 10–5:30.*

CAMDEN TOWN

Although it's becoming increasingly gentrified, Camden Town is still one of the most bohemian and diverse neighborhoods in London. It becomes a serious mob scene on weekends when tens of thousands of people flock to shop the Camden markets, particularly **Camden Lock** (*see* Street Markets in Chapter 7). If crowds give you claustrophobia, visit during the week when you can snooze on the banks of Regent's Canal or enjoy the village's many cool cafés and restaurants in relative peace. The spectacle of the crowd is absent, as are many of the sellers; still, it's a great place to spend a sunny day in London.

To reach Camden Town, take the Northern Line tube and get off at Camden Town. **Camden High Street,** which runs north–south, is the heart of the district. Take a right from the tube station to reach Camden Lock. Stop by the **Regent's Canal Information Centre** (Camden Lock, tel. 0171/482–0523) for the scoop on walking and/or boat tours of the canal. One of the most pop-

Camden Lock, **6**
Church Row, **14**
Fenton House, **15**
Freud House, **13**
Highgate
Cemetery, **3**
Keats House, **4**
Kenwood House, **2**
London Canal
Museum, **5**
London Central
Mosque, **12**
London
Planetarium, **11**
London Zoo, **7**
Madame Tussaud's
Wax Museum, **10**
Open-Air Theatre, **8**
Queen Mary's
Gardens, **9**
Spaniards Inn, **1**

HIGHGATE

N

Hampstead Ln.

Highgate High St.

Waterlow Park

Spaniards Rd.

Hampstead Heath

Bathing Ponds

East Heath Rd.

Heath St.

HAMPSTEAD

Flask Wk.

Keats Gr.

Hampstead High St.

Rosslyn Hill

Pond St.

Fleet Rd.

Parliament Hill

Mansfield Rd.

Highgate Rd.

Chetwynd Rd.

KENTISH TOWN

Haverstock Hill

Maresfield Gdns.

Fitzjohn's Ave.

...hley Rd.

Prince of Wales Rd.

Adelaide Rd.

Finchley Rd.

Primrose Hill

Avenue Rd.

Albert Rd.

Grand Union Canal

CAMDEN TOWN

Prince

Outer Circle

Regent's Park

Broad Walk

Outer Circle

Albany St.

Wellington Rd.

Lord's Cricket Ground

St. John's Wood Rd.

Inner Circle

Chester Rd.

Park Rd.

Lisson Grove

Ivor Pl.

Gloucester Pl.

Baker St.

Outer Circle

Park ...

Portland Pl.

Harley St.

Edgware Rd.

LITTLE VENICE

Marylebone Rd.

0   440 yds
0   400 m

63

ular aquatic journeys travels west from here past Regent's Park and on to Little Venice, near Paddington Station.

PRIMROSE HILL A brief walk south on Regent's Park Road from Chalk Farm tube station will bring you to this spiffy park. A tall hill commands a fine view of central London—check out the plaque identifying the buildings on the skyline. A young, cool crowd, many from nearby Camden Town, hangs out here. If you like dogs, you'll find tons to play with. Every November 5th, the park is the focus of huge Guy Fawkes Night celebrations (*see* Festivals in Chapter 1), complete with fireworks and a huge bonfire. **Primrose Pâtisserie** (136 Regent's Park Rd., tel. 0171/722–7848) makes a fine pit stop for refueling with cakes and coffee. On weekends this West Camden neighborhood also offers a welcome respite from the chaos of Camden High Street.

ISLINGTON

The Royal Borough of Islington is an increasingly stylish area occupying about 6 square miles east of Camden and north of the City. In the old days, before the great amalgamation of London, the village of Islington was a popular stopover for travelers on their way into the budding metropolis. Lots of inns, watering holes, and nightspots cropped up to serve the transient visitors. During Tudor times, the lush, low hills in the wilderness around the village were prime royal romping and hunting grounds, supposedly the favorite of Henry VIII. As London grew and modernity arrived with a bang, Islington was not what you'd call a preferred address. Ugly industrialization consumed a great deal of the countryside, especially along Regent's Canal, which runs through the borough. If you're into that sort of thing, the **Canal Museum** (*see* Museums and Galleries, *below*), not far from the center of Islington, has excellent displays showing the way "canal people" have lived their lives on and along Regent's Canal.

Many immigrant groups—Italian, Lebanese, Bengali, Turkish—have settled in Islington over the past 100 years, giving it the cultural richness in which Islingtonians still take pride. The area has also been a haunt for artists, students, writers, and various other intelligentsia over the years; the list includes some of the bad boys of social commentary—George Orwell, Salman Rushdie, Lenin, and Trotsky. In the 1970s, Islington was regentrified as affluent and artsy liberals flocked here for the boho atmosphere and the palatable housing prices. In the 1980s, property values skyrocketed as people who spent their days nearby in the City getting rich off junk bonds moved in and took over.

Ascending from the depths of Angel tube station—on what is allegedly the longest escalator in Europe—you stumble upon on the main drag, **Islington High Street,** in the heart of the old village. If you head right (north), it quickly turns into **Upper Street,** easily Islington at its trendiest. This busy thoroughfare is lined with a barrage of expensive art galleries, antiques stores, cutesy shops, and eateries with bright awnings and names appended with bistro, patisserie, and brasserie. They've got some great pubs and fringe theater, though, as well as "theater bars" which, since they have theatrical shows of various sorts, are in a particular alcohol licensing category that allows them to serve liquor later than regular pubs.

Islington Markets

Head right from the Angel tube station and follow Islington High Street as it veers off to the right and becomes quite narrow. This marks the beginning of the serious antiques-selling area that eventually funnels onto Camden Passage, a pedestrian-only street and one of the hottest markets around for antiques and plain old junk. Liverpool Road forks off to the left off Islington High Street near the tube station; follow it for about 150 yards and look for Chapel Market on your left. This vibrant street market has some amazing produce and is at its boisterous best in the morning.

Islington is trying to promote itself as a cultural attraction, especially on the basis of its artisan bent. To reach the well-stocked **Discover Islington Visitor Information Centre** (44 Duncan St., tel. 0171/278–8787) hang a right out of Angel tube station and take the first sharp right. Pick up a handy map (10p) as well as free info on all sorts of things going on around the borough. The Information Centre also offers walking tours of the area from time to time, focusing on things like small art galleries or Islington's cultural heritage. The office is open Monday to Saturday 10–5.

CRAFTS COUNCIL This is the primary national organization for promoting contemporary crafts in Britain, largely through rotating displays of different craft mediums such as cloth making or woodworking. Many pieces are quite imaginative and beautiful; it's inspiring to see what human hands can create out of offerings from nature. They also have an art reference library, a small café, and the scoop on the best artisans' shops in the city. *44A Pentonville Rd., tel. 0171/278–7700. Tube: Angel. Sharp left out of station and then next right. Admission free. Open Tues.–Sat. 11–6, Sun. 2–6.*

UPPER STREET If you head north from the tube station along bustling, semi-bohemian Upper Street, you'll soon pass the flashy **Business Design Centre** (52 Upper St., tel. 0171/359–3535) on the left. While it's no great thrill in and of itself, the large hall was built on the site of the formerly important **Royal Agricultural Hall** (nicknamed the "Aggie"), and it retains a few sections of the older structure. The Aggie was built in 1862 to house cattle after Victorian urban planners deemed it uncouth to keep parading live animals all the way from the hinterlands to the Smithfield Meat Market in the city. A thousand tons of cast iron were used to support the magnificent glass roof of the central hall, which also served as a venue for gala balls and receptions.

Continuing north brings you to **Islington Green,** the hub of village life for Islingtonians of yesteryear. Today it's a serene, well-kept grassy spot with benches and a colorful array of flowers. A few blocks past the park looms the **Islington Town Hall,** the center of civic business for this borough of 165,000. The homey 1925 building looks like it could be in the middle of a small town somewhere in Kansas, and inside you can get info on happenings in the area. The **Islington Museum Gallery** (263 Upper St., tel. 0171/477–3851), a few blocks north, is a very small storefront gallery with temporary exhibits on themes reflecting the cultural and artistic diversity of Islington. Admission is free, and it's open Tuesday to Friday 11–3, Saturday 10–5.

CLERKENWELL In the southern reaches of the borough, Clerkenwell was an early 'burb of the City, whose imposing buildings and narrow, congested streets begin in earnest south of the Farringdon tube station. To reach the heart of Islington's Italian community, head north from the tube station along Farringdon Road and take a left on Clerkenwell Road. It gets liveliest north of Clerkenwell Road, along Back Hill and Herbal Hill streets. **St. Peter's Italian Church** (4 Back Hill, tel. 0171/837–1528) holds a beautiful Catholic mass, sung in Italian, at 11 AM on Sunday. The church is only open sporadically on weekdays; try in the morning. On the first Sunday after July 15th, Italians flock here from all over Britain to take part in the colorful **Procession of Our Lady of Mount Carmel,** which winds its way through the streets around the church. The procession is held in conjunction with the equally lively **Clerkenwell Festival,** an arts, crafts, and food fair that spans 10 days in mid-July.

MARX MEMORIAL LIBRARY Head north from the tube station along Farringdon Road, take a right on Clerkenwell Road, and you'll run smack into **Clerkenwell Green,** the centuries-old hangout of London's political radicals, including John Stuart Mill and Vladimir Lenin. Right on the square, the Marx Memorial Library has one of the nation's premier collections of radical books and written artifacts of Marxist history. Lenin, the grand poobah of the 1917 Bolshevik Revolution, had an office in this Georgian building around the turn of the century. *37A Clerkenwell Green, tel. 0171/253–1485. Admission free. Open Mon. 1–6, Tues.–Thurs. 1–8, Sat. 10–1.*

Clerkenwell Green is the place to be if you're a communist in London. When Mikhail Gorbachev came to town in 1984, he drove straight here from the airport to make his first public appearance.

HOUSE OF DETENTION Follow Clerkenwell Close off the north edge of the square and stop by the House of Detention, a wicked 19th-century underground prison that once was the busiest in town, serving more than 10,000 satisfied customers each year. Tunneling through its dark halls takes you past the inmates' dank cells as well as the kitchen and central courtyard. Included in the price of admission is your choice of a human-guided or Walkman tour. *Clerkenwell Close, tel. 0171/253-9494. Admission: £3, £2 students. Open daily 10-6.*

BLOOMSBURY

The British Museum and the University of London impart something of an intellectual atmosphere to the residential Bloomsbury. Yet apart from some blue plaques on **Gordon Square** you're far more likely to find a schmaltzy bed-and-breakfast than any reminders of Virginia Woolf, Vanessa Bell, Lytton Strachey, J. M. Keynes, E. M. Forster, and G. E. Moore—the so-called "Bloomsbury Group" that would assemble in the 1920s and '30s on most Thursday nights to drink and discuss why the Victorian era could not handle sexual, religious, and artistic enlightenment. Sadly, few traces remain of the personalities that brought Bloomsbury renown as the cradle of British philosophical and aesthetic modernism. Drown your disappointment at one of the many wine bars and coffeehouses on **Lamb's Conduit Street,** or go play on the swings at **Coram's Fields** (east of Russell Sq. off Guilford St.). Russell Square tube station puts you right in the belly of the beast; otherwise, it's just a short walk north from Tottenham Court Road or Holborn tube stations to Russell Square.

When you hear the word "lawyer," the immediate tendency is to yawn, grimace, or check your wallet. It's surprising, then, just how pleasant it can be to wander around the **Inns of Court** in Holborn, the heart of legal London. In the 15th and 16th centuries, the Inns of Court were exactly what they sound like—crash pads for lawyers who had business at the city's courts. Eventually, the lawyers took over the hotels and added offices and dining halls. Over time, the various inns were consolidated into just four—Lincoln's, Gray's, Middle Temple, and Inner Temple—and became the focal point of legal work in the city. Today, London barristers (trial lawyers) are still required to maintain an association with one of the inns. Law students must take bar examinations here, and barristers are required to dine in the hall of their inn a certain number of times each year to retain membership; many even have offices here. Similar in style to the courtyards of Cambridge and Oxford, the inns still retain a dignified academic air. Hang out for a while on **Chancery Lane** and watch all the wigged and gowned lawyers heading for court. The legal attire is just one indicator of how differently British and Americans approach the question of law: It's tough to imagine these guys coming on TV and saying, "Have you or a loved one been injured lately?"

Everyone thought they knew what Jeremy Bentham meant when he said he was going to get pickled. Imagine their surprise when, after his death, the founder of University College reappeared in a glass case—embalmed, sitting quietly in his favorite chair and holding his cane.

LINCOLN'S INN Just south of High Holborn and Holborn tube, Lincoln's Inn has beautiful gardens and immaculate lawns, and it's the only inn unaffected by World War II bombings. The impressive architectural features of Lincoln's Inn range from the 15th-century Old Hall to New Square, the only surviving 17th-century square in London. Inigo Jones redesigned the inn's chapel between 1619 and 1623. *Chancery Ln., tel. 0171/405-1393. Tube: Chancery Ln. Admission free. Gardens and chapel open weekdays 12:30-2:30.*

GRAY'S INN Gray's Inn, on the other side of High Holborn from Lincoln's Inn, was blown to bits during the Blitz, and most of what you see today was completely rebuilt in the 1950s—everything except the stained glass and carved oak screen in the main hall. Francis Bacon (1561-1626) kept chambers here and is thought to have designed the impressive gardens. He was later caught taking bribes and was imprisoned in the Tower of London, which led to his retirement from public service. *Holborn, tel. 0171/405-8164. Tube: Chancery Ln.*

THE TEMPLE South of Fleet Street and technically in the City, the Middle and Inner temples (collectively known as the Temple) got their name from the Knights Templar, an 11th-cen-

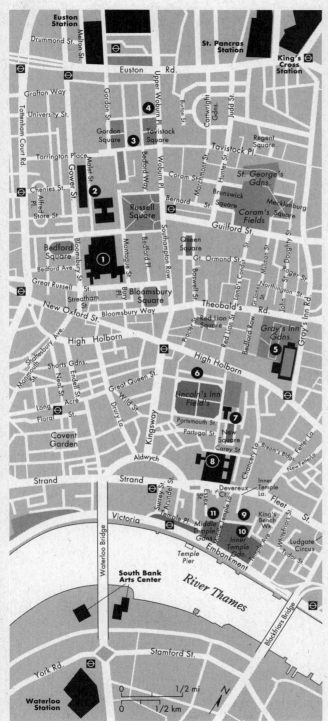

Bloomsbury

British Museum, 1
Gray's Inn, 5
Inner Temple, 10
Jewish Museum, 4
Lincoln's Inn, 7
Middle Temple, 11
Percival David
Foundation of
Chinese Art, 3
Royal Courts
of Justice, 8
Sir John Soane's
Museum, 6
Temple Church, 9
University of
London, 2

tury chivalric order that owned the land here. Sadly, the Inner Temple Hall and the gardens of the Inner Temple are closed to the public. About the only part of the complex that's open to the public are the gardens of the Middle Temple, with entrances on Strand and Fleet streets. If you can sneak a peek inside the Middle Temple Hall, look for the 29-foot-long Bench Table, donated by Elizabeth I. A smaller table nearby, the "Cupboard," is made from wood taken from Sir Francis Drake's ship, the *Golden Hind*. Nearby **Temple Church,** built by the Knights Templar in the 12th century, is one of only three round churches in England and one of Britain's finest examples of Early English Gothic. *The Temple, tel. 0171/797–8250. Tube: Temple. Open daily 10–4.*

ROYAL COURTS OF JUSTICE The impressive Victorian Law Courts lie on the Strand, a block away from the Temple. Don't come expecting tales of horror and gore—the murder trials you read about in the tabloids are held at the Old Bailey (*see* The City, *below*). The Law Courts deal with more mundane cases involving fraud and swindle; if Michael Milken had been tried in Britain, he probably would have modeled his toupee here. That said, it's still fun to wander around the cavernous building with all the duded-out judges and lawyers. *The Strand, tel. 0171/936–6000. Admission free. Open weekdays 9:30–4:30.*

UNIVERSITY OF LONDON University College, the oldest of several colleges and schools that make up the University of London, was once accused of being that "godless college in Gower Street." Today, the college and the university as a whole continue to be places where you can act in ways that the vicar would never condone. Its students have access to probably the best nightlife in the nation—pubs, cafés, and cheap restaurants dot the residential streets around the university, and the lively clubs and action of Soho are just minutes away on foot. University College was founded in 1827 by educators who objected to the fact that Oxford and Cambridge would accept only students indoctrinated by the Church of England. With a curriculum modeled after German universities, University College was the first English school to accept Jews, Catholics, and Quakers. In 1878, the university became the first in England to accept women. The college's main courtyard and portico are in Gower Street, opposite the redbrick University College Hospital. Head inside to check out the Egyptology collection and the permanent display of works by sculptor John Flaxman. The **Percival David Foundation of Chinese Art,** one of several collections administered by the University of London, has a magnificent collection of 10th- to 18th-century Chinese ceramics. *53 Gordon Sq., tel. 0171/ 387–3909. Admission free. Open weekdays 10:30–5.*

HAMPSTEAD AND HIGHGATE

As *The Berkeley Guides,* we would be remiss if we didn't say that, of the many different neighborhoods in London, Hampstead most resembles Berkeley: not really in terms of Berkeley's street weirdos or vociferous ideological ranters (for that, visit Speakers' Corner), but rather in the many cool cafés that set their tables out on the tree-lined sidewalks. Four miles north of central London, Hampstead is a posh, stylish area, popular with writers, musicians, and artists. **Hampstead High Street** is the real heart of the neighborhood, although **Heath Street** is equally evocative. To get here, catch the Northern Line tube to Hampstead.

Hampstead is the best place in London to wear sunglasses, smoke Gauloises, and contemplate love and death over a double espresso.

Besides the Heath, Hampstead is well known for its grand houses, winding streets, and country lanes. On **Church Row,** just off High Street, you'll find some of the finest 18th-century mansions in London. Besides the houses of Freud and Keats, the more famous Hampstead abodes include **Fenton House** (Hampstead Grove, tel. 0171/435–3471), a National Trust building that is now open to the public with displays of 18th-century porcelain and keyboard musical instruments. Hampstead also has some cool little pubs: Consider stopping for a pint at **The Holly Bush** (22 The Mount, tel. 0171/435–2892), north of Hampstead High Street off Holly Hill. More touristy but still interesting is **Spaniards Inn** (Hampstead Ln., on the northwest edge of the Heath), where 18th-century highwayman Dick Turpin is fabled to have done some carousing. East of Hampstead across Hampstead Heath, **Highgate** is another tony residential area. **Highgate High Street,** the main road through this suburb, is lined with boutiques and a few cafés that give it a bohemian flair. If you want to avoid paying the extra 60p it costs to get off at Highgate station (it's in Zone 3), get off at Archway and walk up Highgate High Street past Waterlow Park.

FREUD'S HOUSE The pad of the father of psychoanalysis still feels eerily lived in. Freud spent the last year of his life here, having fled Vienna in 1938 to escape Nazi persecution. Take a peek into his life and try to analyze *his* psyche by inspecting his strange toys, art, and curious knickknacks. You can also check out his preserved library and study—complete with his (in)famous couch—where he spent his final year doing some of his most important theorizing. Ask about the schedule of special exhibits, lectures, and viewings of archive films. *20 Maresfield Gardens, tel. 0171/435–2002. Tube: Finchley Rd. Turn right out of station and head south on Finchley Rd. for 250 yards; turn left on Trinity Walk, and follow it to Maresfield Gardens. Admission: £2.50, £1.50 students. Open Wed.–Sun. noon–5.*

KEATS HOUSE Keats may have been a great Romantic poet, but that didn't help his cause with Fanny Brawne, the girl next door, for whom he pined for years. After his death, their two houses were combined to form what is today an all-encompassing Keats museum, furnished just as it was during the poet's lifetime. Be sure to check out the full-scale plaster "lifemask" of Keats' head, created by a painter friend, for the rare (and somewhat eerie) opportunity of seeing what the long-dead poet *really* looked like. *Keats Grove, tel. 0171/435–2062. Tube: Hampstead. Admission free. Open Apr.–Oct., weekdays 2–6, Sat. 10–1 and 2–5, Sun. 2–5; Nov.–Mar., weekdays 1–5, Sat. 10–1 and 2–5, Sun. 2–5.*

HAMPSTEAD HEATH If you dig traipsing through hill and dale, following narrow paths to nowhere, and crashing through bushes, the 800-acre Hampstead Heath is the place for you. For a big-city park, Hampstead Heath is surprisingly rural—even despite the omnipresent litter. In recent years, use of the park has become something of a sore point between Londoners and uppity Yanks. American ex-pats, it seems, like to play softball on the Heath, a fact that has upset many locals, who complain that the flying balls are dangerous and the game much too loud. However, locals see no problem with cricket (which uses a damn hard red ball) being played on the Heath. It's a much more civilized game, you see, with pressed white suits and time out for tea. For the moment, passionate softball games are still held most weekend afternoons in summer. Otherwise, the principal site on the Heath is **Kenwood House** (Hampstead Ln., tel. 0181/348–1286), a 17th-century mansion with landscaped gardens and a fine collection of paintings, including works by Gainsborough, van Dyck, Rembrandt, Turner, and Guardi. Best of all, admission is free. To reach Hampstead Heath, take the tube to Hampstead and walk ½ mile up Heath Street.

HIGHGATE CEMETERY A light drizzle (not unlikely in London) creates a wonderful gloom in Highgate Cemetery, where a maze of narrow footpaths cuts through a forest of vine-covered Victorian tombstones. The cemetery is divided into two parts: The **Eastern Cemetery** is still in use and contains the somber tomb of Karl Marx, the German philosopher with whom ex-communists all over Eastern Europe would like to have a chat. Just a few feet away, across the gravel path, lies his dialectical opposite, social Darwinist Herbert Spencer. **Waterlow Park,** forming the northern border of Highgate Cemetery, is one of the only parks in London where you'll encounter some formidable hills. These surprisingly steep mounds run down to rush-bordered ponds full of waterfowl. To reach the cemetery and park take the Northern Line, which forks at Camden Town; make sure you're on a train marked HIGH BARNET or MILL HILL EAST. *Swains Ln., tel. 0181/340–1834. Tube: Archway. From station, walk north on Highgate Rd. Admission to East Cemetery: £1. Open daily 10–5.*

East London

THE STRAND AND EMBANKMENT

The Strand, which turns into Fleet Street about ½ mile from Charing Cross, is smelly, noisy, and dirty. And not in an interesting way, either—just a lot of cars in a boring concrete canyon that's crowded by sidewalks and mediocre restaurants. Unless you're a very methodical sightseer or really into carbon monoxide, you could forgo this particular attraction with no adverse effect. The Embankment, on the other hand, is a bit more intriguing. Constructed between 1868 and 1874 by Sir Joseph Bazalgette, the same guy who designed London's sewers, the Embankment was designed to protect the city from flooding (a job now handled by the Thames Barrier). Although it's been abandoned, you'll find some quirky characters hanging out in the shadow of the Embankment, which runs all the way from Westminster to the city. For a detail of the area, see the map of Soho and Covent Garden, *above*.

CHARING CROSS "Charing" is an old English word derived from the French for "dear queen" (chère reine). The story goes that Edward I erected 13 crosses in 1290 to mark the funeral route of his beloved queen, Eleanor of Castile, entombed in Westminster Abbey. Londoners in the 19th century cast copies of the crosses and sunk one in front of Charing Cross station, hence the name. These days, few people notice the somber memorial in what's essentially a tube station parking lot. *Tube: Charing Cross.*

CLEOPATRA'S NEEDLE Although it's not the most dramatic monument in London, Cleopatra's Needle brings home the reality of how vast and far-flung the British Empire was in its heyday. Here, on the Embankment in gray old England, stands a pink granite Egyptian obelisk, carved with hieroglyphics and flanked by benches supported by sculptures of camels. You almost expect General Gordon to ride in from stage left. Carved in Heliopolis in 1450 BC to record the victories of Ramses the Great, it was given to the British in 1819 by the viceroy of Egypt. Even so, it took another 59 years for the obelisk to make its way to Britain: Weighing 180 tons, the needle could not possibly be put on a ship, so it was towed behind in a torpedo-like case, which was lost during a storm at sea. To everyone's surprise, it was recovered soon after and towed to London for immediate display. *Victoria Embankment, opposite the Victoria Embankment Gardens. Tube: Embankment.*

Quirky Victorians buried a time capsule beneath the Embankment's obelisk, containing such oddities as a railway guide, a portrait of Queen Victoria, and a baby's bonnet.

SOMERSET HOUSE The best place to get a good view of 18th-century Somerset House is from **Waterloo Bridge;** the view of the rest of London from here ain't too shabby, either. Constructed between 1776 and 1786 by William Chambers, Somerset House replaced a Renaissance palace used by members of the royal family. The replacement, though, is rather bland and conservative. The construction of Victoria Embankment in the 19th century didn't help—before then, the Thames lapped at the very base of the building. Until 1973, Somerset House was the home of the Registrar General of Births, Deaths, and Marriages, as well as a number of other government offices. Today, the building houses Inland Revenue (the British equivalent of the IRS) and the **Courtauld Institute Galleries.** This gallery, affiliated with the University of London, has a collection of oils from the 15th to 20th centuries. The Impressionist and Post-Impressionist movements, displayed in two rooms, are the best represented. The Cézanne collection is considered the finest in London, as is the collection of Manet's works, including *A Bar at the Folies-Bergère.* Classical works by such artists as Botticelli, Giovanni Bellini, and Rubens are also exhibited. *The Strand, tel. 0171/873–2526. Tube: Temple. Walk west on Temple Pl., turn right on Surrey St., left on The Strand. Admission: £3, £1.50 students. Open Mon.–Sat. 10–6, Sun. 2–6.*

ST. MARY-LE-STRAND Constructed between 1714 and 1717, St. Mary-le-Strand, which stands opposite Somerset House, was the first of 50 churches that Queen Anne ordered built to lure Londoners back to religion following the twin whammies of the plague (1665) and the Great Fire (1666). Twelve churches were about all that anyone could take, however. The architect was Scotsman James Gibbs, who melded elements of Italian Baroque with Christopher Wren's distinctive style. Gibbs probably never intended to surround his church with an unceasing flow of traffic, but those are the breaks. Try not to get run down while gawking. *The Strand, across from Somerset House. tel. 0171/836–3126. Tube: Aldwych.*

ST. CLEMENT DANES Like St. Mary-le-Strand to the west, this church is also an island in a sea of traffic. Built by the ubiquitous Wren, St. Clement Danes has been extensively restored and is the adopted church of the Royal Air Force (RAF). A book inside the church contains the names of 1,900 American fliers killed during World War II. The church's distinctive bells were the inspiration for the nursery rhyme "Oranges and lemons, say the bells of St. Clement's." The bells ring for Sunday services at 9 and 11 AM. *The Strand, by Royal Courts of Justice, tel. 0171/242–8282. Tube: Aldwych. Open daily 8:30–4:30.*

THE CITY

The City is to London what Wall Street is to New York. It smells of money and deals. And like all good capitalist animals, the City answers to the markets and nothing else, not even the rest of London—it's an administrative and legal entity in itself. Taking up more than a square mile in east London, the City is home to the stock exchange, the Bank of England, Lloyd's, and a host of large banking and trading firms. The traditional view of the City has always been that of upper- and upper-middle-class gentlemen in bowler hats carrying brollies and briefcases. That all changed in the headlong rush for money during the Thatcher '80s. Desperately trying to cash in on the market binge, once-staid companies began hiring employees who could produce the goods, even though they may not have attended the right schools. Before you could say "new money," a host of self-made men with "frightful" accents was swaggering through London with wads of cash. Of course, the Old Boy network hasn't dried up and blown away—the snobbery has just grown a little more subtle. In fact, the City's newly made millionaires are still referred to by their upper-class brethren as "barrow boys."

Although the City lies to the east of central London, it actually rests on the original Celtic settlement that the Romans conquered and built up into Londinium. Vestiges of this ancient heritage pop up all over the City, even though the Great Fire of London, which started in a baker's shop in Pudding Lane in September 1666, destroyed almost every building in the area. In the years that followed, architect Christopher Wren redesigned the entire district, building 51 new churches including St. Paul's cathedral, which stood as the focal point of a new city of spires. German bombers wrecked most of Wren's work, however, and post-war London architects managed to brutalize much of the rest. The once-dramatic views of St. Paul's have slowly disappeared behind concrete behemoths.

FLEET STREET Until a decade ago, Fleet Street was synonymous with newspapers and journalists. Almost all of Britain's major papers had their offices here, and Fleet Street pubs were the lairs of hoary old journalists and their sources. The newspapers are all gone now, scattered to cheaper neighborhoods with lower overheads, more computers, and fewer unionized employees. Even so, many people still refer to the British press as Fleet Street. It's not surprising really, since the printed word has a long history here. Wynkyn de Worde printed about 800 books in the area around St. Paul's between 1500 and 1535. Most of the books were for the clergy, the only literate bunch back then, but in later centuries, printers, binders, and stationers all set up shop in the area.

At various times, Fleet Street has acted as everything from a cheerleader for the Empire to a scurrilous Peeping Tom looking to catch Princess Di without a bra. The *Daily Mail* and the *London Standard,* two run-of-the-mill tabloids, operated out of Carmelite Street (down Whitefriars St. from Fleet St.) before moving to Kensington in 1988. Prior to shifting to the Docklands, Rupert Murdoch's *The Sun* and *News of the World* worked out of Bouverie Street, also just off Fleet Street; these papers continue to set the world standard for unscrupulously lowbrow journalism. The *Daily Telegraph,* Britain's most conservative paper, had its offices next to Peterborough Court; the liberal *Guardian* was headquartered on Farringdon Road; the *Observer* was just off Ludgate Hill; and the *Financial Times,* the ultraconservative pink paper, was produced just behind St. Paul's.

OLD BAILEY If you can't afford theater tickets or you're a fan of "Rumpole of the Bailey," go and watch a trial at the Old Bailey, officially known as Central Criminal Court. You can't beat the drama (it's all for real) or the price (it's free). Just line up outside and scan the offering of trials—they're posted on a sort of legal menu du jour at the Newgate Street entrance; start with something light, perhaps a mugging, and then move on to a main course of murder and mayhem. The juiciest trials usually go down in Courts 1–3, the old courts. In the modern Courts 4–19, it's difficult to see unless you're in the front row or actually on trial yourself.

The City

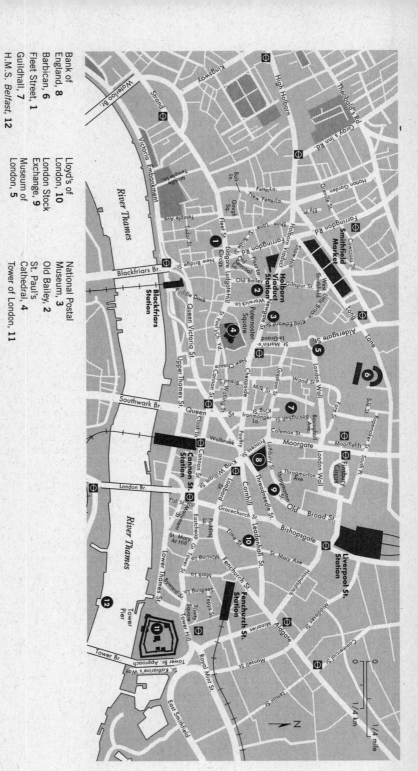

72

While you're waiting for the show to begin, check out Pomeroy's famous bronze statue of Justice atop the building. *Old Bailey, at Ludgate Hill, tel. 0171/248–3277. Tube: St. Paul's, Mansion House, or Blackfriars. Public Gallery open weekdays 10–1 and 2–4.*

Famous defendants tried at the Old Bailey include Oscar Wilde, convicted of homosexuality in 1895; William "Lord Haw Haw" Joyce, who did pro-Nazi radio shows from Berlin during World War II; and Peter "Yorkshire Ripper" Sutcliffe, a serial killer convicted in 1981.

THE BARBICAN This large complex of residential towers and cultural venues was built between 1959 and 1981 in an ill-fated attempt to resurrect central London as a living city instead of merely a place of work. The modern concrete blocks are inordinately ugly and look more like something you would find in Eastern Europe than London. Nevertheless, the Barbican Centre has evolved into one of the city's principal cultural institutions. The **Barbican Hall** hosts a variety of musical performances, including several by the London Symphony Orchestra and the Academy of St. Martin-in-the-Fields. The Royal Shakespeare Company stages regular productions in the **Barbican Theatre,** while smaller companies play in **The Pit.** The **Barbican Cinemas** show great films daily. For details on all of the above, *see* Theater in Chapter 6. There are also some impressive visual arts displays at the **Barbican Art Gallery.** Free music and art exhibitions are usually held in one of the many foyers, and the huge, glass-encased **conservatory,** filled with exotic plants and trees, is open to the public (80p) on weekends noon–5:30. *Silk St., tel. 0171/638–4141 (general info) or 0171/638–8891 (box office). Tube: Barbican or Moorgate. Admission to Barbican Art Gallery: £4.50, £2.50 students. Gallery open Mon. and Wed.–Fri. 10–6:45, Tues. 10–5:45, Sun. noon–6:45.*

LLOYD'S BUILDING The Lloyd's building is the most aggressively "modern" building in the City and certainly one of the most architecturally important structures built in the '80s. The duo that put it up, celebrity-architect Richard Rogers and structural engineer Peter Rice (engineer of the Sydney Opera House and recently awarded the gold medal from the Royal Institute of British Architects), also worked together on the equally revolutionary Pompidou Centre in Paris. The Lloyd's building makes no effort to hide its "builtness," a key element in Rice's project of "humanizing" architecture by reintroducing evidence of human participation in construction. Indeed, you might mistake Lloyd's for a building still under construction. The bright blue structures protruding from the roof look like cranes, and the many tubes and ducts exposed on the exterior look as though they're waiting for their facade. There used to be an observation deck that was open to the public, but for security reasons (read: IRA bombs), it's now accessible *only* if you write well ahead of time to Lloyd's Visiting Department at 1 Lime Street, London EC3M 7HA. Other than that, you can only walk through the courtyard. *1 Lime St., tel. 0171/623–7100. Tube: Monument. Walk north on Gracechurch St., just past Fenchurch St.*

EAST END

The East End is usually derided by Londoners as well as by the tourist crowd. While it is definitely not the most glamorous part of town, it does not fully deserve its brutal reputation. No one denies that the East End is not the "Queen's London" (and they certainly don't speak the Queen's English here), but that's because it is the *people's* London—an ethnically diverse, hardened, very much alive district that's well worth a look. Historically one of the city's poorest areas, the East End has been home over the centuries to immigrant Irish, Jews fleeing persecution on the Continent, and Bangladeshis and Afro-Caribbeans looking for a better life. Recently, many struggling artists have made the East End their home, taking advantage of the large studio/living spaces that old, dilapidated warehouses have to offer.

In the East End, South Asian specialties and Jewish kosher delicacies are served up like nowhere else in London; next door to a bagel shop you can find butchers selling *halal* meat (the Muslim equivalent of kosher) to the East End's growing Islamic population. Not to be missed are the restaurants up and down **Brick Lane:** Bangladeshi, Indian, and other savory cuisines are authentically prepared and offered at reasonable prices, making it one of the best dining thoroughfares in the city.

HAGGERSTON
Geffrye St.
Dun-Loe St.
Cremer St.
Hackney Rd.
Goldsmith's Row
Warner Pl.
Cambridge Heath Station
Cambridge Heath Rd.
Temple St.
Russia La.
Old Ford Rd.
Approach Rd.
Cyprus St.
Globe Rd.
7

SHOREDITCH
Columbia Rd.
Barnet Grove
Gosset St.
Turin St.
Old Bethnal Green Rd.
Vallance Rd.
BETHNAL GREEN
Bethnal Green Rd.
Sceptre Rd.

Shoreditch High St.
Brick La.
Swanfield St.
Red Church St.
Bethnal Green Rd.
Cheshire St.
Dunbridge St.
Weavers Fields
Bethnal Green Station
Colbert Ave.
Cephas St.

Quaker St.
Commercial St.
Buxton St.
Vallance Rd.
Burial Ground
Brady St.
Collingwood St.
Cambridge Heath Rd.
Mile End Rd.
Redman's Rd.
Smithy St.
Jamaica St.

SPITALFIELDS
Lamb St.
6
5
Hanbury St.
Brick Ln.
Greatorex St.
Montague St.
Whitechapel Rd.
Raven Row
Stepney Way
4
Liverpool St. Station
3
Old
New Rd.
Cavell St.
Sidney St.
Middlesex St.
Castle St.
Adler St.
Settles St.
Greenfield Rd.
Myrdle St.
Varden St.
Nelson St.
Commercial Rd.
1 **2**
Houndsditch
Bevis Marks
Whitechapel Rd.
Braham St.
Gowers Wk.
Alie St.
N

Bethnal Green Museum of Childhood, **7**
Bloom's, **1**
Brick Lane, **3**
Christ Church, **4**
Spitalfields Heritage Centre, **5**
Spitalfields Market, **6**
Whitechapel Art Gallery, **2**

The **Tower Hamlets Environment Trust** (150 Brick Ln., tel. 0171/377–0481) is the best source for tapping into the sights, sounds, tastes, and history of Cockney London; the office is open weekdays 10–5. This is a fairly large area, but many cool sights are concentrated in areas well-covered by public transportation. **Spitalfields,** the district that encompasses Brick Lane and a couple of amazing markets, fans out eastward from the front door of Liverpool Street Station. **Whitechapel,** south and southeast of Spitalfields, is home to the renowned Whitechapel Gallery and the excellent Petticoat Lane Market; the sights are best served by the Aldgate and Aldgate East tube stations. **Bethnal Green,** northeast of Spitalfields, has its own tube station on the Central Line. The massive **Docklands** area far to the east along the Thames is served by the **Docklands Light Railway,** which makes connections at Bank, Tower Hill, Shadwell, Stratford, and Bow Road tube stations.

SPITALFIELDS At Bishopsgate, the thoroughfare in front of Liverpool Street station, flamboyant office buildings and construction projects that reflect City-style gentrification meet the western border of the East End. Head north on Bishopsgate and take a right on Brushfield Street. Ahead is one of Spitalfields' main commercial avenues, the ugly and appropriately named **Commercial Street.** The mongo **Spitalfields Market** building will be on your left (see Street Markets in Chapter 7). Across Commercial Street, at the intersection with Fournier Street, is the definitively steepled **Christ Church** (Commercial St., tel. 0171/247–7202), built in 1720 when the area was populated mostly with French immigrants—check out the old French gravestones in the churchyard. Reflecting the diverse composition of today's parish, all announcements and schedules posted outside the church are in both English and Bengali. Christ Church is also the venue for an amazing lineup of concerts that are part of the **Spitalfields Festival** in mid-June.

Head east on Fournier Street a few blocks to **Brick Lane.** A visit to one or more of Brick Lane's ethnic restaurants is obligatory for anyone who likes food. The large, flavorful **Brick Lane Mar-**

ket (see Street Markets in Chapter 7) roars to life here on weekends. A left on Brick Lane and then another quick left will put you in front of the **Spitalfields Heritage Centre** (17–19 Princelet St., tel. 0171/377–6901). They mainly do research on the history of the area's immigrants, and it's only open erratically to the public. If you do happen to arrive when it's open, check out the old synagogue that the center is housed in. The Shoreditch tube station, on the remote East London Line, is at the northern end of Brick Lane—be warned that it operates peak hours and Sunday morning only.

WHITECHAPEL Whitechapel was the heart of the London's Jewish community until the 1950s; prior to World War II the district had about 90,000 Jews compared with today's 6,000. The blocky flats they left behind are being filled slowly by immigrants from Asia, but orthodox Hassidim still walk the streets in their somber black attire. **Bloom's** restaurant (90 Whitechapel High St., tel. 0171/247–6001) is the most beloved kosher eatery in town; the branch up in Golders Green is the place to be on Saturday nights after the Sabbath ends.

Those interested in East End Jewish culture shouldn't miss the **Bevis Marks Synagogue,** London's oldest. In 1701, a Quaker philanthropist had this beautiful structure built to serve newly arrived refugees fleeing persecution in Spain and Portugal. It's now hidden behind a gate in a little nook, surrounded by the tall, flashy buildings of the City. Anachronistic, to say the least. Bevis Marks, at Heneage Ln., tel. 0171/626–1274. Tube: Aldgate. Walk west on Aldgate High St., turn right on Houndsditch, left on Creechurch Ln. (look out for it!), quick right on Bevis Marks. £1 donation requested. Open sporadically.

From the Aldgate East tube station, its a short trek east up Whitechapel Road (also called Whitechapel High Street) to reach the tremendous **East London Mosque** (84–86 Whitechapel Rd., tel. 0171/247–1357), the first building in London built specifically for use as an Islamic place of worship. Today hundreds of Bangladeshi residents congregate here for the Jumma ceremony on Friday afternoon. Admission is free to the mosque, and you can walk the grounds daily 10:30–9 unless there's a service being held. Female visitors should wear pants and some sort of head covering. West from the Aldgate East tube station along Whitechapel High Street brings you past the **Whitechapel Gallery** (see Museums and Galleries, below). Take a right on Commercial Street, just past the museum, if you're headed up to Spitalfields; otherwise, continue past Commercial Street, take a right on Middlesex Street and head north about ¼ mile to the colorful and value-packed **Petticoat Lane Market** (see Street Markets in Chapter 7). Be forewarned: It's a favorite Sunday morning destination for thousands of Londoners.

BETHNAL GREEN It was a fashionable address during Tudor times, but today Bethnal Green is pure East End. The current highlights are a number of nifty parks right around the tube station. The pretty **Bethnal Green Gardens,** in all their flowering glory, are in between the tube station and the **Bethnal Green Museum of Childhood** (see Museums and Galleries, below). If you've got time, ramble in the huge **Victoria Park,** the first park in London created specifically for public use (1842). Head north on Cambridge Heath Road and take a right on Old Ford Road just past the museum; follow it east about ½ mile to the park. To reach the monstrous, grassy expanse (Frisbee heaven) of **Weavers Fields,** head the opposite way (south) on Cambridge Heath Road, take a right on Three Colts Lane, and follow it past all the garages where London taxicabs come to die.

THE SOUTH BANK

Many visitors never venture across the Thames unless they're heading to Waterloo Station. Who can blame them? The South Bank is fairly industrial and lacks the major monuments and shops of central London. It was also bombed flat during World War II, so no one is likely to bandy about clichés like "quaint" to describe it. What the South Bank does offer are some great museums, including the Imperial War Museum (see Museums and Galleries, below), and the South Bank Arts Centre, one of London's major cultural venues.

SOUTH BANK ARTS CENTRE Just across the Thames along Waterloo Bridge is this sprawling, multitier monument to modernist poured concrete. Home to the **National Theatre,** the **National Film Theatre,** the **Royal Festival Hall,** the **Hayward Gallery,** and the **Museum of the Moving Image** (see Museums and Galleries, below), this institution takes its role as a hard-core

The South Bank

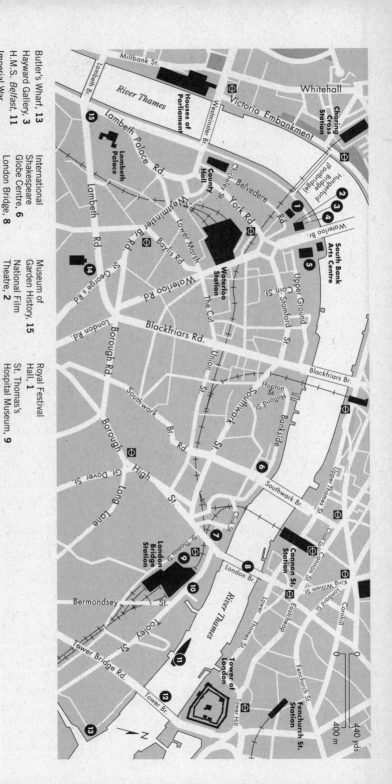

Butler's Wharf, **13**
Hayward Gallery, **3**
H.M.S. *Belfast*, **11**
Imperial War
Museum, **14**

International
Shakespeare
Globe Centre, **6**
London Bridge, **8**
London
Dungeon, **10**

Museum of
Garden History, **15**
National Film
Theatre, **2**
National Theatre, **5**
Queen Elizabeth
Hall, **4**

Royal Festival
Hall, **1**
St. Thomas's
Hospital Museum, **9**
Southwark
Cathedral, **7**
Tower Bridge, **12**

Millbank St.

River Thames

Houses of
Parliament

Whitehall

Victoria Embankment

Charing
Cross
Station

Hungerford
Bridge
(footbridge)

Lambeth Br.

Lambeth Palace Rd.

Lambeth Palace

County
Hall

Chichele St.

Belvedere
Rd.

York Rd.

Waterloo Br.

South
Bank
Arts Centre

Westminster Br. Rd.

Lambeth Rd.

Westminster Br.

Tower Marsh

Baylis Rd.

St. George's Rd.

Waterloo Rd.

London Rd.

Waterloo
Station

The Cut

Upper Ground

Stamford St.

Lower Marsh

Union St.

Blackfriars Rd.

Borough Rd.

Southwark St.

Hopton St.
Holland St.

Bankside

Blackfriars Br.

Southwark Br.

Upper Thames St.

Southwark Bridge Rd.

Borough High St.

Gt. Dover St.

Long Lane

Clink St.

Cannon St.
Station

Cannon St.

King William St.

Lombard St.

Cornhill

Lower Thames St.

Eastcheap

London Bridge
Station

St. Thomas St.

London Br.

River Thames

Tooley St.

Bermondsey St.

Tower Bridge Rd.

Tower Br.

Tower of
London

Tower Hill

Fenchurch St.
Station

Fenchurch St.

N

0   400 m
0   440 yds

"cultural center" seriously. It's as progressive a complex as you could hope for from any quasi-official institution. Thick brochures listing the month's attractions at the center are available in the lobbies of most hotels and from tourist offices. To get here, take the tube to Waterloo Station, then walk north to the complex following the signs.

SOUTHWARK You would never be able to tell that Southwark, directly opposite the Tower of London, is London's oldest suburb, dating back to Roman times. Most of the buildings today are post–World War II, and many of these fell into neglect when London's port facilities moved south. During the Thatcher '80s, Southwark (pronounced "Suth-uk") underwent a boom, and construction began on several huge new complexes. But with Britain again mired in recession, it seems unlikely that Southwark's regeneration can continue. The easiest way to get here is to take the tube to London Bridge Station, which is south of the Thames; otherwise, take the tube to Tower Hill and walk across Tower Bridge.

➤ **ST. THOMAS'S HOSPITAL MUSEUM** • Don't come to this museum if you or a family member are facing surgery anytime soon. The display of a 19th-century operating room, complete with sawdust to soak up the blood, is enough to turn any visitor into a Christian Scientist. The operating room is all that remains of the original St. Thomas's Hospital, which occupied the site from the 13th to the mid-19th century. The hospital was moved to Lambeth, and all the other buildings were demolished; the lone operating theater, which is in a remote loft, was blocked off and forgotten for more than a century. It's been restored to its original, gruesome, and doubtlessly unsterile state. Next door is the herb garret, where medicinal plants were dried and stored. *9A St. Thomas St., tel. 0171/955–4791. Tube: London Bridge. Follow signs from station. Admission: £2, £1.50 students. Open Tues.–Sun. 10–4.*

➤ **INTERNATIONAL SHAKESPEARE GLOBE CENTRE** • Shakespeare staged many of his plays in Southwark at the old Globe Playhouse, which has long since been destroyed. The theater was part of a vibrant entertainment district that featured everything from bear-baiting to dive bars. In those days, people didn't pay £20 a ticket for a theater seat, and they didn't look for neo-Marxist-feminist symbolism in Shakespeare's works. Going to the theater, it seems, was more like going to a baseball game, with people in the cheap seats cracking peanuts and generally acting oafish. With luck, visitors will be able to see just what it was like when a replica of the old **Globe Playhouse** opens within the next year or so. The project is the work of American filmmaker Sam Wanamaker, who has slaved for two decades to reconstruct the outdoor theater, even using the same construction materials and techniques as 16th-century craftsmen. A second indoor theater, the **Inigo Jones Theatre,** is also being built, based on the venerable architect's

In 1574 all theaters were banned from central London, forcing the city's actors to move across the Thames into newly built theaters like the Rose (1587) and the Globe (1599).

17th-century designs. Once complete, both theaters will be used for performances, but it's unclear whether they'll sell peanuts or not. The **Shakespeare Globe Museum** offers a dry, slightly boring look at the old Globe and the surrounding area. *Bear Gardens, tel. 0171/982–6342. Tube: London Bridge. Head south on Borough High St., quick right on Southwark St. and right on Southwark Bridge Rd. Museum admission: £3, £2 students. Open Mon.–Sat. 10–5, Sun. 2–5.*

➤ **SOUTHWARK CATHEDRAL** • Right near London Bridge, a couple of blocks from St. Thomas's Hospital Museum, Southwark Cathedral is the largest Gothic church in London after Westminster Abbey. Construction of this whopper—the fourth church on this site since the 7th century—started in 1220, but it was substantially rebuilt in the 19th century. One of the most interesting parts of the cathedral is the **Harvard Chapel,** named after John Harvard, founder of Harvard College, who was baptized here in 1608. Also check out the original Gothic nave. If you like music, the church choir sings liberally during the 11 AM Sunday service. *Montague Close, off Borough High St., tel. 0171/407–2939. Admission free. Open daily 8–6.*

➤ **LONDON DUNGEON** • If you have a mean streak and can afford the hefty admission price, join the hordes of tourists in line at this museum of warped and weird violence. Who knows, maybe the next rampaging psychopath is right behind you. Lots of blood and gore are the basis of exhibits detailing medieval torture tactics, executions, and general mean-spiritedness; there's also a re-creation of the Great Fire of London (1666). *28–34 Tooley St., tel. 0171/403–7221 or 0171/403–0606 for recorded info. Tube: London Bridge. Walk north from station. Admission: £6.50, £5.50 students. Open daily 10–6:30, last entry 5:30.*

➤ **HMS BELFAST** • One of three branches of the Imperial War Museum (the others are Duxford Airport and the Cabinet War Rooms), HMS *Belfast* was the pride of the Royal Navy during the mid-century, and remains the largest cruiser ever built for the British. It helped shell the Normandy beaches on D-Day and later served in the Far East. Yellow arrows lead you on a clearly marked tour past guns, engines, and a large number of life-size dioramas reconstructing life and war on the ship. The interesting Walkman tour costs a mere 50p. The HMS *Belfast* is moored on the southern bank of the Thames, ⅓ mile west of Tower Bridge. *Morgans Ln., off Tooley St., tel. 0171/407–6434. Admission: £3.80, £1.90 students; free on Fri. Open Easter–Oct.; daily 10–5:20; Nov.–Easter, daily 10–4.*

South London

CHELSEA AND KING'S ROAD

Chelsea extends south from Knightsbridge to the Thames. Much of the neighborhood is residential, although it does have pockets of counterculture funk. Of most interest to hipsters is King's Road, a long boulevard anchored in the northeast by **Sloane Square.** Sloane Square gets interesting on weekend afternoons when the aggressively weird begin to assemble—punkers with brightly dyed 'dos, elaborate makeup, plenty of piercings, and lots of black leather. In the 1970s, **King's Road** *was* the punk movement where the Sex Pistols and other early English punk bands first appeared, and where counterculture clothing shops and record stores operated out of dingy holes. Today, it's gone somewhat yuppie, lined with lots of expensive boutiques and bistros.

South of King's Road, along the Thames, is a short strip called **Cheyne Walk** (pronounced "Chainy"), which once boasted such heavyweight residents as George Eliot (No. 4), Dante Gabriel Rosetti (No. 16), and Mick Jagger (No. 48). Certainly no artists or literary masters roam the streets now. All you'll find is posh family homes and Sloanies walking their privileged Labradors on the privileged streets. You can, however, get a small glimpse into the life of one literary giant. **Thomas Carlyle's House** (24 Cheyne Row, tel. 0171/352–7087) is just as the Carlyles left it more than 150 years ago—Thomas's very own hat is still where he put it before he died, and all the furniture, books, and possessions remain intact. Admission is £2.75, but beware—it's open erratically throughout the year, so call ahead.

RICHMOND AND SOUTHWEST LONDON

Immediately southwest of central London, the Borough of Richmond-upon-Thames (BritRail or Tube: Richmond) is filled with culture and money. Residents live in palatial Victorian homes, many of which have been passed down from generation to generation. A fun way to reach Richmond is on one of the **WPSA ferries** (tel. 0171/930–4721) that depart from Westminster Pier and stop at Putney, Chelsea, and Kew, and then continue on to Hampton Court Palace (*see below*), all for £8 round-trip.

One of the highlights of any visit is **Richmond Hill.** Lined with beautiful houses and antiques shops, the hill enjoys sweeping views over the river. Richmond Hill leads up to **Richmond Park,** 2,470 acres of heathland still roamed by herds of deer. After hoofing it over hill and dale, take a breather at **Richmond Harvest** (5 The Square, tel. 0181/940–1138), a small restaurant hidden on a busy street in the center of town. You may have to look extra carefully, but the search is worth it. Starters run about £2.50, main courses about £5.

KEW GARDENS Started in 1759 by Princess Augusta (wife of Frederick, Prince of Wales), Kew Gardens is the mother of all botanical gardens. People with Zone 1 and 2 Travelcards may need to buy an extra ticket or risk getting slapped with a penalty fare, but it's worth it—Kew is colossal and absolutely amazing. Wild patches, hyperformal patches, lakes, ponds, and paths

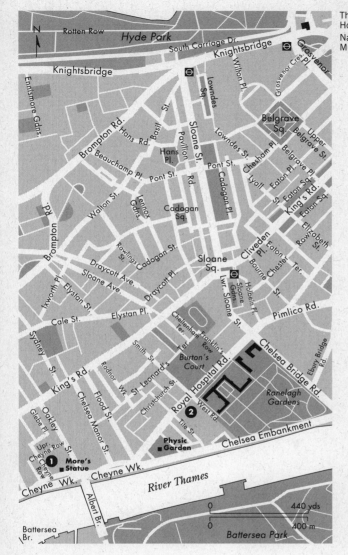

Thomas Carlyle's House, **1**

National Army Museum, **2**

abound. Half a dozen glass greenhouses—many huge and architecturally magnificent—house an immense variety of plants from arctic to tropical vegetation, from huge trees to humble ground cover. Although it's hard to choose favorites, the **Princess of Wales's Conservatory** is especially good. Here in a modernist structure, a tropical jungle has been re-created in lush detail: Mist blows out of pipes every 45 seconds, birdcalls resound from hidden speakers, and the atmosphere is hot and sultry. *Kew and Wakehurst Pl., tel. 0181/940–1171. Tube: Kew Gardens. Follow the clearly marked signs to Victoria Gate. Admission: £4, £2 students. Open Mon.–Sat. 9:30–6, Sun. 9:30–7:30; greenhouses close at 4:30, Sun. at 5:30; shorter hrs off-season.*

HAMPTON COURT PALACE Up the Thames west from Richmond is Hampton Court Palace, party house of English royalty since the early 16th century. The palace was built in

1514, and the great hall in 1532. Henry VIII is said to have rushed construction of the hall by having laborers toil 24 hours a day in shifts, working by candlelight at night. The amazing extravagance of the palace is evident in its size, but the ornate interior and exterior decoration puts its value far beyond comprehension. Within the grounds are the world's first indoor tennis court, massive state bedrooms, and kitchens, plus gardens, canals, a garden maze, and a grapevine that's more than 220 years old. *Hampton Court Bridge, tel. 0181/781–9500. Take London Transport Bus R68 from central Richmond, or take the ferry. Admission: £7, £5.30 students. Open Mon. 10:15–6, Tues.–Sun. 9:30–6 (until 4:30 Oct.–Mar.).*

BRIXTON

Brixton, in south-central London at the end of the Victoria Line, looks pretty funky and is rarely visited by the casual tourist. Another of the city's multi-ethnic areas, Brixton is where many young Londoners venture for raves and to dance to world-beat sounds in the district's innumerable clubs. Another draw is the excellent **Brixton Market,** an open-air affair that grooves Monday to Saturday on Electric Avenue (that's right, the one in the Eddy Grant song), right around the corner from the tube station (*see* Shopping in Chapter 7). Brixton's population is mostly of West Indian and African descent, and primarily working class. In 1981 and 1985, Brixton was rocked by a series of riots that—even though they were dubbed "race riots"—were probably sparked by worsening socioeconomic conditions during Thatcher's everyone-for-themselves '80s. Westminster did take notice, however, and threw some pounds this way to help revive Brixton's economy. The government programs have helped some, but many of the area's problems are too deeply rooted to be cleaned up with any quick-fix solution.

➤ **BLACK CULTURAL ARCHIVES AND MUSEUM** • It's one of the nation's premier collections of art and artifacts concerning the history of black people in Britain. Exhibits—photographs, letters, storyboards, artwork, and other cool stuff—chronicle the plight and achievements of black immigrants from Roman times until today. The art gallery has changing displays of works by locally and widely known black artists. *378 Coldharbour Ln., tel. 0171/738–4591. Tube: Brixton. Turn right out of station and right on Atlantic Rd. Admission free. Open Mon.–Sat. 10–6.*

➤ **BROCKWELL PARK** • Just south of Brixton, the huge, grassy Brockwell Park used to be the gluttonous estate of a wealthy glassmaker. Today it's simply a pleasant green that's open to the public. There's nothing amazing about it—it's just a nice place to while away a few hours on a sunny day, especially by one of the lakes on the western side, close to where the bus drops you off. The park also has sports facilities—swimming pools, tennis courts, squash courts—that can be reserved by calling in advance. *Tel. 0181/674–6141. Tube: Brixton. Take Bus 2 heading south from station along Tulse Hill; look for park on left. Open daily dawn–dusk.*

Museums and Galleries

In addition to the museums reviewed below, the following museums are discussed above: **Barbican Art Gallery** (*see* The City); **Black Cultural Archives and Museum** (*see* Brixton); **British Museum** (*see* Bloomsbury); **Cabinet War Rooms** (*see* Whitehall); **Courtauld Institute Galleries** (*see* The Strand and Embankment); **Fenton House** (*see* Hampstead and Highgate); **Guards Museum** (*see* Buckingham Palace); **HMS *Belfast*** (*see* The South Bank); **Keats House** (*see* Hampstead and Highgate); **Kensington Palace** (*see* Kensington and Knightsbridge); **Kenwood House** (*see* Hampstead and Highgate); **London Dungeon** (*see* The South Bank); **Madame Tussaud's Wax Museum** (*see* Marylebone and Regent's Park); **National Gallery** (*see* Trafalgar Square); **Natural History Museum** (*see* Kensington and Knightsbridge); **Percival David Foundation of Chinese Art** (*see* Bloomsbury); **Queen's Gallery** (*see* Buckingham Palace); **St. Thomas's Hospital Museum** (*see* The South Bank); **Science Museum** (*see* Kensington and Knightsbridge); **Serpentine Gallery** (*see* Hyde Park/Kensington Gardens); **Shakespeare Globe Museum** (*see* The South Bank); **Tate Gallery** (*see* Tate Gallery); **Thomas Carlyle's House** (*see* Chelsea and King's Road); **University of London** (*see* Bloomsbury); **Victoria and Albert Museum** (*see* Kensington and Knightsbridge).

Bank of England Museum. Housed in the Bank of England Building, this multimedia museum has some cool historical artifacts, early photographs, collections of old banknotes, and interactive videos where you can play around with banking matters. The collection lays out the Bank's history and functions, chronicling the institution's importance in helping to build England's financial and trading empire of yore. Special exhibits, which change every few months, feature topics like "Women in the Bank." *Bartholomew Ln., tel. 0171/601–5545 or 0171/601–5792 for recorded info. Tube: Bank. Walk east on Threadneedle St., turn left on Bartholomew Ln. Admission free. Open Oct.–Mar., weekdays 10–5; Apr.–Sept., weekdays 10–5, Sun. 11–5.*

Bethnal Green Museum of Childhood. It's an offshoot of the Victoria and Albert Museum, so it's gotta be good. The collection is all about the life of children and includes toys, games, puppets, dolls, and an amazing assortment of dollhouses. The exhibit that has playthings made from scraps and garbage will make you stop and think. *Cambridge Heath Rd., tel. 0181/980–3204 or 0181/980–2415 for recorded info. Tube: Bethnal Green. Admission free. Open Mon.–Thurs. and Sat. 10–5:50, Sun. 2:30–5:50.*

Camden Arts Centre. This is one of the best places in London to see contemporary European art. Exhibits and shows rotate frequently, and lectures are usually scheduled to accompany the current painting, photography, or sculpture displays. *Arkwright Rd., tel. 0171/435–2643. Tube: Finchley Rd. Walk north (uphill) on Finchley Rd., turn right on Arkwright Rd. Admission free. Open Tues.–Thurs. noon–8, Fri.–Sun. noon–6.*

Canal Museum. Located in a former ice storage house, this museum illustrates the growth and decline of London's canal network. These waterways were once important venues for trade and transportation, and a distinct way of life evolved for the "canal people" who lived and worked on them. Make sure to have a gander at the trippy "narrow boats" of modern canaldwellers on nearby Regent's Canal. *12/13 New Wharf Rd., tel. 0171/713–0836. Tube: King's Cross. Walk north on York Way, turn right at Wharfdale Rd., left on New Wharf Rd. Admission: £2.50, £1.25 students. Open Tues.–Sun. 10–4:30, last entry 3:45.*

Most museums let you bring daypacks in, but upon entry don't be surprised when they stick a wand-like electrical contraption inside to check if you're packing any Semtex, the IRA's high-powered explosive of choice.

Commonwealth Institute. When the British Empire collapsed into the loose political configuration known as the Commonwealth, they threw up a museum to celebrate the fact. Three floors hold displays covering each member country. Unless the target's easy (like Idi Amin), internal political turbulence tends to be glossed over in favor of "modernization," "development," and scientifically aided "progress." Nevertheless, it's this curious gloss-over propaganda that makes the institute so interesting. *Kensington High St., tel. 0171/603–4535. Tube: Kensington High St. or Earl's Court. From Kensington High St.: walk west on Kensington High St. From Earl's Court: walk north on Earl's Court Rd. Admission: £1, 50p students. Open Mon.–Sat. 10–5, Sun. 2–5.*

Cork Street. This street in Mayfair is the center of the commercial art scene in London, with more than a dozen private galleries between Burlington Gardens and Clifford Street. The galleries are open to the public and tend to concentrate on contemporary Western art, although a handful emphasizes material ranging from 20th-century canonical "avant garde" to Australian aboriginal art and contemporary Russian realism. The galleries are close together, so it's easy to hit them all within a few hours. *Tube: Green Park or Piccadilly Circus. From Green Park: head east on Piccadilly, turn left on Old Bond St., right on Burlington Gardens. From Piccadilly: walk northwest 1 long block on Regent St., turn left on Vigo St. (which becomes Burlington Gardens).*

Design Museum. This elegantly laid-out museum houses two floors of 20th-century international design, with an emphasis on mass-produced consumer goods. The Review gallery is hypermodern, displaying the newest in contemporary design. Half of this gallery is dedicated to rotating exhibits of individual designers or design firms. On a separate floor, the Collection gallery has a more historical emphasis. *Butler's Wharf, Shad Thames, tel. 0171/403–6933 or*

0171/407–6261 for recorded info. Tube: Tower Hill. Cross Tower Bridge and head east along the Thames. Admission: £4.50, £3.50 students. Open daily 10:30–5:30.

Dickens House. During the three years (1837–1839) he lived at 48 Doughty Street, Charles Dickens churned out *Oliver Twist* and *Nicholas Nickleby,* and finished up *Pickwick Papers.* The house is now an interesting museum and library. *48 Doughty St., 1 block west of Gray's Inn Rd., tel. 0171/405–2127. Tube: Russell Sq. Head east on Bernard St., turn right at Coram's Fields, left at Guilford St. Admission: £3, £2 students. Open Mon.–Sat. 10–5.*

Hayward Gallery. This is the flagship art gallery of the huge South Bank Arts Centre. It's forte is assembling thorough retrospectives of modern artists such as Magritte, Jasper Johns, Dali, and Toulouse-Lautrec. *Belvedere Rd., tel. 0171/928–3144 or 0171/261–0127 for recorded info. Tube: Waterloo. Admission: £5, £3.50 students. Open Mon. and Thurs.–Sun. 10–6, Tues. and Wed. 10–8.*

Imperial War Museum. As you enter, a large exhibit hall filled with planes, tanks, field guns, and a variety of other war toys sets the tone. This museum outlines the history of Britain's 20th-century wars using weaponry, mementos and reconstructions—including a bomb shelter from the Blitz and a trench from the Great War. For an extra £1.35 (£1.10 students), you can fly with "Operation Jericho" and witness a 1944 raid over France. For £3.90, you can attend "History Evenings" with guest speakers talking on different aspects of wars, particularly World War II. *Lambeth Rd., tel. 0171/416–5000 or 0171/820–1683 for recorded info. Tube: Elephant & Castle. Walk northwest on St. George's Rd. Admission: £3.90, £2.90 students; free daily after 4:30. Open daily 10–6.*

Institute of Contemporary Arts (ICA). Lectures, excellent films, and rotating exhibits of photography, paintings, and architectural drawings make the ICA the HQ for lusty cultural bolshevism. The sales table of the bookshop offers some choice bargains, and you can watch films in the video library. *Carlton House Terrace, The Mall, tel. 0171/930–3647 or 0171/930–6393 for recorded info. Tube: Charing Cross or Piccadilly. From Charing Cross: walk southwest on The Mall. From Piccadilly: walk south on Regent St., turn right on The Mall. Admission for exhibits: £1.50, £1 students. Gallery open daily noon–9; bookshop open Mon.–Sat. noon–10, Sun. noon–9.*

Jewish Museum. This collection of art and artifacts illustrates Jewish rituals and culture, and the history of Jews in Britain. The offerings, many of them precious antiques, include manuscripts, embroidery, silver, and ceremonial dress. Displays tell stories of the persecution of Jews around the world and throughout history. The museum will be moving to Camden sometime in the near future; call for the latest details. *Woburn House, on Tavistock Sq., tel. 0171/388–4525. Tube: Russell Sq. Turn left out of station, a right on Woburn Pl., and walk about 250 yards. Admission: £2.50. Open Sun.–Thurs. 10–4. Closed national and Jewish holidays.*

London Museum of Jewish Life. London's East End was the gateway for most Jewish immigrants arriving in Britain over the centuries, but a larger Jewish community now exists here in Golders Green. This museum display photographs, storyboards, and historical artifacts tracing the immigration, settlement, and lifestyles of local Jews, including reconstructions of an early immigrant home and a garment workshop. They also feature interesting temporary exhibits as well as guided walks through Jewish London. The museum is temporarily closing in the near future for renovations; call for details. *80 East End Rd., in Sternberg Centre, tel. 0181/349–1143. Tube: Finchley Central. Walk west on Regent's Park Rd., turn left on East End Rd. Admission free. Open Mon.–Thurs. 10:30–5, Sun. 10:30–4:30.*

London Toy and Model Museum. Dolls, old rickety toys, and teddy bears provide an historical glimpse at childhood playtime. The antique model fairgrounds, roller coaster, merry-go-round, and mini steam train are also pretty cool; on Sundays, kids only can take rides for real. *21 Craven Hill, tel. 0181/964–8010. Tube: Lancaster Gate. Follow signs from station. Admission: £3. Open Tues.–Sat. 10–5:30, Sun. 11–5.*

London Transport Museum. Located south of Covent Garden tube, the London Transport Museum tells you everything you ever wanted to know about the technological and social history of mass transportation in London—and then some. It's actually interesting for studying mass transportation's impact on both the growth of London and class stratification within it. *39 Wellington St., entrance on Henrietta St., tel. 0171/379–6344. Tube: Covent Garden or Leicester Sq. Admission: £3.95, £2.50 students. Open daily 10–6, last admission 5:15.*

Museum of Garden History. A peaceful little spot of green hidden away from the smoggy, concrete world. The gardens were built to honor Charles I's royal gardeners, who are buried here. All sorts of specialty flora are featured; check out the replica of a 17th-century garden, containing only period plants, in the church courtyard. *St. Mary-at-Lambeth Church, Lambeth Palace Rd., tel. 0171/261–1891. Tube: Westminster. Cross east over Westminster Bridge, walk 2 blocks on Westminster Bridge Rd., turn right on Lambeth Palace Rd. Admission free. Open Mar.–Nov., weekdays 11–3, Sun. 10:30–5.*

Museum of London. Come to this City museum for an extremely thorough look at the history of the city, from the early Stone Age to the present day. A lot of the older material on display was found in the Thames or at modern building sites. The ticket is good for three months, so you can send an unlimited number of cronies in one at a time. *London Wall, tel. 0171/600–3699. Tube: St. Paul's. Walk north on St. Martin's-Le-Grand. Admission: £3, £1.50 students. Open Tues.–Sat. 10–5:50, Sun. noon–5:50.*

Museum of Mankind. Otherwise known as "The Ethnography Department of the British Museum," the Museum of Mankind is housed in a building about 2 miles from the British Museum. The museum specializes in non-Western cultures, particularly the indigenous people of Africa, Australia, the Pacific Islands, North and South America, Asia, and certain areas of Europe. At any given moment there will be one or two feature exhibitions and constantly rotating selections from their massive collection in storage. *6 Burlington Gardens, tel. 0171/437–2224. Tube: Piccadilly Circus. Walk northwest 1 long block on Regent St., turn left on Vigo St. (which becomes Burlington Gardens). Admission free. Open Mon.–Sat. 10–5, Sun. 2:30–6.*

Museum of the Moving Image (MOMI). An impressive television and film museum that traces the history of man's manipulation of light and shadow. Tons of interactive exhibits—plus snippets from groundbreaking flicks—make this a definitively cool museum. Watch yourself fly like the Man of Steel, be a network anchor for one minute, or play "Name That Commercial." A fine place to fry. Mildly embarrassing actors employed by the museum float around, trying to add period flavor. *South Bank Arts Centre, tel. 0171/928–3535 or 0171/410–2636 for recorded info. Tube: Waterloo. Admission: £5.50, £4.70 students. Open daily 10–6.*

National Army Museum. An admirably nondidactic presentation on the life of British soldiers from the Tudor period to the present day, told with videos, models, reconstructions, and mementos. One of the highlights is a huge model—with more than 70,000 toy soldiers—of the Battle of Waterloo. *Royal Hospital Rd., tel. 0171/730–0717. Tube: Sloane Sq. Walk southwest on King's Rd., turn left on Smith St. and continue 6 blocks to Royal Hospital Rd. Admission free. Open daily 10–5:30.*

National Postal Museum. Even if you've never collected stamps, stop by this philatelic extravaganza—it's one of the most important collections of postage stamps in the world. Although it's a medium you have to squint at to see in detail, much of the artwork is absolutely exquisite. Historical exhibits show that transporting mail is an amazing endeavor, actually. *King Edward St., London Chief Post Office, tel. 0171/239–5420. Tube: St. Paul's. Walk west on Newgate St., turn right on King Edward St. Admission free. Open weekdays 9:30–4:30.*

Photographer's Gallery. This is the leading locale in London for contemporary British and international photography. Exhibitions change regularly, and symposia on various topics of photography are occasionally held. Check out the cool shop and print room. *5 Great Newport St., tel. 0171/831–1772. Tube: Leicester Sq. Walk north 50 yards on Charing Cross Rd. and turn right. Open Tues.–Sat. 11–7.*

Royal Academy of Arts. As the oldest institution in London devoted to the fine arts, the Royal Academy stages a number of rotating exhibitions throughout the year. These are typically retrospectives of deceased masters supplemented by an annual Summer Exhibition that's open to any contemporary artist—though of the 14,000 works submitted each year, only 1,300 are selected. The Academy's postgraduate students show off their final exam projects to the public in January. *Burlington House, tel. 0171/439–7438 or 0171/439–4996 for recorded info. Tube: Piccadilly Circus. Walk 300 yards west on Piccadilly. Admission: £5, £3.50 students. Open daily 10–6.*

Saatchi Collection. The megabucks of madman Charles Saatchi fuel this gallery, one of the most coveted venues in the land for young artists (as one of the most influential private collectors, Saatchi has made the careers of a number of young artists). *98A Boundary Rd., tel. 0171/624–8299. Tube: Swiss Cottage. Walk ⅓ mi south on Finchley Rd., turn right on Boundary Rd. Admission: £2, free on Fri. Open Fri.–Sun. noon–6.*

Sir John Soane's Museum. This ex-abode of one of Britain's greatest architects is full of antiquities, gargoyle heads, pediments, and a plethora of other chunks o' buildings. A series of oil paintings, including Hogarth's *The Rake's Progress,* is mounted on a special wall that the museum warden opens occasionally to reveal another wall, hung with dozens of prints of classical ruins. Don't miss the creamy stained glass and tall, narrow ceiling of the Monk's Room. *13 Lincoln's Inn Fields, tel. 0171/405–2107. Tube: Holborn. Walk south on Kingsway, turn left on Remnant St. Admission free. Open Tues.–Sat. 10–5.*

Theater Museum. With fascinating goodies galore, the Theatre Museum illustrates life on the British stage from Shakespeare's time through the present. On exhibit are theatrical memorabilia of every kind, including prints and paintings of the earliest London theaters, early scripts, costumes, and props. It's not all high-brow drama stuff, either—the galleries include art and artifacts of the circus, modern musicals, puppetry, and even rock music (Mick Jagger's jumpsuit always draws a small crowd). *1E Tavistock St., 1 block south of Covent Garden, tel. 0171/836–7891. Tube: Covent Garden. Admission: £3, £1.50 students. Open Tues.–Sun. 11–7.*

Whitechapel Gallery. Cheap rent and big spaces have attracted more than 6,000 artists to East London, making it one of the largest artist colonies in Europe. This large, well-designed venue with lots of natural light is where many major contemporary exhibitions take place in the East End. They have a great lineup of art talks and other special events, even "touch tours" for visually impaired visitors. The café here is trendy (no-smoking, even) and serves a mean cup of vegetarian soup. *80 Whitechapel High St., tel. 0171/377–5015 or 0171/377–0107 for recorded info. Tube: Aldgate East. Walk west on Whitechapel High St. Admission free. Open Tues. and Thurs.–Sun. 11–5, Wed. 11–8.*

Cheap Thrills

Although London is an expensive city, you can find tons of ways to get the most out of the metropolis for a few quid or less. One of the more pleasant ways is to spend a day in one of London's many parks and squares. Picnicking, reading, zoning out, copping some z's, basking in the sun, and, of course, people-watching are only some of the activities you can pursue at Hyde Park, Kensington Gardens, St. James's Park, Green Park, Holland Park, Hampstead Heath, and Regent's Park—to name just a few. The farther afield you get, the less cultivated and less crowded the parks become.

One of the great London freebies is late-night people-watching in the West End, particularly on Trafalgar Square, Leicester Square, and Piccadilly Circus. Tourists, late-night clubbers, prophets of the coming apocalypse, and red-nosed juiceheads stumble past one another under the bright lights and glowing neon.

If you're looking for a good rambling walk, a path runs from the southeastern corner of St. James's Park (Tube: Westminster) through Green Park, Hyde Park (pass through the pedestrian subway at Hyde Park Corner), to the northwestern corner of Kensington Gardens; this 3-mile trail traverses the very heart of the city. Another long, pleasant walk is the 8-mile path along **Regent's Canal.** A particularly pleasant stretch runs from just south of Warwick Avenue tube along the northern edge of Regent's Park to Camden Lock.

The Thames affords the poverty-stricken traveler a number of opportunities for low-budget fun. The best place for a walk along the river is the South Bank. A path runs from Southwark Bridge (opposite St. Paul's) all the way to Lambeth Bridge (south of Whitehall). It's far from the noise and fumes of the city streets, and affords brilliant views of the skyline from St. Paul's to the Houses of Parliament. At dusk, stick around for the great sunsets; you can mull over life's little joys and tragedies as you watch the sky slowly turn a pale magenta.

Many of the Thames's bridges have a special appeal that you can experience for free. The twin gothic pylons of **Tower Bridge** make the structure one of the most widely recognized in the world; if you forgo going upstairs to the gangways, it's free, too. **Waterloo Bridge** was immortalized by the Kinks song "Waterloo Sunset," and as Ray Davies once said, "Waterloo sunset's fine." **Westminster Bridge,** farthest west and south on this cheapskate's tour of the Thames, is where noted Gallic paint-slinger Monet painted all of those scenes of Parliament and Big Ben.

Along the Thames, just in front of the National Theatre (walk south over Waterloo Bridge from Embankment tube or north from Waterloo Station), you can hang out on what, at low tide, might qualify as a little beach. A broad stone stairway makes access easy, plus you get a great view of St. Paul's dome. If the sand is dry enough, you could probably lie down, ignoring the fact that the fetid Thames water washes over this very sand most of the day.

Another boon for the poor in London is the large number of street performers. Prime locales to see buskers (as they're called in Britain) include Leicester Square, the West Plaza in Covent Garden, Carnaby Street in Soho, the Church of St. Martin-in-the-Fields Market, and, of course, the tube, particularly at West End stops.

WHERE TO SLEEP   3

By Rashmi Sadana

London entirely deserves its reputation as an expensive city, and lodging is no exception. During the off-season, your best bet is a dorm bed in a hotel or bed-and-breakfast (B&B) for £45–£60 per week. In summer, most places stop offering a weekly rate and charge a straight £14–£18 per night for a dorm bed—like we said, London lodging ain't cheap. The only true bargains are the city's three campgrounds (*see* Campgrounds, *below*), where hard-core penny pinchers can camp for £4–£5 nightly in London's outskirts, 30–45 minutes by bus or tube from the central sights.

Don't be afraid to haggle for reduced rates on multinight stays; you shouldn't be forced to pay the daily rate if you're crashing somewhere for a week or more.

Budget B&Bs in London are likely to fall significantly short of your expectations: Rather than fresh flowers and plump matrons stuffing you with scones and cream, budget B&Bs are often about chintz, damp rooms, and breakfasts of rolls and tea (and maybe cornflakes and an egg if you're lucky). Further, finding a double room in a B&B for less than £35 a night will be a coup; your best bet is to look around **Bloomsbury,** particularly Russell Square, Montague Street, and Bedford Place, or in the suburbs of north London. Another prime B&B area is **Notting Hill Gate,** especially Pembridge Gardens (just north of the Notting Hill Gate tube station).

If you arrive without motivation or reservations, consider letting yourself be collared by one of the lodging hustlers in Victoria Station—provided they're quoting you a single room for less than £15 per night. Many of these lodging vultures offer free van service from the station to local hotels, which can be a boon if you have yet to figure out London's complicated Underground system (or if you're just feeling tired and lazy). Of course, you should not pay for *anything* without seeing your room first, and do not accept a ride with anyone who gives you the creeps. For women traveling solo, it's best to avoid the hustlers in Victoria Station altogether.

If you're not in the mood to haggle with a wily hotelier (or a hotelier's commission-hungry minion), head to Victoria Station's helpful **Tourist Information Centre Accommodations Service** (26 Grosvenor Gardens), located at the north end of this rather hectic terminal (look up and follow the signs). Though the staff caters to tourists rather than to mangy backpackers, for a £5 fee, they book beds in the £15–£25 range. If you've just arrived at Heathrow Airport, look for the Accommodations Service desk in the tube station that serves Terminals 1, 2, and 3. If you're Type-A and need to make a reservation before arriving in the United Kingdom, get out your MasterCard or Visa and dial the center's staff at 0171/824–8844; they accept over-the-phone bookings weekdays 9:30–5:30. The center also sells the handy *Where to Stay: London*

(£3.50), which lists hundreds of B&Bs and hotels throughout the city. Buy it in person at any of the center's offices or order it over the phone at 0171/824–8844 or 0171/730–3488.

For somewhat longer stays (a few weeks to a few months), head over to the **University of London Accommodation Office**, in the monstrous Senate House building near Russell Square in Bloomsbury. From June to the end of September their "Vacation Letting Service" lists rooms in family homes and flats ranging from £25–£65 per week. To use this service, you must be able to prove that you're a student or that you're affiliated in some way with any university or learning institution worldwide. *Malet St., tel. 0171/636–2818. Tube: Euston Sq. Walk south on Gower St., turn left on Torrington Pl., take first right onto Malet St. Open weekdays 9:30–5:30; also Sept., Sat. 9:30–2.*

A Continental breakfast is tea or coffee, orange juice (if you're lucky), rolls or toast, and jam and butter. An English breakfast includes the above as well as bacon, eggs, and cereal— although different places may have their own interpretations. One warning: Beware of blood pudding, fried toast, and soggy stewed tomatoes.

Renting a flat may be a good idea for exchange students and those whose week-long visit becomes a year-long commitment—although you'll be hard-pressed to find a landlord who doesn't ask for last month's rent and a security deposit, which can be hell to get back if you vacate your flat early. Be ready to part with bushels of cash before you move in. For more info and tips on how to find a place, *see* Longer Stays, *below*.

Hotels and B&Bs

BAYSWATER AND NOTTING HILL GATE

Bars and cheap eateries on **Bayswater Road** cater to the budget and middlebrow travelers who pack the neighborhoods' innumerable hotels. **Queensway**, perpendicular to Notting Hill Gate and Bayswater, is a party-hearty tourist strip lined with pubs that blare "You Shook Me All Night Long" and other sing-along favorites. If you're looking for a more sedate environment, **Kensington Gardens** and **Hyde Park** are just across Bayswater Road.

➤ **UNDER £40** • **Abbey Court/West Point Hotel.** A pleasant hotel on a quiet stretch in the otherwise hectic Bayswater area. The rooms are very neat and clean, and a Continental breakfast is included in the prices. For £2 more you can get a full-blown English breakfast. Singles £22, doubles £34, triples £57. In winter the rates drop by about 30%. *174 Sussex Gardens, W2, tel. 0171/402–0704, fax 0171/224–9114. Tube: Paddington. Walk north on Praed St., turn right on Sussex St., left on Sussex Gardens. 26 rooms, some with bath. AE, MC, V.*

Glynne Court Hotel. The Glynne Court is actually in the Marble Arch area adjacent to Bayswater, right off Oxford Street (London's main shopping drag). For late-night runs to Virgin Records, this is the place to stay. Although it's not the Ritz, the rooms are clean and offered to students at a 15% discount. Singles £30, doubles £40, triples £50. *41 Great Cumberland Pl., W1, tel. 0171/262–4344, fax 0171/724–2071. Tube: Marble Arch. 12 rooms, none with bath. Small charge for AE, MC, V.*

Hyde Park House. The Hyde is one of the nicer hotels in the area, close to the Bayswater and Queensway tube stations and a short walk from leafy Hyde Park. It's on a side street, so noise is not a real problem. Simple singles £20, doubles £30. Both prices include a Continental breakfast. *48 St. Petersburgh Pl., W2, tel. 0171/229–9652 or 0171/229–1687. Tube: Bayswater or Queensway. 14 rooms, some with bath.*

Lords Hotel. Rooms here are basic and a bit shabby, although some have wide windows and balconies (definitely ask for one). Singles start at £24, doubles at £35, triples at £46, all with Continental breakfast. *20–22 Leinster Sq., W2, tel. 0171/229–8877, fax 0171/229–8377. Tube: Bayswater. Walk north on Queensway, turn left on Moscow Rd., right on Chester Gardens. AE, MC, V.*

St. David's/Norfolk Court Hotels. The Regency-style Norfolk Court joined the neighboring St. David's hotel a few years ago; the result is a simple, comfortable art deco–style guest house. Some second-floor rooms have French windows and balconies that overlook the square. Singles £25, doubles £36. A full English breakfast is included. *20 Norfolk Sq., W2 1RS, tel. 0171/723–4963, fax 0171/402–9061. Tube: Paddington. 28 rooms, some with bath. AE, MC, V.*

➢ **UNDER £50** • **The Gate Hotel.** This tiny B&B at the top of Portobello Road is friendly and clean, with reasonably sized rooms furnished with conveniences like refrigerators, TVs, and phones. Singles £33, doubles from £44. *6 Portobello Rd., W11 3DG, tel. 0171/221–2403, fax 0171/221–9128. Tube: Notting Hill Gate. 8 rooms, 5 with bath or shower. Small charge for AE, MC, V.*

➢ **UNDER £60** • **Vicarage.** Run by the same family for nearly 30 years, the Vicarage feels like a real home. It's beautifully decorated, quiet, and overlooks a garden square near Kensington's main shopping streets. Expect to pay about £32 for a single and £54 for a double. Both rates include a full English breakfast. *10 Vicarage Gate, W8 4AG, tel. 0171/229–4030. Tube: Kensington High St. From station, go right on Kensington High St., left on Kensington Church St., and veer left at fork onto Vicarage Gate. 10 rooms, none with bath.*

BLOOMSBURY

This neighborhood just north of Soho was the stomping grounds of the Bloomsbury Group, the famed literary clique that included Virginia Woolf, her husband Leonard, E. M. Forster, Lytton Strachey, and John Maynard Keynes. Today the area has many private hostels and semi-expensive B&Bs. The British Museum, the University of London—which has many colleges dispersed throughout the area, each with its own friendly pub—and a number of excellent bookstores contribute to Bloomsbury's quiet, academic atmosphere.

If you're new to London and trying to decide where to stay, you could do a lot worse than peaceful Bloomsbury.

➢ **UNDER £40** • **Langland Hotel.** To avoid street noise, ask for a room at the back of this yellow-brick hotel. Besides its location near the British Museum, the Langland is run-of-the-mill—nothing more, nothing less. If you opt for the dainty Continental breakfast instead of the whopping English breakfast, you'll save yourself a fiver or so. Singles £25, doubles £40, and triples and quads £16.50 per person. *29–31 Gower St., WC1E 6HG, tel. 0171/636–5801, fax 0171/580–2227. Tube: Goodge St. Walk north on Tottenham Court Rd., turn right on Chenies St., left on Gower St. 27 rooms, some with bath. AE, MC, V.*

Maree Hotel. This family-run hotel is near the British Museum and, like the nearby Langland Hotel, is more clean and modern than fancy. It's also reasonably priced: singles £24, doubles £32, triples £40, quads £48. During the off-season subtract £3–£4 from the prices. If you're lucky, your room will overlook the rose garden out back. *25–27 Gower St., WC1E 6HG, tel. 0171/636–4868. Tube: Goodge St. Walk north on Tottenham Court Rd., turn right on Chenies St., left on Gower St. 31 rooms, none with bath.*

Repton Hotel. The Repton is on a breezy road between Bloomsbury and Russell squares, with small but well-equipped rooms—note the TVs, phones, and tea/coffee-making facilities. If you want the Georgian terrace experience in central London, this is your best and cheapest bet. It's small, so be sure to call ahead. Singles £30, doubles £40, and dorm £12 per person. All rates include a Continental breakfast. *31 Bedford Pl., WC1B 5JH, tel. 0171/436–4922. Tube: Russell Sq. Walk south on Herbrand St., quick right on Guilford St., left on Southampton Row, right onto Russell Sq., left on Bedford Pl. 28 rooms, some with bath. MC, V.*

Ridgemount. The kindly owners, Mr. and Mrs. Rees, make you feel at home, and the public areas—especially the family-style breakfast room—have a friendly, cluttered Victorian feel. Ask for a room that overlooks the leafy garden. Singles £25, doubles from £36. Both include a full English breakfast. *65 Gower St., WC1E 6HG, tel. 0171/636–1141. Tube: Goodge St. Walk north on Tottenham Court Rd., turn right on Chenies St., left on Gower St. 15 rooms, none with bath.*

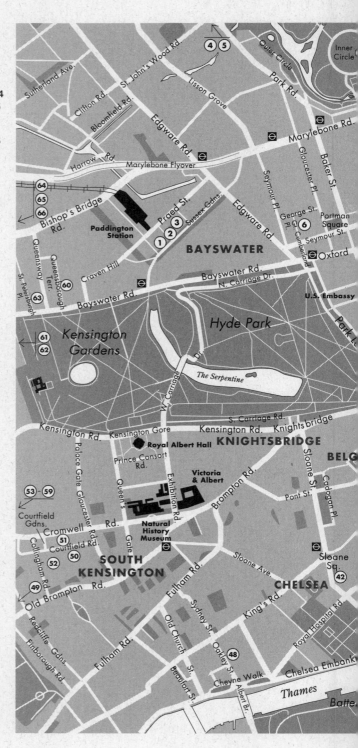

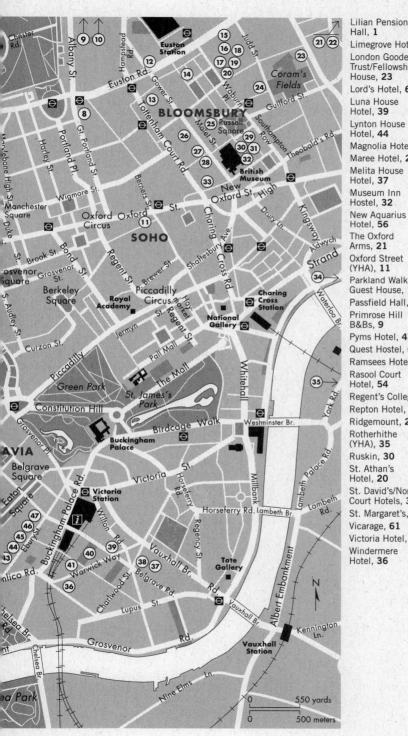

Lilian Pension
Hall, **1**

Limegrove Hotel, **41**

London Goodenough
Trust/Fellowship
House, **23**

Lord's Hotel, **65**

Luna House
Hotel, **39**

Lynton House
Hotel, **44**

Magnolia Hotel, **48**

Maree Hotel, **28**

Melita House
Hotel, **37**

Museum Inn
Hostel, **32**

New Aquarius
Hotel, **56**

The Oxford
Arms, **21**

Oxford Street
(YHA), **11**

Parkland Walk
Guest House, **10**

Passfield Hall, **13**

Primrose Hill
B&Bs, **9**

Pyms Hotel, **43**

Quest Hostel, **60**

Ramsees Hotel, **59**

Rasool Court
Hotel, **54**

Regent's College, **7**

Repton Hotel, **29**

Ridgemount, **26**

Rotherhithe
(YHA), **35**

Ruskin, **30**

St. Athan's
Hotel, **20**

St. David's/Norfolk
Court Hotels, **3**

St. Margaret's, **31**

Vicarage, **61**

Victoria Hotel, **38**

Windermere
Hotel, **36**

St. Athan's Hotel. This simple but charming Edwardian guest house isn't far from Russell Square. Read the newspaper in the comfy TV lounge or grab your umbrella and take a long walk around the smart-looking square. Singles £30, doubles £40; both include a full English breakfast. *20 Tavistock Pl., WC1, tel. 0171/837–9140 or 0171/837–9627, fax 0171/833–8352. Tube: Russell Sq. Cross street and head up Woburn Pl. or Herbrand St. to Tavistock Pl. 51 rooms, some with bath. AE, MC, V.*

➢ **UNDER £50 • Ruskin.** Opposite the British Museum, this family-owned hotel is pleasant and quiet—mostly thanks to double-glazed windows. The rooms are clean, albeit a bit boring; try to get one overlooking the back garden. Singles £34, doubles £49. Both include an English breakfast. *23–24 Montague St., WC1B 5BN, tel. 0171/636–7388, fax 0171/323–1662. Tube: Russell Sq. Walk south on Herbrand St., turn right on Guilford St., cross Russell Sq., left on Montague St. 35 rooms, some with shower. AE, MC, V.*

St. Margaret's. Set on a tree-lined Georgian street, this hotel has been run by a friendly Italian family for years. Its spacious rooms, towering ceilings, and prime location by Russell Square are the main draws. The back rooms have pleasant garden views. Singles £36.50, doubles £48.50 and up. *24 Bedford Pl., WC1B 5JL, tel. 0171/636–4277, fax 0171/323–3066. Tube: Russell Sq. Walk south on Herbrand St., quick right on Guilford St., left on Southampton Row, right onto Russell Sq., left on Bedford Pl. 64 rooms, some with bath.*

➢ **UNDER £65 • Central Club Hotel.** After recent renovations, this centrally located hotel—it's a very short walk to theaters, shops, and the British Museum—gave up its YMCA affiliation and jacked up its rates. You can still get a decent deal on three- and four-bed rooms, but you now must pay for the old Y's amenities—principally the adjacent gym (though guests do have free access to the large swimming pool). The rooms are clean, if basic; more appealing are the on-site coffee shop, self-service laundry, and hairdresser. Singles £33, doubles £60, triples and quads £18 per person. *16–22 Great Russell St., WC1B 3LR, tel. 0171/636–7512, fax 0171/636–5278. Tube: Tottenham Court Rd. Walk 1 block north on Tottenham Court Rd., turn right on Great Russell St. 104 rooms, none with bath. MC, V.*

Harlingford Hotel. You could get lost forever in the Harlingford's maze of stairwells and twisting corridors, pieced together from three Georgian-era buildings. The rooms aren't much to look at, but who cares when you can sack out on a comfy bed and watch cricket on BBC 2. Singles £49, doubles £62, triples £69. All rates include a full English breakfast. Reservations are essential in summer. *61–63 Cartwright Gardens, WC1H 9EL, tel. 0171/387–1551, fax 0171/387–4616. Tube: Russell Sq. Walk north on Herbrand St., turn right on Bernard St., first left on Marchmont St. (it becomes Cartwright Gardens). 44 rooms, most with shower.*

EARL'S COURT AND SOUTH KENSINGTON

Earl's Court and neighboring South Kensington have the highest concentration of inexpensive lodgings in London. While many are skanky, to be sure, there are some tolerable options amid all the dives. An hour's worth of comparison shopping here will save you plenty of moolah: Take the Underground to Earl's Court station (in the west) or Gloucester Road (in the east) and start scouting around. One warning: If you stay in either neighborhood, you'll feel like a real tourist and are sure to run into sweatshirt-clad compatriots by the dozen. The best explanation for this is that many of London's principal museums are in South Kensington, including the Victoria and Albert, the Natural History Museum, and London's Science Museum.

➢ **UNDER £30 • Green Court Hotel.** This place is a bit more polished than the rest of the options on Hogarth Road, though the rooms are still a bit drab. Singles £24, doubles £28. A Continental breakfast is included. *52 Hogarth Rd., SW5, tel. 0171/370–0853, fax 0171/370–3998. Tube: Earl's Court. Cross main road and take first right. 23 rooms, some with bath. AE, MC, V.*

Hunters Lodge Hotel. Hunters Lodge feels more like a low-key hostel, minus the grime and ugly decor. There's absolutely nothing fancy about this place, but the bathrooms are clean and the staff is friendly. Better still (depending on your tastes), the rates include a very full English breakfast. No-frills singles cost £20, doubles £28, triples £36. *38 Trebovir Rd., SW5, tel.*

0171/373–7331. Tube: Earl's Court. From station, go left and left again onto Trebovir Rd. 20 rooms, none with bath. AE, MC, V.

Kingsway Hotel House. Doubles are a bargain at £25 daily or £120 weekly, but this place is as dead as a doornail—you certainly won't find any budget travelers about. Singles are £20 daily, £85 weekly. Knock off £5 from the rates if you book in advance. *11 Eardley Crescent, SW5, tel. 0171/373–6847. Tube: Earl's Court. Exit station on Warwick Rd. and walk south, turn right on Eardley Crescent. 40 beds.*

Ramsees Hotel. The Ramsees is a real bargain by London standards, and it's just a few minutes' walk from the tube. Each room is simple but well-equipped with showers and TVs. Singles £15, doubles £25. *32–36 Hogarth Rd., SW5, tel. 0171/370–1445, fax 0171/ 244–6835. Tube: Earl's Court. Cross main road and take first right. 60 rooms, all with bath. AE, MC, V.*

➢ **UNDER £40** • **Magnolia Hotel.** While this rustic guest house has small, comfortable rooms, the best reason to stay is the neighborhood: It's near the once-hippie, once-punk, now-trendy King's Road, and it's only a short trek from the tube. Singles start at £22, doubles at £35. *104–105 Oakley St., SW3, tel. 0171/352–0187 or 0171/352–3610, fax 0171/352–0187. Tube: South Kensington or Sloane Sq. From South Kensington: walk south on Onslow Sq., turn right on Fulham Rd., left on Dovehouse St., right on King's Rd., quick left on Oakley St. From Sloane Sq.: walk southwest on King's Rd., turn left on Oakley St. 20 rooms, some with bath. AE, MC, V.*

New Aquarius Hotel. Don't expect the disinterested staff at the convenient but basic New Aquarius to read your horoscope, or much else. More inviting are the rooms themselves, most with TVs and airy bay windows. Singles £20–£25, doubles £35–£40. *20–22 Hogarth Rd., SW5, tel. 0171/373–6155 or 0171/370–6582, fax 0171/373–5182. Tube: Earl's Court. Cross main road and take first right. 36 rooms, most with bath. AE, MC, V.*

Rasool Court Hotel. If your idea of street theater is watching an occasional drug bust, consider one of the mildly sleazy hotels near the tube station on Penywern Road. If you're undeterred, this hotel is the best of the lot. Singles start at £20, doubles at £30, and the rates include a Continental breakfast. Don't be afraid to haggle, especially during the off-season. *19–21 Penywern Rd., SW5, tel. 0171/373–8900 or 0171/373–4893, fax 0171/244–6835. Tube: Earl's Court. From station, turn right and take second right. 57 rooms, some with bath. AE, MC, V.*

➢ **UNDER £60** • **Annandale House Hotel.** If you're thinking about splurging, this is the place to do it. The Morris family's stylish, cozy B&B oozes character and is on a Georgian villa-lined road just off posh Sloane Square. The high-ceilinged rooms all come with telephones, TVs, and radios. It's just a two-minute walk from the tube and is easy to reach by bus. Oh, and the breakfasts are outta this world. Singles £35, doubles £50–£75. *39 Sloane Gardens, SW1, tel. 0171/730–6291. Tube: Sloane Sq. 13 rooms, most with bath. Reservations advised. MC, V.*

NORTH LONDON

If you want a taste of bohemian suburbia (i.e., nice neighborhoods with cool cafés) or a homier and less-touristy atmosphere than Earl's Court or Bayswater, try the neighborhoods north of central London, which roughly encompass the massive expanse of trees, ponds, and rolling hills known as the Heath. You may have to sit on the tube an extra few stops or even catch a bus to central London, but that's the price you pay for a quieter, more residential, less stressful experience. Hotel rates are about the same in north London as in most other areas, but you're more likely to get what you pay for here.

If you want a taste of English country-style living while still being near central London, definitely contact **Primrose Hill**. This small B&B association believes that "travel shouldn't be a rip-off"; to prove it, they books guests into beautiful family homes at reasonable rates—£17–£24 per person in single or double rooms. All houses are in or around leafy Primrose Hill and Hampstead, where you'll find London's best parks. Expect cozy rooms, your own latchkey, and scrumptious breakfasts. Book ahead to be safe. *Contact Gail O'Farrell, 14 Edis St., Hampstead, NW1 8LG, tel. 0171/722–6869, fax 0171/916–2240. 15 rooms in various locations.*

➢ **UNDER £40 • Five Kings Guest House.** Although the surrounding neighborhood is quintessentially residential, you're only 15 minutes by foot from both Camden and the Heath. The friendly proprietors run a tight ship—nothing fancy, but very inviting. Singles £18, doubles £32, both with an English breakfast. *59 Anson Rd., Kentish Town, N7, tel. 0171/607–3996 or 0171/607–6466. Tube: Tufnell Park. Walk 3 blocks south on Brecknock Rd., turn left on Anson Rd. 16 rooms, most with bath. MC, V.*

Kandara Guest House. The main reason to stay here is location—smack-dab in the middle of lively Islington, home to good eats, film houses, cafés, and pubs. The guest house is small and basic, with comfy singles (£23) and doubles (£32). An English breakfast is included. *68 Ockendon Rd., Islington, N1, tel. 0171/226–5721 or 0171/226–3379. Tube: Highbury and Islington. Off Essex Rd. 8 rooms, none with bath.*

The Oxford Arms. This traditional pub and inn is the place to stay if you want a neighborhood atmosphere and easy access to local brew. Although it's not the most central address, you're only a five-minute walk from the main road and its frequent double-decker buses. The Oxford's five double rooms are equipped with showers and toilets. The £36 rate includes a decent English breakfast. *21 Halliford St., N1, tel. 0171/226–6629. Tube: Tottenham Court Rd. From station, take Bus 73 to Halliford St. 5 rooms, all with bath.*

➢ **UNDER £50 • Parkland Walk Guest House.** An ideal escape for people who prefer English country living to life in the hectic city. The luxurious Parkland Walk is near Crouch End, which recently made headlines when Bob Dylan almost bought a house here. Modern renovations haven't sanitized the style and character of the Parkland, nor have they obstructed the great views of London. The fresh, delicious food is yet another reason to come. Singles £25, doubles £45 (a bit less if you stay more than two nights). *12 Hornsey Rise Gardens, N19 3PR, tel. 0171/263–3228 or 0171/404–5011, fax 0171/831–9489. Tube: Archway or Finsbury Park. From Archway: take Bus 41 to Crouch End. From Finsbury Park: take Bus 210 to Crouch End. 4 rooms, none with bath. No smoking, reservations advised.*

VICTORIA

Victoria has a billion cheapish hotels, all of which make their living off Victoria Station, an all-in-one BritRail terminal, bus depot, and tube station. The farther from the station you go, the cheaper rooms become. And remember that, because competition for customers is stiff, B&B owners are always ready to cut a deal, especially during the off-season and/or if you agree to stay more than a few nights. A good strategy is to walk down **Belgrave Road,** take a side street such as **Warwick Way,** offer everybody £10 less than they're asking, and see who makes the best counteroffer.

➢ **UNDER £40 • Limegrove Hotel.** Though small and slightly decrepit, the Limegrove compensates with an accommodating staff and a full-blown English breakfast that's served in your room each morning. Singles £22, doubles £32. *101 Warwick Way, SW1, tel. 0171/828–0458. Tube: Victoria. 15 rooms, some with bath.*

Luna House Hotel. Of the many hotels on Belgrave Road, this one is less grotty and more friendly than most. Don't hesitate to barter, especially during the off-season. Singles start at £18, doubles at £30. An English breakfast is included. *47 Belgrave Rd., SW1, tel. 0171/834–5897, fax 0171/828–2474. Tube: Victoria. 17 rooms, some with bath.*

Lynton House, a five-minute walk from Victoria Station, is by far the best of the bunch on hotel-ridden Ebury Street.

Lynton House Hotel. The cozy Lynton—which has been run by the friendly Bateys for the last 30 years—has comfortable rooms equipped with TVs and washbasins and a small common terrace. You may even find a few disheveled backpackers hanging about. Singles £25, doubles from £35. If you're traveling in a group of four or more, consider booking one of their homey self-contained flats (£110 per night). *113 Ebury St.,*

SW1 92U, tel. 0171/730–4032. Tube: Victoria. Cross Buckingham Palace Rd., go west on Eccleston St., left on Ebury St. 14 rooms, some with bath.

Melita House Hotel. This comfortable, family-run hotel is on a quiet street near Victoria station. The furniture's strictly garage sale, but the small rooms are clean. Couch potatoes will appreciate the TVs in each room. Singles start at £24, doubles at £36. An English breakfast is included. *33–35 Charlwood St., SW1V 2DU, tel. 0171/828–0471, fax 0171/932–0988. Tube: Victoria. Walk east on Belgrave Rd., turn right on Charlwood St. 18 rooms, some with shower. AE, MC, V.*

➤ **UNDER £50** • **Chesham House Hotel.** This unassuming B&B is hidden on a row of terrace houses near Victoria Station. The rates are reasonable for the area, and you're only a short walk from the Underground. Singles are £30, doubles are £45, and a double with a shower is £58. All rates include a full English breakfast. *64–66 Ebury St., SW1 W9Q, tel. 0171/730–8513, fax 0171/730–1845. Tube: Victoria. Cross Buckingham Palace Rd., go west on Eccleston St., turn left on Ebury St. 23 rooms, none with bath. AE, MC, V.*

Collin House. Don't come if your idea of a good time is an all-night party where you end up trashing the furniture—the proud, friendly owners of this mid-Victorian B&B would die of grief. Come instead for the spotless rooms, each with a sink and a cushy divan bed, and for the great location between Sloane Square and Victoria Station. Singles with bath cost £34, doubles £48, and a double with a shower is £56. *104 Ebury St., SW1W 9QD, tel. and fax 0171/730–8031. Tube: Victoria. Cross Buckingham Palace Rd., go west on Eccleston St., turn left on Ebury St. 13 rooms, most with bath.*

Ebury House. This is definitely a place where you can relax and make yourself at home (the wood-paneled breakfast room is a great place for a chat). If you'd enjoy an animated conversation with owner David Davies, tell him that England will never beat the Springboks at rugby again. All rooms have TVs and sinks. Singles £35–£40, doubles £45–£50. *102 Ebury St., SW1W 9QD, tel. and fax 0171/730–1350. Tube: Victoria. Cross Buckingham Palace Rd., go west on Eccleston St., left on Ebury St. 13 rooms, none with bath. AE, MC, V.*

Rumor has it that a housekeeper at Ebury House plied one guest with so much breakfast, he exploded. Hmmm.

➤ **UNDER £60** • **Elizabeth Hotel.** This award-winning hotel sits on a quiet, 19th-century square right next to Victoria Station, but it offers little in the way of facilities. On the plus side, some rooms have pleasant views—be sure to ask for one. The ultimate plus: a knockout English breakfast. Singles £38, doubles £55. *37 Eccleston Sq., SW1V 1PB, tel. 0171/828–6812, fax 0171/828–6814. Tube: Victoria. Walk 2 blocks east on Belgrave Rd., turn right on Eccleston Sq. 25 rooms, some with bath.*

Pyms Hotel. This friendly B&B between Sloane Square and Victoria Station is noted for its cleanliness—whatever you do, don't tramp on the white carpet with dirty Doc Martens. A full English breakfast is included in the rates: singles £45, doubles £55. *118 Ebury St., SW1W 9QQ, tel. 0171/730–4986, fax 0171/730–7865. Tube: Victoria. Cross Buckingham Palace Rd., walk west on Eccleston St., turn left on Ebury St. 12 rooms, some with bath. AE, MC, V.*

Windermere Hotel. This white stucco house has many amenities, not the least of which is a convenient location—10 minutes on foot from Victoria Station. Each room has a TV and a phone, and evening meals are available. Singles £46–£55, doubles from £55. *142–144 Warwick Way, SW1V 4JE, tel. 0171/834–5163, fax 0171/630–8831. Tube: Victoria. Walk east on Belgrave Rd., turn right on Warwick Way. 24 rooms, most with bath. AE, MC, V.*

Hostels

England's **Youth Hostel Association (YHA)** operates seven hostels in central London (some are more central than others) and a number out in the boonies (only one of which is really accessible by tube). These Formica-and-linoleum wonders tend to be clean to the point of sterility: Even if the outside looks cool, it's a safe bet that the rooms are basic and bland. And there's

WHERE TO SLEEP

no doubt that space-age bunk beds really pack 'em into shared dorms. Most YHA hostels offer institutional breakfasts and dinners, which are kind on the budget, if not always kind on the stomach. None of the seven YHA hostels listed below has a lockout or curfew, and the reception desks at six are open daily, 7:30 AM–11 PM; the one exception is Highgate Village, where the reception desk is open 1 PM–11 PM. **Astor,** a private hostel firm, has four above-average places in London that cater to international cheapo travelers; show your ISIC student card to shave 10% off the tab. Astor also provides free cereal-and-bread breakfasts. Wherever you stay, reservations are highly recommended in summer, particularly if you want a single or double room in the few hostels that offer such things. Unless otherwise noted, the non-YHA hostels listed below do not have curfews or lockouts and are open 24 hours for check-in.

You do not need a YHA hostel card if you already have a Hostelling International (HI) card. In England the two cards are essentially interchangeable.

Besides the hostels listed below, some London B&Bs offer dorm-style accommodations in addition to their more expensive singles and doubles. (B&Bs can be lifesaving after a few weeks of snoring bunk mates, noisy school groups, and 8 AM wake-up calls.) The following B&Bs charge £10–£17 for dorm beds and are reviewed above: **Central Club Hotel** (*see* Bloomsbury), **Kingsway Hotel House** (*see* Earl's Court and South Kensington), **Langland Hotel** (*see* Bloomsbury), **Lynton House Hotel** (*see* Victoria), and the **Repton Hotel** (*see* Bloomsbury).

Anne Elizabeth House. Situated in "Little Australia," this first-rate, recently renovated hostel has dorm-style accommodations in singles (£10–£21), doubles (£31), and triples (about £40); prices are £2–£4 higher in summer. Many guests stay here for weeks, cooking their meals in the kitchen, doing their laundry in the machines, and loafing around the TV room. Be sure to reserve ahead June–September. *30 Collingham Pl., SW5, tel. 0171/370–4821. Tube: Earl's Court. From station, go right on Earl's Court Rd., quick left on Earl's Court Gardens, quick right onto Collingham Pl. 55 beds. Laundry, luggage storage.*

Chelsea Hotel. This huge private hostel has clean, well-kept rooms and fills up exceedingly quickly (make reservations if possible). A dorm bed runs £10 (£54 monthly), singles £16, doubles £25, triples £39, quads £48. All rates include a Continental breakfast. *33–41 Earl's Court Sq., SW5 9B4, tel. 0171/244–6892, fax 0171/244–6891. Tube: Earl's Court. Walk south on Earl's Court Rd., turn right on Earl's Court Sq. 300 beds. Laundry, luggage storage.*

City of London Hostel (YHA). Formerly the Carter Lane Hostel, the City of London has a great location in the middle of town. Unfortunately, it has zip for character, and it attracts more of a middle-aged set than comparable budget accommodations. Singles, doubles, and dorms are all £14–£22 per person (£11–£18.50 for people under age 18). *136 Carter Ln., EC4V 5AD, tel. 0171/236–4965, fax 0171/236–7681. Tube: St. Paul's or Blackfriars. From St. Paul's: veer south off Cheapside onto Orange St., walk 1 block, cross Cannon St., turn right onto Carter Ln. From Blackfriars: walk 2 blocks north on Blackfriars Bridgeway, turn right on Carter Ln. 91 beds. Laundry, pay phones. MC, V.*

Curzon House Hotel. The Curzon is popular with budget travelers, although at £13 per dorm bed it's no bargain. The front rooms look across the leafy courtyard of a parish church. If you're tired of communal living, the Curzon also has singles for £26 (£120 weekly in winter) and doubles for £34. A Continental breakfast is included. *58 Courtfield Gardens, SW5 0NF, tel. 0171/581–2116. Tube: Gloucester Rd. Walk west on Cromwell Rd., turn left on Ashburn Pl. (which becomes Courtfield Gardens). 62 beds. Kitchen facilities, deposit required for reservations. AE, MC, V.*

Earl's Court (YHA). They really pack 'em in at this joint—the rooms are often stuffed with more than a dozen people. On the plus side, Earl's Court is convenient to the Underground and loaded with budget-travel services. Since it's in a budget part of town, you're also in prime territory for posse formation with other travelers. Beds £16.90 (£14.90 under 18). Continental breakfast is included. *38 Bolton Gardens, SW5 0AQ, tel. 0171/373–7083, fax 0171/835–2034. Tube: Earl's Court. Walk south on Earl's Court Rd., turn left on Bolton Gardens. 154 beds. Laundry, pay phone, bureau de change. MC, V.*

Fieldcourt House. This is one of the cleanest of London's £50-per-week hostels. It's also the sort of place where a number of permanent residents have their tab picked up by the dole. Unfortunately, tons of European school groups constantly roll through, and for the privilege of being bounced from room to room to make way for them, you pay £8–£11 nightly for a dorm bed (£50 per week). Singles are £15 daily and £85 weekly, doubles £24 daily and £135 weekly. *32 Courtfield Gardens, SW5 0PG, tel. 0171/373–0153. Tube: Gloucester Rd. or Earl's Court. From Gloucester Rd.: walk 3 blocks west on Cromwell Rd., turn left on Collingham Rd., right on Courtfield Gardens. From Earl's Court: walk south 2 blocks on Earl's Court Rd., turn left on Barkston Gardens (which turns into Courtfield Gardens). 40 rooms. Deposit required for advance reservations, pay phone.*

Hampstead Heath (YHA). This is one of the best hostels in town, well out of the hustle and bustle of central London yet convenient to the tube. The grounds are beautiful and on sunny days you can play in nearby Hampstead Heath. Single, double, triple, and quad rooms are all £16.50 per person, including breakfast. Ask about special offers during the off-season. *4 Wellgarth Rd., NW11, tel. 0181/458–9054, fax 0181/209–0546. Tube: Golders Green. Walk southeast on North End Rd., turn left on Wellgarth Rd. 200 beds. Laundry, pay phones, bureau de change. 12 beds with wheelchair access. MC, V.*

Highgate Village (YHA). Although getting here is a pain—prepare yourself for a serious uphill trek from the Archway tube station—you'll be rewarded with lodgings in an attractive Georgian house in a quiet neighborhood. It's also just a hop, skip, and jump away from Highgate Cemetery, the Heath, and Flasks (a cool pub just up the road). Since it's one of the cheapest YHA hostels in London, reservations are a good idea. Beds £11.75 (£7.85 under 18). Non-YHA and non-HI members must pay an extra £1.50 per night. *84 Highgate West Hill, N6 6LU, tel. 0181/340–1831, fax 0181/341–0376. Tube: Archway. Walk north up Highgate Hill, turn left on South Grove. 70 beds. Reception open daily 1 PM–11 PM, breakfast £2.60. MC, V.*

International Student House. This fun but monstrously huge establishment sits at the southeast corner of Regency Park, right across from the Great Portland Street tube station. A mellow atmosphere means it's generally full of international students—reservations are almost obligatory. A dorm bed in a clean four-bunk room costs £12.35. Singles are £23.40, doubles £39.50, triples £49.80, all including an English breakfast. *229 Great Portland St., W1N 5HD, tel. 0171/631–3223, fax 0171/636–5565. Tube: Great Portland St. 400 beds. Laundry. MC, V.*

King George VI Memorial Youth Hostel/Holland House (YHA). This haven of the young and weird is a long walk from the tube, but it's right in the middle of a huge, beautiful park; bring your Frisbee and play with local dread heads on weekends. Singles, doubles, and dorms cost £16.90 per person (£14.90 under 18). All rates include a full English breakfast. *Holland Walk, W8 7QU, tel. 0171/937–0748, fax 0171/376–0667. Tube: Holland Park. Turn left as you exit station, walk down Holland Park Ave., turn right on Holland Walk. 187 beds. Laundry, pay phones, kitchen, lockers. MC, V.*

Museum Inn Hostel. This Astor-run hostel is great for exploring Bloomsbury, the West End, and the British Museum (right across the street). Ask for a room overlooking the courtyard in back. Dorm beds are £12–£14 per person. Doubles are a steal at £33. *27 Montague Rd., WC1, tel. 0171/580–5360, fax 0171/589–1590. Tube: Tottenham Court Rd. Walk 1 block north on Tottenham Court Rd., turn right on Great Russell St., left on Montague Rd. Safe deposit boxes, pay phone, kitchen. MC, V.*

Oxford Street (YHA). In the heart of deepest, darkest Soho, this hostel makes a great base for exploring the West End and Whitehall. Imagine the convenience of staggering home from the pub instead of having to deal with the tube. The reception is on the third floor, but watch out for the temperamental elevator—it's good enough to send your bags up in, but it has a reputation for stopping when and where it damn well pleases. Most of the rooms are triples and doubles, with beds going for £16.50 (£13.50 under 18). *14 Noel St., W1V 3PD, tel. 0171/734–1618, fax 0171/734–1657. Tube: Oxford Circus or Tottenham Court Rd. From Oxford Circus: walk east on Oxford St., turn right on Poland St. From Tottenham Court Rd.: walk west on Oxford St., turn left on Berwick St. 82 beds. Breakfast £2.60. MC, V.*

Quest Hostel. This private hostel is near the Queensway tourist strip. Troglodytes will feel right at home—many of the rooms don't have windows. The lone double costs £30, while four- to eight-bed dorms cost £12.50–£13.50 per person, including breakfast. Prices go down a bit during the off-season. *45 Queensborough Terr., W2, tel. 0171/229–7782, fax 0171/ 727–8106. Tube: Bayswater. Turn right as you exit station onto Queensway, left onto Bayswater Rd., left on Queensborough Terr. 86 beds. Safe deposit boxes, pay phone, kitchen. MC, V.*

Rotherhithe (YHA). Although this relatively new hostel is really cool architecturally, it's quite a trek from central London. Fortunately, the neighborhood is interesting in its own right, and the rooms, while pretty shrimpy, all have private baths. Doubles and dorm beds are £17 per person (£13.80 under 18). *Island Yard, Salter Rd., SE16 1PP, tel. 0171/232–2114, fax 0171/237–2919. Tube: Rotherhithe. Walk northeast on Brunel Rd. (which becomes Salter Rd.). Laundry, pay phone, bureau de change. Wheelchair access. MC, V.*

Victoria Hotel. If you simply want to collapse at the end of a long journey, consider this Astor-run hostel near Victoria Station. Occupants are tightly packed into small, dark rooms, and the carpets are threadbare, but at least it's cheap: dorm beds £11–£14 daily, £55–£59 weekly. The common room is crowded, but congenial. *71 Belgrave Rd., SW1, tel. 0171/834–3077, fax 0171/932–0693. Tube: Victoria. Walk 2 blocks south on Buckingham Palace Rd., turn left on Eccleston Bridge (which becomes Belgrave Rd. after ½ mi). 70 beds. Deposit required for advance reservations. MC, V.*

Student Housing

Many university residence halls earn a few extra pounds by throwing their doors open to back-packers and the great unwashed during vacations. Life in college dorms will give you the pleasure of rubbing shoulders with like-minded young expatriates, but the most significant advantage is location: Student housing is often in northwest Bloomsbury, an easy 10-minute walk from London's West End. While the dorms themselves are often spartan, you usually get access to such amenities as saunas, tennis courts, and cheap eats at university cafeterias and pubs. These places fill up fast in summer, and reservations are a must. Student identification, however, is not: Nonstudents typically pay a small supplement to stay in dorms. If you're having trouble finding space in one of the following student dorms, contact the **Vacation Bureau** at King's College (tel. 0171/351–6011). They offer rooms in southwest London and beyond, March 19–April 24 and July 3–September 20. The student rate for a single room is £12.50; nonstudents pay £16.50.

Campbell House. This is definitely one of London's nicer residence halls. It's quiet, clean, and boasts a pleasant courtyard to boot. Singles cost £13.50 nightly, £87 weekly; doubles are £24.50 nightly, £154 weekly. *5–10 Taviton St., WC1, tel. 0171/388–0060 or 0171/ 380–7079. Tube: Euston Sq. Walk east on Euston Rd., turn right on Gordon St., left on Endsleigh Gardens, right on Taviton St. 100 rooms, none with bath. Kitchen, laundry.*

Canterbury Hall. The attractive wood-paneled lobby goes a long way toward disguising the building's true nature as an apartment block. An advantage is that most bathrooms are shared by only two or three rooms. Singles cost £21.15 with breakfast, £24 with breakfast and dinner. *12–18 Cartwright Gardens (address not marked on building), WC1H 9EB, tel. 0171/387–5526. Tube: King's Cross. Walk west on Euston Rd., turn left on Mabledon Pl. 245 rooms, none with bath. Laundry, tennis courts. Open Mar. 21–30, Apr. 16–22, June 27–Aug. 12, and Sept. 5–30.*

Centre Français. This Bayswater outpost of the Centre Français language-school chain offers cheap, clean lodging for weary travelers. Practice your *français* with the scores of French who land here to hone their *anglais*. Dorm beds £13 (£90 weekly), singles £23.20, doubles £40. *61–69 Chepstow Pl., W2, tel. 0171/221–8134. Tube: Bayswater or Notting Hill Gate. From Bayswater: walk north on Queensway, turn left on Moscow Rd., right on Chepstow Pl. From Notting Hill Gate: walk north on Pembridge Rd., turn right on Pembridge Sq., left on Chepstow Pl. 169 rooms. Laundry, pay phones.*

College Hall. This hall in the center of London's student ghetto gives you easy access to university pubs and facilities—it's across the street from the student union and next door to the university branch of Dillon's bookstore. Singles cost £17.50 with breakfast, £23.50 with breakfast and dinner. Nonstudents add £2 to the prices. *Malet St., WC1, tel. 0171/580–9131, fax 0171/636–6591. Tube: Goodge St. or Russell Sq. 200 rooms, none with bath. Laundry, TV room, library. Open Mar. 22–30, Apr. 6–23, July 4–Aug. 13, and Sept. 13–30.*

Commonwealth Hall. Fringe benefits in this modern (read: ugly) high-rise dorm include the use of tennis courts. Singles £18.50. *1–12 Cartwright Gardens (address not marked on building), WC1, tel. 0171/387–0311. Tube: King's Cross. Walk west on Euston Rd., turn left on Mabledon Pl. 400 rooms, none with bath. Laundry, kitchen, tennis courts. Open Mar. 19–25 and June 26–Aug. 26.*

Connaught House. This newly refurbished residence hall overlooks pleasant Tavistock Square. Singles £19.50, including breakfast. *36–45 Tavistock Sq., WC1H 9EB, tel. 0171/387–4120 (front desk) or 0171/387–6181 (reservations). Tube: Russell Sq. or Euston Station. From Russell Sq.: walk north up Woburn Pl. From Euston Station: walk south on Eversholt St. 200 rooms, none with bath. Laundry, TV, kitchen. Open Mar 21–31, Apr. 5–23, and July 1–Sept. 20.*

Hughes Parry Hall. This high-rise dorm has basic, clean singles for £18.50 with breakfast, £22 with breakfast and dinner. *19–26 Cartwright Gardens, WC1, tel. 0171/387–1477. Tube: King's Cross. Walk west on Euston Rd., turn left on Mabledon Pl. 300 rooms, none with bath. Laundry, pay phones. Open Mar. 19–Apr. 24 and June 27–Aug. 31.*

International Hall. The building is uninspired, but you're near Russell Square and the Renoir, a good arty film house. Singles £15.50 with breakfast, £17.50 with breakfast and dinner. Nonstudents add £2 to both rates. *Brunswick Sq., WC1, tel. 0171/837–0746, fax 0171/278–9720. Tube: Russell Sq. From station, go right on Bernard St., left on Brunswick Sq. 500 rooms, none with bath. Laundry, lounge, pub.*

International Student House. Located in an old Regency building, this huge dorm/condo offers basic, inexpensive accommodations to travelers year-round. It's also just a short tube ride from central London. The best deals are long-term: If you pay in advance for an entire month, a dorm bed costs a mere £34 a week. Otherwise, dorm beds are £12.35 nightly, singles £23.40, doubles £39.50, triples, £49.50. *229 Great Portland St., W1, tel. 0171/631–3223. Tube: Great Portland St. From station, go south on Great Portland St. 321 beds. Laundry, pay phones.*

John Adams Hall. This group of Georgian houses has been converted into student lodging and is available at bargain rates during school vacations. While there's nothing luxurious about the complex, it's only a short walk from the British Museum, and Euston Station is across the street. Singles £19, doubles £33. A Continental breakfast is included. *15–23 Endsleigh St., WC1H 0DH, tel. 0171/387–4086 or 0171/387–4796 (ask for Ms. Stubbs). Tube: Euston Sq. 148 rooms, none with bath. Open Mar. 21–Apr. 15 and July 4–Sept. 30.*

Lilian Pension Hall. This Bayswater dorm has two advantages: It's in a more happening area than most student dorms, and it has space year-round for short-term visitors. Singles cost £20, shared twin rooms are £12 per person, and double rooms for couples are £15.50 per person. *Talbot Sq., W2, tel. 0171/262–2081, fax 0171/724–1258. Tube: Paddington. Walk 3 blocks south on London St., turn right on Sussex Gardens, right on Talbot Sq. Number of rooms varies, all with bath. Laundry, pub.*

London Goodenough Trust/Fellowship House. This palatial graduate student and scholars' residence is the place to stay if you want a peaceful academic environment. Singles cost £18 and fill up fast—book at least three months in advance. One bummer: You must have a passport from the United States or from an EU country to stay here. Doubles £32. *Mecklenburgh Sq., WC1, tel. 0171/837–8888, fax 0171/278–5489. Tube: Russell Sq. From station, go right and follow road as it curves right, take first left and then first right. 57 rooms, none with bath. Laundry, library, reading rooms, pay phones.*

Passfield Hall. The residence hall at the London School of Economics is a bit too dumpy for the money, but it'll work in a pinch. Singles £17, doubles £30. *1 Endsleigh Pl., WC1, tel. 0171/387–3584 or 0171/387–7743. Tube: Euston Sq. Walk east on Euston Rd., turn right on Gordon St., left on Endsleigh Pl. 198 beds. Kitchen, laundry.*

Regent's College. The best thing about this converted Regency mansion is that it's smack in the middle of Regent's Park. Beds are of the bunk variety, bathrooms of the locker-room variety. It's reasonably cheap, though—singles £25, doubles £36, triples £39. The college has its own café, bar, cafeteria, tennis courts, and weight room. *Inner Circle, Regent's Park, NW1 4NS, tel. 0171/487–7483. Tube: Baker St. 82 rooms, none with bath. Closed Oct.–Nov. and Feb.–Apr.*

Campgrounds

Camping in London is a weird enough idea to be interesting, and if you don't mind a longish commute, it's practical, too. God knows, it's cheap enough. Two of the three main sites—Tent City and Hackney Camping—are actually inside Zones 1 and 2, which is great for Travelcard holders (*see* Getting Around, by Underground, in Chapter 1). Halfway there, the Underground trip turns into a pleasant train ride through the country.

Camping Eastway Cycle Circuit. This 48-acre nature reserve doubles as a cycling racetrack. It's a 15-minute walk from the tube and a 20-minute tube ride from central London, so be sure to stock up on groceries before coming; the only thing nearby is an expensive snack bar in the sports center across the street. The rates are £5 per person plus £7 per car. Reservations are a good idea in July and August. *Temple Mill Ln., E15, tel. 0181/534–6085. Tube: Leyton. From station, turn left and follow Leyton High Rd. to first set of traffic lights, turn right onto Temple Mill Ln. 100 spaces. Reception open 8–8. Showers, toilets, luggage storage. Open mid-Mar.–mid-Oct.*

Hackney Camping. This huge, empty park on the outskirts of London is ideal for cheap sleeping in a small enclosed grove. Although it's run by the London Tourist Board, it's staffed largely by young French punkers. BYOT (bring your own tent); the rate is £4 per person. *Millfields Rd., E5, tel. 0181/985–7656. Tube: Liverpool St. From station, take Bus 22A and alight at Mill-fields and Mandeville Sts., cross bridge, and follow signs. 200 sites. Showers, toilets, luggage storage, snack bar. Open June 18–Aug. 25.*

Tent City. This west London institution has a number of cots in 14 large tents spread across Wormwood Scrubs. You can choose between men's, women's, and mixed tents, or else pitch your own tent for the same daily price of £5. *Old Oak Common Ln., W3, tel. 0181/743–5708. Tube: East Acton. Walk northeast on Erconwald St., left on Wolfstan St. (which intersects Old Oak Common Ln.). 450 beds. Showers, toilets, luggage storage, snack bar. Open June–Sept. 15.*

Longer Stays

London may be one of the world's most over-touristed cities, but it's also a damn fine place to live, attracting students, writers, artists, and other international folks in droves. While this is great for the town's cosmopolitan flair, it leads to one pressing question: Is it even remotely possible to find a cheap flat? Yes and no. If you have a bit of time and money, you will inevitably find something suitable. The trick is, you'll probably have to stay in a hostel or student dorm for a few weeks to conduct a proper housing search. On the other hand, if you arrive on a Saturday and want to rent something cheap by Monday, you're utterly mad.

One warning: The competition for living space is fiercest in September, when London universities start their first terms and students are desperate for a place to call home.

Generally speaking, flats, simple rooms, and bedsits (very modest studios where the kitchen often consists of a hot plate on top of a microwave) are advertised by their weekly rate. You can get a room for as little as £35 a week if you don't mind having your bathtub in the kitchen and living behind train tracks in Zone 4. While this has a certain romantic ring to it, you'll be better off paying £55–£70 a week for lower-end accommodations in central London—you'll still have to shower in the sink, but at least you'll live within a short walk of the tube in Zone 2 or 3. Keep in mind that the farther you live from the city center, the more expensive your monthly tube pass will be. Zones 1 and 2 are central, and Zone 3 is a bit out; anything beyond will cost you so much money and time that you might as well live in Paris.

The best newspaper for home-finding is *Loot* (£1), which appears at local newsstands six times a week (it's a different color each day). Since it's free to place an ad in *Loot,* it often has the best—and the cheapest—selection of flats and bedsits in London; it also has special sections on student housing and short-term stays. Other places to look for flats and private rooms are the classifieds of the *Evening Standard* (30p), *TNT* (free), and the relatively new *Capital Keys* (free)—all of which can be found at newsstands and in many corner shops.

SHORT-TERM ACCOMMODATIONS One option for short-term stays—anything from a few weeks to a month or two—is a university hall (*see* Student Housing, *above*). The great advantage to student dorms is that you can stay at a very reasonable weekly rate—usually £60–£90 in summer, £40–£60 in winter—while you search for a more permanent place to live. Student dorms are also a great place to meet people. And don't forget about the facilities: tennis courts, laundry rooms, kitchens, gyms, local pubs, shops—you name it.

Otherwise, the best place to start your search is the notice board at the **University of London Accommodation Office.** Although you need a University of London Letter of Admission to view lists of long-term accommodations, from June to September you can view lists of family homes and flats priced at £25–£65 per week—assuming, of course, you have some sort of student or teacher I.D. *Malet St., tel. 0171/636–2818. Tube: Euston Sq. Walk south on Gower St., turn left on Torrington Pl., first right onto Malet St. Open weekdays 9:30–5:30; also Sept., Sat. 9:30–2.*

ACCOMMODATION SERVICES The **Housing Advice Switchboard** (tel. 0171/434–2522) gives advice and referrals for home-seekers. The switchboard is open weekdays 10–6. **Piccadilly Advice Centre** (100 Shaftesbury Ave., tel. 0171/730–3488; Tube: Leicester Sq.) offers similar lodging services. Many accommodation services charge a fee either to prospective tenants (usually two week's rent) or, if you're very lucky, directly to the landlord. One of the latter variety is the **Jenny Jones Accommodation Agency** (40 S. Molten St., tel. 0171/493–4801; Tube: Bond St.). Their lists of flats and bedsits change weekly and include locations throughout central London and beyond. If you don't mind paying a fee, definitely call **Flatsearch** (68 Queensway, tel. 0171/730–7888; Tube: Bayswater). They're a little cheaper than most agencies, charging only one week's rent for a successful search.

FOOD

4

By Lara Harris

There are more than 8,000 restaurants in London, and even the ones serving so-called British cuisine may surprise you. Yes, the phrase "traditional English food" usually means a stale Shepherd's pie, greasy sausages, and soggy peas. Yet believe it or not, it can also mean a delicate seafood dinner that even a French person would approve of. Of course, said seafood dinner may cost upwards of £15, so if you're on a strict budget, you're more likely to explore the greasy depths of pub grub, crisps (what Americans call potato chips), and deep-fried burgers.

Then again, in London you can also choose from a nearly endless variety of ethnic cuisine: That's one of the benefits of having been an imperial capital with far-flung dominions. Wander along **Gerrard Street,** north of the City, and you'll find yourself in a Hong Kong street scene with crates of fresh produce, skinned ducks hanging in shop windows, and the omnipresent stench of yesterday's fish. For that matter, many regional feathers flock together in particular parts of London: Bengali on Spitalfield's **Brick Lane** (Tube: Aldgate East), Indian on Bloomsbury's **Drummond Street** (Tube: Euston Sq.), and Vietnamese on **Lisle Street** (Tube: Piccadilly Circus). Italian, Continental, and Middle Eastern restaurants are ubiquitous.

Trouble is, London is expensive. The cheapest sit-down meals cost at least £4, more likely £5–£7. If you want any sort of ambience you'll pay £8–£14, not including the cover charge (50p–£1) that some restaurants add to the bill. And don't forget the VAT (Value Added Tax), a vexatious 17.5% tax that's added to most checks. (Some restaurants include VAT in their prices and some don't; inspect the menu to avoid paying twice.)

Any lengthy stay in London requires a strategy for eating on the cheap—like making lunch the biggest meal of the day to take advantage of discounted lunch specials. London's pubs typically serve soups and sandwiches for less than £5, and fish 'n' chips or steak 'n' peas for £4–£7. If you can't afford to eat out all the time, acquaint yourself with **Marks & Spencer** (458 Oxford St., tel. 0171/935–7945), a department store that sells surprisingly yummy and diverse prepared meals at decent prices. Look for other Marks & Spencer branches at 258 Edgware Road and 113 Kensington High Street. Alternatively, most of London's neighborhoods have regular fruit and vegetable markets, not to mention specialty stores with all sorts of goodies (*see* Markets and Specialty Stores, *below*).

One final note: If you're looking for a specific restaurant but don't know which neighborhood it's in, check in the handy index at the back of this book. If you're looking for a type of cuisine, check the reference listings at the end of this chapter—have we thought of everything or what?

Restaurants

BAYSWATER AND NOTTING HILL GATE

Full English breakfasts are a rite of passage for visitors: fried eggs, fried toast, fried tomatoes, and fried sausage, followed by the obligatory tank of tea. One meal will harden your arteries for life.

Join the American tourist crowd in Bayswater, a neighborhood full of kebab joints, chippies, and mediocre delis. British trendsetters, on the other hand, like to strut their stuff in Notting Hill Gate, which is a cut above Bayswater when it comes to food.

➤ **UNDER £5** • **Churchill Arms.** This traditional British pub hides an excellent Thai restaurant in an enclosed patio out back. Chow on *khao rad na* (rice with a choice of chicken, prawn, or meat sauce) or *kwaitiew pad thai* (Thai noodles with prawns), both for around £4. Beers range from Grolsch to Singha (£1.50–£2.25). Come dinnertime, add 50p to the prices. *119 Kensington Church St., tel. 0171/727–4242. Tube: Notting Hill Gate. Walk east on Notting Hill Gate, turn right on Kensington Church St. Open Mon.–Sat. noon–2:30 and 6–9:30, Sun. noon–2:30.*

Gallery Café. This hippie and rasta haunt off Portobello's main drag serves up all sorts of vegetarian edibles. Lasagna and moussaka are both £2.50, sweet cakes £1, cappuccino 80p. *74 Tavistock Rd., tel. 0171/221–5844. Tube: Ladbroke Grove. Turn right on Ladbroke Grove, left on Lancaster Rd., left on Portobello Rd., right on Tavistock Rd. Open daily 9–5.*

Geales. If you fancy fish-and-chips, Geales has been serving up some of the best in London for more than 50 years. The homemade fish soup makes an excellent light meal (£1.70); or tackle haddock, plaice, or cod for £4.50. It's not hypergreasy, either—allegedly because Geales pours plenty of beer into the batter. *2 Farmer's Rd., tel. 0171/727–7969. Tube: Notting Hill Gate. Walk west on Notting Hill Gate, turn left on Farmer's Rd. Open Tues.–Sat. noon–3 and 6–11.*

Khan's. It's always busy, so you know it's good. Cane chairs, high ceilings, and cool murals make this a great place to linger over some of London's cheapest Indian food. Chicken *shahi* (in a mild curry sauce) costs a mere £2.85, lamb tikka £3.40. *13–15 Westbourne Grove, tel. 0171/727–5420. Tube: Queensway or Bayswater. Turn left exiting either station onto Queensway, left on Westbourne Grove. Open daily noon–3 and 6–midnight. AE, MC, V.*

➤ **UNDER £10** • **Il Carretto.** The prices are somewhat steep—roast lamb with herbs and garlic costs £6, *frutti di mare al spedino* (seafood skewers) £8—but the place is charming and on a secluded side street; try to score a shrub-shaded sidewalk table. *20 Hillgate St., tel. 0171/229–5040. Tube: Notting Hill Gate. Walk west on Notting Hill Gate, turn left on Hillgate St. Open daily noon–3 and 6–11. AE, MC, V.*

No chippie worth its salt is open on Monday; with most fishermen sitting at home on Sunday, Monday's fish would be more than a day old.

Micro-Kalamaras. Nestled behind Queensway, this charming Greek tavern is a real find, with a homey dining area presided over by a matronly mama. Choose from traditional Greek dishes like *kalamarika* (baby squid; £3.50), cheese pies (£2.40), and zucchini stuffed with chicken (£6). *66 Inverness Mews, tel. 0171/727–5082. Tube: Bayswater. Turn right on Queensway, left on Inverness Pl., left on Inverness Mews. BYOB. Open Mon.–Sat. 7 PM–11 PM. AE, MC, V.*

Savva's. It's not long on atmosphere, but Savva's does a good job with "Greek home-cooking" at reasonable prices. Try to score a table on the raised patio in front or in the sunroom out back. *Kleftikon* (broiled lamb) and *kotopoulo* (baked chicken) both cost £5. The haricot bean casserole (£4.10) is a good vegetarian option. *7 Ladbroke Rd., tel. 0171/727–9720. Tube: Notting Hill Gate. Walk north on Pembridge Rd., turn left on Ladbroke Rd. Open Mon.–Sat. 6 PM–11 PM. AE, MC, V.*

BLOOMSBURY

Once London's literary slum, Bloomsbury is now better known for its thriving Asian and Indian communities. **Drummond Street,** in particular, is lined with east Indian curry houses and southern Indian vegetarian restaurants.

➤ **UNDER £5 • Anwars.** Super-low prices make this simple, Formica-heavy canteen especially popular with students from nearby colleges. The best deals are at lunchtime: yummy mutton biryani for £3, spicy chicken vindaloo for £2.80. *64 Grafton Way, tel. 0171/387–6664. Tube: Warren St. Walk south on Tottenham Court Rd., turn right on Grafton Way. Open daily 11 AM–11:30 PM.*

Those in search of the ultimate curry should dive into the cramped lanes and alleyways of Bloomsbury, which has the highest concentration of Indian restaurants in the entire United Kingdom.

Diwana Bhel Poori House. They serve up fresh southern Indian (read: vegetarian) cuisine on big plates at Diwana, so strict carnivores should head elsewhere. Try the deluxe *dosa* (a crepe, here stuffed with curried veggies, potatoes, and lentils; £4.15) and wash it down with a few mango milkshakes (£1.60)—one is never enough. *121 Drummond St., tel. 0171/ 387–5556. Tube: Euston Sq. Open daily noon–11:30. BYOB. AE, MC, V.*

YMCA. The dining hall at this Bloomsbury YMCA caters to the Indian students staying here, but nonresidents are welcome to line up for the cheap, tasty meals. Breakfast runs £2.30, lunch or dinner £4. *41 Fitzroy Sq., tel. 0171/387–0411. Tube: Warren St. Walk south on Tottenham Court Rd., turn right on Grafton Way, left on Fitzroy Sq. Open weekdays 8–9:15, 12:30–1:45, and 7–8, weekends 8:30–9:30, 12:30–1:30, and 7–8.*

➤ **UNDER £10 • Chutney's.** It's on everybody's short list for London's best vegetarian Indian restaurant. The upstairs dining room is a bit anemic, but downstairs it's all cozy wooden booths and amber light. If you're catching a train at Euston Station, Chutney's is definitely worth the 10-minute walk. The £3.95 lunch buffet (Mon.–Sat. noon–2:45, Sun. noon–10:30) is one of the city's few culinary steals. *124 Drummond St., tel. 0171/388–0604. Tube: Euston Sq. Walk northeast on Euston Rd., turn left on Melton St., left on Drummond St. Open daily noon–2:45 and 6–11:30. MC, V.*

Wagamama. Don't let the long lines put you off; rest assured that the turnover rate of slurping customers is high at this Japanese ramen bar. The menu features a staggering variety of noodles; novice ramen eaters should start with wheat noodle soup (£3.80–£5) or *kare lomen* (rice noodles with lemongrass, onions, and tofu; £4.70). *4 Streatham St., tel. 0171/323–9223. Tube: Tottenham Court Rd. Walk east on New Oxford St., left on Bloomsbury, right on Streatham St. Open weekdays noon–2:30 and 6–11, Sat. 12:30–3 and 6–11, Sun. 2–10.*

BRIXTON AND CLAPHAM

Brixton has the upper hand on Afro-Caribbean joints, while Clapham features a variety of popular watering holes and cafés, especially around **Clapham Common.** In Brixton, there's no particular street littered with restaurants, but rather clusters of places throughout the neighborhood.

➤ **UNDER £5 • Eco.** The food may be identical to that served at its sister restaurant, Pizzeria Franco (*see below*), but the similarities stop there. Franco is loud and lively, while Eco is more subdued, with wooden sculptures and industrial pipes for decor—the essence of hep Clapham. *162 Clapham High St., tel. 0171/978–1108. Tube: Clapham Common. Walk northeast on Clapham High St. Open Mon.–Thurs. 11:30–3 and 6:30–11, Fri. and Sat. 11:30–4 and 6:30–11:40, Sun. noon–4:30 and 6–10:30; closed Wed. lunch. AE, MC, V.*

Phoenix Restaurant. There are plenty of London cafés just like this one, but for the price you can't find a better roast lamb with two veggies (£3.60), or a cheese omelet with chips (£2.80). If deep-fried toast doesn't frighten you, come for a classically greasy English breakfast. Toast and tea are served all day. *441 Coldharbour Ln., tel. 0171/733–4430. Tube: Brixton. Walk south on Brixton Rd., turn left on Coldharbour Ln. Open Mon.–Sat. 6:30 AM–5 PM.*

Pizzeria Franco. Sit outside in the middle of Brixton Market and eat to the sounds of jazz and reggae from surrounding stalls. Franco is high on atmosphere and good on pizza—from the *margherita* (tomato and mozzarella; £3.40) to the *quattro stagioni* (tomato, cheese, ham, and artichoke; £4.70). *4 Market Row, tel. 0171/738-3021. Tube: Brixton. Walk north on Brixton Rd., turn left on Electric Ave., right on Electric Ln., left on Market Row. Open Mon., Tues., and Thurs.-Sat. 8-5:30.*

➤ **UNDER £10** • **The Brixtonian.** The savory Afro-Caribbean menu includes snapper and rice (£4.20), fried plantains (£3), and daily specials priced £6–£9. Lunch is served downstairs in the bar, with wicker chairs and wooden shutters. If you're feeling extravagant, head upstairs for dinner; the extra cost (£13.95 for a set two-course meal) buys white tablecloths and delicacies like Creole peanut soup and quail with paw paw sauce. *11 Dorrell Pl., tel. 0171/978-8870. Tube: Brixton. Walk north on Brixton Rd., turn left on Dorrell Pl. (the street sign's a bit worn). Open Mon.-Wed. 11:30 AM-midnight, Thurs.-Sat. 11:30 AM-1 AM. AE, MC, V.*

CAMDEN

You'll find virtually every national cuisine on offer in Camden, although herds of tourists and wealthy north Londoners may mean forking out a few extra quid. **Camden High Street,** surprise, is the main drag, interspersed with kebab stands, pizza stands, sausage stands, and the odd café. Poke your nose around the corner to **Bayham Street** for eateries that are slightly less clogged with Camden shoppers.

➤ **UNDER £5** • **Thanh Binh.** Delicate Vietnamese prawns (£4.50) and finger-licking-good Mongolian lamb (£3.50) make for a delectable meal. If the twee Vietnamese decor and the chef who sings in the kitchen aren't to your taste, order a chicken with lemongrass lunch box (£3) and hit the road. *14 Chalk Farm Rd., tel. 0171/267-9820. Tube: Chalk Farm. Walk southwest on Chalk Farm Rd. Open Tues.-Sat. noon-2:30 and 6-11:30, Sun. noon-10. AE, MC, V.*

➤ **UNDER £10** • **Belgo.** Don't ask why the waiters are dressed like Benedictine monks in this Belgian diner—it's just one of those things, much like the open kitchen and stark, industrial interior (cement walls, exposed pipes, trendy furniture). Menu highlights include wild-boar sausage with mash and a beer (£5 lunch, £7.95 dinner), and the pot of mussels cooked five different ways (£8.95). Choose from the vast list of Belgian ales (£2.25–£3.25). *22 Chalk Farm Rd., tel. 0171/267-0718. Tube: Chalk Farm. Walk southeast on Chalk Farm Rd. Open weekdays noon-3 and 6-11:30, Sat. noon-11:30, Sun. noon-10:30. AE, MC, V.*

Daphne's. The smell of fresh meat searing on the grill hangs heavy in the air near this backstreet Greek tavern. Very likely it's *shashlik* (skewered lamb) or *ortikia* (quail with lemon and oregano), both £6.25. Standards like moussaka (£5.50) are just as good. If the weather's even remotely pleasant, sit in the rooftop garden. *83 Bayham St., tel. 0171/267-7322. Tube: Camden Town. Walk southwest on Camden High St., turn left on Greenland St., right on Bayham St. Open Mon.-Sat. noon-3 and 6-midnight. MC, V.*

The Lansdowne. You'll find this hip, upmarket pub on the affluent fringe of Camden Town, which means you're paying for atmosphere as well as for fine food. Try garlic bread topped with grilled veggies and goat cheese (£6.50) or roast duck with prunes and potatoes (£8). *90 Gloucester Ave., tel. 0171/483-0409. Tube: Chalk Farm. Walk southeast on Chalk Farm Rd., turn right on Regent's Park Rd., left on Gloucester Ave. Open Mon.-Sat. noon-2:30 and 7-10, Sun. noon-3 and 7-10:30.*

Osmani. There's nothing pretentious about this quiet North African eatery on the edge of Camden's main shopping strip. The *moutzebal* (grilled eggplant with tahini, couscous, and vegetables; £6) is delectable, and the grilled lamb (£7.50) or vegetable couscous (£5) won't disappoint. Make sure you leave room for the succulent lemon tart (£3.50). *46 Inverness St., tel. 0171/267-4682. Tube: Camden Town. Walk north on Camden High St., turn left on Inverness St. Open weekdays 12:30-2:30 and 7-11, weekends 7-11. AE, MC, V.*

Ruby In The Dust. A busy Tex-Mex joint with candles, potted plants, canned funk and jazz music, and psychedelic wall paintings. In the great London tradition, Tex-Mex includes cheese and bacon burgers (£6.25) and desserts like Death by Chocolate (£2.85). The platters of chips and guacamole (£3.95) are slightly more authentic. *102 Camden High St., tel. 0171/485–2944. Tube: Camden Town. Walk southeast on Camden High St. Open daily 10 AM–11:30 PM. MC, V.*

CHELSEA

Chelsea is loaded with semicheap grazing grounds. The problem is finding the good stuff amid all the mediocrity. Stick to the restaurants at the top of **King's Road**, between the Sloane Square tube station and Beaufort Street.

➢ **UNDER £5 • Chelsea Kitchen**. The original owners of the Stockpot restaurants (*see* Knightsbridge, *below*) now own Chelsea's leading venue for dirt-cheap eats. Fill 'er up on curried chicken madras (£2.50) or goulash with chips and mushy peas (£2.90). The ambience is bland, but the prices are too low to complain. *98 King's Rd., tel. 0171/589–1330. Tube: Sloane Sq. Walk southwest on King's Rd. Open Mon.–Sat. 8 AM–11:45 PM, Sun. noon–11:30.*

Sydney Street Cafe. In summer, sit in the expansive courtyard and enjoy the Chelsea ambience. If you're an avowed carnivore, the grilled-steak baguette (£4.95) will satisfy. For those who don't mind a full-throttle grease blast, consider an English breakfast with tea (£4.95), served all day. On your way out, spend some time browsing the surrounding farmers' market. *215 Sydney St., tel. 0171/352–5600. Tube: Sloane Sq. Walk ½ mi southwest on King's Rd., turn right on Sydney St. Open Apr.–Oct., daily 9:30 AM–11 PM; Nov.–May, daily 9:30–5:30.*

➢ **UNDER £10 • Ambrosiana Creperie.** This hep Chelsea restaurant dishes out a variety of both sweet and savory crepes. Pears and cinnamon (£3.50) do nicely for a late breakfast; heartier sorts should try a savory crepe like salami, ratatouille, and cheese (£5.30) or chicken, spinach, tomato, and cheese (£5.20). *194 Fulham Rd., tel. 0171/351–0070. Tube: South Kensington. Walk southwest on Old Brompton Rd. Open weekdays noon–3 and 6–11:30, weekends noon–11:30. MC, V.*

Chapter 11. Huge neo-expressionist paintings provide the backdrop for this dinner-only restaurant. Appealing—albeit pricey—entrées include grilled lemon and pepper chicken (£7.50) and asparagus risotto (£6.50). *47 Hollywood Rd., tel. 0171/351–1683. Tube: South Kensington. Walk ¾ mi west on Old Brompton Rd., turn left on The Little Boltons, right on Tregunter Rd., left on Hollywood Rd. Open Mon.–Sat. 7 PM–11:30 PM. AE, MC, V.*

Pucci's. This English version of an old-style pizzeria has blue-checkered tablecloths and tacky Italian artifacts on the walls. Even so, Pucci's creative pizzas—such as the Four Seasons (mushroom, pepperoni, anchovy, and tomato; £5) and the Siciliana (with eggplant and olives; £5.50)—are a welcome alternative to the generic, overpriced pizza you get on the street. *205 King's Rd., tel. 0171/352–2134. Tube: Sloane Sq. Walk ½ mi southwest on King's Rd. Open Mon.–Sat. noon–midnight.*

THE CITY AND ISLINGTON

Restaurants in the City mainly cater to suited office folk; after all, this is the financial heart of London. Predictably, the area is busiest on weekdays from dawn until early evening, and it slows to a crawl on weekends. There's no lack of sandwich shops, delis, pubs, and restaurants, but if you're not desperately hungry as you explore the City, consider a short tube ride to nearby Islington. Once the center for '70s dropouts, Islington now has a surfeit of young hipsters and happening places to dine, especially on **Islington High Street** (which becomes **Upper Street** just north of the Angel tube station).

➢ **UNDER £5 • Alfredo's.** An amiable vibe and 1920s theme mean Alfredo's is more than your average neighborhood café. Highlights include traditional English breakfasts (£2.60) and homemade pies with two veggies (£2.10). *426 Essex Rd., tel. 0171/226–3496. Tube: Angel. Walk north on Islington High St., veer right onto Essex Rd. Open weekdays 7 AM–2:30 PM, Sat. 7 AM–4 PM.*

East West. Enlightened spiritualists frequent this airy health food restaurant on hectic Old Street. It's the perfect stop for a quick, filling, healthy lunch: Try rice and adzuki beans (£4.50) or the salad (£1.95) and miso soup (£1.70). The couscous cake (£1.75) will satisfy your sweet tooth without promoting tooth decay. *188 Old St., tel. 0171/608–0300. Tube: Old St. Walk east on Old St. Open Mon.–Thurs. 11–9, Fri. and Sat. 11–10, Sun. 11–4. AE.*

Finca. The decor in this Spanish tapas bar resembles a Texas cattle ranch: wooden railings, a big bar, and so on. It may take two or three tapas dishes to fill you full, but the prices are decent: Spanish omelets cost £2.10, prawns with garlic £3.60, *crema Catalan* (a flan-like concoction) £2.10. There's live music every Wednesday and flamenco once a month. *96 Pentonville Rd., tel. 0171/837–5387. Tube: Angel. Walk west on Pentonville Rd. Open Sun.–Thurs. noon–midnight, Fri. and Sat. noon–2 AM. AE, V.*

In the evenings, students get a 20% discount at Ravi Shankar, a southern Indian restaurant with ridiculously friendly prices.

Ravi Shankar. Ravi Shankar won't win any awards for bold interior design, but the food is filling and supercheap. A potato dosa filled with veggies and rice goes for £3.40. If you're especially hungry order Mysore thali, with *dal* (lentils), *bhaji* (deep-fried veggies), rice, and *chapati* (unleavened bread) for £4.70. *422 St. John St., tel. 0171/833–5849. Tube: Angel. Walk south on St. John St. Open daily noon–2:30 and 6–11 (Fri. and Sat. until 11:30). AE, MC, V.*

➤ **UNDER £10** • **The Eagle.** As one of London's new-style pubs this place has the requisite open kitchen, young City folk, and ever-changing menu of Mediterranean edibles. Spanish ham, chorizo, bruschetta, and tomato salad (£7) or the home-salted cod with salsa and mash (£7.50) are both good bets. *159 Farringdon Rd., tel. 0171/837–1353. Tube: Farringdon. Right on Cowcross St., right on Farringdon Rd. Open weekdays noon–3 and 6:30–10:30.*

The Quality Chop House. Traditional British grub in a space unlike any pub, with black and white floor tiles, open booths, and fresh flowers. Test the scrambled eggs and smoked salmon (£6.75) or corned beef hash (£8.75), then treat yourself to a gooey dessert (£3–£3.75). As the English say, a little of what you fancy does you good. *94 Farringdon Rd., tel. 0171/837–5093. Tube: Farringdon. Right on Cowcross St., right on Farringdon Rd. Open Mon.–Sat. noon–3 and 6:30–midnight, Sun. noon–4 and 7–11:30.*

The Fruits of Imperialism

Britain may well boast more Indian restaurants than India itself, so don't deny yourself the pleasure of a London curry house. To generalize shamelessly, southern Indian dishes are heavy on the vegetables, northern Indian on all varieties of curries. Bombay-style restaurants feature plenty of yogurt, Kashmir-style cream and almonds. If you're unwilling to order boldly, most Indian restaurants offer some version of thali, which is not a dish but rather a way of serving: all sorts of curries and sauces in individual bowls on a large tray with rice and breads.

Indian curries in London generally fall into four categories: korma and patia, which are mild, and madras and vindaloo, which are hot. Tikka means that your food has been marinated with spices and then fried, and mughlai indicates a creamy dish prepared with yogurt, almonds, and possibly pistachios. Tandoori refers both to the tangy orange sauces used to marinate meat, and to the clay oven where said meat is suspended on a metal spit so that it cooks evenly on all sides.

COVENT GARDEN

The lively market days of Covent Garden are over; what remains are pricey crafts shops and, for the most part, undistinguished restaurants. Even so, a few gems still exist in this yuppified area. On weekday evenings and Sunday afternoons, get your food to go on **Endell Street** or **Neal Street** and have a picnic while watching street performers on the plaza.

➤ **UNDER £5** • **Food for Thought.** This veggie eatery occupies a small converted basement, giving it a snug feel that's best appreciated on a soggy London night. Covent Garden hipsters frequent Food for Thought for the large portions of fresh vegetarian food, like spinach cauliflower quiche (£2) and pineapple scones (50p). *31 Neal St., tel. 0171/836–9072. Tube: Covent Garden. Turn right on Long Acre, left on Neal St. Open Mon.–Sat. 9–8, Sun. 10:30–4:30.*

Rock and Sole Plaice. This family-run diner—really a cross between your basic fish 'n' chip bar and a pretheater bistro—has no aspirations to be anything other than traditionally British, with options like cod and chips (£3.30) and chicken mushroom pie (£1.95). Expect small crowds after the pubs close on Saturday night. *47 Shorts Gardens, tel. 0171/836–3785. Tube: Covent Garden. Turn right on Long Acre, left on Endell St. Open Mon.–Sat. 11:30–11.*

➤ **UNDER £10** • **Calabash.** Despite its basement location, this excellent African restaurant is cheerfully decorated with vivid tablecloths, bright green plants, and mediocre paintings of Africa. Go for the *yassa* (onion stew cooked with lemon juice and pepper; £6.50) or the dependable groundnut stew (£6.25). Chase it all down with a Nigerian beer (£2) or a bottle of Algerian or Zimbabwean wine (£8 and up). *38 King St., Africa Centre, tel. 0171/836–1976. Tube: Covent Garden. Walk south on James St., turn right on King St. Open weekdays 12:30–3 and 6–11:30, Sat. 6–11:30. AE, MC, V.*

Mars. Definitely on a planet of its own, Mars has funky blue and orange walls and broken-china mosaics, not to mention strangely named, vaguely French food. Menu highlights include Soupe Egberte le Sensitive, a fine-tasting lentil soup (£3.50), and Mr. Jones Goes Back to Basics (avocado, spinach, and ricotta parcels; £6.50). *59 Endell St., tel. 0171/240–8077. Tube: Covent Garden. Turn right on Long Acre, left on Endell St. Open weekdays noon–midnight, Sat. 6 PM–midnight.*

Neal's Yard Dining Room. The windows of this airy "world food" café open onto a cool, peace-love-and-granola courtyard lined with health food stores and juice bars. Partake of some Turkish *meze* (appetizers; £5.50) or Egyptian falafel (£3.65) and seek transcendental oneness. *14 Neal's Yard, tel. 0171/379–0298. Tube: Covent Garden. Walk east on Long Acre, turn left on Neal St., left on Shorts Gardens, right on Neal's Yard. BYOB, no smoking. Open Mon.–Sat. noon–8 (until 5 PM in winter).*

EARL'S COURT

For hash and hookers, Earl's Court is fine. For food, it's pretty grim: loads of nasty kebab shops, greasy chippies, and plain sandwich shops catering to the constant flow of travelers.

➤ **UNDER £5** • **Al Rawshi.** Quick and greasy satisfaction is guaranteed from the chicken or lamb shawarma (£2) and falafel (£1.50) at this tiny Lebanese snack bar. Wash it all down with a variety of fresh fruit juices (£1). *3 Kenway Rd., no phone. Tube: Earl's Court Rd. Walk north on Earl's Court Rd., right on Kenway Rd.*

Benjy's. Breakfast is big and cheap at this dive, which makes it a good place to fill up before journeying out of the culinary black hole that is Earl's Court. The Builder's Breakfast includes baked beans, two sausages, two pieces of toast, bacon, one egg, and as much tea and coffee as you can put down—all for £3.30. *157 Earl's Court Rd., tel. 0171/373–0245. Tube: Earl's Court Rd. Turn left as you exit the station. Open daily 5 AM–9:30 PM.*

Kramps. This unfortunately named restaurant serves up delicious crepes, both sweet and savory. Try the classic sugar and lemon (£1.50), or stretch your palette with chicken Creole (£4.90). Big eaters won't be satisfied, though, without an additional side salad (£2). *6–8 Ken-*

Don't leave Kramps without a two-for-one coupon. As long as you wait at least 24 hours, the coupon gets you two plates of crepes for the price of one.

way Rd., tel. 0171/244–8759. Tube: Earl's Court Rd. Walk north on Earl's Court Rd., turn right on Kenway Rd. Open daily noon–11. MC, V.

➢ **UNDER £10** • **Texas Lone Star.** This over-the-top shrine to Texas will cure the homesick Lone-Star staters before they can say "Sam Houston" (oof). Respectable barbecue ribs (£6) and messy chili burgers (£5.60) are the best deals. The good selection of Mexican beers (£2 a bottle) may force you to postpone your research into English ale. *154 Gloucester Rd., tel. 0171/370–5625. Tube: Gloucester Rd. Walk south down Gloucester Rd. Open Sun.–Wed. noon–11:30, Thurs.–Sat. noon–12:30 AM. AE, MC, V.*

Thai Taste. An elegant oasis amid cheesy food stands and take-away places, Thai Taste feels like a real restaurant, with white cotton tablecloths, proper silverware, and subdued lighting. The entrance is easy to miss, though, so keep a sharp eye out. Order the basil chicken (£5.25) or the beef with black beans, ginger, and black mushrooms (£5.25). Linger afterwards with a Singha beer (£2.50). *130 Cromwell Rd., tel. 0171/373–1647. Tube: Gloucester Rd. Walk north on Gloucester Rd., turn left on Cromwell Rd. Open Mon. 6:30 PM–11:30 PM, Tues.–Sun. noon–3 and 6:30–11:30. AE, MC, V.*

HAMPSTEAD

The wealthy, genteel surroundings—Hampstead Heath is but a step away—ensure that this neighborhood is littered with overpriced bistros and hep cafés. Don't restrict yourself to **Hampstead High Street;** explore the side streets for tearooms and a smattering of mellow cafés. On busy **Heath Street,** which runs right past the Hampstead tube station, fill up on delicious Hungarian poppy seed cake at **Louis Patisserie** (32 Heath St.).

➢ **UNDER £10** • **Ali Baba.** Homey, heartwarming food offsets the dated Egyptian decor. Traditional stews start at £3.50, or try a more filling plate of lamb with rice and nuts (£5.50) or stuffed grape leaves (£3.50). If you're in a rush, there's always take-out shawarma, falafel, and kebabs. *32 Ivor Pl., tel. 0171/723–7474. Tube: Baker St. Walk west on Marylebone Rd., turn right on Gloucester Pl., right on Ivor Pl. Open daily noon–midnight.*

Viva Zapata. The £4.95 all-you-can-eat Tex-Mex buffet is highly recommended for homesick Americans and anyone else with a taste for chili and beans. The staff can be offhand, but they fit in with the laid-back atmosphere, which features plenty of youthful fashion victims. *7 Pond St., tel. 0171/431–9134. Tube: Hampstead. Walk south on Hampstead High St., turn left on Pond St. Open daily 10 AM–midnight. MC, V.*

Zamoyski's. Where else in London can you choose from more than 20 vodkas (£1.40 a shot)? Sample several while working on the Polish *mezze*, nine dishes for a bargain £4.50. Equally worthwhile are the *blinis* (pancakes) with smoked salmon (£4.50) and the *klops* (meat loaf; £5.50). *85 Fleet Rd., tel. 0171/794–4782. Tube: Hampstead. Walk south on Hampstead High St., turn left on Pond St., right on Fleet Rd. Open weekdays 5:30 PM–11 PM, Sat. 6 PM–11 PM, Sun. noon–10:30. AE, MC.*

KNIGHTSBRIDGE

Knightsbridge is a ritzy tourist and shopping area, where chic Londoners drop names like loose change while promenading past designer boutiques. Although there's a wide variety of cuisines on **Beauchamp Place,** off **Brompton Road,** the same can't be said of price ranges: Your best bets for budget dining in Knightsbridge are pubs and sandwich shops.

➢ **UNDER £5** • **La Barraca.** The open windows and doors in the front make this mellow Kensington tapas bar a sort of outdoor café; it's also a popular late-night watering hole. Order calamari (£3.90), garlic chicken (£3.65), or mussels (£3.90). *215 Kensington Church St., tel. 0171/229–9359. Tube: Notting Hill Gate. Walk east on Notting Hill Gate, turn right on Kensington Church St. Open Mon.–Sat. 11 AM–1 AM. AE, MC, V.*

The Stockpot. The Stockpot's English and Continental menu changes twice a day and features simple but tasty dishes like stuffed squash (£2.65) or lamb cutlets with potatoes (£3.95). Finish off your meal with a traditional sweet like the treacle pudding with custard (95p). *6 Basil St., tel. 0171/589–8627. Tube: Knightsbridge. Walk south on Sloane St., turn left on Basil St. Open weekdays 9:30 AM–11:30 PM, Sat. noon–11:30, Sun. noon–10:30. Other locations: 273 King's Rd. (Tube: Sloane Sq.), and 40 Panton St. (Tube: Piccadilly Circus).*

➢ **UNDER £10** • **Caravela.** This Portuguese basement bistro is a great place if you can stomach the outrageous £1.25 cover charge and mandatory 12.5% service charge. Indulge in *sardinhas assadas* (charcoal-grilled sardines; £6.75) or *lulas á marinheira* (squid simmered in tomatoes and onions; £7.95) while being serenaded by Portuguese folk music. *39 Beauchamp Pl., tel. 0171/584–2163. Tube: Knightsbridge. Walk southwest on Brompton Rd., turn left on Beauchamp Pl. Open Mon.–Sat. noon–3 and 7–1. AE, MC, V.*

Luba's Bistro. This Russian restaurant suffers from an overabundance of red-checkered tablecloths and peasant art, but the food is yummy and the helpings are large. They'll even deduct 10% from your bill if you pay before 8 PM. House specialties include Georgian-spiced lamb (£9.95) and buckwheat piroshki (£5.75). *6 Yeoman's Row, tel. 0171/589–2950. Tube: Knightsbridge. Walk west on Brompton Rd., turn left on Yeoman's Row. BYOB. Open Mon.–Sat. 6 PM–midnight. AE, MC, V.*

Scandies. This eatery is a welcome alternative to the swill elsewhere in Knightsbridge. Its Continental menu changes every two weeks, but regular delicacies include the flaked pink trout salad (£4.50) and the spicy lamb casserole (£7). If weather permits, settle down at a sidewalk table. *4 Kynance Pl., tel. 0171/589–3659. Tube: Gloucester Rd. Walk north on Gloucester Rd., turn left on Kynance Pl. Open weekdays noon–3 and 5:30–10:30, weekends noon–3 and 6:30–10:30. AE, MC, V.*

MAYFAIR

Mayfair comprises two distinct neighborhoods, namely Marble Arch and Piccadilly. Marble Arch is known for its sandwich shops and busy shoppers on **Oxford Street** and nearby **St. Christopher's Place, James Street,** and **Wigmore Street**. Piccadilly, London's most popular meeting place, may be a little chaotic for an outdoor picnic, but the people-watching can't be beat (try the steps of the Eros statue right in the middle of Piccadilly Circus). While **Denman Street** is a solid bet for sandwich shops and cafés, there's no particularly good road for restaurant-hunting.

➢ **UNDER £5** • **Malaysia Hall.** Even though this cafeteria-style dining hall is intended for and mainly patronized by Malaysian students, the public is welcome, and you can't do better for so cheap. The set meal—rice topped with any of the excellent, spicy dishes—goes for the ridiculously low price of £1.80. As you can imagine, long lines form. *46 Bryanston Sq., tel. 0171/723–9484. Tube: Marble Arch. Walk west on Oxford St., turn right on Great Cumberland Pl. and keep going for 5 blocks. Open daily 8:30 AM–9 PM.*

New Piccadilly. The decor in this hole in the wall is so weird it's interesting: red and yellow Formica furniture, an old unfinished floor, and a curious collection of "art." Simple, no-frills, British-Italian food like deep-fried chicken Toscana and Escallop Piccadily Garni (veggies and potatoes) both go for £4.50. *8 Denman St., tel. 0171/437–8530. Tube: Piccadilly Circus. Walk northeast on Shaftesbury Ave., turn left on Denman St. Open daily 11:30–9:30.*

Rabin's Nosh Bar. A good kosher nosh is what you can expect from this humble café: sandwiches, bagels with salt beef (£2.55), and *kneidlach* (matzoh ball) or lokshen soup (£2.55). *39 Great Windmill St., tel. 0171/434–9913. Tube: Piccadilly Circus. Walk 1 block northeast on Shaftesbury Ave., turn left on Great Windmill St. Open Mon.–Sat. 11–8.*

Taffgoods. Here you'll find London's cheapest noshes: Bagels with lox and cream cheese cost 90p, salt-beef bagels £1.50. It's possible to eat in, but most order to go. *128 Wardour St., tel. 0171/437–3286. Tube: Piccadilly Circus. Walk 3 blocks northeast on Shaftesbury Ave., turn left on Wardour St. Open Mon.–Sat. 7 PM–4:30 PM.*

West End Kitchen. Comfy green chairs and pine booths impart charm and simplicity rarely found in this busy part of town. Three-course lunch specials—like the Lancashire hot pot with salad and apple crumble—go for £2.95 on weekdays, £3.50 on weekends. Lentil and carrot soup (85p) makes an excellent light lunch. *5 Panton St., tel. 0171/839–4241. Tube: Piccadilly Circus. Walk south on Haymarket, turn left on Panton St. Open Mon.–Sat. 11:30 AM–11:45 PM, Sun. noon–11.*

➤ **UNDER £10** • **Hamine.** Homesick Japanese and local cognoscenti patronize this slick noodle shop. Have a huge bowl of *charsoo ramen* (noodles with rice and pork; £6.50) or one with veggies (£6.50). Either way, you'll leave stuffed. *84 Brewer St., tel. 0171/287–1318. Tube: Piccadilly Circus. Walk north on Sherwood St., turn left on Brewer St. Open weekdays noon–3 AM, Sat. noon–2 AM, Sun. noon–midnight.*

SOHO

Soho, the heart of tourist London, is a happy hunting ground when it comes to restaurants, cafés, trattorias, food stands—just about every type of eatery imaginable. London's best Asian restaurants are in Soho's small Chinatown, on **Lisle Street** (pronounced "Lyle") and **Gerrard Street** between Leicester Square and Shaftesbury Avenue. This is the best place to shop for herbs and bulk produce, fresh fish, meats, teas, and miracle cures. Soho's **Wardour Street** is the place to scout out everything from fast-food stands to chains like Pizza Hut.

Great London Take-Aways

- **Abohammad Restaurant.** Most Queensway kebab takeouts use some kind of disgusting meat loaf for shawarma, but not here. Your £3 buys a kebab as it's meant to be. *102 Queensway, tel. 0171/727–0830. Tube: Queensway or Bayswater.*

- **Bonne Bouche Coffee Shop.** Cheap sandwiches in Marylebone. *2 Thayer St., tel. 0171/935–3502. Tube: Bond St.*

- **Gaby's Continental Bar.** No atmosphere here, only decent grub. Take your food to nearby Leicester Square or Covent Garden. *30 Charing Cross Rd., tel. 0171/836–4233. Tube: Leicester Sq.*

- **Garden Cafe.** A tacky hole-in-the-wall with delicious kebabs (£2.30), falafel (£1.80), and smoked salmon sandwiches (£2.20). *22 Cranbourne St. Tube: Leicester Sq.*

- **The Grain Shop.** The ideal veggie stop if you're milling along Portobello Road: Stews, quiches, and pasta run £1.75–£3.85. The best bargain is spinach pie (£1.20). *269A Portobello Rd., tel. 0171/229–5571. Tube: Notting Hill Gate.*

- **Manzara.** A characterless joint at best, but with some of the finest cappuccino (95p) and almond croissants (65p) in Notting Hill Gate. Grab some food on the way to nearby Kensington Gardens. *24 Pembridge Rd., tel. 0171/727–3062. Tube: Notting Hill Gate.*

- **Maxwell's.** Get ready for a serious blast of grease at this dog-eared fish-and-chips stand. *263 Old Brompton Rd., tel. 0171/373–5130. Tube: Earl's Court Rd.*

➤ **UNDER £5** • **Bar Sol Ona.** You walk through a vibrantly painted hallway and descend into the basement to enter this tapas joint. Choose from a large variety of tapas in three sizes, priced £4 and up. Don't miss happy hour (6 PM–10 PM) with Estrellas beer for £1. *17 Old Compton St., tel. 0171/287–9932. Tube: Leicester Sq. Walk north on Charing Cross Rd., turn left on Moor St., left on Old Compton St. Open Mon.–Sat. 6 PM–3 AM. AE, V.*

Govinda's. There's no proselytizing at this friendly Hare Krishna restaurant, just tasty vegetarian grub at rock-bottom prices. Govinda's is only a block from Soho Square, so you can eat in or order your lasagna (£3.50), *subji* (mixed vegetables with varying sauces; £2), or bean hot pot (£1.80) to go. Every night from 7:30, it's all-you-can-eat for £2.50. If that isn't good enough, on Sunday at 5 PM the Krishnas serve a free—yes, free—feast. No alcohol. *9–10 Soho St., tel. 0171/437–3662. Tube: Tottenham Court Rd. Walk west on Oxford St., turn left onto Soho St. Open Mon.–Sat. 11–8:30.*

Mildred's. This eatery offers above-average veggie food, a genial staff, and a boho hipster clientele. The menu changes daily, but if you spot chili bean burritos (£4.70) or stir-fried veggies with brown rice (£3.40), you're in luck. For dessert, spoon into a bowl of yogurt, honey, and nuts for £2.40. *58 Greek St., tel. 0171/494–1634. Tube: Leicester Sq. Walk north on Charing Cross Rd., turn left on Shaftesbury Ave., right on Greek St. Open Mon.–Sat. noon–11.*

New World. Paper tablecloths, schlocky Chinese lanterns, and tacky Muzak set the stage for weekend dim-sum feasts. The food is cooked Hong Kong–style and served from steaming carts that are rolled through the packed dining room. Pick from a variety of dumplings, noodles, steamed buns, even chickens' feet. It's a great bargain, and if you're not stuffed to the gills for £5, you'd better have that tapeworm checked out. *1 Gerrard Pl., tel. 0171/734–0677. Tube: Leicester Sq. Walk north on Charing Cross Rd., turn left on Little Newport St., and continue 1 block up small alley. Open daily 11 AM–midnight. AE, MC, V.*

The staff at Soho's Wong Kei's (41 Wardour St.) are renowned for their rudeness, so much so that people actually return just to be insulted.

Il Pollo. Pick from an extensive menu of incredibly cheap pastas: basic spaghetti runs £2.60–£2.90, with chicken £4, with veal £3. The atmosphere is jovial and noisy; herds of hungry university students mean you may have to share a table. *20 Old Compton St., tel. 0171/734–5917. Tube: Leicester Sq. Walk north on Charing Cross Rd., turn left on Moor St. Open Mon.–Sat. 11:30 AM–11:30 PM.*

Poons. At this classic hole in the wall, ducks hang in the windows, the food is cheap and tasty, and the staff is friendly. When the place gets busy, waiters don't ask before seating people at your table. Menu highlights include roast duck (£3.90) and noodles with mixed veggies (£3.10). Come with a group of friends. *27 Lisle St., tel. 0171/437–4549. Tube: Leicester Sq. Walk north on Charing Cross Rd., turn left on Newport St., left on Newport Pl., right on Lisle St. Open daily noon–11:30.*

➤ **UNDER £10** • **Harry's Bar.** This is one of the only places in Soho that serves late-night breakfasts (10 PM–6 AM), so you can imagine what a scene it becomes in the wee hours. After a hard evening's clubbing, collapse with a full English breakfast (£5) or Harry's Blowout (£7), a hodgepodge of every breakfast dish on the menu. *19 Kingly St., tel. 0171/434–0309. Tube: Piccadilly Circus. Walk north on Regent St., turn right on Beak St., left on Kingly St. Open Mon.–Sat. 7:30 AM–6 AM. MC, V.*

Italian Graffiti. If it's even vaguely warm enough, sit at a sidewalk table and savor one of Graffiti's inexpensive gourmet pizzas; a large prosciutto-and-mushroom runs £5.50. Graffiti also does a good job with pasta, particularly spaghetti *puttanesca*, with tomatoes, olives, and onions (£5). *163–165 Wardour St., tel. 0171/439–4668. Tube: Oxford Circus. Walk east on Oxford St., turn right on Wardour St. Open weekdays noon–3 and 5:45–midnight, Sat. noon–midnight. AE, V.*

La Reash Cous-Cous House. The sidewalk tables here are great for people-watching. Couscous (£6) is an obvious specialty; a bolder option is the platter of *Mazah* (£9), a collection of yummy small dishes that can feed two easily. *23–24 Greek St., tel. 0171/439–1063. Tube: Leicester Sq. or Tottenham Court Rd. From Leicester Sq.: walk north on Charing Cross Rd., turn left on Moor St. (which leads to Greek St.). From Tottenham Court Rd.: walk south on Charing Cross Rd., turn right on Moor St. Open daily noon–midnight. MC, V.*

Tokyo Diner. Look for the doorway hidden behind flapping fabric; just inside you'll find basic, tasty Japanese food at decent prices. Dive into a steamy bowl of fried rice or stuff yourself with *donburi*, a bowl of sticky rice laced with soya, egg, and onion plus a meat of your choice (£5). *2 Newport Pl., tel. 0171/287–8777. Tube: Leicester Sq. Walk north on Charing Cross Rd., turn left on Little Newport St., right onto Newport Pl. Open daily noon–midnight.*

Van Long. The tasteful decor of this Indonesian and Malaysian restaurant is a welcome respite from the Formica and hanging lanterns of most Soho Asian joints. And the food's excellent, to boot. Indulge in pork slices with bamboo shoots, baby corn, and mushrooms (£5) or the spicy stir-fried prawns (£7). *40 Frith St., tel. 0171/434–3772. Tube: Leicester Sq. Walk north on Charing Cross Rd., turn left on Shaftesbury Ave., right on Frith St. Open daily noon–3 and 6–midnight. AE, MC, V.*

SOUTH BANK AND WATERLOO

For a bit of river culture, grab a sandwich in Gabriel's Wharf and chill out in South Bank, London's answer to Paris's Left Bank. For better value eating, wander farther afield into the urban sprawl of Waterloo.

➤ **UNDER £5** • **The Fire Station.** This huge Mediterranean diner occupies a converted fire station: The old tiles and metal supports remain, but the red engines have been replaced by a huge bar, an open kitchen, and rows of wooden tables. The Italian-Continental menu changes twice daily; spinach papardelle (£4.95) and phyllo pastry with fruit and mascarpone (£3.25) are two delectable possibilities. *150 Waterloo Rd., tel. 0171/620–2226. Tube: Waterloo. Walk south on Waterloo Rd. Open daily 12:30–2:30 and 6:30–11. AE, MC, V.*

Splurging in London

With a few appetizers, wine, dessert, and more wine, some of the places listed in this chapter could become serious splurges—especially if mummy and daddy are paying. Try Belgo (Camden), The Brixtonian (Brixton and Clapham), Caravela (Knightsbridge), Il Carretto (Bayswater and Notting Hill Gate), Chapter 11 (Chelsea), Luba's Bistro (Knightsbridge), and The Quality Chop House (The City and Islington). Then again, if you have the chance why not go for something really special?

• **Alastair Little. The ultimate in modern British cooking. Don't be put off by the sparse interior—it's intentional, darling. Chef Little has made quite a name for himself with delicious Asian and Mediterranean-influenced food. Set lunches, including two courses, start at £10. Sadly, credit cards are not accepted. 49 Frith St., tel. 0171/734–5183. Tube: Leicester Sq.**

• **The River Café. At this superb Italian joint, you pay for what you get: about £20 a head for handmade pasta, charbroiled steaks, fresh fish, and an excellent range of Italian wines (house wines start at £10 a bottle). The riverfront view gives the restaurant a wide-open feel. No credit cards are accepted. Thames Wharf, Rainville Rd., tel. 0171/381–8824. Tube: Hammersmith.**

Marie's. Of the many Thai cafés that have recently popped up in London, Marie's takes the biscuit for tackiness. Never mind the Formica tables and small booths; the lemon chicken with noodles (£2.80) and pad thai with pork, beef, or mixed vegetables (£3) are greasy and satisfying. *90 Lower Marsh, tel. 0171/928–1050. Tube: Waterloo. Walk south on Waterloo Rd., turn right on Lower Marsh. Open weekdays 7 AM–5:30 PM, Sat. 7 AM–2:45 PM.*

SPITALFIELDS

Spitalfields, in the heart of the East End, was once the center of London's Jewish community, but now it's better known for Asian shops, restaurants, and markets. **Brick Lane** and the streets leading from it are where you'll find the best selection.

➤ **UNDER £5 • Bloom's.** Just east of the Aldgate East tube, this classic kosher deli is revered for its selection and rock-bottom prices: plain bagels 10p, salted-beef bagels £2, homemade lokshen pudding only £2. *90 Whitechapel High St., tel. 0171/247–6001. Tube: Aldgate East. Walk east on Whitechapel High St. Open Sun.–Thurs. 11–9, Fri. 11–3. AE, MC, V.*

Brick Lane Beigal Bake. An East End institution, Beigal Bake churns out freshly baked bagels around the clock. Add smoked salmon and cream cheese to your bagel for 90p, or go for thick, succulent slices of salted beef and mustard (£1.50). *159 Brick Ln., tel. 0171/729–0616. Tube: Aldgate East. Walk east on Whitechapel High St., turn left on Brick Ln. Open daily 24 hrs.*

Brick Lane Beigal Bake may be London's only 24-hour anything, and you'd be surprised how many weirdos make a predawn pilgrimage for bagels and lox.

Clifton. If you think Bengali and Indian cuisine are synonymous, Clifton will set you straight. It's one of the more stylish Bengali eateries on Brick Lane, but still cheaper than most; chicken vindaloo or lamb *phal* (hotter than hell) will set you back a mere £3.60. Look for a second branch in the Sweet Mart (118 Brick Ln). *126 Brick Ln., tel. 0171/377–9402. Tube: Aldgate East. Walk east on Whitechapel High St., turn left on Osborn St. (which becomes Brick Ln.). Open daily noon–1 AM. AE, MC, V.*

Lahore Kebab House. Popular with the locals, Lahore serves excellent tandoori dishes in purely functional surroundings. There's a bare sink to wash your hands in before eating, and the staff makes no bones about hurrying customers in and out. Well-spiced lamb *karahi* (seared on a sizzling hot plate) costs £3, mixed vegetable curry £2. Meat kebabs are a steal at 50p a pop. *4 Umberston St., tel. 0171/488–2551. Tube: Aldgate East. Walk northeast on Whitechapel High St., turn right on Commercial Rd., right on Umberston St. Open daily noon–midnight.*

Cafés

Let's be honest—London is not Paris or Berkeley, and cafés don't line the boulevards here. Even so, café-craving foreigners are on the rise in London, prompting an explosion of coffeehouses and nurturing something not unlike a café culture—as long as you don't mind hopping on the tube and doing a bit of walking.

Pimlico Brahms

If you find yourself in Pimlico (between Victoria Station and the Thames), you'd be mad to miss the Brahms Experience. It's a cross between an elegant bistro and a sleek, very hip, very David Lynch diner: candlelight, green velvet curtains, and an arresting view of Battersea Power Station. A plate of fresh mussels goes for £3.50, tiramisù for an unbeatable 50p. Stop in for coffee and watch the beautiful people at play. 147 Lupus St., tel. 0171/834–9075. Tube: Pimlico. Open daily 12–3 and 6–11:45 (Sun. until 11).

Al's Diner. In this City café, bankers and prim grannies peep through the windows, and striped plastic tablecloths and a funky staff round out the picture. Fortify yourself with a smoked salmon bagel (£1.60), or go decadent with cherry pie and custard (£2.20) and a cappuccino (£1). *11–13 Exmouth Market, tel. 0171/837 4821. Tube: Farringdon. Walk west on Cowcross St., turn right on Farringdon Rd., right on Exmouth Market. Open weekdays 7 AM–8 PM, weekends 10 AM–8 PM.*

Bar Italia. See and be seen in Soho's primo coffee bar where ineffably cool Italian waiters serve what's generally considered the best cappuccino (£1.20) in town. Chill at an outside table if the weather permits. Bar Italia is theoretically open around the clock, but the doors sometimes close 5 AM–7 AM. *22 Frith St., tel. 0171/437–4520. Tube: Leicester Sq. Walk north on Charing Cross Rd., turn left on Old Compton St., right on Frith St. Open daily 24 hrs.*

Café Bliss. If the name doesn't say it all, then the almond croissants (90p) and fresh sandwiches—try tomato, basil, and cream cheese for £2.65—will put an end to the debate. Oh yes, there's also a good selection of teas and coffees (around £1). *428 St. John St., no phone. Tube: Angel. Walk south on St. John St. Open weekdays 8–7, weekends 9–6.*

Café Delancey. This excellent whistle-wetter off Camden's main drag serves supremely large cups of coffee for £1.20. The light food menu, however, is standard and a bit overpriced. *3 Delancey St., tel. 0171/387–1985. Tube: Camden Town. Walk south on Camden High St., turn right on Delancey St. Open daily 8 AM–midnight. AE, MC, V.*

Maison Bertaux. Here, at one of Soho's best-loved pâtisseries, you can sit back and enjoy a gooey, flaky almond croissant (£1.20) while watching Soho socialites in action. *28 Greek St., tel. 0171/437–6007. Tube: Leicester Sq. Walk north on Charing Cross Rd., turn left on Old Compton St., right on Greek St. Open Mon.–Sat. 9 AM–7:30 PM.*

Maison Bouquillon. Grand gâteaux and exquisite pastries, most around £1.50, are what this Bayswater café does best. The 30p *physalis* (gooseberry pastries in sugary fondant) are to die for. *41–45 Moscow Rd., tel. 0171/229–2107. Tube: Bayswater. Walk north on Queensway, turn left on Moscow Rd. Open Mon.–Sat. 8:30 AM–9 PM, Sun. 8:30 AM–8 PM.*

Maison Sagne. With its white tile floors, cane chairs, and antique light fixtures, the Sagne seems to wish it were in turn-of-the-century Paris. But, alas, it's only Marble Arch. Linger over a cappuccino (£1.20) and pretend. *105 Marylebone High St., tel. 0171/935–6240. Tube: Bond St. Walk west on Oxford St., turn right on James St. (which becomes Mandeville Pl., Thayer St., then Marylebone High St.). Open Mon.–Sat. 8–6, Sun. 9–7.*

Marnie's. This airy, friendly place in Notting Hill Gate is regularly packed to the hilt. Fill up on bacon and eggs (£1.75) and fresh coffee (£1.40) before an arduous day of bargain-hunting. *9 Portobello Rd., tel. 0171/229–8352. Tube: Notting Hill Gate. Walk north on Pembridge Rd., turn left on Portobello Rd. Open Mon.–Sat. 7:45–4:30.*

Olympic Bakers Pâtisserie. Come to this traditional Greek bakery with a small sitting area for strong black coffee and fresh pastries packed with savory sweets like nuts and honey. Slices of baklava and kataifi start at 50p. *281 Camden High St., tel. 0171/482–1649. Tube: Camden Town. Walk south on Camden High St. Open Mon.–Sat. 8–6, Sun. 9–6.*

Pâtisserie Valerie's. Since its birth in 1926, Valerie's has become a hangout for starving artists and journalists, and the place is packed day and night. Join them with a hot cross bun (£1) or fresh pastry (£1.50 and up). *44 Old Compton St., tel. 0171/437–3466. Tube: Leicester Sq. Walk north on Charing Cross Rd., turn left on Old Compton St. Open weekdays 8–8, Sat. 8–7, Sun. 10–6.*

Primrose Pâtisserie. This Polish café is popular with arty locals, in part because it's far from the maddening crowds on Camden High Street. Delights include the aromatic poppy seed strudel (£1), apple crumble (£1.30), fresh-baked breads, and a variety of salads. *136 Regent's Park Rd., tel. 0171/722–7848. Tube: Chalk Farm. Walk southeast on Chalk Farm Rd., turn right on Regent's Park Rd. Open daily 8 AM–9:30 PM.*

Markets and Specialty Stores

For the best deals, though, especially on produce, you can't beat London's street markets; once you hear a barrow boy bellowing out the bargains of the day, you'll know you've arrived in London Towne. In the East End, the **Old Fruit and Vegetable Market** (Brushfields St.; Tube: Aldgate), held every Sunday 9–3, is especially known for its selection of organic produce. **Berwick Street Market** (Tube: Piccadilly Circus) is one of the best-loved food fares in London's West End. The **Brixton Market** on Electric Avenue (Tube: Brixton) features West Indian delicacies like yams, pig trotters, and unmentionable innards. And then, of course, there's Camden (Tube: Camden Town), with poultry and dairy stalls on **Inverness Street.**

Carluccio's. Mouthwatering pasta sauces and ready-to-eat dishes are prepared fresh every day. You can also pick up the essentials to make your own Italian feast: dried pasta, mushrooms, fresh veggies, cured meats, and all sorts of herbs. *28A Neal St., tel. 0171/240–1487. Tube: Covent Garden. Walk northwest on Neal St. Open Mon.–Thurs. 11–7, Fri. 10–7, Sat. 10–6.*

Fortnum & Mason. For exotic and unusual splurges, wealthy Londoners have flocked to Fortnum & Mason since 1707. Sure, you can buy caviar and truffles elsewhere, but the store's crystal chandeliers and royal red carpets provide a certain *je ne sais quoi*. Don't leave without a peek at the tea shop. *181 Piccadilly, tel. 0171/734–8040. Tube: Green Park or Piccadilly Circus. Open weekdays 9–5:30, Sat. 9–5.*

Harrods. Buy (or simply gawk at) every culinary delight imaginable: beautifully displayed fish and game, exotic fruits and vegetables, wines, more than 300 cheeses, and cakes, including a tempting choice of ready-to-eat dainties. *Knightsbridge, tel. 0171/730–1234. Tube: Knightsbridge. Walk west on Knightsbridge. Open Mon., Tues., and Sat. 10–6, Wed.–Fri. 10–7.*

Neal's Yard Wholefood Warehouse. London's original health food emporium has all sorts of seeds, nuts, fruit, breads, and cakes. There's also an impressive selection of British and Irish cheeses at nearby Neal's Yard Dairy (9 Neal's Yard). *21–23 Shorts Gardens, tel. 0171/836–5151. Tube: Covent Garden. Walk northwest on Neal St., turn left on Shorts Gardens. Open Mon.–Sat. 9–7, Sun. 10–5:30.*

Newport Supermarket. The staff are far from helpful (they're often downright rude), but you can't beat the prices on everything from black bean sauce and bamboo shoots to woks and dragon-painted china. *28–29 Newport Ct., tel. 0171/439–1573. Tube: Leicester Sq. Walk north on Charing Cross Rd., turn left on Little Newport St., right on Newport Pl., right on Newport Ct. Open daily 10–8.*

Selfridges. This is a very modern, chrome and white-tiled Aladdin's cave of ethnic foods and deli delights. It's also a good stop for perishable gifts, and a fine place to shop for groceries if you live nearby. *400 Oxford St., tel. 0171/629–1234. Tube: Bond St. Walk west on Oxford St. Open Mon.–Wed. and Fri.–Sat. 8:30–6, Thurs. 8:30–8.*

Steve Hatt. If you're a fish fiend then this is the place to come—even if only to admire the array of absolutely fresh (and often live) creatures in scales and shells. *80 Essex Rd., tel. 0171/226–3963. Tube: Angel. Walk north on Upper St.; turn right onto Essex Rd. Open Tues.–Sat. 7–5.*

Villandry. Here you'll find French pâté, Continental cheeses, fruit tarts, biscuits, breads, and more. If you must indulge but can't wait, there's a small café in back. *89 Marylebone High St., tel. 0171/487–3816. Tube: Bond St. Walk west on Oxford St., turn right on James St. (which becomes Mandeville Pl., Thayer St., then Marylebone High St.). Open weekdays 9–7, Sat. 9–5.*

Reference Listings

BY CUISINE

AFRO-CARIBBEAN AND AFRICAN

UNDER £10
The Brixtonian (Brixton and Clapham)
Calabash (Covent Garden)
Osmani (Camden)
La Reash Cous-Cous House (Soho)

BRITISH

UNDER £5
Alfredo's (The City and Islington)
Benjy's (Earl's Court)
Chelsea Kitchen (Chelsea)
Geales (Bayswater and Notting Hill Gate)
New Piccadilly (Mayfair)
Phoenix Restaurant (Brixton and Clapham)
Rock and Sole Plaice (Covent Garden)
The Stockpot (Knightsbridge)
Sydney Street Cafe (Chelsea)
West End Kitchen (Mayfair)

UNDER £10
Harry's Bar (Soho)
The Quality Chop House (The City and Islington)

CHINESE AND VIETNAMESE

UNDER £5
New World (Soho)
Poons (Soho)
Thanh Binh (Camden)

CONTINENTAL

UNDER £5
Chelsea Kitchen (Chelsea)
The Fire Station (South Bank and Waterloo)
Kramps (Earl's Court)
The Stockpot (Knightsbridge)
West End Kitchen (Mayfair)

UNDER £10
Ambrosiana Creperie (Chelsea)
Belgo (Camden)
Chapter 11 (Chelsea)
The Eagle (The City and Islington)
The Lansdowne (Camden)
Mars (Covent Garden)
Scandies (Knightsbridge)

GREEK AND MIDDLE EASTERN

UNDER £5
Al Rawshi (Earl's Court)
Lahore Kebab House (Spitalfields)

UNDER £10
Ali Baba (Hampstead)
Daphne's (Camden)
Micro-Kalamaras (Bayswater and Notting Hill Gate)
Neal's Yard Dining Room (Covent Garden)
Osmani (Camden)
La Reash Cous-Cous House (Soho)
Savva's (Bayswater and Notting Hill Gate)

INDIAN AND BENGALI

UNDER £5
Anwars (Bloomsbury)
Clifton (Spitalfields)
Diwana Bhel Poori House (Bloomsbury)
Govinda's (Soho)
Khan's (Bayswater and Notting Hill Gate)
Lahore Kebab House (Spitalfields)
Ravi Shankar (The City and Islington)
YMCA (Bloomsbury)

UNDER £10
Chutney's (Bloomsbury)

ITALIAN

UNDER £5
Eco (Brixton and Clapham)
The Fire Station (South Bank and Waterloo)
New Piccadilly (Mayfair)
Pizzeria Franco (Brixton and Clapham)
Il Pollo (Soho)

UNDER £10
Il Carretto (Bayswater and Notting Hill Gate)
Italian Graffiti (Soho)
Pucci's (Chelsea)

JAPANESE

UNDER £10
Hamine (Mayfair)
Tokyo Diner (Soho)
Wagamama (Bloomsbury)

JEWISH AND EAST EUROPEAN

UNDER £5
Bloom's (Spitalfields)
Brick Lane Beigal Bake (Spitalfields)
Rabin's Nosh Bar (Mayfair)
Taffgoods (Mayfair)

UNDER £10
Luba's Bistro (Knightsbridge)
Zamoyski's (Hampstead)

SPANISH AND PORTUGUESE

UNDER £5
La Barraca (Knightsbridge)
Bar Sol Ona (Soho)
Finca (The City and Islington)

UNDER £10
Caravela (Knightsbridge)

TEX-MEX

UNDER £10
Ruby In The Dust (Camden)
Texas Lone Star (Earl's Court)
Viva Zapata (Hampstead)

THAI, MALAYSIAN, AND INDONESIAN

UNDER £5
Churchill Arms (Bayswater and Notting Hill Gate)

Malaysia Hall (Mayfair)
Marie's (South Bank and Waterloo)

UNDER £10
Thai Taste (Earl's Court)
Van Long (Soho)

VEGETARIAN

UNDER £5
Diwana Bhel Poori House (Bloomsbury)

East West (The City and Islington)
Food For Thought (Covent Garden)
Gallery Café (Bayswater and Notting Hill Gate)
Govinda's (Soho)
Mildred's (Soho)

UNDER £10
Chutney's (Bloomsbury)
Neal's Yard Dining Room (Covent Garden)

SPECIAL FEATURES

BREAKFAST PLACES

UNDER £5
Alfredo's (The City and Islington)
Benjy's (Earl's Court)
Brick Lane Beigal Bake (Spitalfields)
Chelsea Kitchen (Chelsea)
Gallery Café (Bayswater and Notting Hill Gate)
Phoenix Restaurant (Brixton and Clapham)
The Stockpot (Knightsbridge)
Sydney Street Cafe (Chelsea)

UNDER £10
Harry's Bar (Soho)

OUTDOOR EATING

UNDER £5
La Barraca (Knightsbridge)
Churchill Arms (Bayswater and Notting Hill Gate)
Pizzeria Franco (Brixton and Clapham)
Sydney Street Cafe (Chelsea)

UNDER £10
Il Carretto (Bayswater and Notting Hill Gate)
Daphne's (Camden)
Italian Graffiti (Soho)
The Lansdowne (Camden)
La Reash Cous-Cous House (Soho)

Savva's (Bayswater and Notting Hill Gate)
Scandies (Knightsbridge)

EATING AFTER MIDNIGHT

UNDER £5
La Barraca (Knightsbridge)
Bar Sol Ona (Soho)
Brick Lane Beigal Bake (Spitalfields)
Clifton (Spitalfields)

UNDER £10
The Brixtonian (Brixton and Clapham)
Hamine (Mayfair)
Harry's Bar (Soho)

PUBS

By Caitlin Ramey

The English take their drink very seriously, and pubs are where Londoners go to hang out, see and be seen, act out the drama of life, and drink themselves into oblivion. Neighborhood pubs—patronized by local drunks and families—make up the largest group of London's 1,000 or so public houses. If you're a student (or not too old to pretend), most colleges have on-campus pubs for socializing between lectures. While the atmosphere is rarely inspiring, the clientele certainly is, and you won't find cheaper alcohol unless you buy discount cans at an "off-license" (the British equivalent of a liquor store).

The cruelest words in the English language: "Drink up, ladies and gents, time to go. Please lads, come now, drink up."

Once you decide where to drink, the big decision is *what* to drink. Most English pubs are affiliated with particular breweries and are beholden to sell only beers produced by that brewery. Some of the larger chains, identified on the pub's sign outside, include Bass, Chef and Brewer, Courage, Samuel Smith, Guinness, and Whitbread. In contrast, independently owned pubs, called "free houses," are allowed to serve whatever they wish and tend to offer a more extensive selection.

Unless otherwise noted, all pubs listed below are open Monday to Saturday 11–11, Sunday noon–3 and 7–10:30. Exceptions to the rule are wine bars (which charge handsome prices to subsidize their expensive after-hours liquor licenses), some theater or music pubs, and small neighborhood pubs that just don't give a damn. People also head to restaurants for after-hours drinking, since some serve alcohol as late as 2 AM. Of course, the pints are more expensive. And sometimes you must order food, too.

BAYSWATER AND NOTTING HILL GATE

If you want to avoid the American tourist crowd in Bayswater, wander just a little way west to Notting Hill Gate. This is where London's fashionable crowd dines in ever-so-trendy restaurants before winding things up with a refined pint.

The Ashes. It's all you could hope for: Popular, packed, loud, and smoky. Flags from all over the globe cover the ceiling, catering to international tourists who come for pints and animated conversation. *Moscow Rd., no phone. Tube: Bayswater. Walk north on Queensway, left on Moscow Rd.*

The Market Bar. Weird, drippy candles and heavy velvet curtains give this Notting Hill local an almost clubby feel. A mix of young urban trendies, rastas, and punks haunt the bar. *240A Portobello Rd., at Lancaster Rd., tel. 0171/229–6472. Tube: Notting Hill Gate. Walk north on Pembridge Rd., turn left on Portobello Rd.*

Prince Alfred. Every few days, free live music—a rarity in London—turns this place into the wildest pub on Bayswater's main drag. Otherwise, it's relaxed, quiet, and nothing special. *Queensway, opposite Whiteleys Centre, tel. 0171/228–0923. Tube: Bayswater or Queensway.*

Bartenders don't get tipped in pubs. If you want to show appreciation for exceptional service, buy the bartender a drink; after placing an order say, "and one for yourself."

Uxbridge Arms. The King's College set—young, urbane, and slightly drunk—packs this place on weekends. *Uxbridge St., tel. 0171/727–7326. Tube: Notting Hill Gate. Walk west on Notting Hill Gate, turn left on Hillgate St., right on Uxbridge St.*

Windsor Castle. Drinkers of every ilk are welcome, though on warm summer nights the large courtyard out back is packed with students from nearby King's College. *114 Campden Hill Rd., tel. 0171/727–8491. Tube: Notting Hill Gate. Walk west on Notting Hill Gate, turn left on Campden Hill Rd.*

BLOOMSBURY

With its myriad tourist attractions, Bloomsbury is a more likely locale for afternoon tea than a nighttime pub crawl. On the other hand, after blitzing the British Museum, you'll be parched.

The Old Crown. Two blocks south of the British Museum, the Crown serves tasty international nibbles like taquitos (£4.35) and veggie specials (£2.95). The wine list is impressive but expensive. *33 New Oxford St., tel. 0171/836–9121. Tube: Holborn. Walk west on High Holborn, veer right onto New Oxford St. Open Mon.–Sat. noon–midnight.*

Princess Louise. Polished wooden banisters, molded ceilings, and stained glass give this spacious, popular pub a genuine turn-of-the-century feel. The food is a cut above normal pub grub—especially the Thai dishes. *208 High Holborn, tel. 0171/405–8816. Tube: Holborn. Walk west on High Holborn.*

The Sun. Ale aficionados flock here for the city's largest selection of cask-aged "real ales." The Sun's proximity to the University of London means you'll find plenty of students here. *63 Lamb's Conduit St., tel. 0171/405–8278. Tube: Russell Sq. Walk east on Guildford St., left on Lamb's Conduit St.*

University of London Union. When you've had enough of American and Aussie tourist hordes, consort with the pimply natives in this cheap, unpretentious pub. You might be asked for a student I.D. *Malet St., tel. 0171/636–8000 or 0171/580–9551. Tube: Russell Sq. Walk southwest down Russell Sq., turn left on Thornbaugh St., right on Montague Pl., right on Malet St.*

CAMDEN

The Good Mixer. Don't be surprised if you spot a celeb or two hanging out after a grueling recording session at some nearby studio. There's a pool table and lots of smokers, but not much space; arrive early on weekends, or risk being shut out. *Inverness St., tel. 0171/916–7929. Tube: Camden Town. From station, turn right onto Camden High St., left on Inverness St.*

HQ's. Climb up a creaky staircase just off Camden Lock for this large, loftlike room. Food and overpriced beer are served at one end while live bands play at the other. Jazz, soul, and funk music attract a young, mellow crowd, especially on weekends. A cover of £3 is sometimes charged, but you can get in for less before 10 PM. *Westyard, tel. 0171/485–6044. Tube: Camden Town.*

WKD. WKD is one of Camden's trendiest bars, crammed with posers wearing black. After 9:30 PM, there's a cover charge (£3). Check *Time Out* for live music listings. *18 Kentish Town Rd.,* *tel. 0171/267–1869. Tube: Camden Town. Walk north on Kentish Town Rd. Open Tues.–Sat. noon-2 AM, Sun. 7-11 PM.*

World's End. After a busy Saturday at Camden Market, retreat to the world's largest pub (at least according to the management). Needless to say, finding a seat is never a problem. *174 Camden High St., tel. 0171/482–1765. Tube: Camden Town.*

CHELSEA

Hip, upscale, punk, and yuppie all at the same time, Chelsea is really more about wine bars and cafés than pubs. Even so, a handful of unpretentious pubs lies hidden on the alleys and side streets that lead from King's Road.

Admiral Cordington. You'll find an upscale crowd chatting on the outdoor patio of this handsome Victorian relic; note the gas lamps and antique mirrors. Come for a satisfying pub-grub lunch. *17 Mossop St., tel. 0171/589–4603. Tube: South Kensington. Walk east down Pelham St., cross Fulham Rd. to Draycott Ave., left on Mossop St.*

Coopers Arms. Ceiling fans, Persian rugs, and lots of newspapers for public perusal make this a mellow hangout. *87 Flood St., tel. 0171/376–3120. Tube: Sloane Sq. Walk southwest on King's Rd., turn left on Flood St.*

Front Page. This fairly small pub draws a steady crowd of twentysomethings. Checkers seems to be the game of choice. *35 Old Church St., tel. 0171/352–0648. Tube: Sloane Sq. Walk southwest on King's Rd., turn left on Old Church St.*

Henry J. Bean's. If you really must do the Americana thing, do it here. The burgers are the real thing, and you can order cocktails just like in Chicago (the owner's hometown). The drinks cost more than average, but there's a beautiful beer garden out back. *195 King's Rd., tel. 0171/352–9255. Tube: Sloane Sq. Walk southwest on King's Rd.*

The Queen's Arms. A young, beautiful, rich crowd comes here after a heavy day of boutique shopping. *94 Draycott Ave., tel. 0171/589-4981. Tube: South Kensington. Walk east down Pelham St., and cross Fulham Rd. to Draycott Ave.*

The Spaniards Inn (Spaniards Rd., tel. 0171/455–3276), near Hampstead Heath, served Romantic poets Keats, Shelley, and Byron—even Charles Dickens (this guy drank everywhere). Order the incredible chocolate cake and relax outside with a great view of the city.

THE CITY AND ISLINGTON

The City is mainly a daytime drinking area: When the suits leave at the end of the business day, so does the life, such as it is. Regardless, the pubs here are some of the oldest in London—once frequented by the likes of Dr. Samuel Johnson and Charles Dickens. Islington, in contrast, is less stuffy, less wealthy, and more conducive to hanging out.

Cittie of York. This huge, comfy pub is filled with the young white-collar set, but it's also one of the cheapest spots in the City to cop a pint. Cittie has been around since the 17th century, and its bar is reputedly the largest in London. *22 High Holborn, tel. 0171/242-7670. Tube: Chancery Ln. Walk west on High Holborn.*

The King Lud. A young, friendly crowd gathers in this centrally located pub on the east end of Fleet Street. Lots of polished wood lends the place a cozy, if somewhat trendy, feel. *Ludgate Circus, no phone. Tube: Blackfriars. Walk north on New Bridge St.*

Mitre. Skinheads and housewives alike mix at this quiet, relaxed Islington public house. The mood is set by candles and subdued lighting. *Upper St., tel. 0171/254–7890 Tube: Angel. Walk north on Upper St.*

The Ship and Blue Ball. The beer is particularly good here, compliments to the Pitfield Brewery. Definitely try Dark Star, an excellent organic and additive-free brew. *13 Boundary St., no phone. Tube: Old St. Walk east on Old St., veer right onto Austin St., right on Boundary St.*

Slug and Lettuce. The vibe is young and undergraduate in this traditional-looking Islington pub. Bands sometimes hang out here before a gig at the nearby Powerhouse. Come early if you want to lounge on the comfy couches. *1 Islington Green, tel. 0171/226–3864. Tube: Angel. Walk north on Upper St., turn right on Islington Green.*

Ye Olde Cheshire Cheese. One of the oldest pubs in London (*rebuilt* after the Great Fire of 1666), the YOCC has long been a famous haunt of Fleet Street journalists. Charles Dickens, once a parliament reporter for the *Morning Chronicle,* slammed down pints here. *145 Fleet St., tel. 0171/353–6170. Tube: Blackfriars. Walk north on New Bridge St., turn left on Fleet St.*

EARL'S COURT AND KNIGHTSBRIDGE

Earl's Court and Knightsbridge may be popular budget-lodging areas, but that's about it. When night falls, the streets empty—except, of course, for dazed tourists staggering from jet lag and looking for a nearby, no-hassle drink.

Ashebee's. This cool basement wine bar features a hipper than usual crowd. Descend the bright red staircase, order a Chianti, and dig the live accordion music. *22 Hogarth Rd., tel. 0171/373–6180. Tube: Earl's Court. Walk north on Earl's Court Rd., turn right on Hogarth Rd.*

The Grenadier. If you have time to kill before your Victoria connection, take a short tube ride to this tiny, smoky den just off Belgrave Square. *Wilton Row, tel. 0171/235–3074. Tube: Hyde Park Corner. Walk south on Grosvenor Crescent, right on Wilton Crescent, turn right on Wilton Row.*

Hoop & Toy. From the gaslights outside to the beef-and-ale pie on the menu, everything about the Hoop and Toy says Edwardian. It's a free house, with more beer to choose from than usual. *34 Thurloe Pl., tel. 0171/589–8360. Tube: South Kensington. Turn right exiting the station, cross the street, and turn right on Thurloe Pl.*

Prince of Teck. At this Aussie home-away-from-home in Earl's Court, you can nurse a can of Victoria Bitter ("VB" to those in the know) to blend in with the equally large Kiwi and South African contingents. *161 Earl's Court Rd., tel. 0171/373–3107. Tube: Earl's Court. Walk north on Earl's Court Rd.*

SOHO AND COVENT GARDEN

Soho's pub scene is frustrating. Some places make a killing selling overpriced pints to tourists, while others cater to wealthy Londoners with candlelight and fancy pub grub. In deepest Soho, you'll also find a few pubs packed with metal heads, Top-40 heads, and tweed-jacket heads, not to mention American, German, and French tourists.

Coach & Horses. It's here that '50s local character Jeffrey Barnard, of "Jeffrey Barnard is Unwell" fame, spent his life pissed at the bar, observing Soho's "Low Life" for the magazine *Spectator.* Order a bitter and observe for yourself. *29 Greek St., tel. 0171/437–5920. Tube: Leicester Sq. Walk north on Charing Cross Rd., turn left on Shaftesbury Ave., right on Greek St.*

Crown & Anchor. This otherwise standard pub has a noticeably hippie clientele. And no wonder—it's situated in the best part of Covent Garden. Don't miss nearby Neal's Yard Dining Room (*see* Restaurants in Chapter 4). *22 Neal St., tel. 0171/836–5649. Tube: Covent Garden. Walk east on Long Acre, turn left on Neal St.*

De Hems. Although its just steps away from Chinatown, De Hems's theme, if you can't guess, is Dutch; hence the gins and Orangeboom beer in the hands of the youngish, mixed crowd. Suits overrun the pub between 5 and 7 PM. *Macclesfield St., tel. 0171/437–2494. Tube: Piccadilly Circus. Walk northeast on Shaftesbury Ave., turn right on Macclesfield St.*

The Dog House. This little hole in the ground has the hippest divey scene in Soho, full of young and friendly urban funkies: It's cramped, smoky, and loud. *187 Wardour St., tel. 0171/ 434–2116. Tube: Tottenham Court Rd. Open Mon.–Sat. 5:30 PM–11 PM.*

French House. The unofficial Resistance headquarters during World War II, this Soho pub still maintains a distinctly French aura. Predictably, there's a great wine selection—easily the best of any pub in London. *49 Dean St., tel. 0171/437–2477. Tube: Leicester Sq. Walk north on Charing Cross Rd., turn left on Shaftesbury Ave., right on Dean St.*

Institute of Contemporary Arts (ICA). The ICA's café and bar are a cut above what you find in most museums. After you've examined the exhibits (*see* Museums and Galleries in Chapter 2), wander over to discuss your favorite director, poem, or beer, loudly, while wearing black and smoking heavily. *Nash House, The Mall, tel. 0171/873–0057. Tube: Charing Cross. Walk southwest on The Mall. Café open Mon.–Sat. noon–3 and 5:30–9, Sun. noon–9; bar open Mon.–Sat. noon–1 AM, Sun. noon–10:30 PM.*

Lamb and Flag. "The oldest tavern in Covent Garden" sits in an alley just off Floral Street. With the cobblestone courtyard and wee fluffy lamb on the sign outside, you'd never guess people once boxed bare-knuckle upstairs, prompting the pub's nickname, "Bucket of Blood." *33 Rose St., tel. 0171/497–9504. Tube: Covent Garden. Walk south on James St., turn right on Floral St., left on Rose St.*

Porcupine. People invariably spill out onto the sidewalks at this meat market for international students. Come to make new friends. *48 Charing Cross Rd., tel. 0171/836–0054. Tube: Leicester Sq. Walk north on Charing Cross Rd.*

SOUTH OF THE THAMES

With its industrial veneer and general lack of anything trendy, London south of the Thames is the butt of many jokes. Yet the museums are great, the South Bank Arts Centre is nearby, and the pubs are just as nice as anywhere else in the city, thank you very much.

The Fire Station. Housed in—you guessed it—a former fire station, this trendy hot spot serves wines, beers, and fine (if not a bit overpriced) food. *150 Waterloo Rd., tel. 0171/401–3267. Tube: Waterloo. Open Mon.–Sat. noon–11.*

Flower and Firkin. This modern pub right next to the Kew Gardens tube station is the haunt of tourists by day, locals by night. Come for pub grub and terrific home-brewed ale. Funky bands sometimes play on weekends. *Tel. 0181/332–1162. Tube: Kew Gardens. Closed Sun. 3 PM–7 PM in winter.*

Phoenix and Firkin. Voted Pub of the Year in 1993 by the *Evening Standard,* this pub rose from the ashes after part of the Denmark Hill BritRail station burned down a few years ago. It retained some of the station's design and added a microbrewery on the premises. Call for the schedule of live music. *Windsor Walk, tel. 0171/701–8282. Tube: Elephant & Castle. From station, take Bus 68 to Champion Park, alight and walk east on Champion Park (keep alert for train station).*

Willows Wine Bar. This is a lovely candle- and flower-filled pub, an ideal place to linger over a glass of wine or beer. The food selection is good, and the prices are decent. *Denmark Hill Rd., tel. 0171/701–0188. Tube: Elephant & Castle. From station, take Bus 68 or 176 south to Camberwell Green, and walk south on Denmark Hill Rd. Open Mon.–Sat. noon–3 and 5:30–11:30.*

GAY AND LESBIAN PUBS

London has a great gay scene, but pubs are a bit hard to find, especially if you're looking for something that caters exclusively to lesbians. Places like the **Drill Hall** (*see below*) have well-established lesbian or gay nights, but you'll need a magazine like *Time Out* to ferret out current details on pubs that nurture London's sizable community. Another resource is the **London Lesbian and Gay Switchboard** (tel. 0171/837–7324); it's not really an events hot line, but staffers may suggest a good pub or club if asked politely.

The Champion. The predominantly balding and potbellied crowd is big into Cher (a regular on the jukebox), but some younger folk keep this place from getting stale. All in all, it's a good place to end a day at nearby Hyde Park or Kensington Gardens. *1 Wellington Terr., at Bayswater Rd., tel. 0171/229–5056. Tube: Notting Hill Gate. Walk east on Notting Hill Gate Rd. (which becomes Bayswater Rd.).*

The Colherne. This is an in-your-face male pub for the hard core—dress code: black leather. *Old Brompton Rd., at Coleherne Rd., tel. 0171/373–9859. Tube: Earl's Court. Walk south on Earl's Court Rd., turn right on Old Brompton Rd.*

Drill Hall. For most of the week, the Drill Hall is a gay cultural center and meeting place, presenting music and theater (*see* Theater in Chapter 6), but on Monday night it's womyn-only. The folks are friendly, the music is sociable, and the drinks are decently priced. *16 Chenies St., tel. 0171/631–1353. Tube: Goodge St. Head northeast across Tottenham Court Rd. Open Mon. 6 PM–11 PM.*

Duke of Clarence. The fireplace inside and garden outside make this one of London's coziest women's bars. If you'd rather not take the tube and endure the short hike, catch BritRail to the Essex Road station and walk north one block. *140 Rotherfield Rd., tel. 0171/226–6526. Tube: Angel. Walk north on Upper St., turn right on Essex Rd., right on Rotherfield Rd. Open weekdays 5:30–11:30, Sat. 7–11, Sun. 7–10:30.*

Earl's. Although this place draws mostly boys, the attitude is easygoing, upbeat, and comfortable for just about everyone. *180 Earl's Court Rd., tel. 0171/835–1826. Tube: Earl's Court. Open Mon.–Sat. 4 PM–midnight, Sun. noon–midnight.*

King William IV. One of the oldest gay pubs in Britain, King William is patronized by a mixed group—all ages, both sexes. You can drink in the leafy courtyard out back, or breathe clean air in the no-smoking bar upstairs. *77 Hampstead High St., tel. 0171/435–5747. Tube: Hampstead. From station, turn left onto Hampstead High St.*

The Laurel Tree. Just two blocks from the Camden tube station, the Laurel is a friendly gay bar that attracts a mixed crowd. Dance downstairs to ABBA and Rocky Horror hits, or just hang out with a friend and a drink. *Camden High St., no phone. Tube: Camden Town.*

AFTER DARK   6

By Caitlin Ramey

London has a raging after-hours scene that's been setting global trends for decades. Rock music, jazz, raves, you name it, London probably did it first and often does it best. The one bummer is cost: A pint of beer can run you £2, movie tickets are £6–£7, and clubs usually charge covers of £6 and up, up, up. Student and rush tickets soften the blow for theater and classical music, and many dance and live-music clubs distribute half-price flyers on street corners. Even so, there's no getting around the fact that London is an expensive place to play.

First-run movie theaters, jazz joints, dance clubs, and big-name theaters are concentrated around Soho and Covent Garden, but you'll find hip alternative clubs and theaters all over London. A number of publications give detailed rundowns of what's on where—invaluable resources if you plan to stay in London for more than a few days. The best of the lot by far is *Time Out* magazine, published weekly and available almost everywhere for £1.50. If it's happening in London, it's probably listed in *Time Out,* complete with a useful description that will help you wade through the barrage of options. *What's On* (£1) is a cheaper but slightly less comprehensive version of the same thing. Alternatives to these relatively mainstream rags include *New Music Express (NME), Melody Maker,* and *Spin. The Evening Standard,* available at all newsstands, also has all-purpose entertainment info.

Frank Sinatra says "London by night is a wondrous sight," but not from the upper deck of a Night Owl bus—it's prime mugging turf.

In Soho, check the little cards and invites laying in heaps at clothing and record shops for suggestions on where to spend your evening; sometimes these promo cards entitle you to bargain admissions. Student I.D. cards also come in handy at dance clubs and some music venues, which offer "concession" prices to students with identification as well as to OAPs (old-age pensioners) and UB40s, i.e., the unemployed (it's the form one fills out to go on the dole—and yes, it's where the band UB40 got its name). And remember: Theaters and cinemas will only sell you reduced-rate and standby tickets if you can show them one of the above I.D.s.

The Artsline (tel. 0171/388–2227) is a free events-info service for people with disabilities—ask about anything from wheelchair accessibility to dramatic interpretations for the hearing impaired to "touch exhibits" at museums.

Pubs (*see* Chapter 5) generally close at 11 PM, which can be a real pisser. The tube also closes early (about 12:30 AM), so for late-night fun you'd better figure out London's extensive Night Owl bus system (*see* Getting Around London in Chapter 1). Night Owl buses operate on fewer routes and less often than daytime buses, but you still won't wait much more than 30 minutes for your double-decker. To avoid getting mugged, never sit alone on the upper deck of a Night Owl bus. Cab shares are also popular for getting around after the Underground shuts down, though be wary of minicab drivers who chirp "Taxi? Taxi?" outside nightclubs—they often overcharge for late-night trips, especially if they hear a foreign accent. For more details on the taxi scene, *see* Getting Around London in Chapter 1.

Clubbing

Every night of the week, scores of clubs spin contemporary dance music (house and techno), old R&B hits, 1970s funk and disco, and the occasional indie platter. One-nighters ("theme" nights that take place at particular clubs on the same night every week, or move around from club to club) are very popular, but tend to confuse matters with erratic opening and closing times—always check the daily listings in *Time Out* for current info. Some venues that normally stage live music also have dancing with DJs, sometimes after the bands, sometimes before.

The dress code at most of London's clubs is casual; jeans are almost always okay, though some places will specify "no trainers" (athletic shoes). Throughout London, clubs typically open by 10 PM and close around 3 AM (when many liquor licenses expire). Many clubs do have extended hours, but you'll pay handsomely for the privilege of partying into the wee hours. The standard cover charge for dance clubs is £5; you may get a break for arriving early—usually before 11 PM—or for showing a student I.D.

There are plenty of trendy, expensive discos—the sort mainly patronized by tourists and London's rich and beautiful—spread throughout Soho and Covent Garden. Many are right around Leicester Square, and all charge covers of about £10. If you're looking for nothing more than flashing lights, bass-driven dance music, and stylish crowds, try the huge **Equinox** (Leicester Sq., tel. 0171/437–1446), the stylish **Café de Paris** (3 Coventry St., tel. 0171/287–3602) near Piccadilly Circus, or upscale **Stringfellows** (16 Upper St. Martin's Ln., tel. 0171/240–5534), just off Leicester Square. If a bouncer refuses you admission into one of these trendy clubs because you're "not a member," it most likely means your 501s and hiking boots just don't cut it. But, as they say in London, no worries—you'll definitely fit in somewhere else.

Bar Salsa. Brazilian and other Latin bands play to an international crowd on the hot and sweaty dance floor. Salsa and other sexy beats are the norm, along with tequila shots and Corona beer. *96 Charing Cross Rd., tel. 0171/379–3277. Tube: Leicester Sq. Walk north on Charing Cross Rd. Cover: £2–£5.*

Camden Palace. A wide mix of one-nighters—rock, disco, house—draw large dancing crowds throughout the week. The Palace also hosts the occasional live band, often new indie talent. *1A Camden High St., tel. 0171/387–0428. Tube: Camden Town. Cover: £2–£10.*

Electric Ballroom. Londoners hell-bent on cool clubbing attire (especially of the goth variety) have given the Electric Ballroom the fashion thumbs-up. A powerful sound system and a large dance floor provide the setting for some great one-nighters, usually hard rock and glam. *184 Camden High St., tel. 0171/485–9006. Tube: Camden Town. Cover: £4–£5.*

The Fridge. Brixton's major dance venue is like a three-ring circus, often with multimedia displays, live performances, and go-go dancers. They host a couple of gay one-nighters, as well as some cool reggae and roots-oriented gigs. *Town Hall Parade, Brixton Hill, tel. 0171/326–5100. Tube: Brixton. Walk south on Brixton Rd. Cover: £3–£6.*

Gardening Club. All sorts of stylish one-nighters are held in this upbeat and easygoing club. The music is mostly house and techno. *4 The Piazza, Covent Garden, tel. 0171/497–3154. Tube: Covent Garden. Cover: £4–£8.*

Gossips. This subterranean lair has plenty of dark, sculpted corners for late-night liaisons. The music tends toward R&B, funk, and '70s disco—eminently danceable. Patrons are on the younger side of twentysomething. *69 Dean St., tel. 0171/434–4480. Tube: Tottenham Court Rd. Walk west on Oxford St., turn left on Dean St. Cover: £6–£8.*

Heaven. This massive gay club is busiest on weekends. During the week it caters to straights with a variety of one-nighters. Heaven's maze of rooms and hallways is cool for getting lost and remaining anonymous. *The Arches, Villiers St., tel. 0171/839–3852 or 0171/839–2520. Tube: Embankment. Walk up Villiers St. toward the Strand. Cover: £3–£10.*

The Hippodrome. Besides being impossible to miss, this mammoth, centrally located disco features all manner of lights and lasers, an almost dangerously powerful sound system, and tourists galore. More than anything else, come for the spectacle. *Charing Cross Rd., tel. 0171/437–4311. Tube: Leicester Sq. Cover: £8. Closed Sun.*

LA2 at the Astoria. Although the Astoria is normally a live-music venue, it also hosts some cool one-nighters, many of which are gay. When you need a break, head up to the balcony and peer down on the dancing masses. *157 Charing Cross Rd., tel. 0171/434–0403. Tube: Tottenham Court Rd. Cover: £2–£10.*

Limelight. One-nighters in this former church run the gamut—rave, funk, house, rave-gay. Two large dance floors usually play slightly different music, but either way, the mongo sound systems thump religiously. *136 Shaftesbury Ave., tel. 0171/434–0572. Tube: Leicester Sq. Cover: £5–£10.*

Mambo Inn. This long-running and popular one-nighter—actually a two-nighter—is the best of its type. Totally danceable African and Latin grooves are mixed downstairs, while upstairs it's hip-hop and house. The crowd is multi-ethnic and all ages. Arrive early before the queue gets outrageous. *Loughborough Hotel, cnr Loughborough and Evandale Rds., tel. 0171/737–2943. Tube: Brixton. Walk left on Brixton Rd. for ½ mi, turn right on Loughborough Rd. Cover: £3–£4.*

Paradise. Head to Islington's most happening gay club after a crawl through the nearby pubs. Unwind at the pool table or get busy on one of two lively dance floors. *1 Parkfield St., tel. 0171/354–2590. Tube: Angel. Walk north onto Liverpool Rd., quick right on Parkfield St. Cover: £1–£5.*

Turnmills. It host all sorts of one-nighters—*all* nighters on weekends—including some hugely popular gay and rave nights. Have breakfast in the attached café after dancing until dawn. *63B Clerkenwell Rd., tel. 0171/250–3409. Tube: Farringdon. Walk north on Farringdon Rd., turn right on Clerkenwell Rd. Cover: £2–£10.*

Wag Club. The hip-hop, contemporary R&B, and funk mix is dead on, but the smoke machine seems a bit much. Still, on a good night this hypertrendy Soho club does get funky—once you get past the goons at the front door. *35 Wardour St., tel. 0171/437–5534. Tube: Piccadilly Circus. Walk northeast on Shaftesbury Ave., turn left on Wardour St. Cover: £4–£10.*

Live Music

On any given night London hosts a stupefying number of shows, but nothing comes cheap: Covers and tickets cost anywhere from £3 to £20, with most falling in the £5–£7 range. On the upside, you generally get what you pay for. London's jazz clubs are first-rate, as are its rock and indie venues. With so many of Britain's imperial subjects coming home to roost, the international music scene—Caribbean, African, Latin—is nothing to scoff at. Pick up *Time Out, What's On, Melody Maker,* or *New Music Express (NME)* and face the music.

Acts like Madonna and U2 are usually booked at **Wembley Stadium** (tel. 0181/900–1234), an easy walk from the Wembley Park tube station along Olympic Way. Some of pop music's royalty also grace the stage of the **Royal Albert Hall** (Kensington Gore, tel. 0171/589–3203), not far from the Knightsbridge tube stop. The **University of London Union** (Malet St., tel. 0171/580–9551), near the Goodge Street tube stop, regularly hosts local bands for student consumption. Tickets are dirt cheap, but you may have to fake being a student. Smaller gigs are held at colleges around town; check bulletin boards or *Time Out* for the latest. Occasionally, good live music can also be found in pubs, sometimes even for free (*see* Chapter 5).

MAJOR VENUES

Academy Brixton. This Brixton institution is one of the bigger venues for hip indie and established acts. It's not Wembley Stadium, but it can accommodate about 4,000 people. *211 Stockwell Rd., tel. 0171/326–1022. Tube: Brixton. Walk north on Brixton Rd., turn left on Stockwell Rd.*

Astoria. All sorts of good bands play at this midsized theater—lots of rock, some indie, a splash of reggae. Come early and snag a seat in the upstairs bar; it overlooks the stage. *157 Charing Cross Rd., tel. 0171/434–0403. Tube: Tottenham Court Rd.*

Hammersmith Apollo. Formerly called the Odeon, it's still one of London's most famous mainstream venues. *Queen Caroline St., tel. 0181/748–4081. Tube: Hammersmith. Follow signs from station.*

Marquee. Its glory days were in the '60s and '70s, when bands like the Who, the Jam, and the Police played at the Marquee when it was on Wardour Street. In its newer, slightly larger incarnation, the Marquee has a reputation for featuring good indie, goth, and hard rock acts. *105 Charing Cross Rd., tel. 0171/437–6603. Tube: Leicester Sq. or Tottenham Court Rd.*

Town & Country Club. A favorite venue for bands that are big, but not quite ready for Wembley Stadium. The place gets packed with a fine mix of folks, and it's well designed; everyone has a clear view. *9–17 Highgate Rd., tel. 0171/284–0303. Tube: Kentish Town. Walk north on Kentish Town Rd., veer left on Highgate Rd.*

CLUBS

ROCK, POP, AND INDIE **Borderline.** When record companies want to try out new bands, they send 'em to this hip Soho establishment. Who knows, maybe Lilly Lizard or Toenail's End will make it big someday. *Orange Yard, Manette St., tel. 0171/734–2095. Tube: Tottenham Court Rd. Walk south on Charing Cross Rd., turn right on Manette St. Cover: £5.*

Garage. Clear views of the stage and a killer sound system make this a good place to see live rock and indie acts. Some nights there's a DJ and dancing. *20 Highbury Corner, tel. 0171/607–1818. Tube: Highbury & Islington. Cover: £6.*

Powerhaus. Straightforward and no-frills—basically a glorified pub with the simple additions of a ticket counter and stage. The major appeals are pub prices for beer and talented rock, folk, and R&B acts. *1 Liverpool Rd., across from tube station, tel. 0171/857–3218. Tube: Angel. Cover: £5–£10.*

Robey. This dive is great if you want all-night lineups of virtually unknown (but highly dedicated) thrashers. Hard and sweaty is the norm. *240 Seven Sisters Rd., tel. 0171/263–4581. Tube: Finsbury Park. Walk southwest on Seven Sisters Rd. Cover: £5.*

Rock Garden. Simply put: hard, guitar-heavy rock. It's a stepping stone for bands on the rise; U2 gigged here before their big break. *Covent Garden Piazza, tel. 0171/836–4052. Tube: Covent Garden. Cover: £4.*

The Swan. Nightly rock-and-roll livens up this otherwise nondescript pub. You won't recognize any of the bands, but the vibe is good and the music loud. *1 Fulham Broadway, tel. 0171/385–1840. Tube: Fulham Broadway. Turn right out of station. Cover: £5.*

REGGAE AND WORLD BEAT **Africa Centre.** Visiting musicians from Africa and the Caribbean often play here. On other nights, DJs mix it up for a fairly diverse dance crowd. *38 King St., northwest of Covent Garden Piazza, tel. 0171/836–1973. Tube: Covent Garden. Cover: £5–£8.*

Hackney Empire. It's worth the trek to the East End for the reggae, raga, and roots bands that play in this ornate space. *291 Mare St., tel. 0181/688–9291. Tube: Bethnal Green. From station, take LT Bus 253 north on Heath Rd. (which becomes Mare St.). Cover: £2–£13.*

The Rocket. Some great reggae DJs spin the wax here; it's also a popular venue for world beat and roots bands. You can't miss the place—it's the only one on the block with a spaceship on the roof. *Holloway Rd., tel. 0171/ 700–2421. Tube: Holloway Rd. Cover: £3–£12.*

The Vox. Dub, reggae, and other funky beats soothe a multi-ethnic mix of teens, students, urban funkies, and Brixton locals. *9 Brighton Terr., tel. 0171/737–2095. Tube: Brixton. Walk south on Brixton Rd., turn right on Brighton Terr. Cover: £3–£10.*

R&B, FUNK, AND SOUL **Brahms and Liszt.** A slightly upscale wine bar right off Covent Garden. Things loosen up a bit in the evenings with live R&B, jazz, and soul. *19 Russell St., tel. 0171/240–3661. Tube: Covent Garden. Cover: £3–£5; free Sun.–Tues.*

Pizza Pomodoro. This teeny basement eatery is home to some gargantuan live sounds—anything from Motown and '70s disco to classic R&B and jazz. Food and drink prices are on the wrong side of tolerable, which doesn't seem to bother the crowds of energetic thirtysomethings. *51 Beauchamp Pl., tel. 0171/589–1278. Tube: Knightsbridge. Walk south on Brompton Rd., turn left on Beauchamp Pl. Cover: 10% added to bill.*

Orange. Small, friendly, and favored by Aussies and Kiwis. Nightly bands range from funky to folky. *3 North End Crescent, tel. 0171/371–4317. Tube: West Kensington. Walk north on North End Rd., veer right onto North End Crescent. Cover: £5.*

Station Tavern. This West London pub is known for excellent blues bands and the mellow crowds that fill it every night of the week. And you can't beat the price—it's free. *41 Bramley Rd., tel. 0171/727–4053. Tube: Latimer Rd. Turn left out of station.*

Subterrania. Dance all night long at this small but outrageous club that showcases rap, hip-hop, funk, and R&B during the week. Subterrania's DJs rage hard on weekends. *12 Acklam Rd., tel. 0181/960–4590. Tube: Ladbroke Grove. Walk north on Ladbroke Grove, right on Cambridge Gardens, turn right onto Acklam Rd. Cover: £5–£8.*

JAZZ **100 Club.** Twenty years later, the 100 Club has evolved from a seminal punk club to a hip blues and jazz joint. Fortunately, it's still a dive. *100 Oxford St., tel. 0171/636–0933. Tube: Tottenham Court Rd. Walk ½ mi west on Oxford St. Cover: £5–£8.*

606 Club. Pro jazz musicians often come to—and sometimes play at—this basement club following a gig; inexperienced players are often encouraged to join in. It has a nice vibe, although you may have to wait hours for a table on weekends. Make reservations or prepare to stand inside by the bar. *90 Lots Rd., tel. 0171/352–5953. Tube: Fulham Broadway. Walk east on Fulham Rd., turn right on Wandon Rd., left on King's Rd., right on Lots Rd. Cover: £4.*

Bass Clef. This small, happening club brings down the house with its jazz sessions, Latin jazz bands, and African music. It's cozy and popular; get here early or reserve seats in advance. *35 Coronet St., tel. 0171/729–2476 or 0171/729–2440. Tube: Old St. Walk east on Old St., turn left on Coronet St. Cover: £4–£7.*

Bull's Head Barnes. One of the best jazz pubs in town, even if it is far away in Hammersmith. In its defense, the scene is pleasant—right on the Thames—and big names jam here regularly (shows start nightly at 8:30). *Barnes Bridge, tel. 0181/876–5241. Tube: Hammersmith. From station, take LT Bus 9 to Barnes Bridge. Cover: free–£6.*

Jazz Café. A fine way to end a day of carousing in Camden Town. Big-name talents often play here when touring London. Unfortunately, prices lean toward the high end. *5 Parkway, tel. 0171/284–4358. Tube: Camden Town. Cross Camden High St., walk southwest on Parkway. Cover: £5–£12. Closed Sun.*

Palookaville. This small bistro and wine bar has live jazz every weeknight, plus fusion, R&B, and Latin rhythms on weekends. The cover's cheap, and the small dance floor definitely sees action. Arrive before 9:30 PM to avoid the £3 cover. *13A James St., tel. 0171/240–5857 or 0171/836–8363. Tube: Covent Garden. Walk south on James St.*

Ronnie Scott's. This is the leading venue for jazz in London—if they're the best, they'll play here. Its status is, unfortunately, reflected in the prices. Book in advance or get in line early. *47 Frith St., tel. 0171/439–0747. Tube: Tottenham Court Rd. Walk 1 block west on Oxford Circus, turn left on Soho St., cross Soho Sq., continue down Frith St. Cover: £6–£12. Closed Sun.*

Film

If you're looking for big-budget Hollywood flicks on large screens, head straight for Leicester Square. Tickets at the spiffy multiscreen venues here cost £5–£7, and student discounts are as rare as the sun in January. For films in danger of selling out, it's not a bad idea to book in advance over the phone—the catches are you must pay with a credit card and arrive 30 minutes before show time to pick up your tickets. Also remember that while British films open fairly quickly in the States, American-made films are released in London long after their debut in the colonies. Almost every London newspaper lists movie schedules in its entertainment section, though you'll find the detailed reviews in *Time Out* most useful.

If you detest Hollywood blockbusters, London has dozens of repertory cinemas that specialize in seminal, epochal, and downright groovy flicks (though even major venues like the National Film Theatre and the Barbican occasionally show arty, avant-garde films). Not only are repertories cheaper than Leicester Square cinemas, they're much more interesting. While a few charge dinky membership fees of 50p–£1 per year, many have the bonus of bars and lounges where you can sit and deconstruct the latest viewing. Many also let you book tickets over the phone.

On weekends, there are usually late, late shows (starting around midnight) at some of the larger cinemas on Leicester Square.

Londoners aren't known for their love of foreign films, and you'll have to do some digging to find the latest from the Continent. Filling the gap are two highly respected venues: the **French Institute** (17 Queensberry Pl., tel. 0171/589–6211) and the **Goethe Institute** (50 Prince's Gate, Exhibition Rd., tel. 0171/411–3400), both in South Kensington. Most shows cost £1–£4. Some films aren't subtitled, so call ahead if it really matters.

Barbican Cinema. Foreign and arty films are slowly being supplanted by mainstream stuff here—too bad. If you're lucky, you may catch a flick that ties in with an exhibit at the nearby Barbican Art Gallery. Tickets £6, £4 for student standbys (when available). Every Monday, movies cost a mere £3. *Silk St., tel. 0171/638–8891. Tube: Barbican.*

Stand-Up in The City

London had a pitifully weak comedy scene until The Comedy Store opened its doors about 10 years ago. Although London comedians are still understated, dry, and cerebral, today there's also plenty of cussing, physical comedy, and other comic vulgarity that goes over fine with British audiences. Tickets are £3–£5. 28A Leicester Sq., tel. 01426/914433. Tube: Leicester Sq.

Other popular comedy clubs include Comedy at Soho Ho (Crown and Two Chairmen, Dean St., tel. 0171/340–3627), near Leicester Square tube; the Saturday-only Chuckle Club (Shakespeare's Head, Carnaby St., tel. 0171/476–1672), near Oxford Circus tube; and the Red Rose Cabaret (129 Seven Sisters Rd., tel. 0171/281–3051), near Finsbury Park tube.

Camden Plaza. The flicks here are decidedly arty and noncommercial. Both British and foreign films are featured. Tickets £5, £3.80 for first screening of the day, £2.30 students. *112 Camden High St., tel. 0171/485–2443. Tube: Camden Town.*

Electric Cinema. After clawing your way through Portobello Market, wind down with a cheap, esoteric movie. Tickets £5, £4 students. *191 Portobello Rd., tel. 0171/792–0328. Tube: Notting Hill Gate. Walk 2 blocks north on Pembridge Rd., turn left on Portobello Rd.*

Everyman Cinema. Billing itself as "London's oldest repertory," this cozy venue shows an excellent selection of classic, foreign, avant-garde, and almost-new Hollywood titles. Tickets £4.50–£5, £3.50 students. Membership costs 60p a year. *Hollybush Vale, tel. 0171/435–1525. Tube: Hampstead. Walk 1 block south on Heath St., turn right on Hollybush Vale.*

Gate Cinema. Mainstream releases are cheaper here than at Leicester Square cinemas. Tickets £6, £3.50 for first two shows of the day. *87 Notting Hill Gate, tel. 0171/727–4043. Tube: Notting Hill Gate.*

The Gate Cinema features a bargain double bill every Sunday—perfect for a rainy afternoon.

ICA Cinema. Housed within the Institute of Contemporary Arts, this two-screen theater shows practically anything arty and/or esoteric. Tickets for the main screen cost £6.50, £5 on Mondays. Tickets for the miniscreen always cost £4.50. *Nash House, The Mall, tel. 0171/930–3647. Tube: Piccadilly Circus or Charing Cross Rd. From Charing Cross station, walk southwest on The Mall. From Piccadilly Circus station, walk south on Regent St., turn right on The Mall.*

Minema. This place prides itself on showing "only the best" first-run Hollywood crap. The redeeming feature: £4 student tickets. Everyone else pays £6.50. *45 Knightsbridge, tel. 0171/235–4225. Tube: Hyde Park Corner. Walk west on Knightsbridge.*

National Film Theatre. The NFT is one of London's best and cheapest repertory cinemas. Its three cinemas screen more than 2,000 titles each year, including foreign films, documentaries, Hollywood features, and animation. Tickets £4.25, £3.15 students. *South Bank Arts Centre, tel. 0171/928–3232. Tube: Waterloo.*

The National Film Theatre hosts the London Film Festival each November, featuring hundreds of flicks from Europe, India, and Australia; see Festivals in Chapter 1 for more info.

Prince Charles. Come for reasonably recent flicks, as well as some artier ones, at rock-bottom prices. Tickets £1.99, £1.50 for first screenings. *7 Leicester Pl., tel. 0171/437–8181. Tube: Leicester Sq. Walk west on Cranbourn St., turn right on Leicester Pl.*

Renoir. A little bit of everything, from Hollywood classics to obscure international fare. Tickets £5.50, £2.50 students. *Brunswick Centre, Brunswick Sq., tel. 0171/837–8402. Tube: Russell Sq. Walk east on Bernard St., turn left on Brunswick Sq.*

Classical Music

London is home to symphony orchestras that fully deserve their international fame—among them the London Symphony Orchestra, the London Philharmonic, and the BBC Symphony Orchestra. Expect to pay £5–£20 for regular symphony recitals and even more for big-name conductors and events. Plan ahead for things you really want to see, because many of the best performances sell out early. If you don't have tickets reserved, try going about 30 minutes before show time—you may be able to pick up returns (tickets that have been returned by patrons unable to attend). Students *with I.D.* are often eligible for last-minute, bargain-priced standby tickets; check with the venue to inquire about particular shows.

Probably the biggest—and most affordable—classical spectacles are the **Promenade Concerts,** better known as the Proms, held at the Royal Albert Hall (Kensington Gore, tel. 0171/589–3203) near the Knightsbridge tube station. The series runs for eight weeks from

July to September and features a smorgasbord of well-known pieces plus a smattering of new works. Tickets are £4–£30 unless you can score a gallery or arena seat (£2–£3). The last night of the Proms is the capper, a madly jingoistic display of singing, Union Jack–waving, and general merriment (demand for tickets is so high that you must enter a lottery). For ticket info, call 0171/589–8212.

> *On the last night of the Proms, the crowd goes absolutely berserk when the conductor leads rousing choruses of "Jerusalem" and "Land of Hope and Glory."*

In summer, definitely consider an outdoor concert by the lake at Kenwood House in Hampstead Heath or at Holland Park in West London. Venues and programs change yearly; check *Time Out* for the latest details. If you're broke, the **City of London Festival** (*see* Festivals in Chapter 1), held the first three weeks in July, features classical performances, many of which are free, at churches and squares throughout the City.

Barbican Hall. The famous London Symphony Orchestra plays in the music auditorium of the Barbican Centre. Although the emphasis is on classical music, everything from brass bands to smoky jazz acts also plays here. *Silk St., tel. 0171/638–8891 (box office) or 0171/638–2295 (recorded info). Tube: Barbican. Follow clearly marked signs. Admission: £5–£25, £5–£10 for student standbys on day of performance.*

Royal Festival Hall. The South Bank Arts Centre's main music auditorium is also home to the London Philharmonic Orchestra. Free art exhibits and performances take place daily in the foyer. Student standbys are available two hours before most performances. *South Bank Arts Centre, tel. 0171/928–8800 (box office) or 0171/633–0932 (recorded info). Tube: Waterloo or Embankment. Follow clearly marked signs. Admission: £2–£50.*

St. John's. With its excellent acoustics, this beautiful baroque church has rapidly become one of London's leading venues for classical music. *Smith Sq., tel. 0171/222–1061. Tube: Westminster. From station, walk south on St. Margaret St. (which becomes Old Palace Yard, Abingdon St., and Millbank), turn right on Dean Stanley St. Admission: £3–£15.*

St. Martin-in-the-Fields. This ancient church is a cool venue for classical recitals, both acoustically and atmospherically. Evening gigs (£6 and up) feature some impressive names. Look for free recitals on selected weekdays at 1:05 PM; although it's not the Academy of St. Martin-in-the-Fields orchestra playing, it still sounds good. *St. Martin's Pl., Trafalgar Sq., tel. 0171/930–0089. Tube: Charing Cross. Walk west to Trafalgar Sq.*

Wigmore Hall. Chamber music, period music, and all sorts of soothing melodies fill the air of this pleasant forum. The weekly Sunday morning recitals are very popular; coffee and a croissant from the Wigmore Hall café are the perfect complement. *36 Wigmore St., tel. 0171/935–2141. Tube: Bond St. Head north on James St., turn right on Wigmore St. Admission: £3–£18.*

Opera and Ballet

London's most prestigious opera venue is Covent Garden's Royal Opera House (*see below*), where tickets range from £5 (serious nosebleed) to £125 (ouch!). Despite the prohibitive cost for decent seats, tickets for most programs sell out early. If you're prepared to wait in line, the Royal Opera offers returns for one-third the original price. Also check weekly entertainment publications for smaller operas being sung around town—even some Italian restaurants are popular venues.

Performances by major ballet companies start at around £10 and head skyward. Student standby tickets can bring down prices considerably—check with the venues beforehand and be prepared to queue. Prices are slightly lower for the ballet than for the opera, but tickets go faster; reserve ahead. This is doubly true if you want to catch the world-famous **Royal Ballet,** which performs at the Royal Opera House. The **English National Ballet** and visiting international companies sometimes perform at the Coliseum.

Coliseum. English-language operas are what the English National Opera Company does best. Prices here are generally lower than at the Royal Opera Company, and productions are unconventional and often a lot more exciting. The cheapest upper balcony seats, known as "the gods," are better than those at the Royal. Of course, renting a pair of opera glasses for 20p is never a bad idea. *St. Martin's Ln., tel. 0171/836–3161. Tube: Leicester Sq. Walk northeast on Long Acre, quick right on St. Martin's Ln.*

Royal Opera House. This is the classiest venue for opera in London—very popular and quick to sell out. Tickets way up in the upper balcony cost about £5, and you can hear the operas just fine. You can't see a damn thing, though, without opera glasses—drop a few quid on a disposable pair at the shop inside. When operas are sung in a language other than English, they translate them on a video screen above the stage. *Covent Garden, tel. 0171/240–1066. Tube: Covent Garden.*

Sadler's Wells Theatre. Sadler's Wells hosts various ballet companies—including the Royal and the Rambert—as well as regional ballet and international modern dance troupes. Again, prices are much lower here than at Covent Garden venues. *Rosebery Ave., tel. 0171/278–8916. Tube: Angel. From station, turn left and cross Pentonville Rd., walk south on St. John St., veer right onto Rosebery Ave.*

Theater

London is the theater capital of a country that truly loves the stuff, training would-be actors as if they were actual professionals, to be taken as seriously as bankers and academics. The theater sections in *Time Out* and *What's On* run for pages and pages, with everything from Shakespeare to Mike Leigh to Brecht. London is even overtaking New York as the launching ground for new Andrew Lloyd Webber-ish "vehicles," so if you must see a musical, do it here.

London has always been passionate about its theater; when the Puritans tried to ban performances in the 16th century, underground productions simply moved to the new hot-chocolate houses (established specifically to serve the trendy delicacy imported from the Americas) that were springing up everywhere in London Towne.

Theater in London falls into two basic categories: The West End and the fringe. The West End is London's equivalent of Broadway, featuring big-budget productions and musicals like *Cats, Les Misérables, Miss Saigon,* and *Sunset Boulevard.* Information about West End plays is ubiquitous, though publications like *Time Out, The Evening Standard,* and the *London Theatre Guide* (published by the Society of West End Theatres) are the best. Fringe theaters present everything from small productions by prominent playwrights—folks like Sam Beckett, Harold Pinter, Carol Churchill, David Mamet, and Tom Stoppard—to experimental offerings by young local talent. Fringe performances are sometimes pretentious and obscure, but rarely boring.

Modern Dance

If ballet isn't your bag, or if you just don't like the larger halls, dozens of dance productions are held in smaller venues throughout London. Expect tickets in the £3–£10 range and bring your student I.D. The following are London's main dance venues:

- *Riverside Studios. Crisp Rd., tel. 0181/748–3354. Tube: Hammersmith.*
- *The Place. 17 Duke's Rd., tel. 0171/380–1268. Tube: Euston.*
- *Institute of Contemporary Arts. The Mall, tel. 0171/930–3647. Tube: Piccadilly Circus.*

WEST END THEATERS

The principal West End theaters are on Shaftesbury Avenue in Soho and the Haymarket in St. James's, as well as around Covent Garden. Book way in advance if you're planning to see a hit show; reserve tickets at the box office, over the phone using a credit card, or—for a 10%–20% service charge—through ticket agencies such as **First Call** (tel. 0171/497–9977) or **Ticket-master** (tel. 0171/379–4444). You'll also see small ticket outlets in central tube stations and in the West End; convenient, yes, but the commissions are a rip.

Half-price, same-day tickets cost £3–£10 and are sold at the **Society of West End Theatres** kiosk on Leicester Square; it's open Monday to Saturday noon–2 for matinees, 2:30–6:30 for evening shows. The lines are always long, and they only accept cash. One of the best ways for students *with I.D.* to score same-day tickets is to call or visit individual theaters' box offices. The **Student Theatreline** (tel. 0171/379–8900) lists which West End theaters are offering student tickets on a given night. Each day at 2 PM, the Theatreline updates a recording of the evening's options, but then it's up to you to contact the individual theaters.

Adelphi Theatre. *The Strand, tel. 0171/836–7611. Tube: Charing Cross Station.*

Albury Theatre. *St. Martin's Ln., tel. 0171/867–1115. Tube: Leicester Sq.*

Duke of York's Theatre. *St. Martin's Ln., tel. 0171/836–5122. Tube: Leicester Sq.*

Her Majesty's Theatre. *Haymarket, tel. 0171/494–5400. Tube: Piccadilly Circus.*

New London Theatre. *Drury Ln., tel. 0171/405–0072. Tube: Covent Garden.*

Old Vic. *Waterloo Rd., tel. 0171/928–7616. Tube: Waterloo.*

Palace Theatre. *Shaftesbury Ave., tel. 0171/434–0909. Tube: Leicester Sq.*

Palladium Theatre. *Argyll St., tel. 0171/494–5020. Tube: Oxford Circus.*

Prince Edward Theatre. *Old Compton St., tel. 0171/734–8951. Tube: Leicester Sq.*

Prince of Wales Theatre. *Coventry St., tel. 0171/836–5987. Tube: Piccadilly Circus.*

Theatre Royal, Drury Lane. *Catherine St., tel. 0171/494–5060. Tube: Covent Garden.*

FRINGE THEATERS

For the price of one West End blowout you can afford to see three fringe plays, often staged in basements, in pub back rooms, and anywhere else they can squeeze in a small stage and an audience. Fringe theaters generally sell student standbys minutes before show time for £5 and up. Standing-room tickets cost even less.

The Almeida. This old, successful theater maintains high standards for its contemporary and classical offerings. The simple but snazzy bar is great for intermittent refreshments. *Almeida St., tel. 0171/359–4404 or 0171/226–7432. Tube: Angel. Walk ½ mi north on Upper St., right on Almeida St.*

Drill Hall. All sorts of cool plays are here for the watching; its forte is excellent gay/lesbian productions. *16 Chenies St., tel. 0171/637–8270. Tube: Goodge St. Walk northeast across Tottenham Court Rd.*

Etcetera Theatre. A quaint 50-seater best known for its esoteric one-night productions. *Oxford Arms, 265 Camden High St., tel. 0171/482–4857. Tube: Camden Town.*

Greenwich Theatre. This 400-seat theater hosts everything from comedies to classics to the experimental. *Crooms Hill, tel. 0181/858–7755. Docklands Light Railway to Island Gardens, then walk under river via Greenwich Foot Tunnel.*

Hen and Chickens. One of Islington's best theater pubs. There's even live music in the pub a few nights each week. *Highbury Corner, opposite tube station, tel. 0171/704–2001. Tube: Highbury and Islington.*

King's Head. This is one of the oldest, best-known, and most respected venues for pub theater in London. The ancient, high-ceilinged pub (no cover) is an experience in itself. *115 Upper St., tel. 0171/226–1916. Tube: Angel. Walk north on Upper St.*

Lyric Hammersmith Studio. Mainly contemporary works, with plenty of literary adaptations that'll appeal to bookworms. *Kings St., tel. 0181/741–8701. Tube: Hammersmith. From station, cross Beadon Rd., turn right on Kings St.*

New End Theatre. This intimate, suburban theater in Hampstead is known for presenting period works rarely staged in London's bigger venues. The New End also tackles modern politics, both left- and right-wing. *27 New End, tel. 0171/794–0022. Tube: Hampstead. Walk north on Heath St., turn right on New End.*

The Young Vic. The nominal offspring of the Old Vic, this theater showcases cutting-edge productions and actors. In 1995, they'll be doing a series of "trilogy plays," each set sold as a package. *66 The Cut, tel. 0171/928–6363. Tube: Waterloo. Walk south down Waterloo Rd.*

ARTS CENTERS

Both the Barbican and National Theatre are major-league houses, but the productions they stage are often "fringe" in style—partly because they're both state subsidized and housed within larger arts centers.

The Barbican. The Royal Shakespeare Company stages productions of the Bard's great works here on a regular basis. For more modern, intimate, small-time stuff, see what's playing in **The Pit,** although tickets here don't cost any less than for a show in the larger venue. *Silk St., tel. 0171/638–8891. Tube: Barbican. Tickets: £6.50–£22.50, £6–£8 student standbys.*

National Theatre. Guest directors stage a variety of dramatic works here, from cutting-edge stuff to imaginative interpretations of old standbys. The National Theatre also hosts a series of talks and lectures entitled "Platforms" (admission £3.50, £2.50 students). Recent guest speakers include Nadine Gordimer and Arthur Miller. *South Bank Arts Centre, tel. 0171/928–2252 (box office) or 0171/633–0880 (recorded info). Tube: Waterloo. Tickets: £7–£22, £7.50–£10 standbys, £6 students with I.D.*

OUTDOOR THEATER

Outdoor theater in London is not a completely ridiculous, hideous, and cruel idea; believe it or not, the summers can actually be warm. In fact, London hosts two theater festivals that are completely staged in the great outdoors. The **London International Festival Of Theatre** (tel. 0171/490–3964), with performances from all genres, is held every other year June–July, with the next scheduled for 1995. Call after April for ticket info. British Telecom recently began sponsoring the **BT Streets of London Festival** every other year, with free performances by international casts held in locations throughout London. It'll come around next in the summer of 1996; check with a tourist office for schedules.

Regent's Park Open-Air Theatre. Smack dab in the middle of Regent's Park, with a program that ranges from Shakespeare to contemporary offerings. The season runs May–September, with a variety of afternoon and evening performances almost daily. *Regent's Park Inner Circle, tel. 0171/486–2431 or 0171/486–1933. Tube: Regent's Park or Baker Street.*

Poets' Corner

London lacks neither angst nor poets; check Time Out's "Books and Poetry" section for local readings and workshops. Orchestrated readings and stagings are also head at the Voice Box (Royal Festival Hall, South Bank Arts Centre, tel. 0171/921–0906), near the Waterloo tube station. You won't leave disappointed if you're a fan of anti-poetry, grunts, howls, and all-around weirdness. Tickets cost £4.

SHOPPING

7

By Caitlin Ramey

Name your poison, because London rivals any place in the known universe when it comes to shopping. Funky street markets that roar to life on weekends, swank department stores, music stores for the most discriminating ears, shoe stores for the least discriminating feet—it's all here. London may not trumpet its fashion sensibility the way other European capitals do, but there's no disputing that fashion slaves worldwide look to this city for the latest trends.

Be warned: Competition doesn't do much to keep prices low. You can easily blow your wad before blinking; if you plan to head outside London, wait for better deals on woolens, jewelry, and crafts. For what it's worth, *Time Out* magazine lists bargains regularly in their "Sell Out" section, and many of London's stores have huge, gala sales in January and July. Otherwise, street markets are your strongest bet. The vibe is better, and they offer plenty of basic items at bargain prices.

Specialty Stores

CLOTHING

There are plenty of classy wardrobe essentials to buy here. But, as in any city, the best deals are generally hidden in the nooks and crannies of dusty shops or crammed between the

VAT Refunds

If you spend more than £75 in one store, ask about getting a Value Added Tax (VAT) refund. VAT is the European version of sales tax, though in this case it's an extortionate 17.5% of the net price. VAT is always included (read: hidden) in the price, so half the time you don't even realize you're being taxed. Fortunately, foreigners are exempt from VAT if any single purchase exceeds £75; at some tourist-oriented shops, you can claim a refund on purchases of £20 or more, so be sure to ask. To collect your refund, ask the store for form VAT 407, which should be submitted to British customs. At the airport, look for the "VAT Refund" window in the airport departure lounge. Allow eight weeks for processing after that.

assorted junk sold in street markets. If you insist on browsing the high-priced selections at **Harrods** (*see* Kensington and Knightsbridge in Chapter 2), get an early start—crowds can be maddening by midday. Forget Harrods's post-Christmas sidewalk sales: If the cars or buses don't run you over, shoppers in search of the famed blue-light specials will. Other upscale department stores worth exploring include **Selfridges** (400 Oxford St., tel. 0171/629–1234), **Liberty & Co.** (210–220 Regent St., tel. 0171/734–1234), and **Fortnum and Mason** (181 Piccadilly, tel. 0171/734–8040). Prices at these chain stores can be absurd, except during one of their holiday sales. **Marks & Spencer** (458 Oxford St., tel. 0171/935–7954) is less highbrow, offering some of the best bargains on new clothes in London; look for other Marks & Spencer branches on Edgeware Road, Kensington High Street, and in Queensway. Cheaper still is **Debenham's** (334 Oxford St., tel. 0171/580–3000), where you can stock up on underwear and the like.

NEW CLOTHES Clothing boutiques of all shapes and sizes line Oxford Street, Covent Garden, South Moulton Street (Mayfair), King's Road (Chelsea), Kensington High Street, and Knightsbridge. Also check out the **Petticoat Lane Market,** especially between Middlesex and Goulstons streets, where a number of aspiring designers have set up shop (*see* Street Markets, *below*).

American Retro. Despite the name, American Retro sells new, reasonably fashionable men's and women's gear—particularly accessories like belts, bags, and undies. Unfortunately, the prices aren't especially low. *35 Old Compton St., tel. 0171/734–3477. Tube: Piccadilly Circus. Walk north on Shaftesbury Ave., turn left on Wardour St., right on Old Compton St. Open Mon.–Sat. 10:15–7.*

The Cavern. The crafty owner stockpiles various fashion goods in a warehouse, and then brings them out again when the styles come back around. Most stuff is "uncirculated," though some used items do show up from time to time. *154 Commercial St., tel. 0171/247–1889. Tube: Aldgate East. Open Tues.–Thurs. 10–6 , Fri. 11–7, Sat. noon–6, Sun. noon–3.*

French Connection. This is one of those places where people buy their "favorite" and enduring items of clothing—nothing fancy, just comfortable with a relaxed-yet-classy look. The two branches—one for men, one for women—are within a short walk of each other. *Men's shop: 55 Long Acre, tel. 0171/379–6560. Women's shop: 11 James St., tel. 0171/836–0522. Tube: Covent Garden. Open Mon.–Wed., Fri., Sat. 10:30–6:30, Thurs. 10:30–8, Sun. noon–6.*

Hyper-Hyper. This indoor market rents stalls to struggling British designers and is *the* place to come for all varieties of hats, outrageous outfit-making accessories, and serious clubbing attire. Prices tend to be prohibitive, but there are definitely a few bargains to be found. *26–40 Kensington High St., tel. 0171/938–4343. Tube: Kensington High St. Open Mon.–Wed., Fri., Sat. 10–6, Thurs. 10–7.*

Next. This is the British equivalent of The Gap, except that it offers a wider range of styles to suit broader tastes. You won't have too much trouble finding the place: It's ubiquitous, with branches just about everywhere. If you can't make it to the main branch try: 327 Oxford Street (Tube: Bond St.), 54 Kensington High Street (Tube: Kensington High St.), 20 Long Acre (Tube: Covent Garden), 13 King's Road (Tube: Sloane Sq.), or 33 Brompton Road (Tube: Knightsbridge). *189 Oxford St., tel. 0171/494–3646. Tube: Oxford Circus. Open Mon.–Wed. and Fri. 10–6:30, Thurs. 10–8, Sat. 10–7.*

If the soles of your Birkenstocks are wearing thin, retread in Covent Garden at the Natural Shoe Store (21 Neal St., tel. 0171/836–5254).

Red or Dead. This small chain began as a stall in Camden Market. Nowadays, people flock here for the reasonably priced stock of dresses, jeans, jackets, and accessories. Waffle soles are well represented. Other branches are at 36 Kensington High Street (Tube: Kensington High St.) and 186 Camden High Street (Tube: Camden Town). *33 Neal St., tel. 0171/379–7571. Tube: Covent Garden. Open weekdays 10:30–7:30, Sat. 10–7, Sun. 12:30–6.*

Shelly's. Doc Martens and boots are good buys here, and there are plenty of models to choose from. Shelly's also sells outrageous ultramodern footwear—so cutting edge you wouldn't dare to wear them. Other branches are at 14 Neal Street (Tube: Covent Garden), 40 Kensington High Street (Tube: Kensington High St.), and 124B King's Road (Tube: Sloane Sq.). *159 Oxford St., tel. 0171/437–5842. Tube: Oxford Circus. Open Mon.–Wed., Fri., Sat. 9:30–6:30, Thurs. 9:30–8.*

SECONDHAND AND THRIFT CLOTHING **Oxfam** runs charity shops all over Great Britain, with 40 in London alone. Oxfam has the best deals on sturdy clothing, along with all sorts of tchotchkes like hand-carved wooden dishes from Africa, stationery, and even used books. For central area shopping, check out the stores at 23 Drury Lane (tel. 0171/240–3769) and 202B Kensington High Street (tel. 0171/937–6683).

If you'd rather browse for used clothes, head to Camden Lock in Camden Town or King's Road in Chelsea. Both avenues host weekend street markets (*see* Street Markets, *below*) and are lined with shops that stock used jeans, cheap leather jackets, scads of jewelry and accessories, new shoes, abused shoes, and most everything else a consumer could want.

American Classics. Fifties garb figures heavily in this huge collection of jeans, T-shirts, plaids, and bomber jackets. *20 Endell St., tel. 0171/831–1210. Tube: Covent Garden. Walk east on Long Acre, turn left on Endell St. Open Mon.–Sat. 10–6:30. Other branch: 404 King's Rd., tel. 0171/351–5229.*

Flip. Here you'll find basic and funky secondhand work shirts and classy sweaters, plus some jeans and old poodle skirts. *125 Long Acre, tel. 0171/836–4688. Tube: Covent Garden. Open Mon.–Wed., Fri., Sat. 10–7, Thurs. 10–8, Sun. noon–6.*

Glorious Clothing Company. Some of fashion's best hangers-on from decades past—bell-bottoms, earth-tone jackets, and plenty of fringe—are available at this popular shop on Islington's trendiest street. Prices vary from reasonable to silly. *60 Upper St., tel. 0171/704–6312. Tube: Angel. Open Mon.–Sat. 11–6:30.*

High Society. This store offers classic men's suits and women's party dresses. As its name suggests, prices start in the small-investment range and move right up to virtually prohibitive. *46 Cross St., tel. 0171/226–6863. Tube: Angel. Walk north on Upper St., turn right on Cross St. Open Mon.–Sat. 10:30–6.*

Kensington Market. Ferret out a great clubbing outfit from this store's snazzy selection of retro clothes, shoes, and accessories. Some of the stuff dates from the '20s, some from the '50s, and much from the glorious '70s. Gothic and motorcycle types come to this indoor market for denim and leather. *49–53 Kensington High St., tel. 0171/938–4343. Tube: Kensington High St. Open Mon.–Wed., Fri., Sat. 10–5:30, Thurs. 10–6.*

Stock Market. You'll find some jeans and Gap-like flannel shirts, but Doc Martens are the real reason to come—the selection is large and well-priced. If you don't find what you're looking for, try one of the two dozen shoe stores nearby. *234 Camden High St., tel. 0171/768–9912. Tube: Camden Town. Open Mon.–Sat. 10–6.*

BOOKSTORES

The undisputed literary capital of the English-speaking world is, not surprisingly, a Mecca for bookworms. "Here in this enclave there are centuries / For you to waste," wrote poet Randall Jarrell about something completely different but related. It is quite possible to get lost amid the secondhand bookstores on **Tottenham Court Road, Charing Cross Road,** and the adjacent **Cecil Court,** although the hustle of traffic on these streets will return you to London, and reality, soon enough.

NEW BOOKS As far as chains go, one of the best is **Waterstone's,** with a megabranch at 121–125 Charing Cross Road (tel. 0171/434–4291). You're likely to pass at least one of their stores while wandering around town. Poke your head in and ask about author signings and free lectures. The award for most behemoth and chaotic bookstore goes to **Foyle's** (119 Charing Cross Rd., tel. 0171/376–7656); if it's in print, they probably have it. Across the way is **Books Etc.** (120 Charing Cross Rd., tel. 0171/379–6838), another major chain. Rounding out the list of chain stores are **Hatchards** (187–188 Piccadilly, tel. 0171/767–8232) and **Stanford's** (12 Long Acre, tel. 0171/776–9801); the latter specializes in travel books and maps.

Compendium. With its potpourri of political tracts, New Age manifestos, and radical poetry, this alternative bookstore draws a devoted local crowd. Call for the schedule of readings. *234 Camden High St., tel. 0171/485–8944. Tube: Camden Town. Open Mon.–Sat. 10–6, Sun. noon–6.*

Dillons. This colossal, five-story bookstore is smack-dab in the middle of one of London's main student sections. Browsing at length is not only kosher but de rigueur, even though the prices aren't the best. *82 Gower St., tel. 0171/636–1577. Tube: Goodge St. Walk east on Chenies St., turn left on Gower St. Open Mon. and Wed.–Fri. 9–7, Tues. 9:30–7, Sat. 9:30–6.*

Forbidden Planet. Horror, sci-fi, and fantasy fans will fall into this place and never come back. The selection includes all those elusive anthologies you can't find elsewhere. Check out the massive comics section on the first floor. *71 New Oxford St., tel. 0171/836–4179. Tube: Tottenham Court Rd. Open Mon.–Sat. 10:30–6.*

Murder One. It may look dingy and unimposing from the outside, but inside there's a treasure trove of British mysteries and thrillers. For lovers of the genre, or for fantasy and science fiction junkies, this is one shop not to miss. *71–73 Charing Cross Rd., tel. 0171/734–3485. Tube: Tottenham Court Rd. Open Mon.–Wed. 10–7, Thurs.–Sat. 10–8.*

Silver Moon. This friendly, feminist bookshop is London's sisterhood central for literature by and about women. *64–68 Charing Cross Rd., tel. 0171/836–7906. Tube: Leicester Sq. Open Mon.–Wed. and Fri.–Sat. 10–6:30, Thurs. 10–8.*

Soma Books. Explore India, Africa, or the Caribbean without leaving London. Browse among the cookbooks, or feed your mind on art and fiction. There's even something for the little tykes, printed not only in English but in several Indian languages as well. *38 Kennington Ln., tel. 0171/735-2101. Tube: Kennington. Open Mon.–Fri. 9:30–5:30.*

The Turret Bookshop. Owner Bernard Stone has made a name for himself in London with the Turret's excellent small-press poetry selection. Stay awhile and browse. *36 Great Queen St.,*

Specialty Bookshops

- *DILLONS ART BOOKSHOP. This first-class art bookshop is ideal for academics, art students, and poets. 8 Long Acre, tel. 0171/836–1359. Tube: Covent Garden.*

- *FRENCH'S THEATRE BOOKSHOP. This shop has one of London's most comprehensive, if pricey, collections of plays and books about theater from every angle imaginable. 52 Fitzroy St. tel. 0171/387–9373. Tube: Warren St.*

- *GAY'S THE WORD. Everything from the political to the anthropological, with a heavy slant toward gay and lesbian issues. 66 Marchmont St., tel. 0171/278–7654. Tube: Russell Sq.*

- *SPORTSPAGES. It's London's only comprehensive sports bookstore, and the selection of football fanzines is to die for. Caxton Walk, 94–96 Charing Cross Rd., tel. 0171/240–9604. Tube: Leicester Sq.*

- *TRAVEL BOOKSHOP. This is an excellent source for maps, travelogues, and all varieties of travel guides. 13 Blenheim Crescent, tel. 0171/229–5260. Tube: Ladbroke Grove.*

tel. 0171/405–6058. Tube: Holborn. Walk south on Kingsway, turn right on Great Queen St. Open Mon.–Sat. 10–6.

USED BOOKS **Gloucester Road Bookshop.** The titles are well chosen—especially for fiction—in this cozy neighborhood bookshop. For £1, the helpful staff will run a book search for you. *123 Gloucester Rd., tel. 0171/370–3503. Tube: Gloucester Rd. Open weekdays 8:30–10:30, weekends 10:30–6:30.*

Henry Pordes Books. The musty smell here cues visitors to Pordes' great selection of old books—some of the antiquarian variety and some just plain old. Fiction is one of the strongest sections. Prices for paperbacks start at 50p, not including the 10% student discount. *58–60 Charing Cross Rd., tel. 0171/836–9031. Tube: Leicester Sq. Open Mon.–Sat. 10–7.*

Response. Immerse yourself in a secondhand novel at Response's coffee bar, which is basically a nook with a chair and a Mr. Coffee machine. *300 Old Brompton Rd., tel. 0171/370–4606. Tube: Earl's Court. Walk south on Earl's Court Rd., turn right on Old Brompton Rd. Open weekdays 9:30–5, Sat. 9:30–1.*

Skoob. This is one of the most popular used bookstores in town, and the slightly higher prices reflect it (though students do get a 10% discount). While away the hours in the impressive humanities, foreign literature, and political science sections. *15 Sicilian Ave., at Southampton Row, tel. 0171/404–3063. Tube: Holborn. Open Mon.–Sat. 10:30–6:30.*

MUSIC

From postpunk and Rockabilly to rave, London's music scene is first-rate, and plenty of record stores have sprouted up in recent years to meet the growing demand for major and indie music. Chains like HMV and Tower are the same the world over; London's appeal is its small independent stores. Wherever you go, expect to pay £5–£9 for vinyl, £8–£15 for CDs. The prices aren't great, but hard-to-find imports that cost $20 in the United States fetch more reasonable prices here. Bear in mind that London's smaller music stores pay top dollar for collector's items and small-label U.S. 7- and 12-inch records. If you're looking to supplement your budget, you could do worse than hawking your rare LPs in London.

The flagship branches for each chain are **HMV** (150 Oxford St., tel. 0171/631–3423; Tube: Oxford Circus or Tottenham Court Rd.), **Tower Records** (1 Piccadilly Circus, tel. 0171/439–2500; Tube: Piccadilly Circus), and **Virgin Megastore** (14–30 Oxford St., tel. 0171/631–1234; Tube: Tottenham Court Rd.). HMV and Virgin stay open weekdays until 8 PM, weekends until 7 PM. Night owls can browse Tower Monday through Saturday until midnight, Sundays until 10 PM.

Most genres are well-represented in the megastores, but for that homey, special-interest feel, walk down Berwick Street, where you're bound to fall into one of several small independent music shops. Camden Town is also a good place to look. For a sense of the latest buzz in town, *Melody Maker* (75p) and *New Musical Express* (75p)—available at most newsstands—are standard reads.

Black Market. Twelve-inch import singles take up most of the ground floor, sharing some space with Euro music and listening turntables. Follow the booming music downstairs to the basement, housing all varieties of techno, rap, and hip-hop. *25 D'Arblay St., tel. 0171/437–0478. Tube: Oxford Circus. Walk east on Oxford St., turn right on Berwick St. Open Mon.–Sat. 10–7.*

Honest Jon's. Here you'll find an amazing selection of reggae, jazz, soul, and funk. If you have any doubts about buying a disk, take a test listen before plunking down your quid. *278 Portobello Rd., tel. 0181/969–9822. Tube: Notting Hill Gate. Open Mon.–Sat. 10–6, Sun. 11–5.*

Mister CD. There's something from every genre here: country, indie international, jazz, classical. You may have to sift through a lot of crazy stacks, but this is the cheapest place in town. *Berwick St., no phone. Tube: Oxford Circus. Walk east on Oxford St., turn right on Berwick St. Open daily 10–7.*

Music & Video Exchange. The used CDs are tucked away in glass cases, and you have to crane your neck to read the covers, but the substantial markdowns are worth the trouble. A second branch at 229 Camden High Street (Tube: Camden Town) is much the same. Also look for the used camera and guitar equipment shops run by the same people. *38 Notting Hill Gate, tel. 0171/243–8573. Tube: Notting Hill Gate. Open daily 10–7.*

Reckless Records. Nothing but bargains in these aisles: secondhand 12-inch dance singles, classical, reggae, even country music, not to mention rock, soul, and jazz. *30 Berwick St., tel. 0171/437–4271. Tube: Oxford Circus. Walk east on Oxford St., turn right on Berwick St. Open daily 10–7.*

Rough Trade. The fine selection of indie music, grunge, and U.S. imports draws lots of young skinheads to this store in the basement of a skateboard shop. Then again, it could also be Rough Trade's fairly impromptu—and free—performances by bands playing in town. Check *Melody Maker* or *NME* for current listings. *16 Neal's Yard, tel. 0171/240–0105. Tube: Covent Garden. Open Mon.–Sat. 10–6:30.*

Selectadisc. This place is all about indie rock, thoughtfully organized and with a good depth of titles. If you can't find something, ask the helpful staff. *34 Berwick St., tel. 0171/734–3298. Tube: Oxford Circus. Walk east on Oxford St., turn right on Berwick St. Open Mon.–Sat. 9:30–7.*

Stern's African Record Centre. The drum is king in this shop, which features an amazing collection of music from Africa and Latin America. You're not likely to do better for world music in London. Listen to selections on the store's equipment before making a purchase. *116 Whitfield St., tel. 0171/387–5550. Tube: Warren St. Open Mon.–Sat. 10:30–6:30.*

Vinyl Experience. If you're into collecting records, not just buying them, this is the place. They've got some old classics in mint condition, plus a wide selection of old concert posters. *18 Hanway St., tel. 0171/636–1281. Tube: Tottenham Court Rd. Open Mon.–Sat. 10–6:30.*

HOUSEHOLD STUFF

London's department stores have just about all the furnishings and accoutrements you need under one roof: Try **Selfridges** (400 Oxford St., tel. 0171/629–1234), **Liberty & Co.** (210–220 Regent St., tel. 0171/734–1234), or **Harvey Nichols** (109 Knightsbridge, tel. 0171/672–9822). If you've got the cash, browse the designer boutiques clustered in Chelsea, Covent Garden, and Tottenham Court Road. For cheapie-style new furniture slapped together in Singapore or Eastern Europe, check out **Walworth Road** (Tube: Elephant & Castle) or **Holloway Road** (Tube: Holloway Rd.), two streets lined with shops that sell run-of-the-mill but functional household stuff. In a pinch, also check the yellow pages under "Furniture, Secondhand."

Habitat. The furnishings, kitchen stuff, and linens are the store's own designs. Most prices are decent, but it'd be a major investment to furnish your entire flat here. Other branches of this popular chain are at 208 King's Road (tel. 0171/351–1211), King's Mall on King Street (tel. 0181/741–7111), and 191–217 Finchley Road (tel. 0171/328–3444). *196 Tottenham Court Rd., tel. 0171/631–3880. Tube: Goodge St. Open Mon.–Wed. 10–6, Thurs. 10–8, Fri. and Sat. 10–6:30, Sun. noon–5:30.*

Oxfam. This particular Oxfam is heavy on the furniture selection, and if you're willing to trek down south (not that far, really), the deals can't be beat. *23 Streatham High St., tel. 0181/769–1291. BritRail: Streatham High St. Open Mon.–Sat. 10–5.*

Reject Shop. It started as a shop that sold seconds, hence the name. Now the budding chain sells new furniture and other household items at fair prices. The Reject Shop may remind American shoppers of Pier One Imports—vaguely ethnic and lots of blond wood. No tiki lamps, though. Other branches are at King's Road (tel. 0171/352–6352) and 209 Tottenham Court Road (tel. 0171/580–2895). *245 Brompton Rd., tel. 0171/584–7611. Tube: South Kensington. Open Mon.–Sat. 9–6, Sun. noon–6.*

Street Markets

One person's piece of junk is another person's find, and even on a gray day, you'd be hard pressed to find a better way to shop than in London's street markets. They range from those in **Camden Lock** and **Portobello Road,** major attractions in their own right, to the tiny neighborhood markets where locals stock their fridges. An ever-constant cast of characters—young hipsters, families trailing prams, bedouin stallholders, and wide-eyed tourists—make for excellent people-watching. Set aside an entire Sunday to browse among the myriad fruits and vegetables, new and used clothes, bootleg tapes, counterfeit batteries, blank cassettes, old billboards, antique furniture, used clothing, and other assorted funky stuff. Street markets are a weekend pastime, but some stalls and many shops remain open during the week—without the happy chatter, commotion, and congestion of claustrophobia-inducing crowds.

Most street markets have food stalls, and the wafting smells of curry and spices beckon from blocks away with the promise of a cheap lunch.

WEST AND CENTRAL LONDON

BERWICK STREET Soho's thriving fruit and veggie mart is a great place to buy munchies to take to Leicester and Soho squares. Stop by around 5 PM—when the merchants are desperate to get rid of their produce—and you'll walk away with some incredible deals. *Berwick and Rupert Sts. Tube: Oxford Circus, Tottenham Court Rd., or Piccadilly Circus. Open Mon.–Sat. 9–5.*

PORTOBELLO ROAD The Portobello Road market is second only to Camden for liveliness and funkiness. Watch the bongo players, dancers, and other performers at the small courtyard in the middle of the market. The southern end has Portobello's trademark items—antiques. Even if you can't afford the priceless Victorian gems, cool stalls line Portobello for a mile and

Too Weird For Many Words

- *ANYTHING LEFT HANDED. Lefties of the world unite. 57 Brewer St., tel. 0171/437–3910. Tube: Piccadilly Circus.*

- *THE BEER SHOP. The place for specialty brews and do-it-yourself manuals. 8 Pitfield St., tel. 0171/739–3701. Tube: Old St.*

- *GALLERY OF ANTIQUE COSTUMES AND TEXTILES. Too expensive to take seriously, but a great place to rummage through pre-1930 costumes, linens, and tapestries. 2 Church St., tel. 0171/871–0911. Tube: Edgware Rd.*

- *THE HAT SHOP. Shoe-box-size shop filled with everything from garden hats to funeral wear. 58 Neal St., tel. 0171/836–6781. Tube: Covent Garden.*

- *JUST GAMES. The name says it all. 71 Brewer St., tel. 0171/734–6124. Tube: Piccadilly Circus.*

- *THE KITE STORE. More kites than you can shake a stick at. 48 Neal St., tel. 0171/836–1666. Tube: Covent Garden.*

- *THE TEA HOUSE. Buy tea in bulk or purchase one of a hundred fancy teapots and kettles. 15A Neal St., tel. 0171/240–7539. Tube: Covent Garden.*

overflow into the cross streets at the road's northern end, where you'll find fruit, veggies, and secondhand clothes. *Portobello Rd. Tube: Notting Hill Gate. From station walk 3 blocks up Pembridge Rd. Open Fri. and Sat. 8–3. Antiques stalls open Sat. only.*

ST. MARTIN-IN-THE-FIELDS This market exists almost exclusively for tourists. Even so, there are some surprising possibilities (jewelry, ethnic arts, and a few decent clothes vendors) hidden amid all the junk. *St. Martin-in-the-Fields churchyard, off Trafalgar Sq. Tube: Charing Cross. Open Mon.–Sat. 11–5, Sun. noon–5.*

EAST END

BRICK LANE Although it's full of tacky new clothes and cheap fruit, this East End street market has the advantage of being unknown to tourists. Listen to Cockney vegetable-sellers twist the English language as they strut their stuff. Vendors close shop by 2 PM, after which you can have a late lunch at one of the many good curry houses in the area. *Brick Ln. Tube: Aldgate East. Walk east on Whitechapel High St., turn left on Brick Ln. Open Sun. 5–2.*

COLUMBIA ROAD This is London's main open-air market for flowers and plants—colorful, pleasant, and conveniently located near Brick Lane Market. Get here early, as most things close by 2 PM. *Columbia Rd. Tube: Old St. Walk east on Old St., veer north on Hackney Rd., right on Columbia Rd. Open Sun. 9–2.*

PETTICOAT LANE Though not as hip as Camden Market, Petticoat Lane is easily as big, swallowing Middlesex Street and a host of side streets to the east. Unfortunately, this market is also rapidly becoming as popular as Camden—come early or prepare for some heavy crowds. Lots of generally ugly new clothes are up for sale, along with watches, shoes, luggage, handbags, household stuff, and other groovy bric-a-brac. *Middlesex St. Tube: Aldgate East. Walk southwest on Whitechapel High St., turn right on Middlesex St. Open Sun. 9–2.*

SPITALFIELDS MARKET Spitalfields is not exactly on the street, but inside a huge barn-like warehouse. It's run by the same folks who do Camden Lock, and it features 3 acres of produce stands, food stalls, crafts and clothes vendors—even a tiny farm. Performances of various sorts are held periodically on the small stage. *Brushfield St., at Commercial St. Tube: Liverpool St. From station walk north on Bishopsgate, turn right on Brushfield St. Open weekdays 11–3, Sun. 9–3.*

NORTH LONDON

CAMDEN MARKETS Wait a few moments after stepping off the tube to orient yourself in the crushing mob; after all, this is the raging granddaddy of London flea markets, unparalleled in atmosphere and selection. The highlight among the many street markets is indisputably **Camden Lock.** Get your used clothes, Doc Martens, bootlegs, incense, crystals, arty knickknacks, smart drinks, and bongs here. Lots of funky young Londoners come just to hang out, breathe in the scenery, and blow a spliff or two. The lock itself—a pleasant waterway overlooked by a few cafés and more shops—is just past the cluster of sellers north of the Camden tube station. If you're shopping for shoes, don't get duped by the sellers who congregate in front of the station; better deals can be had farther down the street. *Camden High St. Tube: Camden Town. From station walk north up Camden High St. Open weekends 8–6.*

CAMDEN PASSAGE Not to be confused with the very cool Camden Markets, Camden Passage is a narrow alley full of expensive antiques stores. The flea market, which also sells antiques, is at the end of the alley: pretty schmaltzy, very expensive. *Islington High St. Tube: Angel. From station walk north and veer right on Islington High St. Open Wed. and Sat. 8:30–3.*

CHAPEL MARKET This is where locals from Pentonville and Islington come to buy their fruit, flowers, household goods, shampoo, and other daily supplies. This is as untouristy as it gets in central London. *Chapel Market. Tube: Angel. Turn right out of station, left onto Liverpool Rd., left on Chapel Market. Open Tues., Wed., Fri., and Sat. 9–6, Thurs. and Sun. 8–noon.*

SOUTH OF THE THAMES

BRIXTON MARKET Vibrant Electric Avenue—of Eddy *"Romancing the Stone"* Grant fame—is the heart of this sprawling, largely untouristed market. Interesting used clothing, fruits and veggies, books, tapes, and records are here in abundance, as are more mundane wares like soap, batteries, and shampoo. Because of the ethnic makeup of this south London neighborhood, Afro-Caribbean food, handicrafts, and reggae music are out in force. *Electric Ave. Tube: Brixton. Turn left out of station and walk to Electric Ave. Open Mon., Tues., and Thurs. 8:30–5:30, Wed. 8–1, Fri. 8–7, Sat. 8–6.*

EAST STREET This market is popular with south London locals. It's packed and difficult to walk through, but that's part of East Street's appeal. The cocky shouts of vendors alert you to everyday items like film, batteries, and toiletries, as well as cheap hi-fi items like Walkmans and portable speakers. *East St. Tube: Elephant & Castle. From station walk ¾ mi south on Walworth Rd., or take Bus 45, 68, 171, or 176. Open Tues.–Thurs. and Sun. 8–3, Fri. and Sat. 8–5.*

NEW CALEDONIAN Some freaky loophole dating back to the 18th century makes it legal to sell furniture and antiques of questionable origin at this Bermondsey Square market. Presumably it's not all hot, and you can't complain about the prices. Arrive at the crack of dawn to gawk at the finest pieces before they're sold. *Tower Bridge Rd., Bermondsey Sq. Tube: Borough. From station walk east on Long Ln. Open Fri. 4 AM–2 PM.*

OUTDOOR ACTIVITIES

8

By Caitlin Ramey

The salaries of professional athletes may not be as preposterously huge in England as they are in the States, but don't believe for one second that the British aren't serious about sports. If you feel like joining in, *Time Out* (£1.50), available at most newsstands, is a great resource: the "Sport" section lists upcoming events, times, dates, and ticket info. Also at your disposal is the London **Sportsline** (tel. 0171/222–8000), with information on all things athletic for the price of a local call. The **Wembley Complex** (Empire Way, Wembley, Middlesex, tel. 0181/900–1234; Tube: Wembley Park) and **Crystal Palace National Sports Centre** (Ledrington Rd., tel. 0181/778–0131) host headline events of all sorts. To reach the latter, take any BritRail train to the Crystal Palace station.

Spectator Sports

CRICKET

The game looks like a backward form of baseball played by people in golfing clothes, but don't underestimate the strange operational complexities of this ancient English tradition. Since the 12th century, teams of 11 players have battled each other on a massive grassy field (the "pitch") crowned with two wickets (three "stumps" of wood propped together on a stand) placed 66 feet apart from each other. Imagine the dramatic face-off between baseball's pitcher and batter, except there are two batsmen, one in front of each wicket. If the batter manages to hit the ball far enough afield, giving him and the other batsman time to switch wickets (i.e., run like hell), the team scores, and players rotate. Cricket batters get six "tries" (as opposed to three in baseball) and the teams don't switch roles (between fielding and batting) until there are no longer enough team members to fill both batting positions—in other words, when 10 members are "retired." Confused yet? To add insult to injury for the uninitiated, cricket games go on forever, quite literally *three days* for a normal match, one day for the abbreviated version.

It's all very complicated, so don't panic if none of this makes sense. Like baseball, cricket is a mystery to most of the world outside the game's homeland—with the exception, that is, of England's former colonies (excluding the U.S., of course). If this sounds like your cup of tea, matches are held at the **Lord's Cricket Ground** (St. John's Wood Rd., tel. 0171/289–1611 or 0171/266–3825; Tube: St. John's Wood) and the **Oval Cricket Ground** (Kennington Oval, tel. 0171/582–6660; Tube: Oval). Tickets generally cost around £7.

OUTDOOR ACTIVITIES

FOOTBALL

Of all sports, football (what Americans call soccer) probably draws the most passion out of Brits. It all started in Derby in AD 217 as part of a festival celebrating a victory over Roman troops. Since then, more than 140 countries worldwide have fallen in love with the sport, and the Fédération Internationale de Football Association (FIFA), which sponsors the World Cup every four years, boasts more members than the United Nations. Only the United States stubbornly refuses to acknowledge the sport as rightful king.

When it comes to local football, the most popular of London's eight major clubs is probably Arsenal—the only London team, in fact, with a tube station named after it. Other teams with major followings are Chelsea, Tottenham Hotspur, and West Ham United. The football season runs from mid-August to May, and most games are held at 3 PM on Saturdays. Big important matches are held at London's **Wembley Stadium** (*see above*). Tickets, available from each club's box office, run £5–£30, depending on the seats. If rain is even a remote possibility, it's worth a few extra quid to sit in a covered area.

Arsenal. *Highbury Stadium, Avenell Rd., tel. 0171/354–5404 for tickets or 0171/359–0131 for recorded info. Tube: Arsenal.*

Chelsea. *Stamford Bridge, Fulham Rd., tel. 0171/385–5545. Tube: Fulham Broadway.*

Fulham. *Craven Cottage, Stevenage Rd., tel. 0171/736–6561. Tube: Putney Bridge.*

Millwall. *The Den, Cold Blow Ln., New Cross, tel. 0171/232–1222. Tube: New Cross Gate.*

Orient. *Brisbane Rd., Leyton, tel. 0181/539–2223. Tube: Leyton.*

Queen's Park Rangers. *South Africa Rd., tel. 0181/743–0262. Tube: Shepherd's Bush.*

Tottenham Hotspur. *748 High Rd., White Hart Lane Ground, tel. 0181/365–5050. BritRail: White Hart Lane.*

West Ham United. *Boleyn Ground, Green St., Newham, tel. 0181/472–2740. Tube: Upton Park.*

POLO

Depending on whom you talk to, polo either originated in Persia in the 6th century and was subsequently "discovered" by British army officers stationed in India, or the soldiers developed the sport themselves. In either case, polo rapidly gained ground with the upper classes, and has remained the province of the rich, largely because polo is hard on the horses. Players must be able to afford a "string" of steeds, so they can switch mounts during each game, as horse after horse tires of being slammed into other horses at high speeds.

Prince Charlie is an avid polo player who's often criticized for being more comfortable on a horse than with people.

The Guards Polo Club is the choicest of polo grounds, and it's the venue for the **Royal Windsor Cup** in late June. Tickets for big matches start at £10. Keep in mind that the club hosts matches every weekend during summer, and for lesser-known games the charge is only £10 per carload of people. Crafty pedestrians can even watch for free. *Smith's Lawn, Windsor Great Park, tel. 01784/437797. BritRail: Windsor.*

RUGBY

Rugby has driven many a mother to an early grave, because the players take as much body contact as American football players, but without the benefit of pads or helmets. Legend has it that the game was born when a student playing soccer picked up the ball in his hands and ran from one end of the pitch to the other. The game concept hasn't changed much since then: Players move the ball down the field and score goals through some combination of running, passing, and kicking. It's an old sport, steeped in tradition, and rugby's practitioners shun the

150

modern arguments for protection against injury. Perhaps it's this attitude which makes the rowdy spectacle such a satisfying combination of mud, beer, and battle.

The cheapest way to watch rugby is at a Rugby Union club match: Tickets cost £5–£15 depending on the seat. London's principal sides include the **Wasps** (Repton Ave., tel. 0181/900–2659; Tube: Sudbury Town), the **Saracens** (Green Rd., tel. 0181/449–3770; Tube: Oakwood), and the **London Irish** (The Avenue, Sunbury-on-Thames, tel. 0932/783–034). For the latter, take BritRail to Sunbury. The city's only Rugby League team is the **London Crusaders,** based at the **Barnet Copthall Stadium** (Great North Way, tel. 0181/203–4211; Tube: Mill Hill East). Tickets for league matches run £10–£20.

Basketball is up-and-coming in Britain. The top men's team, the London Towers, plays at Wembley Arena on weekends throughout the year. Check listings in "Time Out."

RACING

CAR RACING The world-famous **British Formula One Grand Prix** is held every July to sold-out crowds at **Silverstone Circuit** (Silverstone, Northants, tel. 01327/857271). Tickets are hard to come by and somewhat expensive (£10 and up), so contact the box office as early as possible. To reach the stadium, take BritRail to Northampton and follow the crowds. During the off-season, Silverstone Circuit hosts local and qualifying races on an irregular basis; flip through *Time Out* for the latest. Another popular racing venue is **Brands Hatch** (Fawkham, Kent, tel. 01474/872331), which also hosts motocross races. To reach the Hatch, take BritRail to Swanley.

GREYHOUND RACING Many Londoners love to bet on what they affectionately call "the dogs." Headliner races are held at Wembley Stadium and Wimbledon Stadium, but **Walthamstow Stadium** (Chingford Rd., tel. 0181/531–4255; Tube: Walthamstow) holds several races each week year-round. The cheapest admission is £2.

HORSE RACING While scruffy beer drinkers and quid betters make up the daily crowd, you couldn't keep the Queen herself away from the pomp and ceremony of the **Royal Ascot**, the grandmummy of all British horse races. You'll need to book good seats far in advance for this massive June event, although admission on the day can be had at the front gate for as little as £4—if you don't mind a nosebleed view. For more info contact the **Ascot Racecourse** (Ascot, Berkshire, tel. 01344/22211), within walking distance of BritRail's Ascot station.

If you're lucky, you may spy some of the royal family watching from their private stand at the **Royal Windsor Racecourse** (Maidenhead Rd., Windsor, tel. 01753/865234), best accessed from BritRail's Windsor Riverdale or Windsor Central stations. Other popular tracks within a short train ride of London include **Epsom Racecourse** (Epsom, Surrey, tel. 01372/464348; BritRail: Epsom), **Kempton Park Racecourse** (Sunbury-on-Thames, Middlesex, tel. 01932/782292; BritRail: Sunbury-on-Thames), and **Sandown Park** (Esher, Surrey, tel. 01372/463072; BritRail: Esher). Admission to the above courses runs £3–£8.

TENNIS

The world's most prestigious and ballyhooed tennis event is venerable **Wimbledon,** held for two weeks each year in late June and early July. Tennis enthusiasts around the world plan their trip to Wimbledon months in advance, so if you're reading this in June, *you're too late!* Actually, you may have some luck showing up on the day of a preliminary match and standing in a long line, but forget about the semifinal or final matches. For ticket info, contact the primary Wimbledon venue, the **All England Lawn Tennis and Croquet Club,** situated southwest of central London. Each year you may enter the ticket lottery—wherein the best seats at semifinal and final matches are sold—by writing the All England club for an application between September 1 and December 31. Completed applications must be received by the club by January 31. *Box 98, Church Rd., Wimbledon SW19 5AE, tel. 0181/944–1066 or 0181/946–2244 for ticket info. Tube: Wimbledon Park or Southfields.*

Another London landmark is the **Queen's Club,** which hosts major and minor competitive and exhibition matches throughout the year, including the venerable **Stella Artois Grass Court Championship** in early June. *Palliser Rd., tel. 0171/385–2366 or 0171/497–0521 for ticket info. Tube: Barons Court.*

Participant Sports

London is not the place to come for a tan, but it does periodically get warm enough during summer to think about stepping outside the pub for a stretch. As mentioned before, the **Sportsline** (tel. 0171/222–8000) provides comprehensive information on sports clubs (*see below*), and you can pick up all sorts of sporting gear, from sneakers to rackets to camping supplies, at all-purpose sporting goods stores like **Lillywhites** (Piccadilly Circus, tel. 0171/930–3181; Tube: Piccadilly Circus) and **Olympus Sports** (134 Oxford St., 0171/436–7605; Tube: Oxford Circus).

LONDON ON HORSEBACK

Hankering to stretch someone else's legs on a woodsy trek? Rent a horse from **Wimbledon Village Stables** (24 High St., tel. 0181/946–8579; Tube: Wimbledon) and travel over hill and dale at Wimbledon Common or Richmond Park. It costs about £20 per hour, and the stables are open Tuesday–Sunday 7 AM–6 PM. **Hyde Park Stables** (63 Bathurst Mews, tel. 0171/723–2813; Tube: Lancaster Gate) also rents horsies, but it's steeper at £25 per hour, and reservations are required. They're open Tuesday–Sunday 7:30 AM–6 PM.

LONDON BY BIKE

Lots of people bike in London, but frankly, the traffic-congested streets make for a perilous and carcinogenic ride. Hard-core street bikers tie bandannas over their mouths to filter out the crud from passing traffic, or invest in specially designed gas masks available at bike shops. Biking *is* great in London's parks, but those intending to brave the roads should invest in a good map that points out the less offensive routes through the city. The **London Cycling Campaign** (3 Stamford St., London SE1, tel. 0171/928–7220) does its best to make London a more bike-friendly place. Send for a copy of their *Cyclists' Route Map* (£4.50 including postage), or look for it at bike shops. Send a SASE to the **Cyclists' Touring Club** (69 Meadrow, Godalming, Surrey GU7 3HS, tel. 01483/417217), and they'll send you info on organized bike journeys and races throughout London and all of England.

London Bicycle Tour Company. Weather permitting, this South Bank biking outfit offers two-hour mountain bike tours of various London neighborhoods. Tours run £9.95 including the bike. For £6.95, rent your own bike and go it alone. The helpful staff provides maps and route advice. *56 Upper Ground, Gabriel's Wharf, South Bank, tel. 0171/928–6838. Tube: Blackfriars.*

Yankee Sports

Baseball and softball games are played in a number of parks around town, especially Hampstead Heath. The British Baseball Federation (66 Belvedere Rd., Hessle, North Humberside, London HU13 9JJ, tel. 01482/643551) can point you toward the nearest club; call or send a SASE. Basketball courts are pretty scarce in London, but there are some in neighborhood sports centers as well as at the London Central YMCA (112 Great Russell St., tel. 0171/637–8131; Tube: Tottenham Court Road). Check with the English Basketball Association (tel. 01532/361166) in Leeds to join a club or find a court near you.

Mountain Bike and Ski. Mountain bike rentals cost £6.99 per day or £12.99 for the whole weekend, not including insurance (£1 per day) and the refundable £50 deposit. This central London shop also has a good selection of bikes and bike-related accessories. *18 Gillingham St., tel. 0171/834–8933. Tube: Victoria.*

TENNIS

There are public tennis courts all over London, many administered by neighborhoods or boroughs. Ask at local council halls about ones nearby, as they're often located at neighborhood sports centers (*see below*). Policies and prices vary wildly, though courts generally costs £3–£5 per hour. Sometimes reservations are accepted, sometimes they're required, and sometimes they're not accepted at all. Central London's larger parks also have courts, including Battersea Park, Regent's Park, Holland Park, Clissold Park, and Hampstead Heath. If you're strapped for a partner, check out the **Tennis Network** (195 Battersea Church Rd., London SW11 3ND), which hooks up players by skill level and geographic area if you send them a SASE. Another good resource is the **Lawn Tennis Association Trust** (Queen's Club, London W14 9EG, tel. 0171/385–4233); their pamphlet "Where to Play Tennis in London" lists dozens of public courts and gives the lowdown on reservation requirements and fees. Send them a SASE, and allow three weeks for a response.

SWIMMING

Many of the city's public sports centers (*see below*) have indoor pools, so swimmers need not bend to the whims of London's weather. Many of these pools are open to the public regularly throughout the week. If you arrive with a sport center member, admission usually runs £2–£5 for the day; fees for complete strangers are usually £2–£3 higher, if they let you in at all. Be sure to call in advance. Also remember that many sports centers require swimming caps and protective eyewear, and many do not provide towels. On the plus side, the weight rooms, saunas, and whirlpools are often available for use by guests and nonmembers, too.

The most serious laps in town are swum in the Olympic-sized pool at the **Crystal Palace National Sports Centre** (Upper Norwood, tel. 0181/778–0131; BritRail: Crystal Palace). At the other extreme, some London pools feature fantabulous setups with slides, cascading waterfalls, wave-making machines, and bizarre art objects. A few of the coolest include the **Britannia Leisure Centre** (40 Hyde Rd., tel. 0171/729–4485; Tube: Old Street) and the **Elephant & Castle Leisure Centre** (22 Elephant & Castle, tel. 0171/582–5505; Tube: Elephant & Castle).

Hampstead Heath. Choose from three swimming and sunbathing areas. If you take the tube to Highgate you'll stumble upon the men-only Highgate Pond and the women-only Kenwood

Windsurfing on the Thames

Hyde Park, Battersea Park, and Hampstead Heath have lakes large enough to merit a boat rental. If you're feeling adventurous, the following watersport centers offer rentals and lessons for activities like sailing, rowing, canoeing, and windsurfing:

- *DOCKLANDS SAILING CENTRE. Kingbridge, Millwall Dock, tel. 0171/537–2626. Take the Docklands Light Railway (DLR) to Crossharbour.*

- *SURREY DOCKS WATERSPORT CENTRE. Greenland Dock, Rope St., just off Plough Way, tel. 0171/237–4009. Tube: Surrey Quays.*

- *WOMEN'S ROWING CENTRE. The Promenade, Dukes Meadows, tel. 0181/840–4962. BritRail: Barnes Bridge.*

Ladies Pond. Or, if you prefer mixed bathing, take the tube to Hampstead and the nearby Hampstead Mixed Bathing Pond. Not surprisingly, the latter pool tends to get rowdier than the other two. *Tel. 0171/485–4491. Admission free. Segregated ponds open year-round, daily from dawn–1 hr before sunset. Mixed pond open summer only, daily 10–6.*

Oasis Baths. A spot of water amidst the parched concrete of central London. There's an indoor pool, too. *32 Endell St., tel. 0171/831–1804. Tube: Holborn or Covent Garden. Admission: £2.30. Open weekdays 7:30 AM–8 PM, weekends 9:30–5.*

Serpentine Lido. This Hyde Park oasis is quite popular in summer, even if a couple of famous people have sunk to its murky depths and never come up again, including Percy Bysshe Shelley's first wife, Harriet Westbrook. But rest assured that the lifeguards aren't about to let anyone drown on their watch. *Hyde Park, south side of the Serpentine, tel. 0171/724–3104. Tube: Knightsbridge. Admission: £2.50. Open late June–Aug., daily 10–5.*

Tooting Bec Lido. This is one of England's largest and oldest (1907) pools, a popular haunt on weekends for Londoners of all stripes. *Tooting Bec Rd., tel. 0181/871–7198. Tube: Tooting Bec. Admission: £3 weekdays, £2.50 weekends; free for guests with disabilities. Open late May–late Sept., daily 10–8; last admission 7:30.*

NEIGHBORHOOD SPORTS CENTERS

Almost every neighborhood has at least one gym offering some combination of aerobics classes, weight rooms, trampolines, saunas, solariums, martial arts gyms, swimming pools, squash and badminton courts, and soccer fields. Charges and/or membership fees vary, though they tend to be reasonable. To find the nearest center, look in the phone book under "Leisure Centres," ask at a local borough hall, or call the **Sportsline** (tel. 0171/222–8000). One cheap (but technically dodgy) option is to show up at one of the gyms at universities and discreetly join in—you didn't hear it from us.

Chelsea Sports Centre. *Chelsea Manor St., tel. 0171/352–6985. Tube: Sloane Sq. or South Kensington. Open weekdays 7:30 AM–10 PM, Sat. 8 AM–10 PM, Sun. 8 AM–6:30 PM.*

Jubilee Hall Leisure Centre. *30 The Piazza, tel. 0171/836–4835. Tube: Covent Garden. Open weekdays 6:30 AM–10 PM, weekends 10 AM–5 PM.*

Queen Mother Sports Centre. *223 Vauxhall Bridge Rd., tel. 0171/798–2125. Tube: Victoria. Open Mon.–Thurs. 7:30 AM–7:30 PM, Fri. 7:30 AM–8:30 PM, Sat. 8 AM–5:30 PM, Sun. 9 AM–5:15 PM.*

TRIPS FROM LONDON
9

By Emily W. Miller and Mark S. Rosen

At some point during your stay in London, the realization will hit you like a soggy sausage: As countries go, England is extremely compact, and absolutely nothing is very far from The Big City. Moreover, the country's train and bus networks—though uncomfortably expensive—are extensive, efficient, and easy to figure out. They also make renting a car completely unnecessary, unless you really want to navigate narrow country roads and don't mind paying upwards of £120 per week for the rental (plus nearly £3 per gallon of gas).

By train from London it takes a mere 75 minutes to reach **Bath,** 60 minutes for **Oxford** and **Cambridge,** 70 minutes for **Winchester,** and 90 minutes for **Canterbury.** Only **Stratford-upon-Avon** takes a bit of planning, as there is no direct train from London (there are, however, *plenty* of buses). While you could tackle any of the above on a frenzied day trip, consider staying for a day or two. Heavy summer crowds make it difficult to cover the sights in a relaxed manner. And, more to the point, you'll have the time to explore a very different England, one blessed with quiet country pubs, fluffy sheep, and neatly trimmed farms. No matter where you go, lodging reservations are a good idea June–September, when foreigners (like us) saturate the English countryside.

Short Trips

A number of towns and attractions lie just outside of London proper, within easy day-tripping distance. Nothing in this chapter is more than an hour or two from the capital, yet the following are *really* close—we're talking about 30- to 60-minute bus, tube, or train rides, so stop complaining.

Greenwich

When King Charles II ordered Christopher Wren to build "a small observatory within our part of Greenwich" in 1675, few realized the impact this unassuming building would have on the future of world navigation. Although the **Royal Greenwich** (that's "GREN-itch") **Observatory** is no longer used for astronomical observations (London's bright lights obscure the view), this is the place the BBC is talking about when they announce "Greenwich Mean Time"; it's also the point with which sailors around the globe determine their bearings, using Greenwich as the prime meridian (0° longitude).

The observatory is now part of the **National Maritime Museum** (Romney Rd., tel. 0181/858–4422), which boasts the world's largest collection of maritime artifacts. Paintings, medallions, and other reclaimed wreckage from England's mighty days of thalassocracy are spread throughout three large floors. Admission to both the observatory and the museum is £3.95 (£2.95 students), but smart cookies planning to see all the sights in Greenwich will go for the **Passport Ticket** (£7.95, £5.45 students), which also lets you in to see the *Cutty Sark* (*see below*).

The line in the observatory's courtyard actually splits the world in two. Straddle it and you're standing in two hemispheres simultaneously.

Christopher Wren is also responsible for the design of the **Royal Naval College** (King William Walk, tel. 0181/858–2154), a home for old sailors that now houses some colossal frescoes by Sir James Thornhill (the same guy who painted the dome of St. Paul's in London). And do you remember the **Cutty Sark** (King William Walk, tel. 0181/858–3445), the 19th-century, tea-trading clipper that's pictured on whiskey labels around the world? The real thing sits in dry dock opposite the pedestrian tunnel by the Thames. For £3.25 (£2.25 students), you can climb aboard the decks, peruse a collection of figureheads, or grab hold of the steering wheel and play captain. For info on guided walks and the like, stop by the **Greenwich Tourist Office** (46 Greenwich Church St., tel. 0181/858–6376); it's open year-round, daily 10:15–4:45.

COMING AND GOING The easiest way to reach Greenwich is via Docklands Light Railway (DLR) (tel. 0171/918–4000) to Island Gardens Station; simply take the tube to Tower Hill (District Line) and walk to the DLR terminal at Tower Gateway. Greenwich is in Zone 3, which is not good news for Zone 1 and 2 Travelcard holders. To reach the main sights from the station, walk through the foot tunnel underneath the Thames.

Windsor

Windsor, west of central London along the Thames, is the sort of place where rowboats roll gently upriver, where geese along the riverbank noisily lap up crumbs, and where families stroll with ice cream. Of all the day trips you could make from London, this is one of the best; Windsor Castle and the royal pomp are simply bonuses. That said, the royal presence draws throngs of foreign and English visitors, packing the narrow, cobbled streets of what would otherwise be a charming village.

BASICS The **Tourist Information Centre** is hidden in a nook in the back of Windsor's Riverside Station; call ahead if you want them to book you a bed. *Thames St., tel. 01753/852010. Open Easter–Sept. daily 10–4.*

COMING AND GOING BritRail service from London Waterloo costs £4.80 round-trip and runs every half-hour to Windsor's **Riverside Station** (Datchet Rd., tel. 01753/859644). **Green Line** (tel. 01923/673121) Buses 700, 701, 702, and 703 each take an hour to get from Eccleston Bridge, near London's Victoria Station, to Windsor (£4.35 return).

WORTH SEEING What William the Conqueror originally built out of dirt and wood (and what Henry II rebuilt in stone) has survived countless alterations over the centuries to become today's **Windsor Castle.** And yet the process of restoration continues: A 1992 fire heavily damaged 100 or so rooms in the State Apartments, most of which were for the private use of the queen, who spends most of her weekends here (the castle remains open even when she's in residence).

Whenever the queen is at Windsor, the Union Jack that usually flies from the Round Tower is replaced with the royal coat of arms

The castle is divided into the Lower, Middle, and Upper wards. Many of England's kings and queens are buried in the 15th-century **St. George's Chapel,** the principal structure of the Lower Ward. The chapel is the shrine of the Order of the Garter, a military outfit that makes a floppy procession from the State Apartments to the chapel each June. For a £1.50 fee you can visit the Upper Ward and its **State Apartments,** the **Gallery,** and **Queen Mary's Dolls' House.** The apartments feature an amazing collection of royal portraiture and other paintings, including works by Dürer, Rubens, and Van Dyck. Check out the Gobelin tapestries, too, and the Louis

XVI bed. The Dolls' House, measuring 8 by 5 feet, is a fully functional (electric lights and running faucets) marvel of miniature engineering. Hours vary but it's fairly safe to assume daily 10:30–5 in summer, with longer hours on Sunday and shorter hours off-season. The Gallery closes in January and reopens in May. St. George's Chapel is closed every Sunday. The **Changing of the Guard** takes place daily at 11 AM. *Castle Hill, tel. 01753/831118. Admission: £8, £5 on Sun.*

WHERE TO SLEEP AND EAT If you're actually spending the night in Windsor, there's a **YHA hostel** (Mill Ln., tel. 01753/861710), open February through December 18. It's only a mile from the castle, an easy 20-minute walk west; beds cost £8.70. After roaming the castle grounds, take a break at **Francesco's Pizzeria** (53 Peascod Rd., tel. 01753/863773), home to an excellent flaky, thin-crust pizza (£3–£9). The bottles all over the place evoke Tuscany (kind of); from Central Station, turn right on Thames Street and right again on Peascod Road.

NEAR WINDSOR

ETON Just across the Thames from Windsor, Eton is home to one of England's most exclusive public (read: private) schools. Don't be too impressed: Academic standards are no higher here than at other public schools, though the old-boy network is, indeed, intimidating. Since the school was founded by Henry VI in 1440 for the expenses-paid education of "poor scholars," many Eton graduates have gone on to Oxford, Cambridge, and fame in public life. Eighteen prime ministers, the King of Siam, William Fielding, Percy Bysshe Shelley, Aldous Huxley, George Orwell, and Ian Fleming have all studied at Eton, but who's counting? Eton's 15th-century **chapel** is a highlight, with its famous gold-inlaid pipe organ. From the outside, the chapel casts a beautiful, brooding Gothic silhouette. For a brief glimpse into a day in the life of an Eton brat, check out the semi-interesting **Museum of Eton Life.** *Brewhouse Yard, tel. 01753/863593. Museum admission: £2.20. Open daily 2–4:30 during term, 10:30–4:30 during school holidays.*

RUNNYMEDE In 1215, disgruntled English barons forced King John to sign the Magna Carta on this little island in the Thames, not far from where the rumbling hordes of Windsor castle-seekers roam today. Hence, the variety of camera-friendly memorials: The Kennedy Memorial, donated by the queen to the United States in 1965; a memorial to the unknown Royal Air Force (RAF) dead; and even one put up in 1965 by the American Bar Association to commemorate the 750th anniversary of the Magna Carta signing. Buses 441 and 443 leave every half-hour from Windsor to Runnymede (take Bus 561 on Sunday). Bus 1 toward Ascot is a pleasant alternative, being the only vehicle allowed to travel through Windsor's Great Park; the scenery is worth the trip.

How the Royals Came to Pay Their Way

A fire in November 1992 left about a third of Windsor Castle's Upper Ward destroyed, including St. George's Hall, the private chapel, and the state banqueting room. Fortunately, most of the private collection, including works by Vermeer, Rubens, and Leonardo da Vinci, was saved by a human chain of staffers, soldiers, and even Prince Andrew. When the smoke cleared, the bill for repairing the damage was estimated at more than £56 million. Initially, Queen Elizabeth simply assumed the public would pay. British taxpayers, however, mired in recession and annoyed that the richest woman in England didn't pay taxes herself, told her where she could shove her castle. To raise money for the restorations, the queen ultimately opened Buckingham Palace in London to tourists, which just goes to show that monarchs don't get no respect these days.

Oxford

Home to the world's first English-language university, Oxford today is bustling and crowded, a vast conurbation expanding ever-outward from the university at its center. Once upon a time, cattle herders led their flocks over the shallow junction of the Thames and Cherwell rivers. These days, the horde of buses and foot traffic in the center of town is more comparable to Piccadilly Circus. As a result, Oxford is not nearly as small and idyllic as Cambridge, England's other ivory tower. Blame the heavy industry on Oxford's outskirts, particularly the large Rover car factory. Even so, street performers and flying troops of bone-rattlers (those shaky bicycles associated with English academics) make Oxford a loud, bright, and engaging city. You'll also find that the food and nightlife rank far above that of quiet, sylvan Cambridge.

Oxford student life is a perennial cycle of classes, drinking, punting on the Thames, more drinking, and occasional bouts of studying.

Oxford and Cambridge are the nation's most prestigious universities and the rivalry between the two is intense. You can safely expect an endless stream of comparisons while visiting Oxford's colleges and local pubs. Of course, the enormous number of graduates from both schools who occupy positions of power in Britain points up the fact that what students actually study is largely irrelevant. Both Oxford and Cambridge are *names,* and thanks to their legendary old-boy networks, a degree from either is a virtual guarantee to a future career of power and influence.

BASICS

AMERICAN EXPRESS AmEx, just steps from the tourist office, holds mail and changes U.S. currency without commission for cardholders. *99 St. Aldate's St., tel. 01865/790099. Open Mon. and Wed.–Fri. 9–5:30, Tues. 9:30–5:30, Sat. 9–5.*

BUCKET SHOPS STA Travel (36 George St., tel. 01856/792800), the biggest of Oxford's budget-travel centers, sells ISIC cards, InterRail tickets, and bargain airfares—like Paris round-trip for £70. When the office gets busy, try to scam a bargain off **Campus Travel** (13 High St., tel. 01865/242067). The agency inside the **YHA Adventure Shop** (9–10 St. Clement's St., tel. 01865/247948) offers cheaper transportation fares if you show them a youth-hostel card.

LUGGAGE STORAGE Oxford is one of the few towns in England with train-station lockers (£1–£2).

MAIL The **main post office** (102–104 St. Aldate's St., OX1 1ZZ, tel. 01865/814785) changes money and handles poste restante, if you're willing to wait in a long line.

VISITOR INFORMATION Too small to handle the crowds, Oxford's **tourist office** seems more interested in selling merchandise than in offering helpful guidance. Nearly every map and leaflet on Oxford costs something. *St. Aldate's St., tel. 01865/726871. Open Mon.–Sat. 9:30–5, Sun. 10–3:30.*

Town Versus Gown

Throughout Oxford's history, tensions between the city and the university have often erupted into violence. The most famous and bloodiest event, the St. Scholastica's Day Riots, took place in 1355, beginning with a tavern brawl between scholars and a local pub owner. Over the next three days, colleges were sacked and six students were killed. In the end, the university gained the upper hand because it had royal backing. Despite several attempts on the part of townies to regain control, the university ran things around town until well into the 19th century.

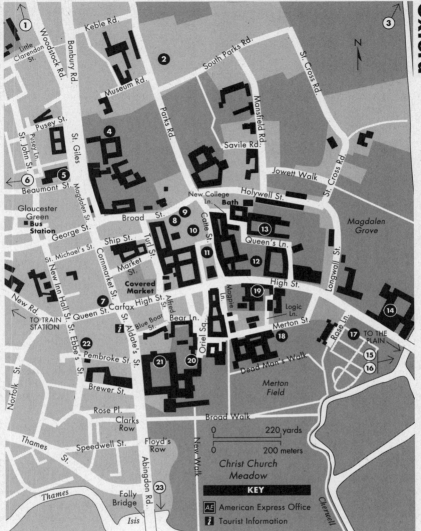

Keble Rd.

Woodstock Rd.

Little Clarendon St.

Banbury Rd.

Museum Rd.

South Parks Rd.

St. Cross Rd.

Pusey St.

Pusey Ln.

St. John St.

St. Giles

Mansfield Rd.

Savile Rd.

Parks Rd.

Beaumont St.

Magdalen St.

Jowett Walk

Holywell St.

Magdalen Grove

Gloucester Green
■ **Bus Station**

George St.

Broad St.

New College Ln. **Bath**

Catte St.

St. Cross Rd.

St. Michael's St.

New Inn Hall St.

Ship St.

Turl St.

Queen's Ln.

Cornmarket St.

Market St.

Longwall St.

Covered Market

High St.

NEW RD.

TO TRAIN STATION

Queen St.

Carfax

High St.

St. Aldate's St.

Blue Boat St.

Alfred St.

Bear Ln.

Magpie Ln.

Oriel St.

Logic Ln.

Merton St.

Rose Ln.

TO THE PLAIN

St. Ebbe's St.

Pembroke St.

Brewer St.

Dead Man's Walk

Merton Field

Norfolk St.

Rose Pl.

Clarks Row

Thames St.

Speedwell St.

Floyd's Row

New Walk

Broad Walk

Christ Church Meadow

Thames

Abingdon Rd.

Folly Bridge

Isis

Cherwell

0   220 yards
0   200 meters

KEY

AE American Express Office

i Tourist Information

N

Sights ●

All Souls College, **12**

Ashmolean Museum, **5**

Bodleian Library, **10**

Botanic Garden, **17**

Carfax Tower, **7**

Christ Church College, **21**

Christ Church Picture Gallery, **20**

Magdalen College, **14**

Merton College, **18**

Museum of the History of Science, **8**

Museum of Modern Art, **22**

New College, **13**

Radcliffe Camera, **11**

Sheldonian Theatre, **9**

St. John's College, **4**

University College, **19**

University and Pitt Museums, **12**

Lodging ○

Brenal Guest House, **15**

Brown's Guest House, **16**

Mrs. O'Neil, **6**

Newton House, **23**

Oxford YHA, **3**

Woodstock Guest House, **1**

COMING AND GOING

BY TRAIN Direct BritRail service to **Oxford Station** from London Paddington takes about an hour and costs £13.30 return. Although the train is convenient, buses are far cheaper. *Botley Rd., tel. 01865/722333.*

BY BUS All long-distance buses stop at **Gloucester Green Bus Station,** about two blocks from the train depot. Bus company offices here have info and timetables. National Express (tel. 01865/791579) travels from Oxford to London's Victoria Coach Station and back every three hours; the earliest bus leaves at 4:35 AM, and the latest arrives at 12:35 AM. The trip takes 90 minutes and costs £9. National Express also offers direct service from Oxford to Birmingham, Heathrow, Gatwick, Southampton, and even EuroDisney.

A better option is **Oxford City Link** (Gloucester Green Bus Station, tel. 01865/711312), with buses to London's Victoria Coach Station every 15 minutes (£8, £6 students). You can also catch an express bus to and from Heathrow and Gatwick airports; one-way costs £8 and £15, respectively.

GETTING AROUND

The town of Oxford and its 40 colleges are inextricably intertwined. The center of it all is **Carfax**—the intersection of Cornmarket, St. Aldate's, High, and Queen streets—where people tend to congregate, and baby strollers battle for space with buses. Streets can be hard to find in the jumbled city center, even with a fairly detailed map; better to invest in an *Oxford A–Z* map (£1.50) or another large, indexed map. With so much to see and do, and so much of it spread over a large area, it's wise to make good use of buses; they're fast, frequent, and fairly cheap.

BY BUS Two main companies, the larger **Oxford Bus Co.** (tel. 01865/711312) and the smaller **Thames Transit** (tel. 01865/727000), vie for business on similar routes. Oxford Bus Co. buses run about every seven minutes during peak times (weekdays and summer Saturdays) and at half-hour intervals at other times. Thames Transit's tan-and-blue minibuses run less frequently but are about 5p–15p less expensive than Oxford Co.'s red double-deckers or green "Nipper" minibuses. Just about any bus labeled CITY CENTER will take you to within ¼ mile of Carfax; most buses to the suburbs also depart from within two blocks of Carfax.

BY BICYCLE Oxford's flat terrain and extensive network of cycle paths make bicycling an ideal mode of transportation. Oxford City Council's *Cycling in Oxford: A Comprehensive Guide* (available free from the tourist office) includes detailed maps of all bicycle paths, and addresses and phone numbers of local bicycling organizations. However, be extremely careful about leaving your expensive mountain bike locked in the town center, because thousands are stolen each year in broad daylight.

WHERE TO SLEEP

Thank your favorite god that Oxford has a good hostel, because finding a cheap bed here is like looking for a running brook in the Sahara. Peak season begins early here, and prices skyrocket in early May. Tons of bed-and-breakfasts (B&Bs) are within bus distance along Iffley, Woodstock, and Cowley roads, but few are within walking distance of the city center. During July and August, just about every bed within 3 miles of campus is filled, so whether you plan on camping or staying in a four-star hotel, book ahead.

➤ **UNDER £30 • Mrs. O'Neil.** This is *the* lodging bargain of Oxford, providing one of the two quiet, immaculate top-floor rooms (one single, one double) is available. Don't just show up; call ahead to reserve. Bed and breakfast is £12 per person. *15 Southmoor Rd., tel. 01865/511205. From Carfax, walk north on Cornmarket St., turn left on Beaumont St., right on Walton St., left on Southmoor Rd.*

➤ **UNDER £40 • Brenal Guest House.** A lucky horseshoe and a sign above the door wishing "Failte" ("Greetings" in Gaelic) cue entrants to the Brenal's distinctly Irish hospitality. Sit by the cozy fire in winter, or lounge in the backyard in summer. Singles £20, doubles (including bath) £36. *307 Iffley Rd., tel. 01865/721561. From Carfax, take Oxford Co. Bus 40 or 42, or Thames Transit Bus 3 toward Rose Hill. Get off at Addison Crescent. 5 rooms, some with bath. Vegetarian meals available.*

Brown's Guest House. Brown's is heartily recommended by the hostel staff, who often send overflow backpackers here for the comfortable beds, plush rooms, and yummy breakfasts. Singles £20, doubles £32. *281 Iffley Rd., tel. 01865/246822. From Carfax, take Oxford Bus Co. Bus 40 or 42 or Thames Transit Bus 3 toward Rose Hill. 8 rooms, some with bath.*

Newton House. A number of bargain B&Bs lurk past Folly Bridge far away from the center, and Newton House is the best of them. Because of its large size—15 spotless rooms with TVs and plenty of light—the Newton is likely to have vacancies, even in summer. Singles £20, doubles £34. *82–84 Abingdon Rd., tel. 01865/240561. From Carfax, walk south on Abingdon Rd., or take Bus 30, 31, 32, or 32A. 15 rooms, some with bath. AE, MC, V.*

HOSTELS **Oxford YHA.** Clean, comfortable, and expertly managed, Oxford's hostel is a model of efficiency, with great kitchen facilities, a pool table, and lots of sightseeing info. Beds fill quickly year-round in this brick Victorian only a mile from Carfax; call a few days ahead, especially in summer, and check-in before 5 PM. Beds £8.70. *32 Jack Straw's Ln., tel. 01865/62997, fax 01865/69402. Bus 72 or 73 from Carfax (on St. Aldate's St. in front of post office); Bus 73 also runs from rail station (weekday evenings after 7 PM and Sun. only). 116 beds. Lockout daily 10 AM–1 PM. Kitchen facilities, laundry. Closed late Dec.–mid-Jan. Wheelchair access. MC, V.*

CAMPGROUNDS **Oxford Camping International.** You'll be vying with motor homes, but hey, it's clean, green, cheap, and open year-round. Two-person tent sites cost £5.75. *426 Abingdon Rd., tel. 01865/246551. From Carfax, take Bus 30, 31, 32, or 32A. 70 sites. Laundry.*

FOOD

Local students may gripe about the lack of decent eats in town, but relative to the rest of England, Oxford has great food, with all ethnicities and price ranges duly represented. If you're strapped, head to supermarkets like **J. Sainsbury** (Westgate Shopping Centre, tel. 01865/722179) and **Tesco** (127 Cowley Rd., tel. 01865/244470), both open Monday–Saturday. At the **Covered Market** (Market St., ½ block east of Cornmarket St.), greengrocers, butchers, and bakers set up shop Monday–Saturday. If you're in a hurry, **Harvey's** (89 Gloucester Green, tel. 01865/793963), conveniently beside the bus station, offers every sandwich combination imaginable.

Vegetarians should cover their eyes when walking past the poachers at the Covered Market; they often display a fresh hare or deer carcass strung up by its hindquarters.

➢ **UNDER £5** • **Café MOMA.** This tiny joint is hidden on a side street beneath the Museum of Modern Art. For £2.40 chow down on salad, or try the "nutroast," a baked loaf of ground nuts, tomatoes, onions, and cheese (£3.80). The best bargain is coffee with the quiche or soup of the day (£1.70). *30 Pembroke St., tel. 01865/722733. From Carfax, walk west along Queen St., turn left on St. Ebbe's St., left on Pembroke St. Open Tues., Wed., Fri., and Sat. 9:30–5:30, Thurs. 9:30–9:30.*

Georgina's Coffee Shop. Toulouse Lautrec posters line the walls in this hip café hidden within the otherwise unfriendly confines of the Covered Market. Great tunes accompany bagels, pastries, and lunch specials like the brie platter (£3.95). *Covered Market, above Beaton's Deli, no phone. Open Mon.–Sat. 9:30–5.*

➢ **UNDER £10** • **Café CoCo.** CoCo's pizza—try the no-cheese Mediterranean for £4.95—is amazing. More adventurous is the warm duck salad (£6.95). *23 Cowley Rd., tel. 01865/200232. From Carfax, walk east down High St., cross Magdalen St., and continue on Cowley after "The Plain" roundabout. Open daily 10 AM–midnight.*

Chang Mai Kitchen. Oxford's best Thai food is served in a ramshackle Tudor building less than a block from Carfax. Despite the classy wood-beam surroundings, most dishes cost £4–£6. **161**

Kemp Hall Passage, 130A High St., tel. 01865/202233. From Carfax, walk east on High St., turn right on tiny Kemp Hall Passage (less than a block). Open Mon.–Sat. noon–2 and 6–11.

The Nosebag. The ever-changing lunch menu features some kind of soup (£1.90), stuffed baked potatoes (£2.80), a cold dish (£4.15), a strictly vegetarian dish (£4.50), and a hot dish (£4.95). Dinners (really just heftier versions of lunch) cost less than £6. Long lines form for both meals; on Saturdays the queue gets ridiculous. No smoking. *6–8 St. Michael's St., tel. 01865/721033. From Carfax, walk north on Cornmarket St., turn left on St. Michael's St. Open Mon. 9:30–5:30, Tues.–Thurs. until 10, Fri. and Sat. until 10:30, Sun. until 9.*

WORTH SEEING

Before publicly embarrassing yourself, you should know that Oxford University isn't one big campus. The 29 undergraduate colleges, six graduate colleges, five permanent halls, and All Souls College—each with its own dormitories and lecture halls—are scattered around town. Many colleges charge a small admission fee to people who want to wander around or take a tour, but there's no harm in trying to pass yourself off as a student and walking determinedly into the colleges.

BOTANIC GARDEN Few gardens are more beautiful or feature a greater diversity of plants than this 300-year-old complex of greenhouses (called "glasshouses" in England). On a cold day, saunter past the rows of rare tropical plants. *High St., across from Magdalen College. Admission free. Open Apr.–Aug., daily 9–5; Sept.–Mar., daily 9–4:30. Greenhouses open daily 2–4. Wheelchair access.*

CARFAX TOWER The last remnant of St. Martin's Church (AD 1032), Carfax Tower minds the corner all by itself now, marking the passage of time with little mechanical figures that dance every 15 minutes. After the 14th-century St. Scholastica's Day Riots, Edward III ordered the tower lowered to prevent townies from showering gownies with rocks, bottles, and flaming arrows. You can get a good view of the town center by climbing up the tower via the dank stairwell. *Admission: £1.20. Open daily 10–6.*

OXFORD UNIVERSITY Oxford University has been a major player in British history for the past 830 years. The establishment of several monasteries in the early 12th century attracted scholarly clerics, and before long they organized themselves into a *studium generale,* offering curriculum along the same lines as the University of Paris. The turning point for the university, however, came in 1167, when the French government expelled all English students from Paris following the assassination of Thomas à Becket, the Archbishop of Canterbury. Lacking a place to study, these students migrated to Oxford and started the first official college.

Most colleges will grudgingly allow visitors to snoop around on weekday afternoons between 2 PM and 5 PM. Be careful to vacate the grounds by 9 PM: The gates shut at 9:05 on the dot, and some unfortunates have been locked in by accident. Another option is student-run **Oxford Student Tours,** which arranges guided walks (£3) on summer afternoons. To catch a tour, look for the guys in funny hats and bow ties hanging around the tourist office. For more info, contact Oxford University General Information (tel. 01865/270000).

➢ **ALL SOULS** • Possibly the most beautiful college, All Souls was originally founded in 1438 by the Archbishop of Canterbury for spiritual and legal studies (interesting combination). Today, the **North Quad** is a whimsical 18th-century interpretation of Gothic spires and pinnacles, featuring Christopher Wren's sundial and John Hawksmoor's famous twin towers (circa 1734). *High St., tel. 01865/279379. Open weekdays 2–4:30 (until 4 in winter).*

➢ **CHRIST CHURCH** • Founded by Cardinal Wolsey in 1525, Christ Church is never referred to as "Christ Church College." Goodness gracious, no—members call it "The House." In fact, everything seems to have a special name here at The House, which many regard as Oxford's snobbiest college. Professors, called "dons" elsewhere in Oxford, are referred to here as "students." The 6¼-ton bell in the clock tower over the entrance is named **Great Tom,** and the quad Great Tom presides over is (big surprise) **Tom Quad.** Every night at 9:05, Great Tom rings 101 times, once for each of the original students (not professors). Near the **Memorial**

Garden you'll find Christ Church's 800-year-old **cathedral,** one of the smallest and most ornate in the country. *Brideshead Revisited* was set here.

A handful of literary and philosophical giants did time at Christ Church, including W. H. Auden, Jeremy Bentham, and John Locke. It was also here, as a college fellow, that Lewis Carroll reputedly lusted after his colleagues' prepubescent daughters, daydreams which led him to write *Alice in Wonderland.* If you have time, take a stroll through quiet, tree-lined paths of **Christ Church Meadow,** alongside the Thames. When school is in session, college "eights" practice their rowing on the "Isis," a nickname for this section of the Thames. The steep admission to the university can usually be dodged by entering the back way off Oriel Square, next to the picture gallery. *St. Aldate's St., tel. 01865/276150. Admission: £2.50, £1 students. Open mid-Apr.–Aug., Mon.–Sat. 9:30–5:30, Sun. 12:45–5:30; Sept.–Apr., Mon.–Sat. 9:30–4:30, Sun. 12:45–4:30.*

➤ **MAGDALEN COLLEGE** • Magdalen (pronounced MAUD-lin) opened its doors to undergrads in 1458 and boasts Oscar Wilde, C. S. Lewis, Peter Brook, and (best of all) Dudley Moore as alumni. The quadrangle is a quiet area, enclosed by ancient vaulted cloisters covered with wisteria. Beyond this lies a deer park, gardens, and the Cherwell River; you can rent punts at the foot of Magdalen Bridge (*see* Outdoor Activities, *below*). **Magdalen Tower,** one of Oxford's most recognizable landmarks, presides over the college grounds. Since the mid-15th century, the beginning of spring has been heralded by the voices of Magdalen's choir from atop this tower. *High St., tel. 01865/242191. From Carfax, walk east along High St. Admission: £1.50 Open daily noon–5.*

➤ **NEW COLLEGE** • The first college built after the bloody St. Scholastica's Day Riot, New College (officially: St. Mary College of Winchester in Oxenford) incorporated a new design feature—the first enclosed quad—to protect students in the event of another town–gown flare-up. The extra caution proved unnecessary, but founder William of Wykeham (Bishop of Winchester and a wealthy, wealthy man) probably didn't feel like taking chances, considering the shortage of well-educated people after the Black Death of 1349. Most of the college and its **chapel** were completed in 1386, with further major additions completed in the 17th century. *Queen's Ln., tel. 01865/248457. From Carfax, walk north along Cornmarket St., turn right at Broad St., right on Catte St., left on New College Ln. Admission: 50p. Open daily 11–5 during school vacations, daily 2–5 when class is in session.*

➤ **UNIVERSITY COLLEGE** • To its embarrassment, University is best known for expelling Percy Bysshe Shelley in 1811, because he wrote and distributed a little pamphlet called "The Necessity of Atheism." After he drowned in Italy, the college had second thoughts and erected a monument for him in the **Front Quad.** This is also where young Bill Clinton dodged the draft,

William Spooner

If you've ever foot your put in your mouth by switching the first sounds of two words in a sentence, you've committed a "spoonerism." The term was coined for the late Rev. William Archibald Spooner, former warden of New College, who regularly langled the manguage without meaning to. We list the top three "classic" spoonerisms, spoken by the master himself:

- *"You have deliberately tasted two whole worms, hissed all my mystery lectures, and you will take the first town drain!"*

- *"Three cheers for our queer old dean!"*

- *"The Lord is a shoving leopard."*

smoked but didn't inhale, and networked like a whirling dervish while on a Rhodes Scholarship. But back to the college: The original foundation dates from 1249, the first proof of any college in Oxford (although Merton claims to be 85 years older). Both the chapel and the hall can be visited during school vacations. *High St., tel. 01865/276602. Admission: £1. Open daily 2–4 during school breaks.*

MUSEUMS AND LIBRARIES Not only do Oxford's museums house some tremendous collections, but almost all of them are free. The exceptions to the rule are the **Museum of Modern Art** (30 Pembroke St., tel. 01865/722733), which badly needs the £2.50 admission fee (£1.50 students); and the **Christ Church Picture Gallery** (tel. 01865/276172; admission: £1, 50p students), with a collection of Rubens drawings and Renaissance paintings by Tintoretto, Van Dyck, and others. All university libraries, with the exception of the Bodleian Library, are off-limits to the general public.

➤ **ASHMOLEAN MUSEUM OF ART AND ARCHAEOLOGY** • The Ashmolean is Britain's oldest public museum, boasting artifacts and masterworks ranging from drawings by Michelangelo and paintings by Pissarro to Bronze Age tools and weapons. The prize for Most Bizarre Objet d'Interet goes to Oliver Cromwell's death mask. *Beaumont St., at St. Giles, tel. 01865/278000. From Carfax, walk north along Cornmarket St., turn left at Beaumont St. Admission free. Open Tues.–Sat. 10–4, Sun. 2–4. Wheelchair access.*

➤ **BODLEIAN LIBRARY AND RADCLIFFE CAMERA** • "Camera" meant "room" in medieval times, and the Radcliffe is one hell of a reading room. So, too, is the library, which owns a copy of every book printed in Britain since printing began—about five and a half million books, give or take a few. Visiting students can't get inside without a signed letter from their university specifically requesting library access, and even then you may have to haggle. The **guided tour** (£3) is your surest bet; about four per day run weekdays 9–5 from the Sheldonian Theatre (*see below*).

➤ **SHELDONIAN THEATRE** • Christopher Wren's marble-covered Sheldonian Theatre, built in 1669, was intended as an appropriately sober venue to confer degrees upon graduates. With its painted ceiling, heavy columns, and enormous pipe organ, it does indeed feel like the sort of place everyone should pass through before graduating into "the real world" (not the MTV show). The cupola provides a decent, if frustrating, glass-enclosed view of central Oxford. The Sheldonian occasionally hosts concerts on Saturday evenings—highly recommended. *Broad St., tel. 01865/277299. Admission: 50p. Open Mon.–Sat. 10–12:45 and 2–4:45 (Dec.–Feb. until 3:45).*

➤ **UNIVERSITY MUSEUM** • One of the world's greatest natural-history museums sits just 20 minutes north of the town center in a massive Victorian Gothic building that it shares with the **Pitt Rivers Museum** (which has masks, hanging sailboats, wooden clothing, and other unclassifiable stuff). University Museum has hundreds of exhibits on just about every facet of nature, but the local dinosaur finds attract the most attention. *Parks Rd., tel. 01865/272950. Admission free. Open Mon.–Sat. noon–5.*

The Bear (Alfred St. and Bear Ln.) is a magnificent 13th-century pub, with walls covered by thousands of ties. You get a free pint if you give up your school, regiment, sporting, or dress tie—assuming they don't already have one like it.

AFTER DARK

PUBS Most pubs in Oxford stay open through the afternoon, serving a post-tutorial pint. All the pubs we list are open Monday–Saturday 11–11 and Sunday noon–3, 7–10:30. **The Head of the River** (St. Aldate's St., at Folly Bridge, tel. 01865/721600) is the biggest "activity" pub in Oxford, with barbecues, snooker play-offs, bucking bronco contests, and even bungee-jumping on summer Saturday nights. A loud crowd on weekends makes **The King's Arms** (40 Holywell St., at Parks Rd., tel. 01865/242369) one of the hottest traditional pubs in the city center. It's also a "free house" (unaffiliated with a particular brewery), so there's a wide variety of real ales. If you can find the tiny 13th-century **Turf Tavern** (4 Bath Pl., tel. 01865/243235)—it's tucked away in a narrow alley—try the mulled wine, cinnamon-spiced and guaranteed to lift even the most discouraged traveler's spirits.

CLUBS *What's On In Oxford,* available free at the tourist office, is an invaluable guide to clubbing around town. **The Jericho Tavern** (56 Walton St., tel. 01865/54502) offers a tremendous variety of known bands in the rock/alternative/indie vein; the cover usually runs £3.50, £3 students. **The Oxford Venue** (196 Cowley Rd., tel. 01865/790501) is the other main outlet for rock-star angst, presenting live music 8 PM–11 PM, and a DJ 11 PM–2 AM. Covers run £3–£5. **Freud** (Walton Rd., at Great Clarendon St., tel. 01865/311171), or FREVD as the sign says, is housed in an enormous converted 19th-century church that still has its stained glass. Nightly jazz starts at 11PM; cover £3. The **Old Fire Station** (40 George St., tel. 01865/794494) is the ultimate one-stop place, with a restaurant, theater, bar, and art museum all under one roof. There's jazz and blues on Friday and Saturday nights. Cover £3.50–£5.

CINEMAS After the recent closing of the much-loved Penultimate Picture Palace, the only remaining theater with any character is **The Phoenix** (58 Walton St., tel. 01865/512526), which shows first- and second-run artsy films.

OUTDOOR ACTIVITIES

PUNTING AND ROWING Boats cost £6 per hour with a £20 deposit at the shop by Folly Bridge, though the owner has been known to raise prices during high-demand periods. A better bet is the friendly **Magdalen Bridge Boathouse,** which charges £7 per hour with a £20 deposit. Both close for bad weather and boat races. *High St. From Carfax, walk east on High St. to Magdalen Bridge. Open daily 10–8; shorter hrs off-season. Life jackets provided on request.*

Cambridge

Even the most jaded dropout won't be able to resist the lure of Cambridge's stone walls, massive libraries, and robed fellows strutting about. Cambridge has produced some of the world's finest scientists, although the register of literary alumni includes John Milton and Virginia Woolf, among others. Stephen Hawking, author of *A Brief History of Time,* today occupies the same faculty chair Isaac Newton once held. But for all the grandeur of ancient academia, Cambridge has plenty of life. You're just as likely to see death-rockers as gray-bearded earls putting down a pint or two in the town's pubs.

Here's a humbling thought: Cambridge University was chartered about 500 years before the United States signed its wee Declaration of Independence.

Like many English universities, Cambridge is composed of a number of smaller colleges (around 35). Since student life is not concentrated on one campus, the center of town is the focal point of the university's social and cultural scene. However, Cambridge isn't all open doors for tourists. University students eat most meals in their respective colleges and many activities, bars, and facilities are only accessible to them. Even though reasonably collegiate-looking visitors can wander through the colleges without getting tossed, the budding Byrons and Newtons who call Cambridge home have to deal with tourist intruders on a daily basis, and are understandably wary.

Cambridge is commonly perceived to be much prettier than Oxford—not because of the superiority of the site, but in the way it's been landscaped. Green lawns stretch to infinity and the surroundings are relatively untouched by encroaching industry. At the first promise of sunshine, many students head to the Botanic Gardens or the banks of the River Cam. Others coast the streets of Cambridge on their '50s-style Pee Wee Herman bikes, maneuvering between the tourists. Occasionally, just occasionally, some studying gets done.

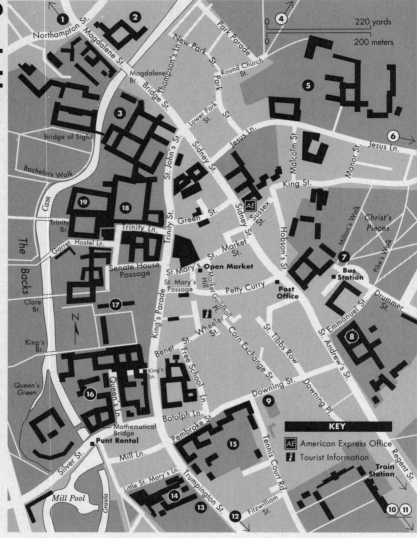

Cambridge

Northampton St.
Magdalene St.
Thompson's St.
New Park
Park Parade
Round Church St.
Park
Magdalene Br.
Bridge St.
Lower Park St.
Jesus Ln.
Bridge of Sighs
St. John's St.
Sidney St.
Malcolm St.
Manor St.
Jesus Ln.
Bachelors Walk
King St.
Cam
The Backs
Trinity Br.
Trinity Ln.
Trinity St.
Green St.
Sidney St.
Sussex St.
AE
Milton's Walk
Christ's Pieces
Pike's Walk
Garret Hostel Ln.
Senate House Passage
St. Mary's St.
Market St.
Open Market
Hobson's St.
Bus Station
Clare Br.
King's Parade
St. Mary's Passage
Market Hill
Petty Curry
Post Office
Drummer St.
King's Br.
N
Bene't St.
Wheeler St.
Corn Exchange St.
St. Tibbs Row
St. Andrew's St.
St. Emmanuel St.
Queen's Green
Free School Ln.
Downing St.
Downing Pl.
Queen's Ln.
King's Ln.
Botolph Ln.
Pembroke St.
Tennis Court Rd.
Regent St.
Mathematical Bridge
Punt Rental
Mill Ln.
Little St. Mary's Ln.
Trumpington St.
Fitzwilliam St.
Train Station
Silver St.
Granta
Mill Pool

220 yards
200 meters

KEY

AE American Express Office

i Tourist Information

Sights ●

Christ's College, **7**

Emmanuel College, **8**

Fitzwilliam Museum, **13**

Girton College, **1**

Jesus College, **5**

King's College Chapel, **17**

Magdalene College, **2**

Pembroke College, **15**

Peterhouse College, **14**

Queen's College, **16**

St. John's College, **3**

Trinity College, **18**

University Botanic Garden, **12**

University Museum of Archaeology and Anthropology, **9**

Wren Library, **19**

Lodging ○

Cambridge YHA, **11**

Carpenter's Arms, **6**

Lyngamore House, **4**

Tenison Towers, **10**

BASICS

AMERICAN EXPRESS 25 Sidney St., Cambridge CB2 3HP, tel. 01223/351636. Open Mon., Tues., Thurs. and Fri. 9–5:30, Wed. 9:30–5:30, Sat. 9–5.

BUCKET SHOPS For £5 and a photo, **Student Travel Association (STA)** issues ISIC and student I.D. cards. STA also books discount airfares. 38 Sidney St., tel. 01223/300247. Open weekdays 9–5:30, Sat. 10–4.

BUREAUX DE CHANGE AmEx has good rates and doesn't charge commission to exchange its own traveler's checks. **Blarney Woolen Mills** is the only money exchange open seven days a week. 13 Trinity St., tel. 01223/314504. Open Mon.–Sat. 9–6, Sun. 10–5.

MAIL The **main post office** sells stamps, cashes checks, processes film, and even has a photo booth. 9–11 St. Andrew's St., tel. 01223/323325. Open Mon., Tues., Thurs., and Fri. 9–5:30, Wed. 9:30–5:30, Sat. 9–12:30.

VISITOR INFORMATION The **Cambridge Tourist Information Centre** gives guided, two-hour walking tours daily and will book lodgings for a £3, refundable deposit. Also check out the fine map and info booklet, "Cambridge: Where to Go, What to See" (£1.65). Wheeler St., behind Guildhall, tel. 01223/322640. Open Mon., Tues., Thurs. and Fri. 9–6, Wed. 9:30–6, Sat. 9–5, Sun. 10:30–3:30; closed Sun. in off-season.

COMING AND GOING

BY TRAIN Two trains per hour leave for London (1 hr, £12.30 return); to reach town from **Cambridge Station,** wait for a Cityrail Link bus or walk 30 minutes down Station Road, turn right on Hills Road (which keeps changing names), and continue straight. Station St., tel. 01223/311999.

BY BUS One advantage of taking the bus to Cambridge is the central location of **Drummer Street** station, near where St. Andrew's Street becomes Sidney Street. The cramped coach office is hectic, but it does have a good supply of timetables. National Express buses run to London (£9.25 return) and other nearby spots. Buy tickets on board, as drivers often give special return fares the office doesn't offer. End of Drummer St., tel. 01223/355554. Office open Mon.–Sat. 8:15–5:30.

BY PLANE **Stansted International Airport** (tel. 01279/662379 or 01279/662520) is as close to Cambridge as it is to London, and is serviced by most national carriers. Hourly trains and Buses 75 and 79 go directly into Cambridge from Stansted for about £7 each way; expensive, yes, but cheaper and closer than a bus from London.

GETTING AROUND

To discourage you from renting a car, the streets change names, are diverted by the colleges, and tend to be packed with cyclists. The narrow arcades in the center get a bit confusing, but orient yourself around the outdoor market on Market Square, and it's easier to remember which college is which. **Geoff's Bike Hire** (65 Devonshire Rd., tel. 01223/65629) rents wobbly steeds for £5 a day (10% discount if you're staying at the adjacent YHA hostel). A few other cycle-hire shops are scattered through town, including **Mike's Bikes** (28 Mill Rd., tel. 01223/312591) and **University Cycles** (9 Victoria Ave., tel. 01223/355517).

The traffic is so bad in Cambridge that the university forbids its students to drive cars within 12 miles of campus. Visitors will also get a better sense of the city center walking and cycling—or punting on the River Cam.

WHERE TO SLEEP

You'd think the university dorms would throw their doors open to student visitors, but no, it doesn't work that way. You have to call each college to find out what its policy is, and generally those that *do* have rooms rent them only to large groups. The tourist office can direct you to colleges most likely to have an available room, but don't count on it. Head instead towards the gaggle of B&Bs around **Tenison Road** and **Devonshire Road,** about three blocks from the train station (walk down Station Rd., hang the first right on Tenison Rd., and continue for a block or two). For something closer to the colleges, try the B&Bs on Chesterton Road and Jesus Lane. Another option is the **YMCA** (Gonville Pl., on Parker's Piece, tel. 01223/356998), which occasionally rents singles (£19) and dorm beds (£15.50). Availability varies dramatically, as preference is given to locals and large groups over individual travelers.

Lyngamore House. With its large, clean rooms and good location across from Jesus Green, one wouldn't expect this to be the cheapest B&B in town, but it is. Call ahead to reserve a room. Singles £15, doubles £25. *35–37 Chesterton Rd., tel. 01223/312369. Take Bus 3 or 5 from train station. 11 rooms, none with bath.*

Tenison Towers. The best B&B within easy walking distance of the train station, Tenison Towers is spankin' clean and affordable, especially for four people. Look for the yellow building on Tenison Road. The sole single is £20, doubles are £28, four-person family rooms £44. *148 Tenison Rd., tel. 01223/566511. From train station, walk down Station Rd., turn right on Tenison Rd. 8 rooms, none with bath.*

HOSTELS **Cambridge YHA.** It's a mere three blocks from the train station, with clean beds, powerful showers, and a mellow international crowd that makes up for the claustrophobia-inducing bedrooms, but *book ahead.* At the very least, phone the moment you arrive; if you call in advance they'll hold your bed until 6 PM. Beds £12. *97 Tenison Rd., tel. 01223/354601, fax 01223/312780. 129 beds. Curfew 11:30 PM, lockout 10 AM–1 PM. Laundry, luggage storage, kitchen. MC, V.*

Carpenter's Arms Backpackers' Accommodations. If only they had more than 14 beds, the competitive prices and central location of Carpenter's could put the YHA hostel out of business. The crowd is young and international, and the owners will even pick you up from the train station if they're not too busy. The rooms are dorm-style, sleep six to eight people, and cost £10 per person. *182–186 Victoria Rd., tel. 01223/351814. From bus station, walk down Drummer St., turn left on Emmanuel Rd. (which becomes Victoria Rd.).*

CAMPGROUNDS **Camping and Caravaning Club Ltd.** Buses don't go often enough to this modern, 13-acre campsite 3 miles south of Cambridge to make it easily accessible from the city center. But it's a sprawling megasite, complete with children's playground and 50 RV hookups. Sites £4.50–£5 per person. *Cabbage Moore, Cambridge Rd., Great Shelford, tel. 01223/841185. From Drummer St., take Bus 102 or 103 to Great Shelford (£1 each way); by car, take A10 and turn left onto A1301. 100 sites. Toilets, showers, washing machines. Closed Nov.–late Mar.*

Toad Acre Caravan Park. The grassy strip to the side of the RVs is peaceful for tent campers, especially when the apple trees are in bloom. Sites £4.50–£5.50 per person. *Mills Ln., Longstanton, tel. 01954/780939. Take Bus 155 or 157 (1 per hr, £1.40 one-way) to Longstanton; by car, drive 5 mi north on A604, turn right onto B1050. 48 sites. Showers, washing machines, dryers.*

Many butcher shops make fresh meat pies, a local specialty, while potatoes grown in the nearby fens are served with almost every dish.

FOOD

The pedestrian zone has plenty of greasy stands and take-out restaurants hidden in little passageways like **Rose Crescent.** For bulk supplies, head for **Market Hill** in the middle of Cambridge, where the open market offers a colorful selection of fruits and vegetables Monday–Saturday. **Cambridge Health Food** (5 Bridge St., tel. 01223/350433) is the place for muesli and other whole-food supplies.

If you like smoky ambience, strong espresso, and Pretty Young Things, **Clown's** (52 King St., tel. 01223/355711) is worth your while, despite the clown memorabilia on the walls. Scarf down gourmet individual pizzas (many under £5) at **7A Jesus Lane** (7A Jesus Ln., tel. 01223/324033), the snazzy former dining room of one of Cambridge's most uptight eating clubs—and still a popular place for college students to chat over a long meal. British yuppies re-create a pretentious American bar-and-grill experience at **Brown's** (23 Trumpington St., near Peterhouse College, tel. 01223/461655); prices are high, but you can get by with a tenner if you order the hot chicken salad (£7.65) or the steak and mushroom pie (£7.25). Meals are served in a glass-enclosed patio, and on sunny days you can even eat outdoors. **King's Pantry** (9 King's Parade, across from King's College, tel. 01223/321551) is a basement vegetarian and whole-food establishment that feels like a friend's living room. Dishes are prepared fresh each day, including vegan and gluten-free entrées. They serve an excellent three-course meal with soup, main course, and dessert for £6.95 (lunch) and £10 (dinner).

WORTH SEEING

Because the city is relatively compact, the main sights are all accessible on foot. For some striking architecture, saunter past the colleges clustered on the west bank of the River Cam, starting perhaps with King's College Chapel and Christopher Wren's library in Trinity College (*see below*). Other colleges worth seeing include **St. John's, Emmanuel, Magdalene, Downing, Jesus** and **Christ's.**

THE COLLEGES Unlike American universities, Cambridge University has no exact center but is spread over many residential colleges. There are few large lecture classes, and students spend most of their scholastic careers attending weekly tutorials—yes, wearing the requisite black robes. The rest of their time is spent keeping up with lengthy reading lists. Many colleges close altogether during final exams, from the fourth week of May until mid-June.

For centuries Cambridge and Oxford have been at odds with each other. These days the huge rivalry comes to a head at two annual sporting events: the Boat Race, when the universities' rowing eights glide down the Thames near Putney; and the rugby match, played before massive crowds at Twickenham in London. Ironically, both rank among the best in the world: Cambridge gave us Newton and Byron, while Oxford gave us Locke and Oscar Wilde. To the outside world, the differences can seem cosmetic, and Brits not privileged enough to attend either school often meld the two names to come up with "Ox-Bridge," a useful, telling adjective.

➤ **KING'S COLLEGE** • King Henry VI founded King's College in 1441 and five years later began constructing its greatest monument, **King's College Chapel.** Calling it a chapel seems a bit insulting; it feels more like a cathedral. Completed in 1536, the 289-foot-long Gothic structure features the world's longest expanse of fan-vaulted ceiling (the spider web–style branches supporting the arches). Peter Paul Rubens' *Adoration of the Magi* hangs behind the altar. During summer there are public recitals—look for a schedule inside. On Christmas Eve a festival of carols is broadcast worldwide. *King's College, tel. 01223/350411. Admission to chapel: £2, £1 students. Open Mon.–Sat. 9:30–4:30, Sun. 10–5.*

➤ **QUEENS' COLLEGE** • Queens' College—founded in 1448 by Margaret of Anjou, wife of Henry VI, and later built up by Elizabeth of Woodville, wife of Edward IV—is a mess of architectural styles. The unspoiled Renaissance cloister court lies beside some ugly, recently constructed buildings funded by Sir John Cripps, owner of the worldwide patent for Velcro™. Legend has it that the so-called **Mathematical Bridge** that crosses the Cam to connect both sides of the college was designed by Sir Isaac Newton and built without screws and fastenings. Not true. A local carpenter named James Essex designed the bridge in 1750, more than 20 years after Newton's death, and yes, he supported the structure with bolts and screws. Visitors can stroll through quietly while term is in session, daily 1:45–4:30.

➤ **TRINITY COLLEGE** • The largest and richest of Cambridge's colleges, Trinity counts among its alumni Lord Byron and Isaac Newton. Trinity is also the third largest landowner in Britain—after the Crown and Church, of course. (It's actually possible to walk from Cambridge to Oxford entirely on Trinity-owned land.) The college's impressive **Wren Library,** designed entirely by Christopher Wren, down to the bookshelves and reading desks, contains an astonishing display of valuable books: one of Shakespeare's first folios and Newton's pocket book, among others. *Wren Library, Trinity College, tel. 01223/338488. Admission free. Open during school year, weekdays noon–2, Sat. 10–2; during vacations, weekdays noon–2. Closed during exams.*

MUSEUMS AND GARDENS **Fitzwilliam Museum.** The permanent collection features paintings and prints from the Renaissance through Impressionism, as well as artifacts from ancient Greece and Egypt. *Trumpington St., tel. 01223/332900. Admission free. Open Tues.–Sat. 10–2 (antiquities and manuscript galleries) and 2:15–5 (painting and sculpture galleries); both galleries open Sun. 2:15–5. Wheelchair access with advance notice.*

University Botanic Garden. This is the perfect place to break the musty monotony of cobblestone, or kill time while waiting for a train. Among its many delights are a glass igloo, a limestone rock garden, and flowers, flowers, flowers. *Cory Lodge, Bateman St., tel. 01223/336265. From train station, turn right on Hills Rd., left on Bateman St. Admission £1.50; free Wed. and daily Nov.–Feb. Open daily 10–5.*

University Museum of Archaeology and Anthropology (UMAA). Cambridge University pioneered the study of social anthropology, and the UMAA traces conceptual progress in the field over the last 100 years. The museum keeps strange hours, so call ahead. *Downing St., near Corn Exchange St., tel. 01223/333516. Admission free. Theoretically open weekdays 2–4, Sat. 10–12:30.*

AFTER DARK

Lord only knows what goes on behind the walls of the colleges late at night, and you'll never know either unless you make friends quickly. Still, there's plenty of culture happening outside the college gates: Great rock bands come through Cambridge regularly, so get a copy of *Varsity* (20p) at a newsstand for current listings. The gay community hurts for public venues in this town; to find out the latest meeting spots contact the **Cambridge Gay Line** (tel. 01223/

Punting on the Cam

To punt means to maneuver a flat, wooden, gondola-like boat through the shallow, vermin-infested River Cam by the "backs" of the colleges. (You get a better view of the ivy-covered walls from the water than from the front.) Mastery of this sport lies in one's ability to control a 15-foot pole, which you use to propel the punt. To avoid the humiliation and failure of losing your pole to the muddy river floor, not to mention outright criticism from people watching along the banks, consider punting at night.

The Granta Inn Punt Hire (tel. 01223/300886) rents punts until 10 PM; during the day, the slightly more expensive Scudamore's Boatyards (tel. 01223/359750) also rents 'em. The "dock" for rentals is between two local pubs, The Anchor and The Mill, at the end of Mill Lane near the Silver Street bridge. Get a bottle of wine, some food, and a small group of people, and you'll find yourself saying things like, "It doesn't get any better than this." Hourly rentals are £4–£8, and all companies require a deposit.

The lazier at heart may prefer chauffeured punting. Cute young Cambridge students wearing Venetian-type straw hats will punt you (sounds risqué, non?) for £4 a head, £15 a group, in 80-year-old boats. They also give a fairly informative spiel on the colleges. Each chauffeur rents his punt independently from Scudamore's Boatyard, so there's no organization to contact; just go down to the dock and wait for the first available boat.

246031) on Wednesdays 6:30 PM–9:30 PM, although the people running the line will usually give advice at other times during the week. The **University Line** (tel. 01223/333313) also has gay listings Tuesday 7:30 PM–11 PM.

PUBS The last official count of pubs in Cambridge came to 28, but surely you'll find more if you look. Right along the Cam near the punt rental, **The Anchor** (Laundress Ln., off Silver St., tel. 01223/353554) is a haven for international students. The outdoor deck is a great place to relax when the sun finally comes out. Indoors, the Anchor hosts live jazz on Tuesday nights. **The Burleigh Arms** (9–11 Newmarket Rd., tel. 01223/316881), the only full-time gay bar in Cambridge, fills up with students on Saturday nights. **The Maypole** (Park St., near Magdalene College, tel. 01223/352999) is *the* place in Cambridge to overhear pretentious conversation; thespians hang out here when they're not working on the latest interpretation of a Beckett play.

MUSIC **The Junction** (Clifton Rd., tel. 01223/412600) hosts local indie bands, jazz, hip hop, house, whatever. If you brought a leotard, you can also join the daily aerobics workout. Tickets range from £3 for small gigs to £7.50 for big-name bands. You'll find everything from jazz and classical to Melody Maker's flavor-of-the-month band at **The Corn Exchange** (Wheeler St. and Corn Exchange, tel. 01223/357851), where tickets usually cost £10.

THEATER AND FILM The **Amateur Dramatic Club (ADC)** (Park St., tel. 01223/359547) presents student-produced plays and late-night arty flicks. You might be able to snag a £5 theater ticket 30 minutes before show time. Late-night films (£3) usually begin at 11:30 PM. The **Arts Cinema** (Market Passage, tel. 01223/302929), affiliated with the ADC, usually shows three different American and European art flicks a day; late-night shows (usually at 11:15 PM) are scheduled about four days a week. Seats cost £3.80 between 5:30 PM and 11 PM, £2.90 at all other times.

Stratford-upon-Avon

We've taken a lot of crap from Stratford locals for our 1994 coverage of the town. We dared to suggest that it's suffocatingly overcrowded—a tourist trap even—and that its soul has been sucked dry by mercenary hucksters looking to make a quick quid off Shakespeare's good name. Well, it still sucks, and we stand by our original take. If you're really that keen on saying you've "done" Stratford, you won't mind the crowds or the lack of cafés, movie theaters, and other forms of cultural life beyond the theater. And while the **Royal Shakespeare Company (RSC)** does stage frequent productions in Stratford, equally prestigious productions run in London—minus the hype and the hordes. That said, the RSC is the best thing going for Stratford, and we unabashedly recommend it.

Stratford is just fine during winter—the crowds thin out, the streets become walkable, and the RSC continues its first-rate program of drama. Even so, don't come expecting to find a sprawling Elizabethan town: Apart from a couple of thatched cottages, the streets of modern-day Stratford are lined with high-fashion clothing stores and the ubiquitous McDonald's. The Shakespeare sights have a certain olde worlde appeal, but even these have been repeatedly reconstructed and restored. To make matters worse, there's no direct train service from London, which means you'll probably end up on one of three daily buses.

BASICS

AMERICAN EXPRESS The American Express office is inside the tourist office and changes money, issues traveler's checks, and holds cardholders' mail. *Bridgefoot, CV37 6GW, tel. 01789/415856. Open Mon.–Sat. 9–6, Sun. 11–5.*

VISITOR INFORMATION At first glance, the **tourist office's** multilingual staff and piles of pamphlets look helpful, but much of the information is geared toward wealthier tourists. In a pinch, come here for lodging reservations and recommendations. *Bridgefoot, tel. 01789/293127. Open Mon.–Sat. 9–6, Sun.11–5.*

TO A34

Clopton Rd.

Birmingham Rd.

Arden St.

Maidenhead Rd.

Stratford-upon-Avon Canal

TO WARWICK CASTLE

Welcombe Rd.

Warwick Rd.

Gt. William St.

Shakespeare Centre

Windsor St.

Henley St.

❷

TRAIN STATION

Meer St.

Union St.

Guild St.

Greenhill St.

Bridgeway

Bus Stop

TO ALVESTON, YOUTH HOSTEL

Wood St.

Bridge St.

i

Bus Stop

Bridgefoot

i **AE**

Grove Rd.

Rother St.

Ely St.

High St.

Sheep St.

Waterside

Bancroft Gardens

Scholars Ln.

Chapel St.

❺

Chapel Ln.

❸

❹

Church St.

Chestnut Walk

Southern Ln.

Avon

Broad St.

West St.

Bull St.

❻

Old Town

❼

Narrow Ln.

College St.

N

Sanctus St.

College Ln.

0   200 yds

0   200 m

New St.

Mill Ln.

❽

KEY

AE American Express Office

i Tourist Information

Anne Hathaway's Cottage, **7**
Hall's Croft, **6**
Holy Trinity Church, **8**
Mary Arden's House, **1**
New Place (Nash's House), **5**
Royal Shakespeare Theatre, **3**
Shakespeare's Birthplace, **2**
Swan Theatre, **4**

A better bet is **Guide Friday,** a local bus-tour company. They have tourist info and free flyers, and the lines are much shorter than at the tourist office. On the downside, they're also trying to sell something: a double-decker bus tour that stops at all five of Stratford's major sights, allowing you to get on and off at will (one runs every 15 minutes). Note that the ticket (£4.50 for students) does not include admission to the sights. Bottom line: Take the pamphlets and run. *The Civic Hall, 14 Rother St., tel. 01789/294466. Office open Mon.–Fri. 9–5:30; tour info. open Mon.–Sat. 9–5:30, Sun. 9:30–5:30.*

COMING AND GOING

There are no direct trains from London to Stratford. Instead, take a train from London Paddington north to Leamington Spa, and then change to the Stratford line; the full trip from London takes three hours and costs £24 return. Stratford's **rail station** (Alcester Rd., tel. 01203/555211) is closed on Sundays October–May, so you'll have to take the bus. **National Express** sends buses every two hours from London's Victoria Coach Station to the bus stop on Bridge Street at Waterside, either directly in front of McDonald's or across the street. The journey takes 2½ hours and costs £13 return. Buses from Stratford to London leave from the same spot at 7:40 AM (7:55 Sat. and Sun.), 10:20 AM, and 4:40 PM. If you're returning from Stratford on a Sunday, make sure you buy your ticket and reserve space on *Saturday* at the National Express desk (tel. 01879/262718) inside Stratford's tourist office (*see* Basics, *above*). Otherwise, buy a return ticket onboard if you don't already have one.

WHERE TO SLEEP

Since nearly every tourist over the age of 40 is magnetically drawn to Stratford, there's no shortage of B&Bs—the hard part is finding cheap ones that aren't booked solid months ahead of time. There are three concentrated pockets of B&Bs: on **Grove Road** near the train station, on **Evesham Road**, the southern extension of Grove Road, and on **Shipston Road,** across the River Avon from the center of town. The hostel and campground are really the only affordable options.

Shakespeare's birthday is traditionally assigned to April 23, 1564. More than 400 years later, it's one of the worst days of the year to look for cheap lodging in Stratford.

All's Well. In a town not noted for genuineness, All's Well is refreshingly unslick. The rooms are plushly decorated, the breakfasts are excellent, and the rates (£15 per person) are fair. *211 Evesham Rd., tel. 01789/299659. From train station, walk toward town, turn right on Grove Rd. (which becomes Evesham Pl. and then Evesham Rd.). 2 rooms, none with bath.*

The Garth House. Unlike most B&B proprietors, Louise Thomas actually caters to backpackers. The double with bath in the back of the house is especially quiet. Doubles cost £28–£30; there are no singles. *9A Broad Walk, tel. 01789/298035. From train station, walk toward town, turn right on Grove Rd. (which becomes Evesham Pl.), left on Broad Walk. 3 rooms, 1 with bath. Closed weekdays Oct.–Mar.*

The Glenavon. Despite the very small rooms, this place is worth considering for its proximity to the train station and friendly service. Bed and breakfast is £15 per person. *6 Chestnut Walk, tel. 01789/292588. From train station, walk toward town, turn right on Grove Rd., left on Chestnut Walk. 15 rooms, none with bath.*

Newlands. This unpretentious B&B is wonderfully quiet, and the rooms are generously large—a surprise considering the prime location. Proprietor Sue Boston loves to give advice on the best plays to see in Stratford. Rooms cost £17.50 per person, £20 per person for rooms with bath. *7 Broad Walk, tel. 01789/298449. From train station, walk toward town, turn right on Grove Rd. (which becomes Evesham Pl.), left on Broad Walk. 4 rooms.*

HOSTELS **Stratford YHA.** While this hostel is in Alveston, 2 miles from Stratford, the walk is easy and actually enjoyable in summer. Clean rooms and helpful management (who'll let you in after curfew if you're coming from a late play) offset the cost: beds £12 (£8.80 under 18), including breakfast. Definitely call ahead to reserve space. *Hemmingford House, Alveston, CV37 7RG, tel. 01789/29709, fax 01789/205513. Bus 18 from Stratford. 154 beds. Curfew 11 PM, lockout daily 11–3. Closed mid-Dec.–early Jan.*

CAMPGROUNDS **Elms Camp.** Elms is the cheapest place around and closer to town than the hostel. The nearby village of Tiddington has a pub and a market. Sites are £2.25 per person, and reservations are advised. *Tiddington Rd., Tiddington, tel. 01789/292312. Bus 18 from Stratford to Tiddington; alight and look for sign pointing to campsite. 50 sites. Check-in by 9 PM. Closed Nov.–Mar.*

FOOD

Finding a reasonably priced, tasty meal in Stratford is nearly impossible. Pubs and greasy fast-food stands will plug the hole in your stomach for cheap. But if you want a full dinner, you'll be eating alongside other tourists and paying heavily inflated prices; try your luck on **Sheep Street** (from the tourist office, turn left on High St. and left again on Sheep St.). Stratford's cheapest sandwiches (£1 and up) come from **Marco's Italian Deli** (20 Church St., tel. 01789/292889).

Although **Café Natural** (Greenhill St., tel. 01789/415741) lacks character, an encouraging mix of locals and visitors gives this lunch-only vegetarian restaurant some life. Try simple dishes like soup (£1.70), quiche (£3.50), and stuffed potatoes (£1.80). Downstairs from the café, **Stratford Health Foods** (tel. 01789/292353) sells supplies in bulk and to go. A "traditional" English establishment with hordes of tourists to prove it, the **Garrick Inn** (25 High St., tel. 01789/292186), built in 1595, still has the cramped feel of an Elizabethan pub. Surprisingly, the food isn't expensive; meals like chicken-and-mushroom pie (£4.50) and gammon steak (£5) are bargains by Stratford standards. There are some good brews on tap, too. An eclectic group of families, twentysomethings, and mostly European foreigners throng **The Vintner Cafe and Wine Bar** (5 Sheep St., tel. 01789/297259), one of the few cool places to just hang out in Stratford. Huge candles stuck in wine bottles dominate the small tables, leaving little room for plates of lasagna (£5.20) or the vegetarian dish of the day (£5.50).

WORTH SEEING

For obvious reasons, the Shakespeare sights are the only reason to visit Stratford. Be prepared, however, for oxygen deprivation at these phenomenally crowded shrines to the immortal dramatist. Conveniently, the Shakespeare Birthplace Trust sells an **all-inclusive ticket** (£7.50, £7 students—some discount, huh?) to the five major sights listed below. If you want to skip Anne Hathaway's Cottage and Mary Arden's House, buy the **three-in-one** ticket (£5, £4 students). For those actually interested in the work of the writer, the **Shakespeare Library** (Henley St., tel. 01789/204016) has original Shakespeare folios and displays on the Bard's life.

At the end of the day, the best way to be alone in Stratford is to walk along the River Avon—most visitors don't make it this far.

ANNE HATHAWAY'S COTTAGE This thatched cottage in nearby Shottery is where Anne Hathaway lived prior to her marriage to William Shakespeare on November 27, 1582. At the time William was a mere 18 years old, while his betrothed was 26; if you count backward from the birth of their child Susana on May 26, 1583, the phrase "shotgun wedding" may come to mind. These days the Tudor furniture pales in comparison with the lovely apple orchard outside. The room attendants are knowledgeable about the history of the cottage, and they tell some great anecdotes—for a tip. From Stratford it's a relaxing 15-minute walk west through open fields; follow the signs from Evesham Place (at the south end of Grove Rd.) or take a frequent bus from the Bridge Street bus stop. *Tel. 01789/292100. Admission: £2.20. Open Mar.–Aug., Mon.–Sat. 9–5:30, Sun. 10–5:30; Nov.–Feb., Mon.–Sat. 9:30–4, Sun. 10:30–4.*

HALL'S CROFT One of the least-visited sights on the Shakespeare trail, Hall's Croft has a tenuous connection to the bard's dramatic life—it was the home of his daughter, Susana, and her husband, Dr. John Hall. Of the 17th-century antiques on display, Dr. Hall's medical instruments are certainly the coolest. The house itself is more architecturally interesting, actually, than either of Shakespeare's homes, and because it's about two blocks from the center of town, it's less busy. *Old Town, tel. 01789/292107. Admission: £1.80. Open Mar.–Oct., Mon.–Sat. 9:30–5:30, Sun. 10:30–5:30; Nov.–Feb., Mon.–Sat. 10–4:30, Sun. 1:30–4:30.*

HOLY TRINITY CHURCH Shakespeare's remains are buried beneath the altar of this traditional Gothic church—not in Westminster Abbey's Poets' Corner, as many think. Will's wife and family rest in peace next to him; above hovers a bust by Gheerart Jansen, made immediately after his death in 1616 and believed to be one of only two likenesses created in Shakespeare's time. *Trinity St., at College Ln., no phone. Admission: 50p, 30p students. Open Apr.–Oct., Mon.–Sat. 8:30–6, Sun. 2–5; Nov.–Mar., Mon.–Sat. 8:30–4, Sun. 2–5.*

MARY ARDEN'S HOUSE The "home" of Shakespeare's mother is probably inauthentic and definitely boring. Fortunately, the mostly undecorated Tudor farmhouse has been expanded to include the slightly more interesting **Glebe Farm,** where falconers display their art with live birds. To reach the house and farm, take the train from Stratford to Wilmcote (a five-minute ride) and follow the signs from the station. *Wilmcote, tel. 01789/293455. Admission: £3.*

NEW PLACE (NASH'S HOUSE) Shakespeare bought New Place in 1597 for £60 (big money at the time) and died here in 1616 at the age of 52. It's called Nash's House after the man who married Shakespeare's granddaughter. Inside, a small museum features artifacts from prehistoric Stratford, though the attached garden is much more interesting. *Chapel St., at Chapel Ln., tel. 01789/292325. Admission: £1.80. Open Mar.–Oct., Mon.–Sat. 9:30–5:30, Sun. 10:30–5:30; Nov.–Feb., Mon.–Sat. 10–4:30, Sun. 1:30–4:30.*

SHAKESPEARE'S BIRTHPLACE The birthplace of the Bard has become a sick shrine of vicious camera-snapping tourists trying to elbow their way in and capture that Kodak moment. This small, heavily restored home is usually too crowded to allow for a casual stroll—which is frustrating because the biographical material is actually interesting. The **Shakespeare Centre,** adjacent to the house, contains exhibits based on recent Stratford productions of Shakespeare. *Henley St., tel. 01789/204016. Admission: £2.60. Open Mar.–Oct., Mon.–Sat. 9–6, Sun. 10–6; Nov.–Feb., Mon.–Sat. 9:30–4:30, Sun. 10:30–4:30.*

AFTER DARK

Stratford's nightlife *is* the Royal Shakespeare Company (RSC), the grandmammy of all Shakespeare companies. The RSC presents nightly performances on two main stages, the **Royal Shakespeare Theatre** and the **Swan Theatre,** featuring about five or six different plays in any given week—not all of them by Shakespeare. A third stage, **The Other Place,** runs smaller, more modern productions during high season. If you don't mind standing during a performance, you can buy tickets for as little as £4.50; tickets to the balcony start at £8.50. If the show hasn't sold out, students can buy discount tickets at 7:15 for about £10. Or, to be safe, you can get up early and catch one of the 20 or so tickets held for day-of-performance sales; be there when the box office opens at 9 AM. The RSC also runs a **Theatre Exhibition** (£1.70, £1.20 students) upstairs from the theater, giving a good history of the staging of Shakespeare plays. Both theaters also conduct **backstage tours** (tel. 01789/296655, ext. 421) Monday–Wednesday and Friday at 1:30 and 5:30, Sunday at 12:30, 1:45, and 2:45. Tickets for these year-round tours cost £4 (£3 students). Try to book in advance, as groups fill the tours quickly. Otherwise, meet at the stage door following the evening's entertainment for 30-minute **post-performance tours** (£3). *Southern Ln., tel. 01789/295623 (box office) or 01789/269191 (24-hr ticket info). Performances usually held Mon.–Sat. at 7:30 PM; additional matinees Thurs. and Sat. at 1:30.*

> *Throw back a pint or two at The Dirty Duck (Waterside, tel. 01789/297312), Stratford's thespian hangout. Everybody from Olivier to Gielgud to Brannagh has drunk here, and some have left signed photographs on the wall to prove it.*

Canterbury

Chaucer's *Canterbury Tales,* **the ultimate** chronicle of church hypocrisy and gender politics in medieval England, tells us more than enough about pilgrims on their way to visit Canterbury Cathedral. Yet it says precious nothing about the eponymous city itself (Chaucer died before his characters could get here). All we know is that in Chaucer's day, horsebacked hundreds made their way from London across harsh terrain in bad English weather to visit the shrine of the martyr Thomas à Becket, killed by knights of Henry II in AD 1170. It's also clear that the stupendous cathedral in which the deed was done—and the surrounding town, with its curving streets and tightly packed Tudor-style

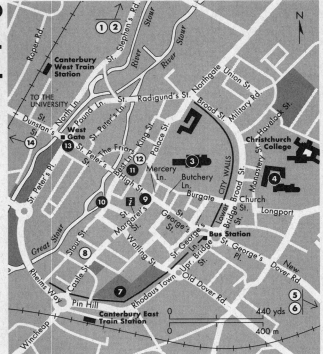

Canterbury

Sights ●
Canterbury
Cathedral, **3**
Canterbury Heritage
Museum, **10**
The Canterbury
Tales, **9**
Dane John
Monument, **7**
Royal Museum Art
Gallery, **11**
St. Augustine's
Abbey, **4**
West Gate
Museum, **13**

Lodging ○
Alverstone House, **5**
Canterbury YHA, **6**
Dar Anne, **14**
Drew Gallery, **12**
Georgian Guest
House, **8**
St. Stephen's
Guest House, **2**
Trevelyan House, **1**

The concept of Thomas à Becket being murdered in his own holy domain intrigued T. S. Eliot to write "Murder in the Cathedral." In the film version, Richard Burton played Becket opposite a deliciously malicious Peter O'Toole as Henry II.

buildings—keeps the tourists thumping in by the bus-load. Canterbury may be encircled by a Roman wall, but it's the city's medieval aspect that prevails—which is quite a feat considering that Canterbury was heavily damaged in the blitz of 1941.

BASICS

BUREAUX DE CHANGE The hostel changes, the tourist office changes, the post office changes, everybody changes—but most have sucky rates made worse by high commissions. Banks—where you get a vastly better rate if you change traveler's checks rather than cash—are scattered along High Street and all of its aliases. **Thomas Cook** (9 High St., tel. 01227/781199) changes Thomas Cook traveler's checks for free.

LUGGAGE STORAGE The **East Kent Roadcar Company** in Canterbury's bus station (*see below*) stores luggage from 8:15 to 5 for £1 per bag.

MAIL Canterbury's largest **post office** (28 High St., tel. 01227/475280) is often disturbingly crowded. If you're in a hurry, try the one at the corner of Church Street and Lower Bridge Street. Both offices are open weekdays 9–5:30, Saturday 9–12:30.

VISITOR INFORMATION The **Tourist Information Centre** offers free lodging guides downstairs and a Book-A-Bed-Ahead office upstairs; the 10% deposit charged for booking ahead is applied to your bill. The office also sells hiking and biking maps. *34 St. Margaret's St., tel.*

176

01226/766567. From Canterbury East station, turn right and follow city wall, left on Watling St., right on St. Margaret's St. Open Mon.–Sat. 9:30–5.

COMING AND GOING

Canterbury is encircled by a medieval city wall and is so small that you can walk anywhere in less than 20 minutes. The main road that bisects the city center changes names as it progresses (presumably to confuse tourists): It's known as St. Peter's Street in the west, High Street in the center, St. George's Street in the east, and New Dover Road even *farther* east. If you walk northwest on this main road for 1 mile or take Bus 604, you'll reach the entrance to the University of Kent. The YHA hostel is on New Dover Road, ½ mile southeast of the city.

BY TRAIN **Canterbury East** is a major stop between London and the ferry/Hovercraft port in Dover. Trains leave London's Victoria Station every 30 minutes on weekdays, hourly on weekends. The trip takes 1½ hours and costs £12.30 round-trip. *Station Rd. E, off Castle St., tel. 01227/454411. Ticket window open Mon.–Sat. 6:10 AM–8 PM, Sun. 6:45 AM–9 PM.*

BY BUS The main bus station's entrance is on the corner of St. George's Lane and St. George's Place, near the shopping district on High Street. **National Express** coaches leave about every two hours for London's Victoria Coach Station (£11 round-trip). *Tel. 01227/634822 or 01227/766151 for recorded info. Open Mon.–Sat. 8:15–5:30.*

WHERE TO SLEEP

An abundant number of B&Bs line New Dover, London, and Whitstable roads. Canterbury is a popular place and most B&Bs are tiny, so reserve ahead for all of them. You won't find any under £12 per person—especially during summer, when the only recourse for the strapped is the ever-popular YHA hostel. If you're into spending more for private bath and/or a little luxury, **St. Stephen's Guest House** (100 St. Stephen's Rd., tel. 01227/767644) charges £18–£21 per head and is a 10-minute walk from town.

➢ **UNDER £30** • **Alverstone House.** The pink rooms in this pretty brick house are nicely laid out, with flowery bedspreads and clean sheets. They only have doubles (£30) and triples (£40); people traveling alone can stay in a double for £20. *38 New Dover Rd., tel. 01227/766360. From bus station, turn right onto St. George's Pl. and continue straight for ¾ mi. 5 rooms, none with bath.*

Dar Anne. Theresa and Dennis Morey love students, and their place is always filled with young people. The house is intimate and, despite the traffic outside, surprisingly quiet. Theresa is a vegan, so herbivores don't get that sidelong look when they ask for no sausage with their breakfast. Students pay £12 for singles, £22 for doubles; everyone else pays a few pounds more. *65 London Rd., tel. 01227/760907. From Canterbury East, follow Rheims Way/St. Peter's Pl., turn left on St. Dunstan's St., left on London Rd. 3 rooms, none with bath.*

Drew Gallery. This is the sweetest deal in the city center, with one single (£15), one double (£30), and one room that'll fit four (£48). You can practically touch Canterbury Cathedral from here (from one room you can even gaze at it while scrubbing in the shower). *16 Best Ln., tel. 01227/458759. From bus station, turn left onto High St., right on Best Ln. 3 rooms, none with bath.*

Trevelyan House. This tiny B&B prefers to admit women only. If they're not full—a rare occurrence—they might consider housing a man or two. It looks like all the other houses on the block, but inside it's quite pleasant. Singles and doubles cost £14 per person. *18 St. Stephen's Rd., tel. 01227/765635. From Canterbury East, follow Rheims Way/St. Peter's Pl., turn left on St. Dunstan's St., right on North Ln. 2 rooms, none with bath. Closed Oct.–Mar. and May.*

➢ **UNDER £40** • **Georgian Guest House.** The stiff owner has better things to do than show you a room, but the rooms themselves are truly lovely, with oriental rugs, antique beds, and fireplaces that don't work but look damn nice. It's nicely located within the city walls, and well worth the £16 a head. *69 Castle St., tel. 01227/761111. From High St., turn on St. Margate St. toward tourist office. 4 rooms, none with bath.*

HOSTELS **Canterbury YHA.** This place is often full, so make every effort to book a week or two in advance. If you do arrive without reservations, don't despair: the proprietors will always refer you to another cheap bed. Dorm beds £8.90 (£5.95 under 18). A standard breakfast costs an extra £2.60. *54 New Dover Rd., tel. 01227/462911. From Canterbury East, turn left on Station Rd. East, right on Castle St., go straight through town, right on High St., and continue straight for 1 mi. 72 beds. Curfew 11 PM, lockout 10 AM–1 PM. Luggage storage.*

CAMPGROUNDS **St. Martin's.** A huge number of sites guarantees little privacy. Of course, if you want to meet people, that should be no problem—a lot of characters hang out at the on-site shop. The campground is in a rural area 1½ miles out of town and just ¼ mile from a main road. Two-person tent spaces cost £4.57 per person. *Bekesbourne Ln., tel. 01227/463216. From Canterbury East, right onto Rhodaus Town, right on Church St., right on Longport/St. Martin's Hill, continue for 1½ mi, then right on Bekesbourne Ln. 250 sites. Hot showers, laundry. Closed late Oct.–late Mar.*

FOOD

High Street is the main drag for both good eats and tourist crap, while cheaper places lurk just off High Street along its smaller lanes and alleys. **Stowaways** (53 St. Peter's St., tel. 01227/764459) is a Tudor-era tearoom with an adjoining fish restaurant serving such oceanic delights as a half-dozen oysters in garlic (£3.95) and poached salmon with Hollandaise sauce (£8.95). **The Counting House** (9 Castle St., tel. 01227/781325), a busy eatery far from the High Street mania, cooks up an omelet with fries and a salad for about £3, and a hearty ploughman's lunch (£3) with cheddar or brie. Don't skip dessert—this place knows chocolate. One of the funkier restaurants in town is **Fungus Mungus** (34 St. Peter's St., tel. 01227/463175), where you can gorge on a filling open-face sandwich with Stilton and mushrooms (£2.95) or one of their many mushroomy main courses (£4.95 and up). They also serve beer on tap for £1.70. **The Black Cat** (41 St. Peter's St., tel. 01227/456402) is a purple-painted rasta café that serves Afro-Caribbean food; try the brilliant Puerto Rican chicken in spicy hot sauce (£4.95). All sorts of tropical juices sell for £1.10.

WORTH SEEING

Canterbury's small size makes it easy to see everything in one day. To avoid the crowds, get an early start, and remember that most attractions are less crowded an hour or even a half-hour before closing time. For a good overview, consider a 90-minute walking tour offered from the tourist office daily at 11 AM and 2 PM (£2.40, £1.70 students). On summer evenings only, the more exciting **Ghost Walks** offers excellent tours of the city center (£2.30, £1.60 students).

If you must have museums, the **Royal Museum Art Gallery** (High St., above library, tel. 01227/452744) hosts temporary exhibits ranging from interesting to embarrassing—but at least they're free. It's open Monday–Saturday 10–5. For a fine view over Canterbury, climb up Pin Hill to **Dane John Monument,** a short walk from Canterbury East station.

CANTERBURY CATHEDRAL As you come through the main entrance, built to commemorate Henry V's victory at Agincourt, the view across and up the cathedral is dizzying, with row upon row of towering pointed arches. Try to imagine what someone who never saw a skyscraper thought when they first encountered this building. The cathedral, as it exists today, is the product of several periods of architecture and various architects. The oldest part of the church is Norman, built by Archbishop Lafranc over the ruins of St. Augustine's church. This construction was hasty and insufficiently small, so it was replaced by an even larger building between 1096 and 1130. Immediately after Thomas à Becket's canonization in 1173, a new Gothic-style choir was installed.

Archbishops have traditionally been enthroned at **Trinity Chapel,** on St. Augustine's chair behind the altar. Inside the chapel are the tomb of Henry IV and his wife, Joan of Navarre, and an effigy of Edward the Black Prince. Beneath the chapel is the crypt where Thomas à Becket was first buried and where Henry II completed his penance for the murder. The northwest transept is the site of Becket's murder (a marker indicates where he fell more than 800 years ago). Becket, a dissident priest who disagreed with King Henry II's meddling in the church's business, was murdered in 1170 by four of Henry's knights seeking the king's favor. Becket's assassins probably entered by the door from the cloisters, which contain amazing vaults that are ornamented with paintings of just under 1,000 heraldic shields.

By 1172, Becket had been canonized St. Thomas of Canterbury, which did little to appease the French ruling class (who took the murder of Becket, a French citizen, as a personal affront). It was only a matter of time before the pressure on Henry II, who felt enormous remorse at the death of his (former) old friend, became too great, and he relinquished a great deal of power to the church. Subsequently, Canterbury Cathedral was made the hub of English Catholicism. *Sun St., at St. Margaret's St., tel. 01227/762862. Admission free. Open Easter–Sept., Mon.–Sat. 8:45–7, Sun. 12:30–2:30 and 4:30–5:30; Oct.–Easter, Mon.–Sat. 8:45–5, Sun. 12:30–2:30 and 4:30–5:30.*

CANTERBURY HERITAGE MUSEUM Medieval Canterbury was full of clergymen, many of whom fell ill as a result of poverty and poor living conditions. To cope with this growing problem, the lord mayor ordered a **Poor Priests Hospital** built specifically for the purpose of treating sick clergymen (ironically, the help they received in this drafty building actually worsened their condition). This one-time hospital is now the site of the popular **Canterbury Heritage Museum,** which exhibits a somewhat boring collection of local artifacts left by pilgrims at Canterbury. *Stour St., tel. 01227/452747. From tourist office, turn right down Hawks Ln. Admission: £1.50, £1 students. Open June–Oct., Mon.–Sat. 10:30–5, Sun. 1:30–5. Closed Christmas and Good Friday.*

Chaucer isn't the only literary ghost haunting Canterbury: Joseph Conrad is buried in Canterbury Cemetery, while the head of Sir Thomas More (author of "Utopia") lies in St. Dunstan's church on St. Dunstan's Road.

THE CANTERBURY TALES Canterbury's attempt to re-create a historically accurate, multisensory version of Chaucer's stories has resulted in "The Canterbury Tales," which is more like a second-rate Chuck E. Cheese Pizza Time Theatre à la medieval England. Multilingual, radio-controlled headphones guide you from room to room, where excerpts from Chaucer's *Canterbury Tales* are illustrated by moving plywood cutouts. The stories are funny, but it's cheaper (and more fulfilling) to read the book. *St. Margaret's St., next to tourist office, tel. 01227/454888. Admission: £4.50, £3.75 students. Open daily 9:30–5:30.*

ST. AUGUSTINE'S ABBEY In AD 589, Pope Gregory I bought Augustine the monk a one-way ticket from Rome to England with the goal of converting the pagan Saxons. Augustine and his 40 followers were so successful, they even converted Ethelbert, King of Kent, to their way of thinking, and established Canterbury Cathedral. Augustine also built this quiet, stoic abbey. As you wander around today's grassy ruins, enough stones and walls remain to evoke the former whole—a cloister, church, and refractory. *Lower Chantry Ln., at Longport Rd., tel. 01227/767345. From bus station, turn right on St. George's Pl., left on Chantry Ln. Admission: £1.20, 90p students. Open Mon.–Sat. 9:30–6, Sun. 2–6.*

WEST GATE MUSEUM Inside West Gate (the medieval, double-towered city gate at the end of St. Peter's St.) is tiny **West Gate Museum,** with exhibits on Canterbury's historical defenses, its Roman walls, and examples of the chains and manacles used on the prisoners who were once detained here. Even if you hate museums, come for the great views from between the battlements. *St. Peter's St., no phone. Admission: 60p, 40p students. Open Mon.–Sat. 11–12:30 and 1:30–3:30.*

AFTER DARK

To the Church of England, gluttony is a deadly sin, but beer drinking is not, and many pub owners have set up shop in the shadows of the cathedral. When you go pub-crawling, try to avoid lingering on the streets after 11 PM; the sometimes less-than-tolerant Canterbury police seem to enjoy getting a little harassment in before the end of their shift. Also remember that most pubs in Canterbury are open Monday–Saturday 11–11, Sunday noon–3 and 7–10:30.

PUBS **The Black Griffin.** With hardwood floors and lots of windows, this big pub is breezy and mellow in the daytime. At night things liven up with a jukebox and occasional live music. A pint on tap costs £1.79. *40 St. Peter's St. tel. 01227/455563.*

Three Compasses. Both the owners and patrons of this pub are the most relaxed in town. It's dark and wood-paneled, and a good place to swallow down a pint (£1.44). *18 St. Peter's St. tel. 01227/452211.*

University of Kent Bars. Each of the four colleges—Darwin, Keynes, Eliot, and Rutherford—has its own bar, and each has its own unique crowd. *From Canterbury, take any bus about 2½ mi up St. Dunstan's St. to university entrance, turn left at road just before second bus stop, enter the courtyard (keeping to the left), and ask someone where the bar is. All open daily 5 PM–11 PM.*

CLUBS **The Bizz.** On Friday and Saturday nights, this venue is an "over 30s" club called The Works. The rest of the week it's The Bizz, alternating between indie music and heavy house. *15 Station Rd. E, across from Canterbury East station, tel. 01227/462520. Cover: £2–£4. Open Tues.–Sat. 9 PM–2 AM.*

THEATER AND CINEMA The **Marlowe Theatre** (The Friars, off St. Peter's St., tel. 01227/767246) stages first-rate London shows as well as crappy pop bands and cheesy British slapstick plays. Before spending £4–£9 on a ticket, pick up a copy of "Fifteen Days," the Marlowe Theatre calendar, to gauge what's on. Amateur drama and performance art get top billing at the University of Kent's **Gulbenkian Theatre** (University Rd., tel. 01227/769075), where tickets cost £3–£9. In addition, free concerts are performed in the Gulbenkian's foyer on various days during the school year between noon and 2 PM. **Cinema 3,** which shares the same box office as the Gulbenkian, shows avant-garde oldies and some big-budget Hollywood flicks for £3.30 (£2.20 students).

OUTDOOR ACTIVITIES

BIKING If you're interested in mountain biking, pick up an Ordnance Survey map from the tourist office; it shows altitude contours in the **North Downs.** The **Canterbury Cycle Mart** (19 Lwr. Bridge St., tel. 01227/761488) rents 10-speed mountain bikes for pollution-free jetting around town. The cost is £10 per ½ day, £15 a day, £50 a week. A MasterCard or Visa number, or £100 cash deposit, is required.

Bath

Bath's history has been shaped by its hot springs, which pour out of the earth at a steady 116° F. In the 1st century AD, the Romans dedicated the township to the goddess Sul Minerva, named it Aquae Sulis (Waters of Sul), and constructed an intricate series of baths and pools around the hot springs. Centuries later, Bath became synonymous with elegance, engendering a social scene second only to London's. The Royals have always shown a preference for the town: Queen Elizabeth I brought a certain prestige to the baths with her visit in 1574, while Queen Anne's visits to the waters in 1702 and 1703 established the "Bath season." In subsequent years, architect John Wood (1704–1754) gave Bath its distinctive, harmonious look; using the yellowish "Bath stone" cut from nearby quarries, he created a city of crescents, terraces, and Palladian mansions. Today, Georgian row houses, the color of clotted cream, curve through the city like scalloped paper cutouts.

Get your hands on a copy of Jane Austen's novel "Persuasion," much of which is set in Bath, for an insight into the town's high-society past.

Sadly, you can no longer bathe in the springs (although you can drink the horrible-tasting mineral water if you so desire). Instead, what makes a visit worthwhile are the museums, parks,

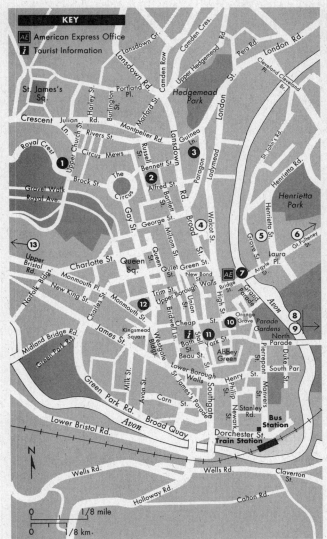

KEY

AE American Express Office

i Tourist Information

Sights ●
Bath Abbey, **10**
Building of Bath
Museum/British
Folk Art
Collection, **3**
Museum of
Costume, **2**
Pulteney Bridge, **7**
Pump Room, **11**
Royal Crescent
(No. 1), **1**
Theatre Royal, **12**

Lodging ○
Bathwick Hill
YHA, **6**
The Georgian
Guest House, **5**
The Limes, **8**
Membland, **9**
Woodville
House, **13**
YMCA, **4**

and architecture. The only caveats about coming to Bath are that lodging is expensive, and you'll probably hear more American accents than you might like.

BASICS

The exceptionally efficient **Tourist Information Centre** (The Colonnades, 11–13 Bath St., tel. 01225/462831), open Monday–Saturday 9:30–5, gets miserably crowded in summer. Come early to book a room, as the bargains go fast. **American Express** (5 Bridge St., 1 block from Pulteney Bridge, tel. 01225/444747) offers regular cardholder services and cashes all traveler's checks free of charge (£2 commission on cash exchanges). **Lloyd's Bank** (23 Milsom St., tel. 01225/310256) has good rates and charges a 1% commission (minimum £3) on most transactions. **Lockers** are available for £1.50–£2 on Platform 1 of the train station, which closes in the wee hours but reopens about 5 or 6 AM (in time to retrieve your things and catch an early train). Lockers outside the bus station are accessible 24 hours. The main **post office** (New Bond St., tel. 01225/445358) is open Saturday until 1 PM in addition to its standard weekday hours.

COMING AND GOING

BritRail (tel. 01272/294255) makes the 75-minute trip from London's Paddington Station to **Bath Spa Station** for £24.50 round-trip. National Express (tel. 01225/464446) runs nine coaches daily to and from London for £18 round-trip. Buy National Express tickets at Bath's **bus station** (Manvers St., across from train station), which also dispatches **Badgerline** (tel. 01225/464446) coaches to neighboring towns.

WHERE TO SLEEP

Seek bargains in Bath and ye shall find them, so long as you don't mind creative accommodations and/or a short bridge-crossing into town. The tourist office has a bulky accommodations brochure, but the hostel's short list of cheap B&Bs is better. In summer, it's wise to book far in advance. Also note that many B&Bs require an advance deposit for phone reservations.

The Georgian Guest House. This is about as close as you can get to the city center without spending a small fortune. Singles and doubles cost £17–£18 per person. *34 Henrietta St., tel. 01225/424103. From stations, walk up Manvers St. to Grand Parade, cross Pulteney Bridge to Great Pulteney St., turn left on Henrietta St. 9 rooms, none with bath. AE, MC, V.*

The Limes. The guest rooms are large and decorated with white chenille bedspreads and some fine wood antiques. Pulteney Road is busy, but street noise is not a problem. Rooms £12 per person. *1 Pulteney Rd., tel. 01225/311044. From stations, walk up Manvers St., turn right on North Parade, cross bridge, right on Pulteney Rd. 2 rooms, none with bath.*

Membland. Peter and Katey Moore, the young proprietors of Membland, make you feel like family. Rooms are £15–£20 per head, depending on the season and the amenities you require. If you arrive in the evening after they get off work, they may pick you up at the train station. *7 Pulteney Terr., tel. 01225/336712. From stations, walk up Manvers St., turn right on North Parade, cross bridge, right on Pulteney Rd. 2 rooms, 1 with bath.*

Woodville House. Tom and Anne Toalster's classic Bath house, right next to Victoria Park and the Royal Crescent, is the best deal around. You cannot smoke here, but you can laze around in sunny rooms with views and comfy beds. You also get breakfast and the use of a TV room. Rooms £13 per head (£18 if you're alone). *4 Marlborough Ln., tel. 01225/319335. From stations, walk to Bath Abbey, turn left on Cheap St., right on Monmouth St. (which becomes Upper Bristol Rd.), right on Marlborough Ln. 3 rooms, 1 with bath.*

HOSTELS **Bathwick Hill YHA.** This Italianate building has a mellow backpacking atmosphere and lots of info on what's going on in Bath. You'll definitely want to take a bus to get up the steep hill. The hostel is open year-round and all day long (no lockout). Reservations are essential in summer. Beds £7.75 (£8.15 July–Aug.). *Bathwick Hill, tel. 01225/465674. From stations, take Badgerline Bus 18 directly to hostel; or walk ¾ mi east of city center (follow signs for university), then walk ½ mi up Bathwick Hill from Pulteney Rd. roundabout. 121 beds. Laundry, pay phone.*

YMCA. It's closer to the center of town than the YHA hostel, but the atmosphere is less lively. At least the bare-bones rooms are clean (as are the coed bathrooms). Dorm beds £9.50, singles £12, doubles £22. *Broad Street Pl., tel. 01225/460471. From stations, walk up Manvers St., veer left onto High St. at Orange Grove roundabout, left on Broad St. (look for YMCA sign leading down alley to right). 86 rooms, 40 dorm beds. Laundry, £5 key deposit. Closed Christmas–early Jan.*

CAMPGROUNDS The closest plot of grass to pitch a tent on is 3 miles west of Bath at **Newton Mill Touring Centre,** which has laundry and shower facilities and is open year-round. Catch

Bus 5 from the bus station and alight at Twerton (ask the driver), then walk through the playground down the footpath. Sites £3.35 per person. *Newton St., Loe, tel. 01225/333909.*

FOOD

You'll find plenty of burger stands around the Theatre Royal, Sawclose, and Kingsmead Square. If you'd rather create your own gustatory masterpiece, there's a fancy **Waitress** supermarket in The Podium shopping center on High Street, opposite Broad Street, and a cheaper **Somerfield** market in the Southgate Shopping Centre behind the bus station.

The Canary Restaurant (3 Queen St., tel. 01225/424846) sits on a quiet cobbled street lined with flowers. Eggs Benedic— yes, their spelling—costs £3.85, pasta and vegetarian dishes £6, Somerset rabbit £4.75. Gourmet sandwiches are the specialty at **Fodder's** (9 Cheap St., tel. 01225/462165), a small take-away in the center of town. Choose from prawns in garlic-mayo (£2.10), pâté de campagne (£1.80), vegetarian fillings, and the ordinary lineup of deli meat—but skip the anemic

You can probably live quite happily without ever sampling the famous "Bath bun," a teatime treat that's degenerated into a tourist attraction.

guacamole. **Scoffs** (20 Kingsmead Sq., tel. 01225/462483), a whole-food bakery and café, has a mouthwatering array of vegetarian dishes, breads, and cakes, most priced £1–£4. The atmosphere at **Caffe Piazza** (The Podium, tel. 01225/429299), located upstairs in a ritzy, modern mall, is far from authentic Bath, though the food is authentic Italian. Pasta Bolognese and carbonara go for around £5, and pizzas with creative toppings cost £5–£6. Considering the land of haute cuisine is just across a narrow body of water, it's troubling that good French restaurants like **Tilley's Bistro** (3 North Parade Passage, btw Abbey Green and North Parade Bridge, tel. 01225/484200) haven't infiltrated the English food scene. Entrées like fresh lemon sole, sliced pork tenderloins in a Dijon mustard cream sauce, and vegetarian and vegan dishes all cost around £6. For lunch try a set two- or three-course meal for £5.50 and £6.60, respectively.

WORTH SEEING

BATH ABBEY In one form or another, Bath Abbey has been around for 1,200 years; what started as a Norman church eventually evolved into this 15th-century Gothic abbey. Stained glass windows at the eastern end portray Christ's biography, though the abbey is better known for its spindly, fan-vaulted ceiling—don't forget to look up. If you don't mind the £2 admission (£1 students), explore the subterranean **Heritage Vaults**, with some slightly cheesy exhibits on the abbey's history. In summer, also check for flyers advertising organ recitals. *High St., tel. 01225/422462. Open Mon.–Sat. 9–7, Sun. 1–2:30 and 4:30–5:30. Sun. services at 8 AM, 9:15, 11, 12:15 PM, 3:15, and 6:30.*

BUILDING OF BATH MUSEUM AND BRITISH FOLK ART COLLECTION If "Norm" makes you think *This Old House* instead of *Cheers,* you'll dig the architectural displays and minutiae at the **Building of Bath Museum** (tel. 01225/333895). If not, the small print and paucity of big pictures make it a bit of a struggle. The **British Folk Art Collection** (tel. 01225/446020) next door contains various pieces done in the 18th and 19th centuries by regular people (thereby called crafts). *The Cantess of Huntingdon's Chapel, The Paragon, off Broad St. Combined admission: £3.50. Both open Tues.–Sat. 10:30–5; shorter hrs off-season.*

ROMAN BATHS AND MUSEUM OF COSTUME The Romans built their luxury baths here between the 1st and 5th centuries AD, on sites with springs already spurting from the earth. The bath network is well preserved, and the smell of sulfur, the looming Roman statuary, and the murky green pools make it easy to imagine what it was like to be a Roman on holiday in Bath. You can't go pool-hopping here, but you can sample some vile-tasting mineral water at the overpriced **Pump Room**, above the Roman Baths. Be forewarned: This is one of the most popular admission-charging attractions in England, and the crowds can get pretty scary. If you have some extra time, buy a combined admission ticket and visit the **Museum of Costume** (Bennett St., tel. 01225/461111), one of the most prestigious and extensive collections of historical costumes in Britain, covering more than 400 years of fashion. The museum is housed in the Assembly Rooms, a series of elegant chambers built in 1771. *Abbey Church-yard, tel. 01225/461111. Admission: £5. Combined ticket with Museum of Costume: £6.60. Both open Sept.–July, daily 9–6; Aug., daily 9–7 and 8–10.*

AFTER DARK

The Bath club scene is lively, if somewhat yup-scale, which explains the £2–£6 cover many pubs charge for live music. **The Loft** (off Queen Sq., next to Theatre Royal, tel. 01225/466467), is one live music venue that never has a dress code. **The Hub** (The Paragon, tel. 01225/446288), up from Broad Street, is another cool and casual place to hear live bands, anything from garage to funk. **The Hat and Feather** (14 London St., near Hedgemead Park, tel. 01225/425672) is a student-oriented pub with live bands every Friday night. **The Garrick's Head** (St. John's Sq., next to Theatre Royal, tel. 01225/448819) has two bars: The Green Room (it's painted red) is Bath's gay bar, and the Nash Room next door is not. University students schmooze at the unpretentious **Island Club** (Terrace Walk, tel. 01225/462238), which plays everything from rave to ABBA. Live bands along the lines of The Pogues characterize the scene at **The Bell** (Walcot St., tel. 01225/460426).

For highbrow theatrics, slink on over to the famous **Theatre Royal** (Sawclose, tel. 01225/448844), with comedy and plays starring fancy British actors like Derek Jacobi, Simon Callow, and Pauline Collins. The box office is open Monday–Saturday 10–8. If you simply want a peek at the old, illustrious theater (admission: £2), come at 11 AM on Wednesday or Saturday, or call 01225/448815.

OUTDOOR ACTIVITIES

Though Bath feels like a minimetropolis, its surrounding area is green and lined with paths for walking and biking. Ask at the tourist office for pamphlets about the 80-mile **Avon Cycleway**, which takes you through a string of rural country villages, or the **Bristol and Bath Railway**

The Square, the Circle, and the Crescent

Bath wouldn't be Bath without its distinctive, elegant 18th-century Georgian architecture, most of which was conceived by John Wood the Elder, an architect obsessed. Wood saw Bath as a mythical city destined for greatness along the lines of Winchester and Glastonbury. He nurtured the myth that Bath was founded by Prince Bladud, ostensibly with the help of an errant pig digging in the ground for acorns (Wood later put stone acorns along the roofs of some of his houses). Wood sought an architectural style that would do justice to his great concept, and found it in the Palladian style, made popular in Britain by Inigo Jones.

Influenced by nearby ancient stone circles as well as by round Roman temples, Wood broke loose from convention in his design for Bath's outstanding Circus, a full circle of houses broken only three times for intersecting streets. After the death of Wood the Elder, John Wood the Younger carried out his father's plans for the Royal Crescent, an obtuse crescent of 30 interconnected houses overlooking Victoria Park—the first curved row houses in Britain. Stop in at No. 1 Royal Crescent for a look at one of these Georgian homes decked out in period style. Tel. 01225/428126. Admission: £3, £2.50 students. Open Mar.–Oct., Tues.–Sun. 10:30–5; Nov. 11–Dec. 11, Tues.–Sun. 10:30–4.

Path, a 12-mile route along an old railway line, with great views and scenery. The "Diary of Guided Walks in Avon" leaflet describes—you guessed it—guided walks that cost £1–£2. The hostel has a pamphlet called "Country Walks Within 5 Miles of Bath Abbey" that gives *detailed* descriptions on the best local strolls. Otherwise, rowboats and punts on the River Avon cost £5 per person and can be rented at the **Bath Boating Station** (Forrestere Rd., tel. 01225/466407).

Winchester

History, history, and more history: That's all anyone hears about when they walk into an English tourist office. But Winchester, the "ancient capital of England," really takes the historical cake. The first king of England, Egbert, was crowned here in AD 828, and Winchester's Great Hall (allegedly the home base of King Arthur and his Knights of the Round Table) was the seat of government until the Norman Invasion in 1066. Even William the Conqueror, though coronated in London first, thought it prudent to repeat the ceremony here. He also brought a fair amount of prestige to the city by commissioning the local monastery to produce the Domesday Book, a record of the general census taken in England in 1085.

The longer you spend in Winchester, the less you'll want to leave. Its YHA youth hostel is one of the best in England, streams and rivers flow through the center, and centuries-old bells stir the air on Sunday mornings.

Not surprisingly, Winchester is spotted with some incredible old buildings. Not only the fantastic cathedral, but also Winchester College and several original Tudor Houses (which look like they were built without a straightedge) remain standing in feats of sheer carbon-dated stubbornness. Although Winchester goes out of its way to preserve its past, it also warmly welcomes the future in the form of fast-food chains and retail clothing outlets along otherwise photogenic High Street. Happily, the city's blend of medieval and mall culture is fairly fluid and inoffensive.

BASICS

Winchester's **tourist office** (The Guildhall, Broadway, tel. 01962/840500) is one of the nicest, neatest, and best-stocked around; it's also open year-round. **Lloyd's Bank** (High St.) and **Barclay's Bank** (Jewry St.) have poor rates for cash, but good rates for traveler's checks (both charge a 1% commission with a £3 minimum). The main **post office** (Middle Brook St., tel. 01962/54004) is open Saturday mornings until 12:30 in addition to its standard weekday hours.

COMING AND GOING

Winchester is on a direct BritRail line from London Waterloo (hourly, 70 min, £14 round-trip) that continues to Portsmouth and Southampton. There's no local information number, and all inquiries are directed to the central switchboard in Southampton (tel. 01703/229393). Buy tickets at the kiosk on Station Road. The **bus station** on Broadway, across from the tourist office, is where National Express (tel. 01329/230023) and Stagecoach buses pick up and drop off passengers. Buy your ticket from the tourist office or the driver.

WHERE TO SLEEP

If you're feeling decadent and have the funds to support it, **The Wykeham Arms** (75 Kingsgate St., tel. 01962/854411) is a luxurious place to eat, drink, be merry, and pass out. You can have it all for the low price of £60 for a single, £70 for a double. Budget-friendlier B&Bs lie southwest of the cathedral, especially along Christchurch Road and its intersecting streets. Many B&Bs don't have signs, so pick up the accommodations pamphlet (it's free) from the tourist office.

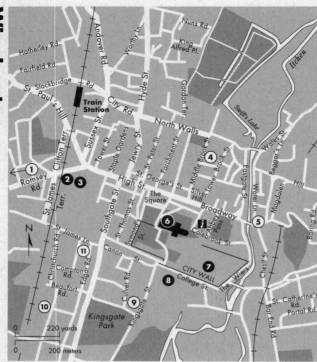

Winchester

Sights ●

Gurkha/Royal Hussars/Royal Green Jackets/Light Infantry Museums, **2**

The Great Hall, **3**

Winchester Cathedral, **6**

Winchester College, **8**

Wolvesey Castle, **7**

Lodging ○

Friar's Crag, **10**

Mrs. N. Bassett, **4**

Mrs. T. Robinson, **11**

The Old Mill YHA, **5**

Shawlands, **1**

The Wykeham Arms, **9**

Friar's Crag. With a grandfather clock, two large dogs, and a cat, this B&B has a homey feel. The immaculate condition of the house is indicative of owner Mrs. Patton's vigilance. Singles £15, doubles £25. If you stay for more than one night, doubles are reduced to £20. *12 Christchurch Rd., tel. 01962/854272. From bus station, Bus 19, 21, 44, 47, or 69 to Ranelagh Rd., walk to Christchurch Rd., and turn left. 3 rooms, none with bath.*

Mrs. N. Bassett. Mrs. Bassett is an older woman with plenty of character. She runs a great B&B in the center of town and charges £15 per person year-round. Hidden in a row of brick houses, hers is the one with flowers blooming in the yard. *64 Middle Brook St., tel. 01962/862222. From station, walk down City Rd./North Walls, turn right on Middle Brook. 3 rooms, none with bath.*

Mrs. T. Robinson. Mrs. Robinson's brick house lies on a quiet residential street near the cathedral. The airy, flowery rooms with old-fashioned dressing tables go for £16 per single, £29 per double. *106 Edgar St., tel. 01962/852502. From station, walk up City Rd./North Walls, turn right on Jewry/Southgate St., right on St. James St., left on Edgar Rd. 2 rooms, none with bath.*

Shawlands. Even if you look schlumpy, Bill and Kathy Pollock will treat you like the queen or king you are—which is some compensation for the 2-mile trek to the suburbs. The very comfortable rooms go for £16–£18 per person, with multinight discounts. *46 Kilham Ln., tel. 01962/861166. Take any bus heading up Romsey Rd., get off at Battery Hill, walk to next stoplight (Kilham Ln.), and turn right. 5 rooms, 2 with bath.*

HOSTELS **The Old Mill YHA.** During the day it's a National Trust tourist attraction. But after 5 PM this 18th-century mill on an island in the middle of the River Itchen becomes the most amazing youth hostel in the south. Views of the river from the garden are top-notch. Book way ahead, because it's fairly small (31 beds). Beds cost £6.30. *1 Water Ln., tel. 01962/853723.*

From tourist office, turn right on Broadway and cross bridge. Closed winter and Sun. and Mon. in spring and fall.

FOOD

Stick with the basics at markets like **S. Sainsbury** (Middlebrook St., off High St.) or **Gateway** (Broadway). Ethnic restaurants are strangely absent in the town center, though a few cluster near the train station. Pubs, many located on Broadway, offer a cheap alternative to the town's few decent restaurants.

The brand new **Cathedral Refectory** (Cathedral Yard, tel. 01962/853224), open daily 9:30–5, serves snacky foods like tomato, pesto, and sheep's cheese with green salad (£2.90), and Welsh rarebit with watercress salad (£2.90). Inside the landmark God Begot House, **Richoux of London** (101 High St., tel. 01962/841790) serves a mean vegetable stir-fry (£5.50) as well as fancy sandwiches (£4–£5) in carpeted, cushioned, Tudor luxury. **The Spinning Wheel** (42 High St., at Market Sq., tel. 01962/865709) will fill you up with giant sandwiches (£2) and quiche (£1.25); it's open daily 8–4:30. **Muswell's** (9 Jewry St., tel. 01962/842414), trying for an American café feel, serves a tasty Cajun chicken breast as well as tuna melts, each for around £5.

WORTH SEEING

Once upon a time, Winchester was the nation's capital, before it was so rudely supplanted by London. Although the town's glory days are over, it's still chock full of majestic sights. The majority, including the military museums, are clustered within a half-mile radius of the cathedral. If you're not already staying at the YHA hostel (*see* Where to Sleep, *above*), you can (and should) check out its grounds, especially the mill. For nonguests, it costs 60p to tour the grounds, which are open April–September, daily 11–4:45 and on weekends in October.

THE GREAT HALL This hall has been the site of crucial historical events for centuries: Parliament held its first meeting here in 1246, Sir Walter Raleigh was tried here for treason *twice* (he got the death sentence here in 1603), and the infamous Judge Jeffreys sentenced Dame Alice Lisle to be burned at the stake for sheltering a fugitive after Monmouth's Rebellion in 1685. These days, most visitors come to check out the Great Hall because of an event that didn't happen here. To the right, just past the entrance, hangs a painted wooden disc about 18 feet in diameter. This is purported to be the Round Table of King Arthur fame, but don't you believe it. The hall was built early in the 13th century, and for 150 years a blank table hung on the wall. In a fit of extraordinary egotism, Henry VIII commissioned the table to be painted, making the Arthurian figure in his own likeness. It's fun to pretend, anyway, that this was the hall in which Arthur feasted with Lancelot, Galahad, and the lads. *Upper High St., at Castle Hill, tel. 01962/841841. From station, walk down Station Rd. (stay left at fork) and follow signs. Admission free. Open Apr.–Oct., daily 10–5; Nov.–Mar., daily 10–4. Wheelchair access.*

WINCHESTER CATHEDRAL Westminster Abbey may have royalty buried within its walls, but Winchester Cathedral is still a strong contender for the Most Prestigious Dead Award, with the remains of Saxon kings, the Viking conqueror King Canute, his wife Queen Emma, and even Jane Austen. This Norman cathedral, originally built in 1079, also has the distinction of being one of the longest churches in Europe.

The church's **library** houses an illuminated, 12th-century copy of the Winchester Bible, as well as a copy of Bede's 8th-century *Historia Ecclesiastica*. The Vulgate (Latin) bible, printed on the skins of more than 250 calves and elaborately decorated with gold leaf and cobalt-blue lapis lazuli, is embellished with painstaking detail (check out the patterns on the subjects' stockings). Also on display is a 17th-century, American-made (in Massachusetts) bible translated into the language of the Native American Algonquin tribe; a Ptolemaic map of the world (circa AD 150); a pair of 17th-century globes; and the massive private library of the late bishop of Winchester, George Morley.

The **Triforium Gallery** holds, among other less interesting trinkets, the Shaftesbury Bowl, a glass bowl from the 10th century that is believed to have held the heart of King Canute, who died in Shaftesbury in 1035. Occasionally, a jarring announcement cackles over the loudspeakers, reciting the Lord's Prayer and asking you to join in. *5 The Close, tel. 01962/853137. Cathedral admission free (£2 donation requested). Open daily 7:15–6:30. Library admission: £1.50, 50p students. Open Easter–Sept., Mon. 2–4:30, Tues.–Sat. 10:30–1 and 2–4:30; Oct.–Easter, Wed. and Sat. 10:30–4:30.*

WINCHESTER COLLEGE Bishop William of Wykeham, who has his own chapel in Winchester Cathedral, founded Winchester College in 1382. Take a tour of this 600-year-old landmark for £2, or wander around the courtyards alone, confronted only occasionally by signs reading PRIVATE, KEEP OUT. At some point, make your way across the courtyards and through the giant, space-age glass doors into the college **chapel** for an up-close look at the stained glass windows and the delicately vaulted ceiling. On you way in or out of college, look for the inconspicuous yellow house next door where Jane Austen finished her novel *Persuasion,* and died at the tender age of 42. *College St., tel. 01962/868778.*

WOLVESEY CASTLE No, you can't go into that fantastic manor house next door—the current Bishop of Winchester lives there. But you can check out the ruins of Wolvesey Castle, which was once home to Winchester's medieval bishops, as well as the site of Mary Tudor and Phillip of Spain's wedding party. At the time it was built, Wolvesey was the largest private dwelling in England. So much for the humble clergy. *College St., tel. 01962/854766. Admission: £1.50, £1.10 students. Open Apr.–Sept., daily 10–1 and 2–6; Oct., daily 10–4.*

MUSEUMS If you walk through the garden at the Great Hall and up the stairs, you'll see several cannons and tanks parked outside a nondescript building. This is the **Gurkha Museum** (admission £1.50), which tells the story of the mercenary regiment recruited by the British from the Gurkhas, who live in Nepal and northern Bengal. (The Gurkhas are among the most feared and revered military units ever, and have seen action from the Falkland Islands to the Far East.) Learn about their symbolic Kukri knives, traditionally worn in battle, then buy one in the gift shop (it's a safe bet that U.S. customs won't be impressed). Some great hats are on display in the **Royal Hussars Museum** (admission £1.50), in the same building. The highlight is the actual armoire wherein a trooper hid for three years (!) after getting lost behind enemy lines during World War I. *Peninsula Barracks, Romsey Rd., tel. 01962/861781 or 01962/842832. Gurkha Museum open Tues.–Sat. 10–5. Royal Hussars open Tues.–Sun. 10–5.*

Winchester still maintains a number of almshouses that provide food and shelter for the elderly, as they have for hundreds of years. Look for the alms recipients as you wander around town, dressed in their traditional black gowns with silver badges.

The Royal Greenjackets Museum (admission £2), across the courtyard, has guns, medals, swastikas, and a book labeled EX LIBRIS ADOLF HITLER (From the Library of . . .). Pretty scary. **The Light Infantry Museum** (admission £1), in the same building, has spoils from more recent conflicts: the civil war in Northern Ireland and the Persian Gulf War. *Peninsula Barracks, Romsey Rd., tel. 01962/863846 or 01962/864176. Open Tues.–Sat. 10–5, Sun. noon–4.*

AFTER DARK

Winchester, although well-suited to day-tripping tourists, is fairly dull at night. The entire nightlife scene consists of a handful of pubs and the **Theatre Royal** on Jewry Street, which features bedroom farces and an occasional Shakespeare play between screenings of second-run films. Since the pubs are the only source of entertainment for most people, the prices for beer range "from reasonable to extortionate," as one tourist-office employee put it.

PUBS Although the patrons at the **India Arms** (High St., tel. 01962/852985) sometimes fight, the pub has a good jukebox and usually packs 'em in. If it's centuries-old beer stains you're after, try the pints at **The Royal Oak** (Royal Oak Pass, tel. 01962/861136), which has the distinction of being the oldest verifiable pub in Britain (more than 900 years!). If you just want a quiet beer, drop into **The Old Vine** (8 Great Minster St., tel. 01962/854616) and enjoy the serenity of a traditional pub that's never too busy.

Index

Notes

Notes

Notes

Notes

Notes

Notes

Prizes: On or about 2/1/96, Promotions Mechanics, Inc., an independent judging organization, will conduct a random drawing from among all eligible entries received, to award the following prizes:

(4) Grand Prizes—$2,000 cash and a Jansport® World Tour backpack, approximate retail value $2,180, will be awarded to entrants from the United States and Canada (except Quebec).

(1) One Grand Prize — £1,000 and a Jansport® World Tour backpack, approximate retail value £1,090, will be awarded to entrants from the United Kingdom and the Republic of Ireland.

Winners will be notified by mail. Due to Canadian contest laws, Canadian residents, in order to win, must first correctly answer a mathematical skill testing question administered by mail. Odds of winning will be determined from the number of entries received. Prize winners may request a statement showing how the odds of winning were determined and how winners were selected.

To receive a copy of these complete official rules, send a self-addressed, stamped envelope to be received by 12/15/95 to: "Big Bucks and a Backpack" Rules, PMI Station, P.O. Box 3569, Southbury, CT 06488-3569, USA.

Eligibility: No purchase necessary to enter or claim prize. Open to legal residents of the United States, Canada (except Quebec), the United Kingdom, and the Republic of Ireland who are 18 years of age or older. Employees of The Random House, Inc. Group, its subsidiaries, agencies, affiliates, participating retailers, and distributors and members of their families living in the same household are not eligible to enter. Void where prohibited.

General: Taxes on prizes are the sole responsibility of winners. By participating, entrants agree to these rules and to the decisions of judges, which shall be final in all respects. Winners must complete an Affidavit of Eligibility and Liability/Publicity Release, which must be returned within 15 days or prize may be forfeited. Each winner agrees to the use of his/her name and/or photograph for advertising and publicity purposes without additional compensation (except where prohibited by law). Sponsor is not responsible for late, lost, stolen, or misdirected mail. No prize transfer or substitution except by sponsor due to unavailability. All entries become the property of the sponsor. One prize per household.

Winners List: For a list of winners, send a self-addressed, stamped envelope to be received by 1/15/96 to: "Big Bucks and a Backpack" Winners, PMI Station, P.O. Box 750, Southbury, CT 06488-0750 ,USA.

Random House, Inc., 201 East 50th Street, New York, NY 10022

Complete this form and mail to:
"Big Bucks and a Backpack" Contest, PMI Station, P.O. Box 3562, Southbury, CT 06488-3562.
Entrants from the United Kingdom and the Republic of Ireland, mail to: Berkeley Guides Backpack Contest, Random House Group, P.O. Box 1375, London SW1V 2SL, England.

Mail coupon to be received by 1/15/96.

NAME _____

ADDRESS
_____
_____

COUNTRY _____   **TELEPHONE** _____

WHERE I BOUGHT THIS BOOK
_____

A T-SHIRT FOR YOUR THOUGHTS . . .

After your trip, drop us a line and let us know how things went. People whose comments help us most improve future editions will receive our eternal thanks as well as a Berkeley Guides T-shirt. Just print your name and address clearly and send the completed survey to: The Berkeley Guides, 515 Eshleman Hall, U.C. Berkeley, Berkeley, CA 94720.

Your Name _____

Address _____

_____ Zip _____

Where did you buy this book? City _____ State _____

How long before your trip did you buy this book? _____

Which Berkeley Guide(s) did you buy? _____

Which other guides, if any, did you purchase for this trip? _____

Which other guides, if any, have you used before? (Please circle)
Fodor's   Let's Go   Real Guide   Frommer's   Birnbaum   Lonely Planet
Other _____

Why did you choose Berkeley? (Please circle as many as apply)
Budget information   More maps   Emphasis on outdoors/off-the-beaten-track
Design   Attitude   Other _____

_____

If you're employed: Occupation _____

If you're a student: Name of school _____ City & state _____

Age _____ Male _____ Female _____

How many weeks was your trip? (Please circle) 1 2 3 4 5 6 7 8 More than 8 weeks

After you arrived on your trip, how did you get around? (Please circle one or more)
Rental car   Personal car   Plane   Bus   Train   Hiking   Biking   Hitching
Other _____

When did you travel? _____

Where did you travel? _____

_____

The features/sections I used most were (please circle as many as apply):
Basics   Where to Sleep   Food   Coming and Going   Worth Seeing   Other

The information was (circle one):
Usually accurate   Sometimes accurate   Seldom accurate

I would _____ would not _____ buy another Berkeley Guide.

These books are brand new, and we'd really appreciate some feedback on how to improve them. Please also tell us about your latest find, a new scam, a budget deal, whatever—we want to hear about it.

For your comments:

_____

_____